Cardinal Choices

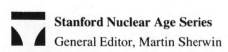

Stanford Nuclear Age Series
General Editor, Martin Sherwin

ADVISORY BOARD
Barton J. Bernstein, David Holloway, and Wolfgang K. H. Panofsky

Cardinal Choices

*Presidential Science Advising
from the Atomic Bomb to SDI*

Revised and Expanded Edition

A CENTURY FOUNDATION BOOK

Gregg Herken

STANFORD UNIVERSITY PRESS
Stanford, California 2000

Stanford University Press
Stanford, California

© 1992, 2000 by The Century Foundation
(formerly The Twentieth Century Fund)

CIP data appear at the end of the book

In memory of
Isidor Isaac Rabi
physicist, patriot, science adviser

Foreword

Although the importance of scientific information to national decision making continues to increase, recent administrations have failed to reestablish anything resembling the strong, independent expert group—the President's Science Advisory Committee—that once provided the executive branch with scientific counsel. In this edition of *Cardinal Choices,* Gregg Herken has brought the story up to date, explaining that the experiences of President Clinton's science adviser, Jack Gibbons, former director of the Office of Technology Assessment, were similar to those of D. Allen Bromley, Assistant to the President for Science and Technology under President Bush. While both appointments reflected an awareness of the increasing national concern with issues such as the environment, science education, and technological competition, both also involved a quite limited conception of the appropriate role for scientific advice. Overall, Herken believes that recent presidents are falling short when it comes to what is needed to deal with the critical questions facing us today.

The relationship between American presidents and science always has had a surprisingly idiosyncratic flavor. Chief executives from Franklin Roosevelt to Ronald Reagan have adopted very different approaches to dealing with the scientific community. Herken, who is Historian and Curator, Space History Department, of the National Air and Space Museum at the Smithsonian Institution, traces the history of presidential science advising—in its way an astonishing story. One might have predicted, I think, that the advance of scientific knowledge and the extension of its implications for other areas of government would ensure an ever-expanding role for science advising in the executive branch. Instead, the history of science advising has been uneven. There have been times when there was systematic provision of high-level analysis, times when government relied on fragmented, competing advice from the scientific establishment, and times when well-placed individuals had direct access to and influence on the president.

Regrettably, the issues that drive the presidential agenda all too often have little to do with the long-term forces, such as science, that shape the nation's future. Certainly, the effects of scientific developments should be high on any list of national concerns. Indeed, as economic competitiveness has emerged as a powerful political issue, one might expect the connection between scientific progress and economic growth to force a reappraisal of federal organization in this area. Since economists are securely linked—for example, through the Council of Economic Advisors—to the highest level of executive decision making, why aren't scientists?

Herken's comprehensive history of the tensions between the cultures of science and government draws upon declassified documents and interviews with the principals, providing a useful guide to the difficulties in the relationship. We remain grateful to him for his continuing contribution to the historical literature and to our understanding of science, government, and policy making.

Richard C. Leone, President
The Century Foundation, formerly
The Twentieth Century Fund
February 1999

Preface

Since the discovery of nuclear fission in 1938, the importance of scientists and their inventions has been evident to governments. The advent of nuclear weapons, as well as more recent physical phenomena—including the "greenhouse" effect, pollution of the oceans, and depletion of the ozone layer sheltering the earth—has focused the attention of the public, as well as the state, upon the critical contribution of scientists.

But beyond being discoverers and inventors, scientists have played another role in government that has received much less attention: as advisers. Since the eve of the Second World War, American scientists have had a crucial part in helping their government decide what C. P. Snow, the late British physicist and novelist, called the "cardinal choices" that modern leaders must make.

This is a book about the advice that scientists have given the president of the United States on such choices. It is not, strictly speaking, a study of science policy, which concerns why and how the government sets priorities in its support of science. Nor does it pretend to be a comprehensive history of presidential science advising. Rather, its focus is on the role that scientists have played in advising the president on what Snow defined as the "choices that in the broadest sense determine whether we live or die."[1]

Since the discovery of atomic fission, those choices have most prominently concerned nuclear weapons: their development, the planning for their possible use, and the efforts and hopes directed toward their control. It was "in the making of weapons of absolute destruction," Snow noted in his celebrated Godkin lectures at Harvard in 1960, that the role of scientists in the making of cardinal choices was revealed "at its sharpest and most dramatic."[2] Less than two years after Snow's lectures on "Science and Government," the publication of Rachel Carson's Silent Spring showed there were choices outside the realm of nuclear weaponry—more subtle, but no less cardinal—where scientists might also give advice.

It seems remarkable today, when the influence of science and technology is so pervasively felt, that more than a decade after the end of the Second

World War there had yet to be established a direct channel of communication between the nation's scientific community and the president. The early history of presidential science advising is thus the story of a few energetic individuals who sought to influence the government's policies when there was no established way for the citizen-scientist to approach the White House. Initially, their intent was to alert the president to the fearsome potential of atomic energy; as time went on, and both the arsenal of bombs and their implications continued to grow, this effort shifted to an attempt to persuade the president not to proceed with the next generation of nuclear weapons.

President Dwight D. Eisenhower's creation of the President's Science Advisory Committee (PSAC) in 1957 opened the first direct channel between scientists and the Oval Office. Under Eisenhower, advising the president became for the first time a systematic and formal enterprise for scientists. Yet the type of advice—and, ultimately, its fate in the government—would continue to be strongly dependent upon the individual scientist or scientists closest to the president.

The decade after Sputnik witnessed a steady waning of the importance of the president's scientists. PSAC's accelerating decline in the 1960s was due in part to the controversy over the Vietnam War, which divided the scientific community as much as the rest of the nation, and to an equally contentious debate over development of the antiballistic missile. In each case, an increasing number of the nation's scientists, including former members of PSAC, came to disagree with, and ultimately to openly oppose, the government's policies.

Relations between scientists and the White House reached their nadir with President Nixon's abolition of PSAC and the post of science adviser early in 1973. Numerous subsequent proposals for reestablishing a PSAC-like entity in the White House would be rebuffed, and the science advisory process itself has become increasingly fragmented among competing branches of government.

Today, growing public concern about a host of urgent, unresolved issues affecting the global environment as well as the nation's security—ranging from the unchecked AIDS epidemic to the potentially catastrophic problem of global warming—has directed attention anew to proposals both for re-creating PSAC and for fundamentally reforming the way that scientific advice reaches the president.

It is to the proposition that the history of cardinal choices contains lessons for the future of presidential science advising that this book is dedicated.

Acknowledgments

In the writing of this book I became grateful to many people. For reading, and commenting on, portions of the manuscript I would like to thank David Aaron, Finn Aaserud, Bruce Abel, William O. Baker, Don Baucom, Barton Bernstein, Hans Bethe, D. Allan Bromley, Harvey Brooks, Harold Brown,

Paul Doty, Sidney Drell, Lee DuBridge, John Gibbons, William Golden, Andrew Goodpaster, Carl Kaysen, Bill Lanouette, Franklin Long, Gordon MacDonald, William Nierenberg, Wolfgang Panofsky, Frank Press, Victor Reis, Simon Ramo, George Rathjens, Jack Ruina, Glenn Seaborg, Frederick Seitz, Guyford Stever, Jerome Wiesner, and Herbert York. Several of the above also provided copies of documents used in my research. Don Hornig, Richard Garwin, David Beckler, and Ed David were especially conscientious—and constructive—critics. The errors that remain—of fact, omission, or interpretation—are my responsibility.

Marcia Bystryn, the Twentieth Century Fund's former assistant director, Pamela Gilfond, my editor at the Fund, and Beverly Goldberg, its publications director, were unfailingly cheerful and diplomatic. Dan Kevles was kind enough to invite me to be the Mellon visiting professor at Caltech during 1987–1988, where I was given both the time and the resources to work on the manuscript. Herbert York, now director emeritus of the University of California's Institute on Global Conflict and Cooperation, and Allen Greb generously included me in the activities of the IGCC, where I was senior research associate from 1985 to 1987.

Finally, I would like to thank old friends at my alma mater, the University of California, Santa Cruz, as well as my colleagues at the Smithsonian Institution, for their encouragement, support, and words of wisdom. For this updated edition, I would like to thank Martin Sherwin and, at Stanford University Press, Muriel Bell and Pamela MacFarland.

Washington, D.C.   G. H.
January 2000

Contents

PART I   *Urgent Appeals, 1939–1952: The Advent of Nuclear Weapons*

Chapter 1
"A Closely Knit Group of People"
The Decision to Build the Atomic Bomb   3

Chapter 2
"No Acceptable Alternative"
The Decision to Use the Atomic Bomb   17

Chapter 3
"Necessarily an Evil Thing"
The Debate over the H-Bomb   34

Chapter 4
"A Point of No Return"
The Opportunity for a Nuclear "Standstill"   49

PART II   *Fragile Hopes, 1953–1960: The Impetus toward Arms Control*

Chapter 5
"Racing toward Catastrophe"
Atoms for Peace and War   69

Chapter 6
"An Age of Danger"
From the Killian Report to Sputnik   82

Chapter 7
"A Vested Interest in This Field"
The President's Science Advisory Committee and the Test Ban   101

Part III   *Guarded Futures, 1961–1988: The Perils
              and Promises of New Technology*

Chapter 8
"Where a Fresh Start Is Badly Needed"
Politics and Science in the Kennedy Administration   127

Chapter 9
"A Nation Cannot Be Built with Gadgets"
Johnson, Hornig, and the Vietnam War   146

Chapter 10
"No Longer as Adviser but as Citizen"
The Crisis of Science Advising under Nixon and Ford   165

Chapter 11
"We Want You to Know of Our Judgment"
Science and Conflict in the Carter Administration   184

Chapter 12
"The President Doesn't Care about Wavelengths"
The Reagan Revolution and the Origins of SDI   199

Conclusion
Speaking the Truth to Power
The Future of Presidential Science Advising   217

Appendixes

A. Einstein-Szilard Letter to President Roosevelt (proposal to build an
   atomic bomb), August 2, 1939   229

B. Fermi-Rabi Letter to the AEC: "An Opinion on the Development of the
   'Super'" (written to oppose the hydrogen bomb), October 30, 1949   231

C. The Golden Report: "Mobilization of Science for War" (report on the
   president's science adviser), December 18, 1950   233

D. The Disarmament Panel's Proposal for a Nuclear "Standstill": "The
   Timing of the Thermonuclear Test" (excerpts), Fall 1952   235

E. The Teapot Report on ICBMs: "Recommendations of the Committee
   on Strategic Missiles," February 10, 1954   239

F. Killian's Charter for PSAC, December 1957   241

G. Ruina-Gell-Mann Paper: "Ballistic Missile Defence and the Arms Race"
   (argument against the ABM), December 1965   243

H. Rathjens-Ruina Memorandum to Henry Kissinger: "A Moratorium on the Testing of Multiple Warheads" (proposal for a MIRV ban), June 2, 1969   247

I. Garwin Letter to President Carter (defense of a comprehensive test ban), August 15, 1978   250

J. The "Insert": President Reagan's Announcement of SDI, March 23, 1983   253

K. Members of SAC/ODM and PSAC, 1951–73   256

Notes   263

Bibliography   341

Index   351

I

*Urgent Appeals,
1939–1952:
The Advent of Nuclear
Weapons*

1

"A Closely Knit Group of People"

The Decision to Build the Atomic Bomb

A rguably the most "cardinal" choice of modern times—the decision to build the atomic bomb—might not have been made by an American president except for the joint effort of two émigré physicists, one born in Hungary, the other in Germany. Due in large measure to the timely and inspired intervention of Leo Szilard and Albert Einstein—and other foreign-born scientists who would join Szilard's ad hoc "association" for promoting the atomic bomb to the American government—the United States turned out to be the only serious entrant in what was originally thought to be a race with Germany to build the world's first nuclear weapon. Theirs would be the first in a long history of efforts by scientists to warn the government of promising or threatening developments, and, later, to speak the truth to power.

While ultimately successful, the repeated and increasingly desperate efforts of this informal coterie of scientists to awaken President Franklin Roosevelt to the possibility of the atomic bomb identified what today seems a stunning omission in the organization of the American government between the wars: the absence of any systematic means whereby scientific and technical advice could reach the president. Because of Einstein and Szilard, and because of the atomic bomb, this situation had begun to change dramatically with the onset of the Second World War.

"The merest moonshine. . ."

As with many discoveries in science, the advent of atomic weaponry is only partly a story of scientific inspiration and invention. It is also—and perhaps just as much—an account of missed opportunities, unforeseen consequences, and the unexpected difficulty that scientists had in persuading governments to heed and ultimately to share their concern about the atom.

In retrospect, it seems remarkable that governments did not recognize sooner the destructive potential of atomic energy. In *The World Set Free,* a novel published on the eve of the First World War, more than thirty years before Hiroshima, H. G. Wells accurately forecast the discovery of artificial radioactivity and its military use.[1] Wells's book, which tells of a nuclear war that destroys most of Europe's major cities in 1956, leading eventually to establishment of a world government, was the first to use the term "atomic bomb"—describing the weapon as "the crowning triumph of military science, the ultimate explosive, that was to give the 'decisive touch' to war."

Nearly twenty years later, in the fall of 1933, physicist Leo Szilard had his own sudden inspiration of how atomic energy might be the means of realizing the alchemist's ancient dream of transmuting one element into another —a moment of epiphany that reportedly occurred while Szilard was waiting for a traffic light to change at a London intersection. The transmutation of matter would be possible, Szilard realized, if an element existed that, when bombarded by neutrons, emitted two or more of the particles for each one that it captured. The not incidental byproduct of such a phenomenon, he knew, would be a titanic release of energy in a self-sustaining atomic reaction.

At the time Szilard had his insight, most scientists considered the natural elements hardly less fixed or immutable than the stars. Just a few weeks earlier, at a meeting of the British Association for the Advancement of Science that Szilard attended, Lord Rutherford, one of the most eminent physicists of his generation, branded the "idea of power from atomic transmutations . . . the merest moonshine."

Initially more bemused than alarmed by the prospect of nuclear fission, Szilard informed colleagues in Europe and America of his idea in a March 1934 letter, enclosing a few pages of Wells's prophetic novel along with the latter's observation that "the forecast of the writers may prove to be more accurate than the forecast of the scientists."[2]

Indeed, some six years earlier, Szilard had been influenced by another of Wells's works—a political tract titled *The Open Conspiracy,* which presented the case for a true meritocracy: a world governed by scientists and other experts. Since then, Szilard had proposed to colleagues that they create their own real-life *"Bund,"* or association, which he described as "a closely knit group of people whose inner bond is pervaded by a religious and scientific spirit"—the purpose of which would be to "take over a more direct influence on public affairs as part of the political system, next to government and parliament, or in the place of government and parliament." Szilard's efforts to bring together such a *Bund* of scientists in Germany in the early 1930s was, however, preempted by Hitler's rise to power.[3]

With exemplary thoroughness, Szilard proposed in his 1934 letter that his hypothesis concerning atomic transmutation be tested by experimenting with each of the ninety-two known elements in the periodic table—beginning with hydrogen and ending with uranium—in each case bombarding a sample with neutrons to see if it emitted more of the particles than it captured. Szilard found no lack of scientific curiosity about this idea among his colleagues, but neither he nor they had much enthusiasm for conducting the laborious and time-consuming experiment.[4]

Lack of funds for research further delayed and finally sidetracked the proposed experiment. At the time he wrote the letter, Szilard had been in England barely nine months—having fled Germany only a day before the Nazis closed the border—and was living in an inexpensive London hotel. The amount of money that he calculated as necessary for the experiment—approximately $8,000—could not be raised through either private or public sources. Federal support for basic research remained a relative rarity throughout the Great Depression. Instead, scientists looking for financial backing turned to wealthy science-minded patrons, many of whom supported experiments and inventions with the expectation of financial gain.

The delay in conducting his experiment proved fortuitous, as Szilard himself later admitted. (Szilard joked after the war that all those who failed to look into atomic transmutation should have been awarded the Nobel Prize—but for peace, not physics. Thus, had atomic fission been discovered by German scientists in 1934 instead of four years later, the outcome of the war and the course of history might have been altogether different.)

"A remote possibility. . ."

The fact that uranium—the last element of the periodic table then known to science—undergoes fissioning under neutron bombardment was not discovered by scientists until an experiment in the Berlin laboratory of German physicists Otto Hahn and Fritz Strassmann near the end of 1938, less than a year before the outbreak of the war in Europe. Beyond the ranks of a small number of scientists, neither in Germany nor in other countries was the potential military significance of the Hahn-Strassmann experiment immediately appreciated.[5]

That realization came more than two months later even for Szilard, who had left London for New York, where he and Enrico Fermi—an Italian physicist and another recent émigré from fascism—discussed the possibility of atomic chain reactions during Szilard's visit to Fermi's lab at Columbia University. Until that time, Szilard had had difficulty convincing Fermi that uranium was the element they were after.

Both scientifically and temperamentally more conservative than Szilard, Fermi considered it only "a remote possibility" that uranium would give off more neutrons than it captured—a one-in-ten chance, he told Szilard. (Ironically, Fermi and a colleague had accidentally induced fission in uranium during a 1934 experiment at their lab in Italy, but neither recognized it at the time.) It had taken Isidor Rabi, Szilard's friend and Fermi's colleague at Columbia, to convince the Italian that the prospect, even if remote, was worth investigating.[6]

Rabi, born of East European Jewish immigrants, had grown up on the Lower East Side of New York.[7] At Columbia, Szilard relied upon Rabi's streetwise pragmatism to put Fermi's theoretical objection to the uranium experiment in perspective. "Ten percent is not a remote possibility if it means that we may die of it," Rabi pointed out to Fermi.[8]

Szilard and another Columbia physicist, Walter Zinn, obtained financial backing for their experiment from a nonscientist who would subsequently play an important role in the development of nuclear weapons: Lewis Strauss, an investment banker with the prestigious New York firm of Kuhn, Loeb. Strauss's boyhood dream of becoming a physicist had collided with the pressing financial needs of his family, for whose sake he left school to make a living selling shoes—an enterprise from which he graduated in progressive steps to Wall Street. Made independently wealthy by his investments, Strauss's continued amateur interest in science manifested itself in support for scientific experiments. In 1936, for example, Strauss had provided funding for an experimental refrigerator pump invented by Szilard and Einstein.[9]

By early 1939, Szilard, Strauss, Rabi, and Fermi, together with two other recent émigrés from Hungary—Edward Teller, a professor of theoretical chemistry at George Washington University, and Eugene Wigner, a Princeton physicist—had banded together to form what Szilard, in a February letter to Strauss, described as "an 'association,'" the purpose of which was to discreetly promote the scientific investigation of nuclear fission in the United States.

Szilard's loosely confederated atomic bomb "association" was in reality the *Bund* of select scientific talent he had first thought of organizing in Germany. But unlike Wells's "open conspiracy," Szilard's *Bund*—to which he gave the ambiguous title Association of Scientific Collaboration—was deliberately kept small and its purpose disguised. Indeed, Szilard confided to Strauss his hope that "the newspapers at least might soon forget about uranium."[10]

On the evening of March 3, 1939, in Pupin Hall, Columbia's physics building, Zinn and Szilard performed their own experiment to see if uranium would emit more neutrons than it captured. In the procedure, extra neutrons released by a lump of uranium would register as tiny flashes on a cathode-ray tube. "All we had to do was to lean back, turn on a switch, and watch the screen of a television tube," Szilard recounted years later. "We watched them for a little while and then we switched everything off and went home." For Szilard, the experiment ended the long uncertainty about the future of atomic energy: "That night there was very little doubt in my mind that the world was headed for grief."[11]

"We could not assume responsibility . . ."

Having verified the possibility of a self-sustaining nuclear chain reaction, the association—now consisting of Szilard, Teller, Wigner, Fermi, and Rabi—debated for weeks whether to publish the results of their research, which they feared would alert the world to the military possibilities of atomic energy. While Szilard and Teller urged continued secrecy, Fermi championed the cause of scientific freedom. Finally, word that French physicist Frédéric Joliot and his colleagues were about to publish the results of a similar experiment forced the hand of the American scientists. They left the decision regarding secrecy up to the dean of the Columbia physics department, George Pegram. Pegram's mind was made up when Rabi, who had just returned from a visit to the University of Illinois, told him that a physicist there—Maurice Goldhaber—already knew of the experiment and its results. Rabi's announcement caused Pegram to think that the secret was already out. What neither Pegram nor Rabi knew was that Szilard had informed Goldhaber, who—like the scientists at Columbia—had been sworn to secrecy about the news.[12]

The publication of two scientific papers on fission during the coming weeks spurred the association's concern with awakening friendly governments to the danger of atomic energy. Wigner was the first to insist that officials of the U.S. government be told, arguing that the matter was so "serious . . . we could not assume responsibility for handling it." Although Szilard reportedly found Fermi "very cool" to his idea of a government-funded crash program to find out if the reaction they observed would be self-sustaining, and hence practical for the construction of a bomb, he convinced Fermi that it would be a good idea to contact higher authority about the results of their experiment. Since atomic power had obvious potential application for the propulsion of ships, particularly submarines, the association agreed that the U.S. Navy was the most logical candidate for the news.

But Fermi's attempt to inform the Navy in the spring of 1939 was summarily rebuffed. Navy officials were not only ignorant of the Italian's scientific credentials but suspicious of his motives because of his national origins. By the end of July, convinced that the Navy had proved a blind lead, Szilard resolved to enlist the best-known man of science at that time—Albert Einstein—in his clandestine association.

Ironically, Szilard's decision was inspired neither by Einstein's international reputation as a physicist nor by their friendship as scientists and inventors but by Einstein's personal acquaintance with the queen of Belgium. One of Szilard's earliest fears was that the Germans would get the material for an atomic bomb from the Belgian Congo, which had the world's largest reserves of high-grade uranium ore. Enlisting Wigner as a chauffeur—Szilard never learned to drive—the two Hungarians searched out Einstein at a vacation cabin on Long Island to enlist him in their secret atomic *Bund*.[13]

To Szilard's surprise, the occasion was the first Einstein had heard of the chain reaction of uranium. After suggesting some revisions, Einstein agreed, somewhat reluctantly, to sign the draft of a letter Szilard had written—addressing it not to the queen directly but to a member of the Belgian cabinet. By the end of the meeting, however, Wigner had persuaded Einstein and Szilard that, as Americans and as scientists, they should not divulge such sensitive information to foreigners without first notifying the U.S. government. The trio agreed to send the letter instead to the State Department, with an attached memorandum indicating their intention to forward the letter to Belgium after two weeks, unless instructed otherwise.[14]

Szilard evidently had second thoughts about the wisdom of this approach, because he sent neither letter. He decided instead to approach the American government—less formally but at a higher level—about the prospects for an atomic bomb.

The greatest difficulty that scientists faced in speaking the truth to power in America, Szilard found, was making their voices heard. As Szilard discovered, there existed in 1939 little communication between the scientific community and the federal government.

Neither the creation by Congress of a National Academy of Sciences in the course of the Civil War nor the establishment (under the academy's sponsorship) of a National Research Council in 1916—the result of the pressure of another war—had managed to open such a channel. Although the academy's charter requires that it "shall, whenever called upon by any department of the Government, investigate, examine, experiment, and report upon any subject of science or art," in practice it and the National Research Council received few such summonses. Apart from sporadic requests for technical advice from the individual military services—requests that increased in frequency with the partial mobilization of science for the First World War—technical advice was neither generally offered by scientists nor actively sought by the U.S. government. This situation had begun to change only slowly by the start of the Great Depression.[15]

Partly in response to the urgings of his secretary of agriculture, Henry Wallace, President Roosevelt established a Science Advisory Board shortly after assuming office in 1933. Wallace's proposal had behind it not the sort of concerns that animated Szilard but a vision of how science might contribute to the nation's economic recovery from the Depression. As a former Iowa hog farmer, Wallace looked to science specifically for advances in agriculture and in predicting the weather.[16]

The Science Advisory Board established during the Roosevelt administration was semiprivate, receiving part of its financial support from the Rockefeller family until 1935, when it was absorbed into a recognized government agency—the National Research Board—as part of the consolidation of the New Deal. Even then, its original emphasis upon practical applications remained. At the time of Szilard's appeal, the top-ranking scientist in the government—the director of the National Bureau of Standards—was physicist Lyman Briggs, an expert in soil science.[17]

"This requires action. . ."

Facing this wall between the scientific community and the government, Szilard even briefly considered making a secret appeal to the government through one of the era's most prominent American heroes—Charles Lindbergh. Szilard drafted a letter asking Lindbergh to lend his support to government research into a vaguely defined, new, and vastly more powerful kind of weapon. But not wishing to draw too much attention to the military potential of uranium, Szilard's description of the atomic bomb was so oblique that it was virtually indecipherable to anyone not already acquainted with the idea. Further, Szilard was so put off by Lindbergh's noninterventionist sympathies at the outbreak of war that he decided against sending the letter.[18] Instead, his ambition now was to include the president of the United States in his atomic bomb "association."

Making another trip to Long Island in early August—this time with Teller as chauffeur—Szilard explained to the ever-patient Einstein his latest plan for informing the American government about the prospects for an atomic bomb. Acknowledging the disadvantage of never having written to a president, Szilard was tentative about both the form and the content of the letter. "How many pages does the fission of uranium rate?" he mused. Szilard drafted two versions of the letter—one short and one long—to go to Roosevelt over Einstein's signature. Einstein agreed to sign both versions, leaving to Szilard the decision as to which would go to Roosevelt.[19]

In what were still guarded and often Delphic terms, the two-page, single-spaced letter called for "watchfulness and, if necessary, quick action on the part of the Administration." Alluding both to the promise and the threat inherent in a fission reaction, the letter warned that, in addition to atomic power for peaceful purposes, it was "conceivable— though less certain—that extremely powerful bombs of a new type may thus be constructed." This fearsome prospect led Szilard and Einstein to their first specific proposal:

> In view of this situation you may think it desirable to have some permanent contact maintained between the Administration and the group of physicists working on chain reaction in America. One possible way of achieving this might be for you to entrust with this task a person who has your confidence and who could perhaps serve in an unofficial capacity.

The duties of the unofficial adviser that they urged upon Roosevelt included directing government efforts in "securing a supply of uranium ore for the United States," as well as speeding up research then going on at universities and in private laboratories around the country. For this set of tasks Szilard evidently thought himself best suited.

The next obstacle facing Szilard was how to get the document before the president. Some weeks earlier he had sought advice on contacting the government from Gustav Stolper, once an internationally known Berlin economist and a former Reichstag member, who had joined those fleeing Hitler's Germany and was now settled in New York. Stolper in turn telephoned Alexander Sachs, another economist and an adviser to the Roosevelt administration. It was Sachs who, after hearing the scientists' story, convinced Szilard that he should go directly to the president with the news—even offering to deliver the letter to Roosevelt himself. (Initially, Sachs had suggested financier Bernard Baruch, MIT President Karl Compton, and Lindbergh as other possible go-betweens, on the grounds that, as Sachs later said of the bomb and Roosevelt: "No scientist could sell it to him.")[20]

Sachs delayed passing the letter along to the White House until he could arrange a personal meeting with the president. Ushered into the Oval Office on October 11, Sachs patiently but inexpertly tried to explain to Roosevelt the science behind the bomb—leaving the president baffled and uncomprehending until Sachs pointed out that it was likely others would get the bomb unless American scientists built it first. Once Roosevelt saw the relevance of the Einstein-Szilard letter to the conflict then going on in Europe, he told Sachs: "Alex, what you are after is to see that the Nazis don't blow us up." The president instructed his aide and confidant, "Pa" Watson: "This requires action."[21]

Despite Roosevelt's encouraging response to Sachs, the action that followed was neither immediate, dramatic, nor productive of any visible results. The scientists learned that the president had simply forwarded their request to a committee of the National Bureau of Standards composed of Briggs, its chairman, and a representative apiece from the Army and Navy. Resigned to the fact that the Briggs committee would be their next major hurdle, Szilard asked his two colleagues and countrymen in the atomic bomb association, Teller and Wigner, to join him in presenting their case for a scientific "facilitator" for the project at the committee's first meeting, on October 21, 1939.

Perhaps because Szilard remembered how funding had been a major impediment to the fission experiments he proposed in 1934, the trio stressed that a "crash program" of experiments necessary to prove the feasibility of an atomic chain reaction would likely cost no more than a few thousand dollars. Most of the money they requested was for graphite blocks needed to shield what Szilard had come to call the atomic "pile." (Wigner even assured Briggs that, since the experiment would leave the blocks undamaged, the government could have the graphite back after the experiment was over.)

Despite the modest cost of the proposed experiment, the Army representative on the committee, Colonel Keith Adamson, remained fundamentally unconvinced of the value of an atomic bomb. Rarely was a new weapon used soon after its development, Adamson protested, since it generally took two wars "before one can know whether the weapon is any good or not." Wigner interrupted what Szilard described as the Army official's "rather longish tirade" on how it was not weapons but the morale of troops that ultimately determined victory in a war. He professed that Adamson's point was "very interesting, since he had always imagined that weapons were important, and this was why he assumed the Army had always asked for such a large appropriation." Now that he understood how it was actually morale that won wars, Wigner suggested that perhaps the Army's budget could be cut to pay for the project.

Evidently stung by Wigner's argument, Adamson and the committee withdrew their opposition to the experiment. Still, the scientists remained worried at meeting's end that they had failed to convey to the government their own sense of urgency about proceeding with the bomb. As his own narrow escape from the Nazis had shown, Szilard reminded his colleagues, it was sometimes less important to be cleverer than your opponent than to be just one day ahead of him.[22]

"Swimming in syrup . . ."

Szilard's concern that the United States was losing the race for the atomic bomb increased in the following months as no sign was forthcoming that the government had decided to act on the committee's recommendations. In the interim, Einstein had returned to the Institute for Advanced Study at Princeton and Fermi to his lab at Columbia, where he was engaged in research on his real scientific interest, cosmic rays and the physics of elementary particles. Only Szilard and Wigner remained preoccupied with atomic energy and anxious about the protracted silence from Washington.

Their further attempts to prod the government into action on the atomic bomb, Wigner recalled, was like "swimming in syrup." "We heard nothing from Washington at all," Szilard recollected. In March 1940, after repeated entreaties, Szilard convinced Einstein to write another letter to be delivered by Sachs. Szilard hoped the letter would convey the heightened sense of urgency he and the others felt about the bomb. "Since the outbreak of the war," the letter warned, "interest in uranium has intensified in Germany."[23]

The following month the Briggs committee—now aptly renamed the Uranium Committee—met again, in response to Sachs's renewed urging. Fermi, Teller, Wigner, and Szilard decided at this time to impose a kind of voluntary censorship on publishing the results of their own research on fission.[24]

Some seven months after Roosevelt had received Szilard and Einstein's letter, progress toward an atomic bomb still seemed glacial to Szilard. The military representatives on the Uranium Committee now agreed that atomic fission might be a useful way to generate electricity or to propel ships in some indeterminate future, but they discounted fears of an atomic bomb. Briggs worried that should they approve a large sum of money for an experiment on the advice of foreign scientists, and should that experiment then fail, the committee would become the target of a congressional investigation.

Szilard's chronic anxiety lifted somewhat that summer when, partly as a result of the scientists' importuning, the Uranium Committee was disbanded and the fission project put under the leadership of Vannevar Bush, head of the National Defense Research Committee (NDRC), which had been created that June in anticipation of America's entry into the war.[25]

A prototypical Yankee with a seafaring ancestry, Bush was trained in mathematics and engineering. But his temperament was better suited to the active life of public service than to the quiet, reflective world of academe. During the First World War, Bush worked for the Navy on the fledgling science of submarine detection. In peacetime, his inventions included an electronic switching mechanism for telephones that made automatic dialing possible and an early version of the analog computer. In 1939, Bush left his teaching post at MIT to become president of the Carnegie Institution of Washington, D.C. By the outbreak of the Second World War in Europe, Bush was also head of the National Advisory Committee on Aeronautics. The inspiration for the NDRC was his personal contribution to mobilizing science for victory in the war.[26]

Upon first hearing of the project proposed by Fermi and Szilard, Bush reportedly expressed the hope that it would fail. At this early stage in the evolution of nuclear physics, it was not yet known whether the number or rate of neutrons emitted by uranium would be sufficient to sustain an atomic chain reaction. Even if the proposed experiment showed a self-sustaining fission reaction to be feasible, it was still possible that the reaction would not occur at a sufficiently rapid rate to produce a nuclear explosion. If that were the case, atomic energy might be used to generate electricity and to drive ships, but not to power a bomb.

The declining fortunes of war in Europe provided another boost to Roosevelt's preparedness drive, and hence also to the atomic bomb. In June 1941—when German troops were victorious on the continent and had begun advancing deep into Russia—James Conant, a chemist and former president of Harvard University, became the second of Roosevelt's de facto science advisers when he replaced Bush as head of the NDRC. Conant was recruited to NDRC because Bush had created a larger, umbrella organization—the Office of Scientific Research and Development (OSRD)—which was to oversee development of new weapons, including the atomic bomb. As head of OSRD, Bush reported directly to Roosevelt; as head of NDRC, Conant reported directly to Bush.

In July, Bush gave needed momentum to the fledgling atomic bomb project when he advised Roosevelt that the weapon—assuming it could be built—might well have a decisive effect not only on the war but in shaping the subsequent peace. Protesting that since he was "no atomic scientist . . . most of this was over my head," Bush had already asked the National Academy of Sciences to judge whether atomic energy was likely to have military application. As Bush noted in his memoirs, Roosevelt seemed to accept his counsel readily, and even uncritically: "Roosevelt did not attempt to delve into the subject to balance one piece of advice against the other."[27]

But the impetus that Bush gave to the project at this stage did not necessarily reflect faith in its ultimate success, or even a discernible sense of urgency on the president's part. When Bush personally delivered the National Academy's tentatively positive verdict on the feasibility of an atomic bomb to the White House on November 27, 1941, it was another two months before Roosevelt sent back the report, pinned to which was a brief note indicating his assent.[28]

Nor did the fact that Roosevelt gave the green light to the atomic bomb project remove the many technical obstacles in the way of proving the bomb's feasibility.

By late 1941, Szilard was in a state approaching despair. "Somehow we did not seem to be able to get the things done which we knew needed to be done," he recalled. A few months after the Japanese attack on Pearl Harbor, Szilard vented his frustration in a bitter and accusatory letter to Bush: "In 1939, the Government of the United States was given a unique opportunity by Providence; this opportunity was lost. Nobody can tell now whether we shall be ready before German bombs wipe out American cities." Even the usually diffident Fermi became livid about the delays, the cause of which he attributed to the slow-moving federal bureaucracy set up to direct research. "If we brought the bomb to them all ready-made on a silver platter, there would still be a fifty-fifty chance that they would mess it up," he told Szilard.[29]

The scientists' frustration was in part a reflection of their inexperience in dealing with the government. But it also stemmed from the fact that, despite their efforts to accelerate the pace of the bomb project, Szilard and his colleagues felt themselves unable to affect events. Ultimately, it was not Szilard and his *Bund* but Bush and OSRD who moved things along. Following the president's terse note of January 1942, giving the go-ahead to the project, Bush—who had meanwhile been in touch with British scientists concerning their atomic bomb research, and was impressed by its progress—ordered that fission research be pursued as a priority.[30]

"The reaction is self-sustaining. . ."

In the fall of 1942, the scientists' work was put under the direction of the Army and Brigadier General Leslie Groves, who gave it the official code name, the

Manhattan Engineer District, and imbued it with a new sense of urgency. Initially, few in Szilard's association saw the involvement of Groves and the military in the bomb project as a portent of more rapid progress. Einstein even predicted that the Army would prove the greatest obstacle yet to research on atomic energy. Fermi, too, feared that the military's involvement would actually hinder the bomb's development. "A general is a man who takes chances," he told Szilard. "Mostly he takes a fifty-fifty chance; if he happens to win three times in succession he is considered a great general."[31]

In September 1942, at the University of Chicago, Szilard once again vented his frustration to colleagues with a broadside titled "What Is Wrong with Us?" Szilard argued that his original scientific *Bund* had erred in putting the responsibility for the bomb project in the hands of bureaucrats in Washington, with the result that the Germans were now likely to build the first nuclear weapon. "We may have to answer before history the question why we tolerated an arrangement which we knew could not work," he predicted. Szilard also hinted that the scientists might wish to go to Roosevelt personally to urge that they be given direct responsibility for building the bomb, on the grounds that "those who have originated the work on this terrible weapon and those who have materially contributed to its development, have, before God and the World, the duty to see to it that it should be ready to be used at the proper time and in the proper way."[32]

The long-awaited climactic moment for the atomic bomb association finally came some six weeks later, more than three years after Szilard and Einstein drafted their letter to Roosevelt. On the afternoon of December 2, 1942, Fermi, Szilard, and some forty other scientists gathered for the start of the world's first nuclear reactor, which they had constructed in secret on a squash court underneath the bleachers of the University of Chicago's Stagg Field.

The mood of the scientists was surprisingly restrained—even detached—considering the significance of their experiment. At the precise moment when the uranium in the pile was about to achieve criticality, giving off enough neutrons to sustain a chain reaction, Fermi suspended the tension by breaking for lunch. Afterward, resuming the experiment—and following a quick calculation with his slide rule—Fermi quietly and smilingly confirmed to the scientists around him their collective triumph with the simple announcement, "The reaction is self-sustaining." Wigner thereupon unceremoniously produced a bottle of Chianti from a brown bag. "We each had a small amount in a paper cup and drank silently, looking at Fermi," remembered one witness.[33]

As had been the case after the fission experiment at Columbia almost four years earlier, Szilard's enthusiasm was almost immediately tempered with concern over the ultimate consequences of the scientists' discovery. Shaking hands with Fermi when the two men were alone, Szilard told his colleague that "this day would go down as a black day in the history of mankind."[34]

"We were all green. . ."

Within a year of the experiment at Stagg Field, the enterprise launched by the Einstein-Szilard letter had grown into the most ambitious scientific and technological undertaking in history. The Manhattan Project ultimately cost more than $2.5 billion and drew upon the talents of some ten thousand of the nation's brightest scientists, engineers, and technicians. In the process it revolutionized the nature of warfare and created an entirely new peacetime industry.

Years after the war, some of the charter members of Szilard's *Bund* conceded that the letter to Roosevelt possibly had been more an obstacle than a spur to the American effort to build the bomb. Robert Oppenheimer, who became scientific director of the Los Alamos laboratory built by the Army in the New Mexican desert, thought that nuclear research in Britain—which was already well under way by 1940—would eventually have led America and its allies to develop the bomb first in any case.

Arthur Compton, head of the atomic scientists at the University of Chicago, argued in 1956 that the actual effect of the Uranium Committee "was to retard rather than to advance the development of American uranium research." Thus, the committee's work, Compton wrote, "seemed to imply"—wrongly, he thought—"that the nation's interests with regard to fission would be looked after."[35]

In a 1984 interview, Isidor Rabi was of a similar opinion, that progress toward the bomb had been slowed rather than accelerated by the intervention of Szilard and what a mutual friend called "the Hungarian conspiracy." Rabi believed, in retrospect, that the naiveté of Szilard, Teller, and Wigner concerning how a democracy works had led them to adopt the wrong approach in getting the project started. Had Szilard gone to Berkeley's Ernest Lawrence, the inventor of the cyclotron, instead of to Einstein, Rabi argued, Lawrence's contacts and organizing talent would have immediately mobilized the government and the scientific community behind the bomb project. The first bomb might then have been ready a full year earlier. "The Germans owed a lot to Szilard," Rabi said ironically.[36]

Indeed, Szilard himself subsequently acknowledged that his and his colleagues' attempts to awaken Washington to the threat of the atomic bomb showed that "we were all green. We did not know our way around in America, we did not know how to do business, and we certainly did not know how to deal with the government." Szilard, however, blamed the delays in starting work on the bomb not on the scientists' disorganization but on secrecy—which, paradoxically, he had been among the first to insist on. Had the scientists been able to freely discuss the atomic bomb among themselves, he later claimed, the weapon might have been ready for use as early as the spring of 1944.[37]

Even those among Szilard's colleagues who credited him with providing the vital spark for the Manhattan Project conceded that his irascible personality and erratic nature sometimes proved more a hindrance than a spur to its success. Robert Serber—who gave the first briefing on the bomb to the scientists brought together at Los Alamos in April 1943—recalled forty years later that the scientists had deliberately excluded Szilard from the initial meeting with Groves: "They wanted to keep him away from Groves. Because he had some crazy ideas and might make Groves think that the whole thing was the idea of a bunch of nuts."[38]

A more significant cause of the delay in getting the Manhattan Project started was the difficulty that scientists had in transmitting the urgency about the atomic bomb to the president. Despite Roosevelt's receptivity to the Einstein-Szilard letter, more than six months passed before the government acted upon the letter's initial recommendation by establishing the Uranium Committee to oversee atomic research. Nearly a year went by before Roosevelt followed the scientists' advice in appointing Bush the unofficial project "facilitator."

Although its approach was both unorthodox and unsophisticated, Szilard's *Bund* provided the impetus for starting work on the atomic bomb. Credit for actually building the weapon, though, properly belongs to Bush and Conant, the OSRD, the scientists at the Los Alamos laboratory, and the Army's Manhattan Project under the direction of Groves. Organization, as much as inspiration, was necessary to make the bomb.

In the subsequent view of many scientists, Roosevelt's choice of Bush, and Bush's creation of the NDRC to replace the overly cautious Briggs and the Bureau of Standards, were the only factors that ensured the atomic bomb would be ready in time to use against Japan. The Germans, it turned out, were never as close to developing a bomb as Szilard and others had feared.[39]

By early 1944, three separate mammoth facilities were producing uranium or plutonium for the first atomic bombs. By the end of that year, the founder and charter members of the atomic bomb association had relaxed enough to think beyond the scientific challenges and consider the next logical stage of the Manhattan Project. It "became possible for the physicists to take a more detached view," Szilard wrote, "and some of us began to think about the wisdom of testing bombs and using bombs."[40]

2

"No Acceptable Alternative"

The Decision to Use the Atomic Bomb

While scientists were unquestionably the best equipped to advise on technical questions pertaining to the atomic bomb, decisions concerning the weapon's use in war primarily involved matters of military strategy and postwar policy, and, as such, were largely outside the realm of their expertise. Nonetheless, as Leo Szilard argued as early as 1942, many of those "who originated the work on this terrible weapon" felt they had a responsibility to see that it was used "at the proper time and in the proper way." Early in the war the question of the bomb's use had rarely surfaced in the discussions of those building it; following the surrender of Germany, it became a growing focus of concern for scientists like Szilard.

"Truman just did not move in the same circles. . ."

In the spring of 1945, even before it was certain that any atomic bomb would work, Szilard discussed with colleagues at the University of Chicago the possibility that the United States might wish to refrain deliberately from using the weapon in the war—or, alternately, that this country would at least warn the enemy prior to its use. But again Szilard found it frustratingly difficult to reach the authorities with his concerns. Discouraged from visiting Los Alamos, he had already been sidelined by Groves. A subsequent attempt to discuss the postwar implications of atomic energy with others in the Manhattan Project met with a similar, summary rebuff. Szilard resolved instead to try once more to approach the president directly. As he later wrote, "There was no point in discussing these things with General Groves or Dr. Conant or Dr. Bush, and because of secrecy there was no intermediate level in the government to which we could have gone for a careful consideration of these issues."[1]

That March, in desperation, Szilard turned again to Einstein for assistance. For a third and final time the famous mathematician and physicist agreed to sign a letter written by Szilard to the president. Using Einstein's letter as an introduction, Szilard arranged to see Eleanor Roosevelt on May 8, 1945, a meeting he hoped would be a step toward gaining the president's attention. Szilard intended to use the occasion to present Franklin Roosevelt with a lengthy memorandum he had written, titled "Atomic Bombs and the Postwar Position of the United States in the World." But FDR's death on April 12 thwarted this plan.

In his remarkably prescient memorandum, Szilard argued that use of the atomic bomb in the war, without warning, might provoke a nuclear arms race with other nations—specifically Russia. Such a race, he warned, would assume an increasingly desperate nature, leading in time "to a rapid accumulation of vast quantities of atomic bombs in both countries"—the very situation that in Wells's 1914 novel had resulted in war.[2]

Szilard's memorandum also cautioned that the only hope of preventing an atomic arms race and eventual war was some system of international control of the bomb, the groundwork for which would need to be established before the weapon was used for the first time. Another, related concern, which Szilard only alluded to in the document, was how to maintain in peacetime the talented team of scientists the nation had assembled during the war.

How to approach Roosevelt's successor, Harry S. Truman, posed new and unanticipated problems for Szilard. "I knew any number of people who could have reached Roosevelt," he noted after the war, "but I knew nobody offhand who could have reached Truman; Truman just did not move in the same circles."[3] Szilard's solution was reminiscent of the indirect approach that had first put him into contact with Stolper, and then Sachs, in his effort to reach Roosevelt. Informed that there was a mathematician on the Chicago faculty who had connections with the Democratic political machine in Kansas City, Szilard was subsequently able to arrange an interview with the Missourian in the White House.

But Szilard's renewed hope of a personal meeting with the president was again destined for disappointment—this time just outside the Oval Office. Having been warned of Szilard's proselytizing, Truman left word with his appointments secretary that Szilard was instead to see James Byrnes, the new president's as yet unannounced choice for secretary of state. Scarcely daunted, Szilard and two colleagues from Chicago boarded a train that night for Byrnes's home in South Carolina.

On May 28, 1945, Szilard showed Byrnes his memorandum, which the latter obligingly read in his presence. According to Byrnes's account, Szilard's chief complaint was that "he and some of his associates did not know enough about the policy of the Government with regard to the use of the bomb." Szilard's assertion in the memorandum that "this situation can be evaluated only by men who have first-hand knowledge of the facts involved, that is, by the small group of scientists who are actively engaged in this work," plainly irritated Byrnes, who sometimes described his role in the Roosevelt administration as that of "assistant President." No doubt galling, too, was Szilard's proposal that he and his colleagues submit their ideas on how the bomb should be used to a special subcommittee of the Cabinet that did not include the secretary of state. "His general demeanor and his desire to participate in policy making made an unfavorable impression on me," Byrnes later said of Szilard.[4]

It was Szilard's turn to be disappointed during this visit when Byrnes abruptly dismissed his proposal that the United States inform the Russians of the bomb before its use. Groves had already assured him that there was, in any case, no uranium in Russia, Byrnes told Szilard. Groves's belief that the Russians had access to deposits of only very low-grade uranium ore in their own country—and lacked the technology to develop even those—was behind the general's estimate that it would take the Russians from ten to twenty years to develop their first atomic bomb. For the same reason, Groves believed the growth of the Soviet nuclear arsenal would thereafter be indefinitely slowed by the West's near-monopoly of atomic raw materials, which his own efforts during the war had been directed at guaranteeing.

Szilard himself initially believed that international control of the raw materials needed to make atomic bombs might be a way to prevent the spread of the weapon after the war. But he soon abandoned the idea as utopian, since any nation that wanted the bomb desperately enough would find the means and materials necessary to build it. While Szilard conceded that it was entirely possible the Russians were deficient in high-grade uranium, he pointed out to Byrnes that low-grade uranium ore—which the Soviets might have in abundance—could also be used.

Szilard also challenged Byrnes's clear inference that the Russians lacked both the know-how and the industrial capacity to build something as complex as the atomic bomb. Szilard believed, correctly, that Groves underestimated the Russians' technological prowess and overestimated the difficulties they would have in getting uranium.[5]

Nonetheless, Byrnes remained unmoved by Szilard's argument and, according to the latter, "showed complete indifference" to the subject of the future control of bomb. For his part, Szilard professed to being "completely flabbergasted" by Byrnes's assertion that America's use of the atomic bomb against Japan might make the Russians "more manageable" in upcoming discussions on the fate of postwar Europe. Nor was he placated when Byrnes raised the possibility that America's monopoly of the bomb could eventually force the Russians out of Szilard's homeland. Byrnes's suggestion "offended my sense of proportion," Szilard later wrote. "I was not disposed at this point to worry about what would happen to Hungary."[6]

The contentious encounter between the eccentric physicist and the southern politician ended with neither persuaded of the other's views. Depressed, Szilard and his colleagues returned to Chicago to learn that Groves was furious at the scientists for going outside of channels in their abortive approach to Truman. Although the Manhattan Project director cited the need to maintain secrecy as the reason for his objection, Szilard suspected Groves's real worry was that the scientists might persuade the government not to use the bomb in the war. Szilard believed that this concern, and not security, was also the real reason why the Army discouraged contact between scientists at the University of Chicago and their counterparts at the secret laboratory in the New Mexican desert. As Szilard later noted, he and his colleagues were tipped off to the imminent test of the first atomic bomb when Groves suddenly forbade telephone calls between the Chicago lab and Los Alamos.[7]

"We did not even speak the same language. . ."

Szilard was, to be sure, not the only scientist worried about the government's seeming indifference to the postwar implications of atomic energy. The previous summer, Danish physicist Niels Bohr, Szilard's mentor, had approached British Prime Minister Winston Churchill with a proposal that the West inform the Russians of the atomic bomb before using it in the war. Churchill's response was a quick and gruff rejection. "We did not even speak the same language," Bohr recalled of the meeting.

Bohr's subsequent interview with Roosevelt went better—prompting him to mistakenly believe that the president shared his views on international control of the bomb.[8] But a secret agreement that Roosevelt signed with Churchill in September 1944 pledged the United States to cooperate with Britain exclusively on matters concerning atomic energy. Roosevelt agreed with Churchill at a later meeting that Bohr should be watched.[9]

Despite their role as de facto science advisers to both Roosevelt and Truman, Vannevar Bush and James Conant fared little better than Szilard or Bohr in their attempts at influencing postwar policy on the bomb. The recommendation that Bush and Conant made to Roosevelt in the fall of 1944—urging the president to avoid binding the government to an Anglo-American "duopoly" of the bomb, and proposing instead "a free interchange of all scientific information on this subject"—was, as events would show, simply disregarded.[10]

While most of the people who knew about the bomb probably considered the question of its postwar fate premature, Szilard and his colleagues at the University of Chicago continued their efforts to force the government to think about the problem. In June 1945, in response to growing pressure from these scientists, Groves agreed to forward the recommendations of the Franck Report to the Pentagon and War Secretary Henry Stimson. This report by a panel of seven scientists, headed by Chicago's James Franck, appealed for international control of the bomb and sought to discourage any hope of an enduring American monopoly on the weapon after the war.

The Franck Report also went further than either Szilard's March memorandum or an earlier study by scientists—the 1944 Jeffries Report on the postwar implications of atomic energy—in urging that the president, rather than ordering the atomic bomb dropped on a city, approve a noncombat "demonstration . . . in an appropriately selected uninhabited area." Such a demonstration—*"before the eyes of representatives of all the United Nations, on the desert or a barren island,"* the Franck Report emphasized— would prove the bomb's power to friend and foe alike and yet avoid a needless mass slaughter of humanity.[11]

"A rehearsal demonstration. . ."

Ironically, Roosevelt had been one of the first to consider the possibility of a noncombat demonstration of the bomb, in lieu of its military use, during a conversation in late September 1944 with Vannevar Bush. A week later, Bush and Conant endorsed the idea of a demonstration, either of the bomb itself or of radiological warfare, in a memorandum to the president: "This demonstration might be over enemy territory, or in our own country, with subsequent notice to Japan that the materials would be used against the Japanese mainland unless surrender was forthcoming."[12]

Two months later, unaware that the subject had already been discussed by the president and his advisers, Alexander Sachs proposed what he called "a rehearsal demonstration" of the bomb before an international assembly of scientists. Bush, Conant, and Sachs all later claimed that Roosevelt seemed favorably disposed toward the idea of a demonstration—certainly as a prelude, and possibly as an alternative, to military use of the bomb. But if so, the president's interest in a demonstration was not conveyed to Vice President Truman before Roosevelt's death.[13]

Perhaps the first among the actual builders of the bomb to propose a demonstration was physicist Robert R. Wilson, who had toyed with the idea in a March 1943 conversation with Robert Oppenheimer at Los Alamos, where work was about to begin on the weapon. Oppenheimer at that time was more concerned with whether the bomb would work than with the prospect of using it in the war. Oppenheimer also expressed doubts, Wilson remembered, that the bomb, even if it worked, would be a militarily useful weapon.[14] Nonetheless, Oppenheimer on this occasion seemed willing to entertain the idea of a demonstration—though he was "very negative," Wilson recalled, to the suggestion that the Russians also be invited.[15]

More than a year later, in late 1944, when the defeat of Germany seemed assured, Wilson again raised the question of a demonstration, this time at a general meeting of scientists at Los Alamos. At this gathering, Oppenheimer challenged the practicality of a demonstration, Wilson said, but again did not dismiss the idea outright.

Several weeks after the surrender of Germany, in June 1945, it was Oppenheimer who brought up the subject of a demonstration in a conversation with Wilson. This time, Wilson recalled, Oppenheimer actively opposed the idea as impractical, raising the question of what would happen if the bomb were a dud. With the test of the implosion "gadget" less than a month away, Wilson told Oppenheimer facetiously, "We could always kill the envoys."[16]

What would come to be known as the demonstration option also subsequently appealed to several other scientists. At the University of Chicago, Arthur Compton had, early on, given tentative support to the idea. Several possibilities for the demonstration were even proposed by those who knew of the upcoming test. Among them was detonating the bomb far out at sea, in sight of observers on board a U.S. Navy ship, including representatives from Japan and possibly Russia. Other ideas were to drop the bomb in Tokyo Bay or explode it harmlessly but dramatically above Mount Fuji—in full view of the capital's inhabitants and the emperor. The most ambitious suggestion was to invite international observers to witness the effect of the weapon upon an uninhabited "model city" specially constructed for the purpose in a remote area of the United States.[17]

The option of demonstrating the atomic bomb instead of—or at least prior to—dropping it on a city in Japan was also being discussed at the Pentagon by the spring of 1945. Lewis Strauss, who had become an aide to Secretary of the Navy James Forrestal, had an especially imaginative suggestion for demonstrating the atomic bomb in a sparsely settled area of Japan. Remembering a particular grove of cryptomeria trees near the village of Nikko on the main island of Japan, which he and his wife had visited years earlier on a vacation, Strauss proposed that the bomb be detonated above the trees after the village had been warned and evacuated. Strauss's theory was that once the Japanese saw the flattened cryptomeria, a tree associated in folklore with the nation itself, they would come to the appropriate conclusions about the inevitable fate of their empire if the war continued.[18]

A major argument of the sponsors of the demonstration option was the unique effects expected from the atomic bomb. Well before the first actual test, the scientists building the bomb were aware of the unprecedented spectacle—and hazard—the weapon portended. A memorandum Oppenheimer wrote in May 1945 regarding "the radiological effects to be expected from the special bomb" speculated that the atomic test would theoretically release enough radioactivity to kill a billion human beings if it were evenly distributed. But Oppenheimer predicted that so-called prompt radiation of gamma and x-rays from the bomb would be lethal only within a half mile of the explosion, while "injurious" to people out to a mile radius. The danger from "fallout"—the long-lived fission products created by the bomb, as well as the radioactive debris caught up in the expanding fireball—was considered less predictable, since it depended upon the height to which the debris cloud rose and the weather at the time of the explosion.[19]

Several weeks earlier, Groves had asked Oppenheimer for assurances that the shock wave from the bomb would not damage buildings far from the point of explosion and lead to lawsuits against the government. Oppenheimer wrote back in June that "there will be some rather marked sound effects as far away as fifty or sixty miles, but these will be rather freakish in nature and should not be accompanied by shattering of windows." (Enrico Fermi, on the other hand, speculated that the bomb might blow up all of New Mexico. Just in case, Groves prepared a press release attributing the deaths of a large number of scientists to an unexpectedly powerful explosion of an unidentified nature.)[20]

Even before the bomb was tested, most of those building it recognized that the searing light and heat of the atomic explosion would be its most impressive, if not necessarily most lethal, effect. The light from the bomb was expected to be as much as a thousand times more intense than the sun at midday. Estimates were that the temperature at the center of the explosion would be several million degrees Fahrenheit—rivaling that at the surface of the sun—and that the heat of the atomic fireball would be felt by observers even several miles away.[21]

In Washington on May 31, 1945, while final preparations for the atomic test were under way in New Mexico, the demonstration option was briefly raised at the fourth meeting of the Interim Committee, the seven-member group that Secretary of War Henry Stimson had assembled to advise the Truman administration on the use and future of the atomic bomb. In addition to Stimson, Bush, Conant, and Byrnes, the committee included Undersecretary of the Navy Ralph Bard, Assistant Secretary of State William Clayton, and President of MIT Karl Compton. Stimson aide George Harrison acted as secretary for the group.

Despite the fact that the idea had been discussed the previous year by Bush and Conant, and more recently by scientists at Los Alamos and the University of Chicago, the demonstration option was not formally considered by the committee. It was only briefly discussed over lunch, mostly by Byrnes and the committee's scientific panel, consisting of Oppenheimer, Fermi, Arthur Compton, and Ernest Lawrence.

Compton, who still favored the demonstration, received little encouragement from the scientific panel or Byrnes and let the issue drop.[22] Practical considerations underlay the Interim Committee's decision to reject the idea of a demonstration. But Oppenheimer may also have opposed it for a specific pragmatic reason that went unremarked at this meeting.

In 1984, Robert Serber, Oppenheimer's close friend and confidant, disclosed that "Oppie" had privately explored the demonstration option with high-ranking representatives of the Army Air Force, only to find them "adamantly opposed" to the idea. "They could never send an observation plane or any kind of plane over Japan without it being attacked," Serber said the officers told Oppenheimer. Accordingly, Army Air Force leaders declared that they would refuse any order that sent a bomber crew on a perilous mission over Japan without the intention of doing serious harm to the enemy. But Oppenheimer opposed the demonstration primarily, Serber speculated, because the two men shared the view that the bomb had to be used against people to have the necessary psychological effect: "We believed the shock would end the war. And the shock would be much less if it was a demonstration. Some guy would come back and say it was a big explosion and they wouldn't believe him."[23]

The topic of the demonstration came up again in mid-June 1945, when the Franck Report was discussed among the scientific panel of the Interim Committee, in a final meeting at Los Alamos. Again the idea was opposed on practical grounds. Oppenheimer objected that the bomb might not work and that a dud could be captured by the Japanese and used against Americans invading their homeland. Another concern was that the enemy, if given sufficient warning, might move Allied prisoners of war onto the announced target site.[24]

While noting that "opinions . . . are not unanimous," the report that the scientific panel gave Stimson on June 16 was unequivocal in its rejection of the demonstration option. That report, written by Oppenheimer as the panel's chairman, noted that the scientists could "propose no technical demonstration likely to bring an end to the war; we see no acceptable alternative to direct military use."[25]

"A light not of this world . . ."

The test of the plutonium "gadget" the following month, at a spot in the desert that Oppenheimer had dubbed Trinity Site, both confirmed some scientists in their opinion that a demonstration might compel the Japanese to surrender and awakened second thoughts among a few previous doubters.

As Oppenheimer predicted, the most impressive thing about the explosion just before dawn was the brilliant light—visible over an area of three states.[26] The bomb temporarily blinded several observers some ten thousand feet away, one of whom compared it to "a close flash of lightning on a dark night."[27] Correspondent William Lawrence of the *New York Times* described it as "a light not of this world, the light of many suns in one." Isidor Rabi remembered it as "the brightest light I have ever seen or that I think anyone else has ever seen. It blasted; it pounced; it bored its way into you." "One sees this monstrous globe of fire expanding," said another witness of the atomic test. "You can't restrain the question, will it stop?"[28]

As predicted, the heat of the bomb's thermal pulse, which was felt up to ten miles from ground zero, was the other effect most vividly remembered by those at Trinity. A spectator more than five miles away compared it to standing a few feet from a campfire. The shock wave that arrived a few seconds after the light and heat made less of an impression, though it still unsettled some scientists, including one expert on conventional explosives. "Although I had expected it, the intensity of the blast startled me," wrote Maurice Shapiro in his report to Groves. "My impression at the time was that an enemy observer stationed about 20 miles from the scene of delivery would be deeply impressed, to say the least."[29]

Three witnesses were so awed by the Trinity test that the following day they sent Navy Captain William Parsons, head of the Ordnance Division at Los Alamos, a memorandum, titled "Proposal for a Modified Tactical Use of the Gadget," which recommended an altogether different kind of "demonstration." Because the radiant energy from the bomb was, they wrote, "very much greater than was originally estimated"—so much so, they noted, that it had awakened and momentarily blinded a sleeping serviceman some ten miles away—they urged that consideration be given to using the bomb's light itself as a weapon.

Their memorandum suggested that the plane carrying the bomb be preceded over the target by another plane, which would drop "a parachute equipped dummy bomb—provided with super powerful sirens, unusual lights, etc." to prompt those on the ground to look up. The real bomb would then be dropped, fused to explode high in the air. "It is our feeling," the three explained, "that nobody within a radius of five miles could look directly at the gadget and retain his eyesight."[30] Left unresolved was whether this bizarre variation on the demonstration option would be instead of or in addition to military use of the bomb against Japan. In any event, unknown to the authors of the memorandum and to scientists at the University of Chicago and Los Alamos, the report of the scientific panel to Stimson a month earlier had already rendered the question of a demonstration moot.

"No claim to special competence. . ."

Although during his meeting with Byrnes, on May 28, Szilard appeared relieved that Oppenheimer would be advising the government on the use of the bomb, he had meanwhile grown pessimistic again that "Oppie" could— or would—prevent the bomb from being dropped on Japan. The scientists who built the weapon, Szilard now felt, had a vested interest in seeing it used.[31]

In fact, Szilard and Oppenheimer were by this time on opposite sides not only of the question of whether and how the bomb should be used—but also regarding the role that scientists should play in the decision. Whereas Szilard had told Byrnes that scientists were the best qualified—indeed, perhaps the only ones qualified—to advise the government on the use of the bomb, Oppenheimer's report to Stimson on behalf of the scientific panel expressed an entirely different view: one that epitomized the dominant pre-war attitude of the scientific community in America concerning the proper relationship of scientists to their government. "With regard to these general aspects of the use of atomic energy," Oppenheimer had written,

> it is clear that we, as scientific men, have no proprietary rights. It is true that we are among the few citizens who have had occasion to give thought-ful consideration to these problems during the past few years. We have, however, no claim to special competence in solving the political, social, and military problems which are presented by the advent of atomic bombs.[32]

The report of the scientific panel had implicitly rejected the notion of a government of experts represented by Szilard's *Bund*. Far from the "open conspiracy" that Szilard originally envisioned, the atomic bomb project had been transformed by wartime secrecy and the federal bureaucracy into a closely knit, highly secretive elect—one from which Szilard himself, ironical-ly, was now excluded. It was not Szilard and his idealistic *Bund,* but the Interim Committee and its scientific panel—especially Bush, Conant, and Oppenheimer—who now spoke for science in the Truman administration.

Further evidence of the Bund's isolation was the fact that another issue still being debated by Szilard and his colleagues at the University of Chicago—the wisdom of alerting the Japanese to the existence of the bomb prior to its use—had already been discussed and rejected by the Interim Committee in its May 31 meeting. It was agreed there, as Stimson noted with emphasis, that *"we could not give the Japanese any warning."* Instead, Conant had proposed that when used the bomb should be dropped on "a vital war plant employing a large number of workers and closely surrounded by workers' houses." The same practical difficulties that stood in the way of a demon-stration worked against the proposed warning. As Oppenheimer and others pointed out, the plane carrying the bomb might be shot down; worse, Amer-ican POWs might be brought into the target area.

What had been nearly a year's discussion among the scientists on the twin questions of the demonstration and advance warning was reduced to a few sentences in Oppenheimer's June 16 report to Stimson:

> Those who advocate a purely technical demonstration would wish to out-law the use of atomic weapons, and have feared that if we use the weapons now our position in future negotiations will be prejudiced. Others empha-size the opportunity of saving American lives by immediate military use, and believe that such use will improve the international prospects, in that they are more concerned with the prevention of war than with the elimina-tion of this specific weapon.

He and the other panel members found themselves "closer to these latter views," Oppenheimer wrote.

By his own admission, Oppenheimer's views on the demonstration changed after the war. Although he had originally ridiculed the idea as "a nuclear firecracker," Oppenheimer in a 1957 interview seemed willing to entertain the argument that a demonstration might have compelled the Japanese to surrender: "We didn't know beans about the military situation," Oppenheimer said of the scientific panel. "We didn't know whether [the Japanese] could be caused to surrender by other means or whether invasion was really inevitable."[33]

The summary verdict rendered by the scientific panel's report meant that the rival view of those scientists who supported the demonstration—or warning the Japanese—reached no higher than Stimson's office. Arthur Compton, entrusted with delivering the Franck Report to Stimson at the Pentagon on June 12, simply left it with Stimson's aide after he and Franck were denied a chance to see the secretary of war. Stimson apparently did not see the report until after the issue of how to use the bomb had already been decided.[34]

When he passed along the Interim Committee's recommendations to the president later that month, Stimson did not mention the demonstration or advance warning. As a result, Truman probably remained unaware of the debate among scientists on the bomb's use and of the continuing lobbying of scientists at the University of Chicago and Los Alamos for warning Japan.

Stimson on his own brought up the question of "whether it was worthwhile to try to warn Japan into surrender" in a meeting with the president on July 2. But the paper that he gave Truman on this occasion made no specific mention of the atomic bomb and discussed only in vague terms the kind of warning he had in mind. Stimson merely wished to impress upon the enemy, he wrote, the "varied and overwhelming character of the forces we are about to bring to bear on the islands," as well as the "inevitability and completeness of the destruction which the full application of this force will entail." The entry in Truman's private journal for July 25 suggests that the president mistakenly believed that the Japanese would be notified of the impending atomic raids: "The target will be a purely military one and we will issue a warning statement asking the Japs to surrender and save lives." (In fact, while leaflets were dropped on other Japanese cities warning of further attacks after the bombing of Hiroshima and Nagasaki, neither of those cities received advance notice of the atomic raid.)[35]

The Navy's representative on the Interim Committee, Ralph Bard, had urged Truman at the end of June to warn the Japanese about the bomb before using it. Yet Bard's appeal, too, was unavailing. The Potsdam ultimatum, issued by Byrnes on July 26, threatened the Japanese with "prompt and utter destruction" unless they surrendered, but made no explicit mention of a pending atomic attack or of the new weapon. Since an average of one Japanese city a day was then being ruined by conventional bombing, Byrnes's wording did not attract particular attention.[36]

"Based upon purely moral considerations. . ."

Although he had been one of the earliest sponsors of a demonstration, Szilard changed his mind as the deadline for the decision on the bomb approached. He had become convinced that an unannounced demonstration, just as much as actual use of the bomb against a city in Japan, would inevitably trigger a nuclear arms race with Russia. Szilard's about-face on the demonstration was also prompted in part by his belief that the argument of the Franck Report against military use of the bomb wrongly rested upon utilitarian rather than ethical grounds.[37] The "time has come," Szilard decided in early July, "for the scientists to go on record against the use of the bomb against the cities of Japan" on moral grounds.[38]

Believing another attempt at a personal intercession with Truman would be futile, Szilard hoped that the unified protest of those who had built the weapon might make a difference. In mid-July, he sent to scientists at Chicago and Los Alamos a petition urging that the atomic bomb not be used against Japan until the surrender terms offered to the enemy had been made public and the Japanese had been given a chance to surrender. In a letter accompanying the petition to Oppenheimer at Los Alamos, Szilard acknowledged that his effort might be a noble but empty gesture on behalf of the scientists' reputation in history, since it was unlikely at this late date to alter the course of events. "But I have no doubt," Szilard wrote, "that from a point of view of the standing of the scientists in the eyes of the general public one or two years from now it is a good thing that a minority of scientists should have gone on record in favor of giving greater weight to moral arguments."[39]

Only sixty-eight out of the more than one hundred and fifty scientists at the University of Chicago chose to sign Szilard's petition—even though a subsequent poll taken by Compton showed that the majority there favored either a prior "experimental demonstration" in the United States, or an unspecified "military demonstration in Japan . . . before full use of the weapon is employed."[40] (At Los Alamos, where the first bomb had just been tested, Oppenheimer refused to let Szilard's petition circulate— allegedly justifying his decision, according to Edward Teller, on the grounds that "scientists had no right to use their prestige to try to influence political decisions.")[41]

The clash between Oppenheimer and Szilard over the petition was emblematic of their different views on the role—and responsibilities—of scientists in advising the government on the decision to drop the atomic bomb. To those actually assigned responsibility for that advice, including Groves, the scientific panel, and members of the Interim Committee, the moral agonizing of Szilard and his colleagues doubtless seemed both presumptuous and largely beside the point.

When he sent his petition to Groves, Szilard requested that it be forwarded on to Stimson and Truman "as promptly as possible." But the general held on to the document for nearly a week before sending it to the sec-retary of war. Because the president was by that time in midocean on the cruiser *Augusta,* returning from the Potsdam conference, and since Truman had, in any case, already made the decision to use the bomb, Stimson saw no purpose in sending the petition further. Neither it nor the result of Compton's poll was received by the president until after the bombing of Hiroshima. Indeed, not until August 17, more than a week after the second atomic bomb had been dropped and following Japan's offer to surrender, did Szilard's petition reach the White House.[42]

"A feeling of relief. . ."

Even though he and his associates failed to prevent the use of atomic bombs against cities in Japan, Szilard continued to hope, in the wake of the Japanese surrender, that a *Bund* of scientists might yet influence the Ameri-can government's postwar policy regarding the atom. It was for this reason, Szilard wrote, that his reaction to the news of Hiroshima was "a feeling of relief. . . . A component of this relief is that we were completely bottled up in our discussions—it was not possible to get real issues before the public because of secrecy. Suddenly the secrecy was dropped and it was possible to tell people what this was about and what we were facing in this century."[43]

But Szilard's sense of relief was short-lived. His notion of the *Bund* was to become a victim of the secrecy that Szilard himself had helped to bring about. Upon informing Groves of his intention to make the petition pub-lic—part of his personal effort to stimulate postwar debate on the bomb—Szilard was promptly told by the Army that because the petition was still a secret document, notwithstanding the war's end, it "did not fall within the purview of such information which could be released without jeopardy."[44] Should the petition become public as a result of his efforts, Szilard was warned, he would face prosecution under the espionage laws for disclosing classified information.[45]

To be sure, Szilard was not alone among scientists in feeling like a prophet without honor in the land, both his advice and his warnings having been disregarded. Neither Szilard's *Bund,* which had first brought atomic energy to the government's attention, nor the scientific leaders of mammoth organi-zations like the Office of Scientific Research and Development and the National Defense Research Committee, which had overseen early work on the bomb, were accorded a voice in deciding the weapon's fate once hostili-ties had ended.

Even Bush and Conant, whose technical advice on the bomb had been eagerly sought by two presidents during the war, found themselves power-less to influence the government's postwar policy on atomic energy. Bush's recommendation that the United States approach the Russians openly on the bomb was no better received by Truman in the fall of 1945 than it had been a year earlier by Roosevelt. Although Truman publicly credited Bush with being his chief adviser on atomic policy, the president's decision to exclude the Russians from postwar cooperation on the atom was actually in direct opposition to Bush's views.[46]

In a personal letter to Conant in November, Bush despaired of Truman's decision to dissolve the Interim Committee against his and Conant's advice, particularly since no definite plan had yet been worked out for the postwar control of the bomb. Bush also hinted that Truman's choice of a long-time friend and speechwriter, Judge Samuel Rosenman, as an adviser on the bomb was sufficient cause for both men to consider resigning from the government: "If Rosenman is to be considered the principle adviser on atomic energy matters to the administration, I thought it was high time the rest of us stepped out."[47] Bush felt "really excluded from the group considering this matter of policy on atomic energy," he had confided to Conant a few days earlier.[48]

Not only on the atomic bomb but on the broader question of the postwar organization of science for defense in the still undeclared cold war, Truman seemed unconcerned by his isolation from the two men who, since Roosevelt's time, had served as the main bridge between the White House and the nation's scientific community. Like the Interim Committee, the Office of Scientific Research and Development was another early casualty of the peace. Shortly after the surrender of Germany, Bush himself had begun urging that OSRD be disbanded as part of a demobilization effort intended to restore freedom to scientific research. But Bush evidently did not expect that Truman, in agreeing to abolish OSRD, would balk at his suggestion to give scientists and scientific research a more prominent postwar role.

"We kept silent. . ."

In November 1944, when victory finally seemed assured, Franklin Roosevelt had asked Bush to begin thinking about the postwar status of science in the United States. Roosevelt was primarily concerned with adapting scientific knowledge gained during the war to commercial processes and medical research. But Bush interpreted the president's instructions as justifying a wider mandate. The end result, a 192-page report titled *Science: The Endless Frontier,* was Bush's blueprint for the postwar reorganization of science in the government, and was given to Truman some two months after Roosevelt's death.[49]

Although the president publicly praised Bush's report, Truman rejected its principal recommendation, which would have meant a dramatic increase in government support for basic scientific research. Other suggestions by Bush received similarly short shrift. The creation of a National Science Foundation (NSF), which Bush urged, was first delayed by Congress—fearful of the new power the organization might give the president—and subsequently vetoed by Truman himself when Congress refused to give him the authority to appoint the NSF's director and to overrule the actions of its governing board. Similarly, a proposed Research Board for National Security was objected to by the administration's budget director, who feared losing control of the national treasury to fund-hungry research scientists.[50]

Because the abolition of OSRD meant there would no longer be a central clearinghouse in the government for scientific advice on military matters, Bush proposed, in May 1946, the establishment of a Joint Research and Development Board (JRDB) in the Pentagon to coordinate weapons research. No sooner was the JRDB created, though, than interservice rivalry rendered it largely ineffective. Jealous of their prerogatives in the area of weapons procurement, the military also blocked establishment of a proposed Division of National Defense in the National Academy of Sciences.[51]

Only a year after the dissolution of the Manhattan Project, the responsibility for overseeing defense-related research was once again in the hands of the individual services, as variously represented by the Office of Naval Research, the Army Research Office, and the Air Force's Office of Scientific Research. At the end of 1946, when the U.S. Atomic Energy Commission (AEC) was established, responsibility for advice pertaining to nuclear weapons policy was assigned to the AEC's General Advisory Committee (GAC).[52]

By this time as well, deteriorating relations between the president and two of the original architects of the Manhattan Project, Bush and Conant, meant that the logical representatives of the nation's scientific community were virtually shut out of Truman's inner circle. Indeed, when the president decided to order his own study of science's proper place in the government, he had pointedly ignored Bush and picked as its director John Steelman— Truman's long-time friend and a former public relations consultant. Truman's decision to assign Bush a spot on Steelman's committee seemed an intentional snub, one that prompted Bush to submit his resignation—which Truman, however, refused to accept.[53]

Truman's personal relationship with other scientists—including Oppenheimer, the best-known and most respected scientist in the country after the war—reflected a like degree of suspicion and even distrust. Following a strained meeting in October 1945 between the president and the physicist, during which Oppenheimer reportedly spoke with some anguish of the guilt he felt over the Hiroshima bombing, Truman rejected a 1946 appeal from Bush that he meet once more with the dean of America's atomic scientists— whom the president privately described as a "cry-baby."[54]

Other attempts by scientists to see Truman on matters of atomic policy never got as far as the Oval Office. In the winter of 1947, a request for a meeting with the president from Niels Bohr got only as high as Gorden Arneson, Stimson's former aide, who had become the Pentagon's liaison with the State Department on atomic energy. Arneson dutifully listened for

more than two hours in Bohr's unheated apartment to the physicist's animated plea for more "openness" with the Russians, but subsequently
reported to the Pentagon that he had been more impressed by Bohr's dedication and earnestness than by the logic of the scientist's argument.[55]

The following year, Albert Einstein was met by a low-ranking foreign
service officer when he made another of his frequent appeals on behalf of
international control of the atom. (Einstein had already publicly acknowledged regret for his role in bringing the atomic bomb to Roosevelt's attention. Had he realized how far behind the United States the Germans were in
building the bomb, Einstein said after the war, he would never have signed
Szilard's letter to the president.)[56]

Einstein's political views received no more sympathetic a hearing in the
government than Bohr's. His interrogator sent a report to the State Department noting that the inventor of the relativity theory "seemed naive in the
field of international politics and mass human relations. The man who pop-
ularized the concept of a fourth dimension could think in only two of them
in considerations of World Government."[57]

Szilard, for his part, had meanwhile abandoned hope that scientists
might influence the government by petitions or personal appeals. Instead,
his energies were increasingly directed toward stimulating public discussion
of the bomb's implications. In articles he wrote for the newly established
Bulletin of the Atomic Scientists, as one of the founders of the prodisarma-
ment Council for a Liveable World, and through the so-called Angels Project—an early exchange of Soviet and American scientists—Szilard became
an active and outspoken critic of the Truman administration's policy of
secrecy and monopoly on the bomb. Still espousing faith in an "open conspiracy" of scientists, Szilard also continued to promote the cause of international cooperation. But as he had already discovered, the success of his
Bund in building the atomic bomb had not been matched in its attempts to
control the weapon.[58]

In reality, it was not to the scientists but to the military—and specifically to
General Leslie Groves—that Truman turned after the war for advice on
what to do about the atomic bomb. Groves' prediction of a "preclusive"
atomic monopoly, lasting ten to twenty years—in contrast to the brief
respite of three to five years predicted by Szilard and most other scientists—
was the estimate on which Truman and Byrnes, and ultimately even Bush
and Conant, based their expectations of a more tractable Soviet Union after
the war. (Like the majority of scientists, Bush and Conant originally sided
with the three-to-five year figure. But in 1946, evidently convinced by
Groves of his mistaken belief that the Russians lacked access to high-grade
uranium, both men changed their estimate to agree with the general's prediction of a much longer "breathing spell.")[59]

Moreover, with the exception of individuals like Einstein and Szilard,
the majority of atomic scientists were initially little interested in shaping the

postwar policies of their government. He and most of his colleagues "refused the numerous requests to speak over the radio or before groups on what the atomic bomb was and what it might mean to the world," Szilard noted. "We kept silent."[60]

"A reluctant lobby. . ."

One notable exception to this silence was the outcry American scientists raised against legislation originally endorsed by the Truman administration for the postwar control of atomic energy. Scientists unfamiliar with the workings of the government joined in creating the Federation of Atomic Scientists for the purpose of defeating a bill that would have given control of the atom to the military. In the spring of 1946 they threw their support instead behind legislation establishing the civilian AEC.[61]

The success of this so-called reluctant lobby emboldened some scientists to approach the government with advice on what to do about the atomic bomb. By late 1946, even Oppenheimer would probably have disagreed with his pre-Hiroshima disclaimer that atomic scientists felt "no proprietary rights" with regard to what was done with the bomb. More than a year after the war's end, the apathy of scientists regarding their role in the government was ending—albeit slowly.[62]

Oppenheimer himself would play a key role in drafting the original American proposal for international control of atomic energy that was presented to the United Nations in June 1946. Isidor Rabi, along with other members of Szilard's original *Bund,* had meanwhile also joined other public advocates of international control of the atom.[63]

But the familiar question of how to make their voices heard now confronted Oppenheimer and Rabi, as earlier it had Einstein and Szilard. Szilard's experience had shown that petitions and personal appeals were at best an uncertain avenue of approach; most failed to reach the White House. Moreover, even were a scientist finally to be admitted to the Oval Office, there was no guarantee that he or she would subsequently be able to defend or promote the scientists' cause within the administration.

The result was that the American scientific community, already split over what to do about the riven atom, was likewise divided in its efforts to influence the policies of the Truman administration. By 1949, while Szilard continued to lobby for international control of the atom in virtual isolation, several of the *Bund*'s charter members, including Rabi, Fermi, Teller, and Strauss, found themselves on opposite sides of another key question: whether to proceed with development of the next, more powerful generation of nuclear weapons.

3

"Necessarily an Evil Thing"

The Debate over the H-Bomb

The part they played in the development of the atomic bomb left many in the American scientific community with mixed feelings about their subsequent relationship to the government. On the one hand, scientists enjoyed a new sense of power and prestige because of their contribution to the war effort; on the other was a feeling of frustration and even helplessness at their inability to control the forces they had brought into being.

After Hiroshima, the view that they had "no proprietary rights" to a say in what was done with their inventions was no longer automatically accepted among atomic scientists. But disagreement continued over whether it was presumptuous to claim that their expertise extended beyond the technical realm to the political, military, and ethical implications of nuclear weapons.

While this question had arisen only belatedly in the case of the atomic bomb, it was, from the outset, at the center of the controversy over whether to proceed with development of the hydrogen superbomb, or the Super, as it was also known.[1]

"A far more difficult development. . ."

Many years before an atomic bomb was known to be feasible, scientists were aware that if the fission bomb proved possible, an even more powerful and terrible weapon might also be built. As early as 1932, experts in Russia as well as the West were acquainted with the thermonuclear process of

34

fusion—in which two atoms of a light element combine under very high temperatures to form one atom of a second, heavier element. These scientists realized that a fusion reaction, if it could be made to occur, would release tremendous—indeed, literally stellar—amounts of energy on earth. In 1938, Hans Bethe, a theoretical physicist at Cornell University, proved that it was the fusion of hydrogen into helium that fueled the energy of the stars—a discovery for which he would be awarded the Nobel Prize some twenty-nine years later.

By early 1942, Edward Teller and Enrico Fermi had come to recognize that a fission reaction might be capable of generating the enormous heat necessary to spark the fusion of deuterium, an isotope of hydrogen.[2] Teller and Fermi envisioned a superbomb of virtually limitless power that would use an atomic bomb as its trigger. Work on the atomic bomb was abruptly suspended for a few weeks that summer as a result of Teller's speculation that the temperatures generated by a fission reaction might ignite the hydrogen in the atmosphere and oceans and cause the light elements of the earth's crust to burn—in effect, converting the entire planet into an exploding star.[3]

Most scientists agreed that building an atomic bomb was a prerequisite to developing the Super. Still, at the inaugural meeting of scientists at Los Alamos in the spring of 1943, Teller had made a plea for proceeding directly with an all-out effort on the H-bomb. One of the first buildings to be erected at Los Alamos was a laboratory designed to study the physical properties of deuterium, the fuel to be used in the H-bomb. (When it was later realized that there was little or no chance of developing the hydrogen bomb before war's end, however, the building was converted to a warehouse.)[4]

Despite the numerous scientific and engineering hurdles still to be overcome in building the fission "gadget," Teller remained single-mindedly committed to the H-bomb.[5] For his colleagues, the Super seemed an unlikely prospect until after the end of the war. Still, even the possibility of the hydrogen bomb raised concern. In a September 1944 memorandum to Roosevelt, Vannevar Bush and James Conant argued that invention of the Super would make it impossible to maintain a postwar monopoly of nuclear weapons.[6]

The H-bomb was discussed as well at the Interim Committee meeting of May 31, 1945, where Oppenheimer, noting that the Super would be "a far more difficult development" than the fission bomb, estimated that "a minimum of three years would be required to reach production." On the other hand, Oppenheimer noted, an H-bomb would be staggeringly powerful: While the atomic bomb was expected to be equivalent to 2,000 or possibly 20,000 tons of conventional explosives, a hydrogen bomb "might produce an explosive force equal to 10,000,000–100,000,000 tons of TNT."[7]

Within days of Japan's surrender, and before Soviet-American relations had begun to deteriorate, Secretary of State James Byrnes informed Oppenheimer "that he and the rest of the gang should pursue their work full force" on both improved atomic weapons and the superbomb. In response to Byrnes's urgings, a postwar meeting of the Interim Committee's scientific panel was convened to discuss weapons development. In late September, Oppenheimer submitted the panel's "Proposal for Research and Development in the Field of Atomic Energy," which contained a four-page discussion of the prospects for a hydrogen bomb.[8]

"A superbomb can be constructed. . ."

As was evident from the scientific panel's report, the H-bomb was already a subject of heated controversy among atomic scientists. A War Department aide informed Byrnes that he "understood from Dr. Oppenheimer the scientists prefer not to do that (superbomb) unless ordered or directed to do so by the Government on the grounds of national policy." In a letter to Secretary of Commerce Henry Wallace, scientific panel member Arthur Compton revealed how strongly the panel objected to proceeding with the H-bomb: "We feel that this development should not be undertaken, primarily because we should prefer defeat in war to a victory obtained at the expense of the enormous human disaster that would be caused by its determined use."[9]

Unconvinced that there was any need for the H-bomb, and eager to return to civilian life, several of the scientists whom Isidor Rabi had once described as "the first team" at Los Alamos began to leave the New Mexico lab: Bethe returned to Cornell; Oppenheimer to teaching at Berkeley and Caltech. When Teller learned that the superbomb would not be given high priority at the lab, he assumed a professorship at the University of Chicago.

Meanwhile, the secret of the superbomb was proving even more elusive than Oppenheimer had predicted. In April 1946, some of the Manhattan Project's veterans held a three-day, top-secret seminar at Los Alamos on the state of research into the H-bomb. While some progress toward the Super had been made at the lab, not all of the discoveries were encouraging.[10]

Scientists at Los Alamos had yet to determine even the feasibility of a hydrogen bomb. Answers to the questions of how—and whether—to proceed with the H-bomb awaited further calculations, which in turn required faster and more sophisticated computers. Another obstacle, acknowledged at the April 1946 conference, was the fact that "undertaking of the new and important Super Bomb Project would necessarily involve a considerable fraction of the resources which are likely to be devoted to work on atomic developments in the next years." Nonetheless, the final report of the conference had concluded: "It is likely that a superbomb can be constructed and will work."[11]

That summer, Teller, now in charge of the Los Alamos group working on the H-bomb, proposed a second, altogether different design for the weapon—designated TX-14, but known both at the lab and by its inventor as the Alarm Clock. (*His* Alarm Clock, Teller reportedly boasted, would awaken the world.[12])

Subsequent calculations suggested that Teller's Alarm Clock would fail to generate sufficiently high temperatures to sustain a thermonuclear reaction. Further, there was an even more fundamental problem with the Alarm Clock: its size. Estimates were that the bomb would be as tall as a three-story building and weigh between forty and one hundred tons: small enough to be taken by ship or submarine to a coastal city or harbor, but far too large to be carried by the Strategic Air Command's bombers to targets deep within the Soviet Union. The search continued at Los Alamos for a more practical, deliverable hydrogen bomb.[13]

In the fall of 1947, Teller and his colleagues at the Los Alamos lab proposed building yet another type of bomb—a hybrid fission-fusion weapon. The boosted fission bomb, or "Booster," would use the energy from an atomic explosion to ignite a small amount of thermonuclear fuel inside the fission bomb. The energy released might be double that of a pure-fission weapon. By the summer of 1948, the Booster had been added to a list of experimental atomic weapons to be tested in the Pacific three years later. But the Booster did not seem capable of achieving the scientists' goal of a deliverable bomb with the explosive force of one million or more tons of conventional explosives.[14]

Progress toward that goal had been stalled since at least the summer of 1947, in part because Los Alamos still lacked computers capable of modeling the intricate dynamics of a thermonuclear explosion. While most of his colleagues at Los Alamos believed that the search for the H-bomb had hit a dead end, Teller proved unwilling to abandon his efforts—though he reluctantly conceded, in a report that September, "that the decision whether considerable effort is to be put on the development of the TX-14 or the Super should be postponed for approximately two years; namely, until such time as these experiments, tests, and calculations have been carried out."[15]

"The highest national policy. . ."

Despite the fact that a decision to proceed with the H-bomb would be—in the words of the 1946 Los Alamos report—"a matter so filled with the most serious implications [that it should] properly be taken only as part of the highest national policy," President Truman as late as the fall of 1949 seemed oblivious of the work being done on the hydrogen bomb. National Security Council (NSC) Executive Secretary Sidney Souers left an Oval Office meeting that October with the impression that the president knew nothing at all of the H-bomb.[16]

In contrast, since its creation in January 1947, the AEC General Advisory Committee, headed by Robert Oppenheimer, had kept the commission informed in detail about the search for the secret of the H-bomb. In 1949, the GAC consisted of Manhattan Project veterans Oppenheimer, Fermi, Rabi, and Conant, physicists Oliver Buckley and Lee DuBridge, metallurgist Cyril Smith, electrical engineer Hartley Rowe, and chemist Glenn Seaborg.[17]

With Truman's dissolution of the Interim Committee and its scientific panel shortly after the surrender of Japan, the president had cut himself off from the best source of technical advice on nuclear weapons. Moreover, Henry Stimson and James Byrnes, to whom Truman had turned for political advice on the atomic bomb, were also now gone. Stimson had retired from government service in September 1945, at the age of seventy-eight. Little more than a year later, following a lengthy dispute with Truman over the conduct of foreign policy, Byrnes, too, had left the administration. Possibly because he saw Bush and Conant as Roosevelt appointees—or simply because of a conflict of personalities—Truman continued to ignore the two scientists who had been Roosevelt's de facto science advisers. Bush had meanwhile left the government to return to the Carnegie Institution.[18]

On most matters concerning the atomic bomb and atomic energy, Truman continued to rely for advice on the military, particularly former Manhattan Project director General Leslie Groves. Even after Groves had handed stewardship of the Manhattan Project over to the AEC in early 1947, his influence on American nuclear weapons policy was still evident—for example in the complacency with which the White House continued to regard the prospect of a Soviet atomic bomb.

As late as February 1948, when he retired from the Army, Groves's confidence in an enduring American atomic monopoly remained so strong that he publicly announced he was "not a bit worried" about a Russian bomb. "It is an oxcart-versus-automobile situation," Groves observed of the Soviet-American arms race a few months later. Groves's confidence remained unwavering, despite warning voices elsewhere in the government. In July 1949, for example, a group of experts representing the Pentagon, the AEC, and the CIA reported that the Russians would probably have their first atomic bomb by mid-1950 and were likely to have as many as 30 weapons by 1955, with a total arsenal of 150 bombs by mid-1957, at which time Soviet uranium reserves would probably be exhausted. Truman, however, chose to abide by Groves's estimate that it might be another decade before the Russians had a single bomb.[19]

To be sure, not all in the American government were as complacent as Truman and Groves about the prospect of a Soviet bomb. In spring 1949, the Air Force and the AEC established a secret Long-Range Detection Program, Project Centering, to monitor foreign nuclear weapons development. The program reportedly owed its origins in no small part to the concern of AEC Commissioner Lewis Strauss and others that a Soviet nuclear test might go undetected. Strauss claimed that he even offered to finance the project with his own money when the CIA and the Air Force showed no interest.[20]

Project Centering relied on a fleet of modified B-29 bombers to detect fallout injected into the upper atmosphere by nuclear explosions, supplementing the acoustic and seismic detectors that the Army had deployed since 1947 to measure the results of American atomic testing. The inauguration of the project proved especially timely. On September 3, 1949—barely two weeks after the program was begun—one of its planes, flying at 18,000 feet, picked up the first signs of low-level radiation from an unidentified "foreign source."

The initial reading of the sample was ambiguous. A top-secret CIA memorandum written six days later speculated that the probable source was either a Soviet atomic test or a recent volcanic eruption in northern Japan. But subsequent samples collected by other planes as well as by ground stations in Alaska and Washington, D.C., showed readings of higher intensity, which American analysts judged "consistent with the view that the origin of the fission products was the explosion of an atomic bomb."[21]

A team of U.S. experts headed by Vannevar Bush subsequently concluded that the Russian bomb, like the Trinity "gadget," had been put on a tower and that the explosion had taken place within one or two days of the end of August "somewhere over the northern part of the continent of Asia." Detailed analyses conducted over the next few days by scientists working for the Air Force, the CIA, and the AEC identified fission products that could have been produced only by an atomic explosion—ruling out the possibility, raised by Groves, that there had been a laboratory accident in Russia or the meltdown of an experimental nuclear reactor.[22]

Follow-up studies by Navy scientists and the CIA confirmed that the weapon tested in Russia was similar in both design and efficiency to the plutonium-implosion bombs the United States had tested in New Mexico and dropped on Nagasaki. (In the early 1990s, it was revealed that Russia's first atomic bomb was an almost exact copy of the U.S. bomb tested at Trinity. The design for the weapon had been stolen by Soviet spies.)[23]

The irrefutable evidence of a Russian bomb notwithstanding, Truman, Groves, and Defense Secretary Louis Johnson were initially disbelieving that the Soviets had broken the American monopoly. The president subsequently demanded—and got—a signed statement from Bush and his colleagues attesting that the fallout they analyzed was from an actual atomic explosion and not the results of a lab experiment gone awry. Even so, Truman's public announcement of the news on September 23 pointedly described the event as "an atomic explosion"—not specifically the test of an atomic bomb. As late as January 1953, Truman was telling the press that he doubted the Russians had either atomic or hydrogen bombs.[24]

"Unusual and even extraordinary steps. . ."

The dawning realization in Washington that the Soviet Union knew the secret of the atomic bomb gave a new and sudden urgency to the American search for the Super. Foremost in urging the government to give priority to development of the hydrogen bomb were Lewis Strauss and Edward Teller. The two men founded their own *Bund*-like association of scientists and nonscientists to promote the H-bomb, which Strauss described as the next necessary "quantum leap" in the development of nuclear weapons.[25]

Unlike Szilard's atomic *Bund,* however, Strauss and Teller's H-bomb lobby enjoyed the immediate support of influential political allies in Washington. One of the lobby's first recruits was Senator Brian McMahon, chairman of the powerful Joint Committee on Atomic Energy. Teller's contacts with high-ranking Air Force officers also guaranteed the lobby a valuable source of support in the Pentagon. Moreover, Strauss was now an AEC commissioner, appointed by Truman.

What proved to be an early impetus—as well as a sustaining fear—behind the H-bomb lobby was Strauss's belief that the Russians, "from the beginning," he wrote, had decided to "leapfrog" the Manhattan Project by simultaneously pushing ahead with research on both atomic and hydrogen bombs—as Teller had unsuccessfully urged the scientists at Los Alamos to do in 1943. Princeton mathematician-physicist John von Neumann as well as Berkeley physicists Ernest Lawrence and Luis Alvarez shared Strauss's suspicion that the Russians, by following this dual approach, had been able to match and perhaps even to pull ahead of the United States in the search for the H-bomb.[26]

In early October 1949, Strauss wrote to his fellow commissioners asking them to support his call for accelerated development of the H-bomb. While the assumption had always been that the United States had the lead in the nuclear arms race, Strauss argued, now "only the fact that we began sooner can be relied upon absolutely." Strauss recommended that "we immediately consult the General Advisory Committee to ascertain their views as to how we can proceed with expedition."[27]

Lacking any real information about the status of the Soviet nuclear weapons program, the H-bomb lobby relied on anecdote and rumor to support its contention that the United States might already be behind in the race for the Super. But because of the shock occasioned by the unexpected appearance of the Russian atomic bomb, their hypothesis attracted ready converts in Washington.

McMahon viewed the possibility that the Soviets were ahead of the United States less as conjecture than as a matter of established fact: "As you know, there is reason to fear that Soviet Russia has assigned top priority to development of a thermonuclear super-bomb," McMahon began a letter to the AEC on October 17, 1949. In it, the senator speculated that the Russians might have an H-bomb only two years hence and urged the commission to recommend that the American Super be pursued with all possible speed. He and his committee were in agreement, McMahon wrote, "that the current situation dictates unusual and even extraordinary steps to push ahead these projects."[28]

"A weapon of genocide. . ."

Called to Washington on October 28, less than two weeks later, to advise on whether the "Commission was making all appropriate progress in assuring the common defense and security," the members of the GAC began three days of deliberations on what should be done about the H-bomb.[29]

The first question raised by Oppenheimer at the GAC meeting was not whether the Russians might already be ahead but whether an H-bomb was ever likely to prove feasible. As the GAC's scientists knew, work had begun at Los Alamos earlier that month on a new approach to the problem of igniting thermonuclear fuel. Even if this approach worked, however, it represented only part of the solution to the problem of building the Super. While Teller had meanwhile resumed work on his Alarm Clock, recent calculations revealed new problems with both it and the boosted fission bomb. The growing concern at Los Alamos was that neither device would work.[30]

But whether the H-bomb could be built was not the only, or even the dominant, concern at this meeting. Oppenheimer and his colleagues concluded that "an imaginative and concerted attack on the problem has a better than even chance of producing the weapon within five years." Instead, the meeting initially focused on whether the H-bomb's potential value as a weapon outweighed its real costs to the rest of the atomic armaments program.[31]

Viewed in this light, it soon became clear that the H-bomb might make little practical sense as a weapon of war. As the GAC noted, the Super and Teller's Alarm Clock each required large amounts of tritium, which would be produced in nuclear reactors being used to make plutonium for fission bombs. Thus, a decision to speed up work on the H-bomb meant slowing the rate at which atomic bombs were being added to the nation's nuclear arsenal—an arsenal that, at approximately 250 bombs in 1949, was not only smaller than the public imagined but also still "insufficient," in the recent assessment of the Joint Chiefs of Staff, to meet military requirements. Partly for that reason, the Joint Chiefs had thus far shown little interest in promoting the H-bomb.

Further, improvements that had already been made in atomic bombs— and more advances that were anticipated—promised to increase their strategic importance. The type of atomic bomb being mass-produced in 1949 had more than twice the yield but used less than half the fissionable material of the weapon dropped on Nagasaki. An advanced, pure-fission weapon already on the drawing board would have a destructive force equivalent to half a million tons of conventional explosive—more than thirty times the yield of the weapon that had devastated Hiroshima.[32]

In addition, because tritium decays relatively rapidly, H-bombs, unlike atomic bombs, would have a limited "shelf life." Opponents of the H-bomb argued that using nuclear reactors to make tritium would be a far less efficient allocation of scarce resources—particularly since it remained far from certain that the H-bomb could be made to work. Even constructing a reactor specifically to make tritium, the solution proposed by some members of the H-bomb lobby, would still mean a delay of years in the superbomb program.[33]

On the morning of October 30, the attention of the GAC turned from the technical questions of whether the H-bomb could be built and what it might cost to the broader concern of whether it would be proper to build it. As members of the committee knew, the weapon being considered would release energy equivalent to ten million tons of TNT. Teller had compared the destructiveness of such a bomb to that of a meteor striking the earth, a major earthquake, or the eruption of a large volcano—calculating that it might destroy every structure within a radius of ten miles.[34] The committee properly recognized that Truman's decision on the H-bomb might conceivably decide—indirectly, unintentionally, but nonetheless literally—the fate of the earth.

They were particularly "alarmed," the scientists noted in their draft report, by "the possible global effects of the radioactivity generated by the explosion of a few super bombs of conceivable magnitude." Specifically, their fear was that the neutrons given off by an H-bomb detonated in the upper atmosphere would transform ordinary nitrogen into radioactive carbon-14. Estimates were that ten to one hundred H-bombs exploded at a high altitude would produce the radioactivity of ten thousand to one hundred thousand fission bombs. Exploding H-bombs closer to the earth, on the other hand, would create an unknown quantity of lethal, long-lived radioactive fallout.[35]

In their report to the AEC on October 30, Oppenheimer and five of his colleagues—Conant, Rowe, Smith, DuBridge, and Buckley—decided on ethical grounds to oppose the H-bomb unconditionally. "In determining not to proceed to develop the super bomb," they wrote in a summary of their views drafted by Oppenheimer and Conant, "we see a unique opportunity of providing by example some limitations on the totality of war and thus of limiting the fear and arousing the hope of mankind." While they endorsed accelerated production of advanced atomic bombs, as well as further work toward the fission-fusion Booster, the majority report of the GAC unanimously opposed going ahead with the H-bomb as carrying "much further than the atomic bomb itself the policy of exterminating civilian populations." The superbomb, they warned directly, "might become a weapon of genocide."[36]

"It would be folly. . ."

The two remaining members of the committee, Rabi and Fermi, took a different approach in a letter, entitled "An Opinion on the Development of the Super," which they appended to the GAC's majority report. Rabi and Fermi denounced the H-bomb in language even stronger than Conant's, as "necessarily an evil thing considered in any light."[37] But, unlike the majority report, their single-page statement, which Rabi had the larger role in drafting, was intended to offer Truman a realistic alternative to outright and unilateral renunciation of the H-bomb. Rabi and Fermi urged the president to announce simultaneously that the United States would not go ahead with the H-bomb and to "invite the nations of the world to join us in a solemn pledge not to proceed in the development or construction of weapons of this category."

The course of action that Rabi and Fermi recommended to Truman was, in essence, a conditional renunciation of the H-bomb, coupled with what they believed to be a verifiable ban on thermonuclear testing. Such a ban on the testing of H-bombs was practical, Rabi and Fermi argued in their letter, because "even without control machinery, it appears highly probable that an advanced stage of development leading to a test by another power could be detected by available physical means—namely, the airborne-sampling that had discovered the test of the Soviet fission bomb."[38]

If the Russians refused to accept a ban on the testing of H-bombs, Rabi and Fermi pointed out, then the United States could proceed with a clear conscience and the full support of its scientific community to develop the weapon. On the other hand, if the Soviets accepted the ban and later violated it with a surreptitious test that the United States discovered, Truman could authorize a crash program to build the Super. Since even proponents of the H-bomb conceded that it would probably take many tests before any nation had a deliverable weapon, cheating would not give the violator a decisive advantage; the American effort might even benefit from an analysis of the fallout from a Russian test, if that test were successful. In the meantime, "we would have in our possession, in our stockpile of atomic bombs, the means for adequate 'military' retaliation for the production or use of a 'super,'" Rabi and Fermi argued.

Oppenheimer and his colleagues on the GAC were almost certainly aware that the test ban which Fermi and Rabi proposed was more likely to be acceptable to Truman than an unconditional renunciation of the H-bomb. GAC member Cyril Smith and John Manley—the GAC's recording secretary and an associate director at Los Alamos, who was also at the October 30 meeting—later independently observed in interviews that members of the committee regarded the Rabi-Fermi proposal as both technically workable and even politically astute, since it responded to growing international concern about the spread of nuclear weapons.

But as AEC commissioner Gordon Dean wrote in his office diary, at the time, ethical objections to the Super dominated the October 30 meeting:

> In the discussions leading to the GAC's conclusion, many things were said, arguments advanced, which do not appear in their written report. They were, I think it is fair to say, visceral reactions. The moral implications were discussed at great length. It was pointed out that this was something different in kind rather than in degree and that the general tenor of the discussion was that it is just too big and must not therefore be built."[39]

In a letter to Conant earlier in the month, Oppenheimer conceded that pragmatism was not the sole, or even the most important, consideration motivating his opposition to the H-bomb:

What concerns me is really not the technical problem. I am not sure the miserable thing will work, nor that it can be gotten to a target except by oxcart. . . . What does worry me is that this thing appears to have caught the imagination, both of the Congressional and military people, as the answer to the problem posed by the Russians' advance.

While scientists "have always known it had to be done; and it does have to be done," Oppenheimer argued, "that we have become committed to it as the way to save the country and the peace appears to me full of dangers."[40]

Ironically, barely five years before, Oppenheimer had discouraged Szilard from circulating a petition at Los Alamos opposing the atomic bombing of Japan, allegedly on the grounds that scientists had no right to use their prestige to try to influence political decisions. Now, in the case of the H-bomb, Oppenheimer seemed to adopt the premise of Szilard's petition that scientists needed to go "on record in favor of giving greater weight to moral arguments." While Oppenheimer reportedly told Rabi and Fermi that he was willing to sign either their statement or the majority report, he ultimately signed only the latter—a decision that Rabi subsequently attributed to his friend's "martyr complex."[41]

Conant was plainly sympathetic to Oppenheimer's point of view. One of the most vocal opponents of the Super at the October 30 meeting, he declared that the country would go ahead with the weapon "over my dead body."[42]

The fact that Oppenheimer and Conant based their stand against the H-bomb on moral grounds rather than on any of the many practical objections to the weapon—including the still unresolved technical obstacles, the problem of its unwieldy size, the lack of a compelling military rationale, or the sacrifices the program necessarily entailed for the atomic arsenal—made their opposition to the weapon a futile gesture, as they probably realized it would be. Oppenheimer had acknowledged as much in his letter to Conant, which noted that "two experienced promoters," Teller and Lawrence, were already rallying support for the H-bomb in Washington and concluded with the prophetic prediction that "it would be folly to oppose the exploration of this weapon."[43]

Upon submitting the GAC's majority report and the Rabi-Fermi letter to AEC Chairman David Lilienthal, Oppenheimer told Lilienthal that he and his colleagues would be interested in meeting personally with either the commission or the president, if necessary, to defend their stand against the H-bomb. Lilienthal raised no objection to Oppenheimer's proposal, but admitted uncertainty about the most propitious timing for a meeting with Truman.[44]

The president apparently remained oblivious to the developing controversy. When Strauss made a personal plea for the H-bomb to the NSC's Souers in the days immediately following the Soviet atomic test, Souers discovered that Truman seemed still unaware of work on the Super.[45]

"Missionaries for the project. . ."

Strauss had been caught off guard by the vehemence of the GAC's opposition to the Super. After reading the majority report and the Rabi-Fermi letter, the five-member commission split over the question of whether to proceed with the H-bomb. Three commissioners—Lilienthal, physicist Henry Smyth, and Sumner Pike, like Strauss an investment banker—sided with the GAC in opposing development of the H-bomb. Strauss, on the other hand, joined Commissioner Gordon Dean, a lawyer, in urging that American scientists proceed with the work necessary to test the feasibility of the H-bomb.

On November 9, the commissioners sent Truman the GAC's reports as well as their own divided opinions on the hydrogen bomb, to which they appended a cover memorandum noting that some outside scientists "have become missionaries for the project." The memorandum gave the odds as "better than even" that the H-bomb could be developed in as little as three years, but admitted there was "no certainty of success." While Dean, in his personal statement to the president, broached the possibility of a vague "secret diplomatic" approach to the Russians to ascertain if they would be willing to join the United States in forgoing development of the H-bomb, neither he nor his colleagues mentioned the test-ban idea proposed by Rabi and Fermi.[46]

When Oppenheimer, Conant, Fermi, and Rabi attended a commission meeting in early November to personally present their case against the H-bomb, they failed to persuade Strauss and Dean to change their minds—and, despite Oppenheimer's earlier suggestion to Lilienthal, made no effort to apprise Truman of their views. Instead, Strauss and McMahon gave the most sanguine view of the H-bomb yet in letters to the president later that month. Predicting that it might take as little as two years to perfect the weapon, Strauss warned once again that "a Russian enterprise started some years ago may be well along to completion."[47] After meeting with Teller and Lawrence, General Omar Bradley, chairman of the Joint Chiefs, decided to advise Truman that the military felt the nation would regard as "intolerable" any situation in which the Russians alone had the superbomb.[48]

On November 19, with the AEC unable to agree about the H-bomb, Truman appointed a special committee of the NSC consisting of Lilienthal, Secretary of Defense Louis Johnson, and Secretary of State Dean Acheson as its chairman to "consider all phases of the question." When the "Committee on the Super-bomb" convened for the first time several weeks later, the meeting was brief and inconclusive—due "to the acerbity of Louis Johnson's nature," Acheson wrote of the most fervent champion of the H-bomb on the committee.[49]

The secretary of state met with Oppenheimer and Lilienthal on his own during the next several weeks to discuss what should be done about the H-bomb. Both Acheson and Gordon Arneson, his atomic energy adviser, professed to find Oppenheimer's moral arguments unpersuasive. "I've listened to Oppie as carefully as I know how," Acheson told Arneson. "But I don't know what the hell he's talking about. How do you disarm an adversary by example?" Arneson believed that Oppenheimer, like Lilienthal, was unwilling as a matter of principle to entertain any alternative that might lead to the H-bomb.[50]

By year's end, positions had only hardened in the H-bomb debate. The GAC, although under increasing criticism from the H-bomb lobby, refused to amend its position opposing the weapon. Instead, a new concern animated its members that winter. "We have the impression that our reasons for not developing a super bomb at this time, irrespective of a Russian development of super bombs, have not been completely understood," John Manley wrote to the AEC on December 3.[51] Manley belatedly listed the practical questions for opposing the H-bomb that had been overlooked, or at least downplayed, in the majority report because of its emphasis on the immorality of the Super. Among these was the issue of whether the superbomb would be of greater military value than existing atomic bombs; whether the super would be cheaper or more expensive than the fission bomb; and whether an American thermonuclear test might not "materially assist a corresponding Russian development" by unwittingly giving away the secret of the Super.[52]

When the superbomb committee met a second and final time, on the morning of January 31, 1950, it was for the purpose of drafting a recommendation to go to the president. At the beginning of the H-bomb debate, Acheson had briefly entertained an idea similar to that proposed by Rabi and Fermi: a Soviet-American moratorium on superbomb research lasting from eighteen months to two years, with the United States prepared to consider forgoing development of the weapon unilaterally if necessary. But the secretary of state had since changed his mind—apparently convinced that this proposal, like that of the GAC, was too utopian.[53]

Acheson also realized that even a decision to proceed merely with determining the feasibility of the H-bomb would be necessarily more than just a limited step; once taken, the next step—development of the weapon—might be all but irresistible, given the pressure then building for the Super. Some two weeks earlier, Acheson had confided to a colleague in the Truman administration that "we should be quite honest and say that in advising this action, we are going quite a long way to committing ourselves to continue down that road."[54]

Nonetheless, the superbomb committee decided against giving Truman any such warning in its report, which urged that the president order the AEC "to proceed to determine the technical feasibility of thermonuclear weapons." The committee also recommended that Truman, in announcing his decision, emphasize that it was for "continuing work . . . rather than give the impression of suddenly beginning something wholly new." Only Lilienthal, the sole dissenting voice on the superbomb committee, raised the question of whether Truman was being informed of the full implications of the decision he was about to make on the H-bomb.[55]

While the report of Acheson's committee conceded that an "all-out effort leading to both a feasibility test and quantity production of 'supers' would seriously impair the efficiency and output of the fission bomb program," it also asserted, somewhat misleadingly, that "there appear to be no advocates for this type of effort." One question that had long been at issue in the H-bomb debate—whether the United States was ahead of or behind the Russians—was subtly resolved in favor of the H-bomb lobby by reference to "the probable fission bomb capability and possible thermonuclear bomb capability of the Soviet Union."[56]

No mention was made by either the AEC or the superbomb committee of the proposal by Rabi and Fermi, which had been included in the AEC report sent to Truman the previous November. Instead, the idea of a thermonuclear test ban was only briefly alluded to—and then just as promptly rejected—in Acheson's report, which objected to it on the mistaken grounds that a ban would have to be "coupled with a plan for the necessary safeguards to insure that the renunciation was in fact being carried out—these safeguards necessarily involving an opening up of Soviet territory."

"Moral considerations are not germane. . ."

The fate of the superbomb was decided in a brief meeting at the Oval Office on the afternoon of January 31. When Lilienthal tried to enumerate the arguments for not proceeding with the H-bomb, Truman simply cut him off.[57] At this decisive White House meeting, the host of technical, strategic, and political issues that had absorbed the attention of both sides in the H-bomb debate for the past several months were either passed over, unwittingly misrepresented, or willfully ignored. Most significant, the ethical argument that Oppenheimer and the GAC majority had made against the H-bomb was dismissed outright. Thus, the AEC, in its own recommendation to Truman, agreed with the report of Acheson's committee that "moral considerations are not germane to the limited objective covered by this problem, i.e., the development and test of the weapon to determine its feasibility."[58]

Even before the January 31 White House meeting, Truman had evidently already made up his mind to proceed with the H-bomb. More than a week earlier, the president had confided to the NSC's Sidney Souers that he made the decision after reading a memorandum from the Joint Chiefs. (The memorandum, which had been sent to the superbomb committee, was apparently forwarded to the White House by Louis Johnson without the knowledge of Acheson and Lilienthal.) Truman concluded that the Joint Chiefs' argument—which likewise dismissed "moral objections" to the H-bomb and recommended its development "as a matter of top priority"—"made a lot of sense," he told Souers.[59] A decision he had made the previous month, to expand the facilities for the production of atomic bombs, also made his choice easier, the president told those assembled in the Oval Office. As Truman would subsequently confess to a long-time friend, "there actually was no decision to make on the H-bomb."[60]

Truman's observation was more accurate than he knew. Behind the argument of the scientists belonging to the H-bomb lobby lay the untestable hypothesis that the Russians were probably already ahead in the race. On the other side in the H-bomb debate, scientists like Oppenheimer and Conant chose to emphasize moral rather than practical objections to going ahead with the superbomb. Substantive, nonpolemical arguments for and against proceeding with the superbomb—including the test-ban proposal of Fermi and Rabi—were never really put before Truman.[61]

To be sure, the highly charged political atmosphere of the time—a consequence not only of the advent of the Soviet atomic bomb but of the recent coming to power of a Communist government in China—made a verdict against the H-bomb difficult for any president. But the advice that Truman got—or, rather, failed to get—on the H-bomb meant the outcome was never in any doubt.

The significance of the January 31 decision was readily apparent to the antagonists in the superbomb debate, even if not yet to the president himself. In publicly announcing later the same day that he planned to leave the AEC by mid-April to return to investment banking, Strauss observed that the "issues involving national security which were my primary concern are now resolved as I had hoped and recommended."[62]

Lilienthal encountered a different mood entirely when he "carried the news in to the GAC" of Truman's H-bomb decision. "It was like a funeral party—especially when I said we were all gagged," he wrote in his journal that night.[63] Neither Oppenheimer nor any other member of the GAC had followed up on his earlier offer to acquaint Truman personally with their reasons for opposing the Super. Now the committee realized it was too late. When a few of its members spoke about resigning to protest the president's decision, Lilienthal advised them against taking such a drastic step.[64]

Significantly, Truman's only acknowledgment of the GAC's role in the H-bomb decision came some two weeks later, in the course of a farewell celebration at the White House for Lilienthal. Referring to a recent television show on which Lilienthal, Oppenheimer, Bethe, and Einstein had appeared, the president told Lilienthal he agreed with the departing AEC chairman that "we need men with great intellects, need their ideas. But we need to balance them with other kinds of people, too."[65] In the wake of the H-bomb decision, Truman's remark seemed a subtle reminder that he regarded scientists more as dreamers than advisers.

4

"A Point of No Return"

The Opportunity for a Nuclear "Standstill"

President Truman's decision to proceed with the Super against the urgings of the General Advisory Committee was a victory for the H-bomb lobby and a setback for those scientists officially charged with responsibility for advising the administration. Within weeks of Truman's January 31 decision on the Super, the GAC's prediction of mounting pressure to build the weapon was borne out: The next cardinal choice confronting the president would be whether to launch an "all-out" effort on the hydrogen bomb.

"A matter of the highest urgency. . ."

Some two weeks before President Truman made his decision to proceed with the H-bomb, Gordon Dean responded to what he told his fellow AEC commissioners was "the best argument that has been made against the 'Super.'" Dean sought to quiet GAC member Lee DuBridge's fears that the administration was about to launch "a 'crash program' on the super bomb." "No one has proposed it and it is no answer to describe the [current] program as a 'crash' program," argued Dean, who would soon replace David Lilienthal as AEC chairman. The Joint Chiefs, too, had recently disavowed any interest in an "all-out" effort to develop the H-bomb.[1]

But in the coming weeks the forces pushing for a crash program on the H-bomb grew, as the GAC and Lilienthal had predicted. Less than a week after Truman gave the go-ahead to determining the feasibility of hydrogen bombs, proponents began urging the president to expand the project beyond research and development to include the building of superbombs.

In early February 1950, Robert LeBaron—a chemical engineer who had been appointed head of the Military Liaison Committee, the link between the Pentagon and the AEC—requested that the commission authorize production of enough tritium to allow not only testing of several possible versions of the H-bomb but also immediate production of the most successful model. Dean, an early advocate of the weapon, agreed.[2]

Behind the urgency that LeBaron claimed for the H-bomb project was the startling news received a few days earlier that Klaus Fuchs, the shy British scientist who did some of the calculations for the plutonium-implosion "gadget" at Los Alamos, had been arrested in England as a spy for the Russians. Members of the H-bomb lobby were quick to use the news to urge acceleration of the superbomb project.

The unsettling possibility that Fuchs had given the Russians not only the secret of the atomic bomb but also vital information that might help them discover the secret of the Super was raised by Strauss—who informed the president by letter on February 1 that Fuchs, in addition to his wartime work on the plutonium bomb, had taken part in the April 1946 superbomb seminar at Los Alamos.[3] The possibility that Fuchs knew a great deal about the H-bomb was also brought to the attention of the White House by the Federal Bureau of Investigation. On the same day as Strauss's letter, FBI Director J. Edgar Hoover telephoned the NSC's Sidney Souers to say that because of Fuchs, the Russians might have "gotten going on the hydrogen bomb even before the other."[4]

Meanwhile, at the Pentagon, Defense Secretary Louis Johnson spread the alarm. After Strauss had shown him four secret documents on the H-bomb that Fuchs had had access to, Johnson personally telephoned Truman to point out the significance of the information that presumably had been compromised. In response, Truman agreed with AEC commissioner Sumner Pike that the Committee on the Super-bomb should be reconvened in emergency session to consider what additional steps might be taken to speed the weapon's development.

What had hitherto only been hinted at in Washington was finally spelled out in a memorandum that LeBaron and two Army colleagues on the Military Liaison Committee—Major General Kenneth Nichols and Brigadier General Herbert Loper—sent to Johnson on February 20. LeBaron's memorandum raised the specter of a Soviet nuclear weapons program advanced to the point at which the Russians' stockpile of atomic bombs might already exceed that of the United States "both as to yields and numbers." Even more disturbing was the possibility that the Russians had tested not only an atomic bomb but also a hydrogen bomb, before Project Centering, America's Long-Range Detection Program, became operational. The memorandum speculated that what Groves had once regarded as a fatal flaw in the Soviets' nuclear weapons program—the scarcity of high-grade uranium in Russia—had, ironically, actually turned out to be an asset, since a dearth of the raw materials needed to make atomic bombs had forced the Russians "to balance that shortage by development of weapons of higher efficiency per ton of ore available, e.g., a thermo-nuclear weapon." This prospect led LeBaron and his colleagues, in turn, to the most frightening conclusion of all—namely, "that Russia's thermo-nuclear weapon may be in actual production."[5]

Subsequently read by the Joint Chiefs of Staff, LeBaron's memorandum had an electrifying effect in the Pentagon. Whereas just the previous month the Joint Chiefs had urged against a crash H-bomb program on the grounds that it would hinder the development of atomic bombs, they now endorsed immediate and all-out development of hydrogen bombs, even if it meant sacrifices in the production of fission bombs.[6]

On February 24, Johnson sent LeBaron's memorandum and the Joint Chiefs' recommendation directly to the president—adding his own voice to the chorus of alarm urging a crash effort for the H-bomb in "view of the extremely serious, in fact almost literally limitless, implications to our national security."[7]

In early March, Acheson's Committee on the Super-bomb—hurriedly reconvened, and with Dean replacing Lilienthal as AEC chairman—promptly seconded the plea that development of the H-bomb now be "regarded as a matter of the highest urgency." The committee further recommended that Truman order the AEC to prepare for "quantity production of materials needed for thermonuclear weapons"—even as Acheson privately acknowledged that "there are no known additional steps which might be taken for further acceleration of the test program."[8]

For others as well, a crash effort to build the H-bomb seemed a leap into a void. On the same day as Acheson's recommendation, the NSC advised Truman that "it is simply not known whether the thermonuclear process will work at all or under what conditions." It was, Souers concluded, "nearly futile" to attempt to estimate when the first H-bomb would be ready.[9] Nonetheless, the following day, March 10, 1950, Truman approved the all-out program for the H-bomb.

In his memoirs, Truman indicated that a crucial factor in his decision was the superbomb committee's conclusion that some of the work on the H-bomb also would benefit the production of atomic weapons. "Thus there would not be a total loss even if it turned out that the process failed to work," he wrote.[10]

"The model considered is a fizzle. . ."

Following Fuchs's arrest there could be little question of opposition to a crash program for the H-bomb—unlike the situation the previous month, when Truman had announced his decision to proceed with research on the

Super. In contrast to his earlier choice, Truman's second decision on the H-bomb was deliberately kept from the public. The president specifically instructed the NSC that the crash effort for the H-bomb was to remain top-secret.[11]

In making his second H-bomb decision, Truman also did not seek the opinion of the GAC, which since January 31 had been effectively cut out of the administration's internal deliberations on the superbomb in any case. Yet the GAC's scientists were presumably the best qualified to put Fuchs's treason, LeBaron's memorandum, and Johnson's call for the all-out effort in proper perspective.

The GAC knew, for example, that Johnson's claim regarding how Fuchs had learned "everything" about the Super while at Los Alamos, and likewise the claim—made at various times to Truman by Strauss, Johnson, and Hoover—that Fuchs had given the Russians the "secret" of the hydrogen bomb, were less damning than they appeared, since scientists at the lab still had no clear idea of how to build a hydrogen bomb. Furthermore, since Fuchs had left Los Alamos in mid-June 1946 to return to England, he had had no access to the superbomb research being done in America.[12] Finally, by the time of Truman's second H-bomb decision, scientists at Los Alamos knew that the information on the superbomb which their erstwhile colleague had gathered at the lab led down the wrong road, to a design that would not work.[13]

Calculations begun by Los Alamos scientists in the winter of 1949-1950, and verified by the first of a new generation of high-speed computers in the following months, revealed that the early figures on which Teller based his original concept for the H-bomb had greatly underestimated the amount of tritium needed to initiate a thermonuclear reaction. As Bethe—one of those who discovered the error—later wrote, the results of the 1950 discovery "were entirely opposite to the 1946 assumption . . . and made the economic soundness of the H-bomb program highly questionable." Bethe claimed that "the theoretical work of 1950 had shown that every important point of the 1946 thermonuclear program had been wrong. If the Russians started a thermonuclear program on the basis of the information received from Fuchs, it must have led to the same failure."[14]

The tentative efforts of GAC scientists to set the record straight about what the Russians might have learned from Fuchs went largely ignored or unheeded in the Truman administration. At a meeting of Pentagon and State Department officials on February 27, Oppenheimer responded to LeBaron's claims of dramatic Russian progress on the H-bomb with the observation that "if they had been able to make any advances on the basis of information given them by Dr. Fuchs they were marvelous indeed."[15] But Oppenheimer's skepticism regarding Fuchs's contribution was evidently not communicated to Truman.

When the same group gathered a week later, Conant, too, wondered aloud "whether the estimates regarding the atomic and hydrogen bomb potentialities might not be suffering from overcompensation." He "could not help but believe," Conant said, "that the H-bomb capabilities were far too optimistic." AEC Commissioner Henry Smyth likewise protested at this meeting that he knew of no recent intelligence that would justify a speeded-up program for the Super. Even Teller later complained that the wording of Truman's order "to continue" work on the H-bomb had given the false impression that "we could produce a hydrogen bomb by tightening a few last screws." Teller subsequently described the state of knowledge about the H-bomb at this time as "thermonuclear fantasies."[16]

Despite Truman's approval of the all-out effort, scientists at Los Alamos remained stymied on how to proceed, with the result that prospects for the H-bomb seemed more distant than ever. Following an April 1950 meeting at Princeton, mathematicians Stanislaus Ulam and John von Neumann reluctantly conceded of the original concept that "the model considered is a fizzle."[17] The following month, Ulam wrote to his colleague admitting that "the thing gives me the impression of being miles away from going."[18]

"The new Super. . ."

It was not until almost a year later, in the spring of 1951, that the pursuit of the H-bomb was suddenly revitalized when a new and ultimately successful design for the weapon was proposed by Teller and Ulam. The new design relied on the effects of x-ray radiation from the fission trigger to compress and ignite the Super's thermonuclear fuel.[19] Teller presented his idea for the "new Super" at a meeting of Los Alamos scientists and AEC officials in Princeton in mid-June 1951.[20]

In the wake of the Princeton meeting, work began almost immediately at Los Alamos on a practical test of Teller's new concept. The success of a test code-named George, part of the Greenhouse series in the Pacific some five weeks earlier, had also provided new encouragement for those working on the Super. The device tested in George—nicknamed the "cylinder" by Los Alamos scientists—proved that a small thermonuclear reaction could be induced by a fission explosion.[21] Also in May there had been a successful demonstration of the Booster in a test code-named Item on the Pacific atoll of Eniwetok, and a triumphant series of tests—Operation Buster—the previous fall in Nevada of improved atomic weapons that the GAC and Oppenheimer had once looked upon as a possible alternative to the Super.[22]

With the news of the Teller-Ulam breakthrough, the last remaining obstacles to the hydrogen bomb began to disappear, while the pressures on Truman to commit his administration wholeheartedly to the Super became unrelenting.

Former opponents of the H-bomb also began to feel this pressure. In the summer of 1950, Senate outrage at Pike's initial stand against the H-bomb nearly prevented his renomination as AEC commissioner and forever ruined whatever chance he might have had of becoming AEC chairman. Strauss and Teller privately accused Oppenheimer of deliberately sabotaging the project. By the end of the summer of 1951, Teller was lining up support in the Air Force and among members of the Joint Committee on Atomic Energy for a proposed second nuclear weapons laboratory, to be located in the Livermore valley near Berkeley, away from the influence of Oppenheimer and Los Alamos.[23]

Less than a week after Dean had briefed him on the suddenly improved prospects for the H-bomb that summer, Truman authorized the AEC to begin building an experimental device incorporating the Teller-Ulam invention. The decisive test of the principle behind the new Super, code-named Mike, was scheduled to take place in the Pacific during late summer or early fall of 1952.[24]

"Mobilizing science for war. . ."

There is no evidence that Truman consulted with the scientists who had opposed going ahead with the H-bomb before he gave his approval for Mike. But it is likely that few, if any, of that number would have been willing to vocally oppose Mike at this point, so unpopular would such a stand have been. For many, like Oppenheimer, the development of the hydrogen bomb probably now seemed all but inevitable.

Although Truman had disregarded the GAC's advice on the H-bomb, most veterans of the Manhattan Project remained available to him as advisers. For example, despite his return to the Carnegie Institution, Bush continued to serve as a science adviser to the Pentagon. Previously chairman of the Research and Development Board, Bush was also made a consultant, in March 1951, to project Vista, a controversial Pentagon-funded study of the role nuclear weapons might play in the defense of Western Europe. Conant—who, after protesting bitterly to Rabi that the H-bomb "would just louse up the world even more," had returned to Harvard—also remained an adviser on defense issues, serving as a member of the GAC until his term expired in July 1952.[25]

As Rabi had argued earlier, many scientists felt that Truman's innocence of scientific matters made it all the more important that the members of the GAC and other scientists continue to act as advisers to the administration—even if their advice was frequently ignored.[26] For some scientists, like Bethe, a sense of responsibility to the country contended with a visceral dislike of weapons like the H-bomb, prompting them to attempt to steer a middle course. Having turned down Teller's plea that he take over direction of the superbomb project at Los Alamos, Bethe nonetheless returned to the lab in the summer to work on the hydrogen bomb.[27]

Coincident with the improving prospects for the Super, the political complexion of the GAC also began to change. To replace Fermi, Rowe, and

Seaborg—all of whom would leave as their terms expired in summer 1950—Dean chose three politically conservative candidates: Willard Libby, a chemist at the University of Chicago; Walter Whitman, a chemical engineer at MIT; and chemist Eger Murphree, a former OSRD official and later president of Standard Oil Development Company.[28] Neither the new nor the old GAC scientists approached or were summoned by the White House to give advice, however.

Truman's estrangement from the country's scientific community was becoming an increasing concern for some in his administration as early as summer 1950—particularly with the outbreak of the Korean War that June. Despite the president's periodic emphasis upon retaining civilian control over the growing arsenal of nuclear weapons, and the looming specter of the H-bomb, responsibility for technical advice on issues relating to the nation's security remained almost exclusively in the hands of the military.

The effectiveness of the Joint Research and Development Board, which Bush in 1945 hoped would coordinate military-related research by the Pentagon, had been undermined by the effects of interservice rivalry a few years after the war's end. The National Science Foundation which Bush had proposed in his 1945 report, *Science: The Endless Frontier,* was finally approved in May 1950 after many sessions of tortured debate in Congress. It was, however, concerned primarily with granting federal money for basic research and had little or no responsibility for overseeing applied research by the military services.[29]

Worried by the administration's dependence on the Pentagon for technical advice on both military and nonmilitary questions, Truman's budget director, F. J. Lawton, urged the president in October 1950 to explore new ways the nation's civilian scientists could contribute to victory in Korea and, ultimately, in the cold war. At Lawton's suggestion, Truman appointed William Golden—an investment banker and Strauss's former assistant in the AEC—to investigate the idea.[30]

Golden's report, "Mobilizing Science for War: A Scientific Adviser to the President," was sent to Truman some six weeks later, on December 18, 1950. The report urged the president to appoint a prominent scientist as his personal science adviser, with a staff and an office in the White House. Such a step, Golden advised, "would be very favorably received in the scientific community and would represent a substantial element of progress in the war mobilization effort." Golden wrote that the president's science adviser "must be extraordinarily competent both technically in order to comprehend the major programs and integrate them in his mind, and administratively, in order to avoid distraction by seductive details or special pleaders." He also noted that the adviser "may wish to select a small advisory committee of scientific specialists to support and assist him or he may call on the National Academy of Sciences to serve him in this way."[31]

Ironically, Bush had been one of the first to suggest that the president should have a personal science advisor, after a 1949 Research and Development Board study on the mobilization of science for a national emergency. However, perhaps because Bush realized that Truman was unlikely to adopt one of its principal recommendations—reestablishment of the civilian OSRD—the report was evidently never sent to the White House. Two years later, when Lawton chanced upon Bush's report, the budget director used it as a justification for his own proposal.[32]

While Truman was sympathetic to Golden's recommendations, opposition to a White House science advisory committee and a presidential science adviser was almost immediately forthcoming from Congress, whose members feared both the program's cost and its potential infringement upon their authority. The newly created National Science Foundation, similarly worried that a science adviser in the White House might intrude upon its own barely established prerogatives and funding, was another source of opposition. Even Golden's friend Strauss, concerned that the president's science adviser might challenge the authority of the AEC, criticized the report. Perhaps because they had already witnessed Truman's cavalier treatment of scientists, or because they feared an even greater diminution of their roles as advisers, Bush and Conant, too, now opposed the idea of a single science adviser.[33]

There was also disagreement within the government and the scientific community over which individual should serve as the first science adviser. Both of the candidates most frequently mentioned for the post—Caltech president Lee DuBridge and Bell Labs president Mervin Kelly—informed Golden they were not interested in the position. Originally, Oppenheimer had been at the top of Golden's list. But as the controversy over the physicist's role in the H-bomb decision mounted, his name was quietly dropped. Moreover, Oppenheimer told Golden that he "had no enthusiasm" for the idea of a presidential science adviser—since, as he wrote, he "doubted the possibility of any individual having a synoptic comprehension of all the research programs."[34]

The possibility that Truman might soon have a scientist in the White House as his personal adviser was finally ruled out when Golden, seeking to salvage his proposal from its critics, approached General Lucius Clay, the vain and temperamental hero of the 1948 Berlin airlift, about putting the proposed Science Advisory Committee and its chairman under the authority of the Office of Defense Mobilization, where Clay was assistant to ODM's director, Charles Wilson.[35]

Although Clay at first objected vehemently to this arrangement—reportedly suggesting, instead, that the scientist in question be considered *his* adviser—a ten-member Science Advisory Committee (SAC) was finally established in April 1951 under the auspices of ODM. In another compromise, Oliver Buckley, the sixty-five-year-old former president of Bell Labs and veteran of the GAC, was chosen as the first head of SAC/ODM. For reasons of temperament, age, and illness—Buckley had recently been diagnosed as suffering from Parkinson's disease—he proved from the outset a well-intended but reluctant and generally ineffective leader of the new committee. While Buckley agreed to serve as chairman of the SAC, at his request the post did not include responsibility as the president's science adviser.[36]

Despite the president's approval of Golden's report and his interest in mobilizing science to win the war in Korea, Truman proved no more eager to listen to SAC/ODM than to the GAC. Thus, although the SAC usually met monthly—and occasionally forwarded specific recommendations to the president through Wilson or his successor, Arthur Flemming—Truman never actively sought its advice.

While the committee's charter gave it the right to report directly to the president if its members thought the occasion warranted, no such request was forthcoming from SAC/ODM while Buckley was chairman. In June 1952, when Buckley left the committee because of his illness, DuBridge agreed somewhat reluctantly to assume the chairmanship part time.[37] On one issue SAC/ODM did go to the president under DuBridge's leadership. Reportedly at Oppenheimer's urging, its members asked Truman in the summer of 1952 to make the committee independent of ODM by attaching it to the more influential NSC, thereby moving the scientists symbolically closer to the White House. But on this matter, too, Truman declined the scientists' advice.[38]

"Swan song. . ."

Although its recommendations on the H-bomb had thus far been either rejected or ignored by Truman, the GAC had not entirely abandoned hopes of influencing the president's policies on atomic energy. With the end of Truman's presidency in sight, and the terms of the committee's three remaining charter members—Oppenheimer, Conant, and DuBridge—to expire in the summer of 1952, the GAC was also feeling a certain sense of urgency. Accordingly, that spring, veterans of the original committee met to draft a letter to the president that would summarize the GAC's achievements and recommend specific steps for the future.

Conant wanted what he called the committee's "swan song" to contain a warning to Truman about the difficulty of making decisions on matters as technical and controversial as the hydrogen bomb. Specifically, he suggested the GAC's letter call attention to the disquieting implications of Project Gabriel, the AEC study of the effects of radioactive fallout, which had been thus far ignored by the president in the furor caused by the H-bomb debate. For his part, Oppenheimer wanted to highlight the remarkable expansion of the nation's atomic stockpile that had taken place since the committee was founded—the nuclear arsenal had grown from just thirteen weapons in 1947 to approximately a thousand some five years later—and to emphasize the further dramatic leap in destructiveness that the H-bomb portended.[39]

The final version of the GAC letter—which Oppenheimer drafted and sent to Truman in mid-June—emphasized past progress and future danger equally, but contained little either specific or new by way of advice, and no clear warning. Instead, in apparent reference to the H-bomb decision, the committee's veterans simply cautioned Truman against the temptation of accepting "partial and misleading technical estimates, because the relevant facts are not always currently available." While denying that they had ever gone beyond their charter by offering advice on policy questions "except in those few instances where the Commission asked us as informed citizens for an expression of our views," the committee also reminded the president that such "decisions of policy, if they are to be wisely taken, require a sound evaluation of scientific factors in their relation to the military and strategic situation."[40]

"Much has changed"

With SAC/ODM quiescent, and the GAC's most experienced members about to leave the committee, there seemed less opportunity than ever for scientists to influence the policies of the Truman administration—even though the thermonuclear device to be tested in Mike was nearing completion at Los Alamos and the war in Korea had slipped from triumph to stalemate. Yet the crash effort for the Super presented a third and, as it turned out, final opportunity for Oppenheimer and his colleagues to attempt to express their views.

In April 1952, as part of his administration's reexamination of American foreign policy in the wake of the H-bomb decision, Truman had asked Acheson to appoint a Panel of Consultants on Disarmament to investigate new approaches for slowing, or even stopping, the nuclear arms race. In addition to Bush and Oppenheimer, its chairman, the panel's members were New York attorney Allen Dulles; John Dickey, the president of Dartmouth College; and Joseph Johnson, head of the Carnegie Endowment.[41]

Possibly because of the political storm clouds already gathering around Oppenheimer—who would be advised by Dean the following month that he was under investigation by the Justice Department for suspected Communist affiliations in his youth—the initiative in the panel fell to Bush. Even before the group was formally assembled, however, Bush had decided on his own to raise the sensitive question of whether it might still be possible to stop the H-bomb.

What Bush proposed was actually only a postponement of Mike until after the upcoming presidential election. However, as Bush pointed out in confidential discussions with Acheson, such a postponement could mean leaving the question of whether to proceed with the H-bomb up to Truman's successor. Thus, Bush suggested that the next president might wish to pursue what he called a nuclear "standstill agreement"—a moratorium on all tests, nuclear and thermonuclear, by the United States and the Soviet Union for a period of one or possibly two years, during which time both countries would strive for a broader agreement aimed at reducing the number of nuclear weapons in their arsenals. In essence, Bush's proposal was a revival of the test-ban idea originally suggested by Rabi and Fermi.[42]

Bush broached the idea of the standstill to Acheson that April, bringing it up with the full panel in May. On June 9, the panel sent the secretary of state a memorandum outlining the arguments for and against a postponement of Mike until after the election. It emphasized that Mike would be

> something more than one more in a series of scientific tests. It will be impossible to conceal the fact that this event has taken place, and very difficult to conceal the fact that it is an event of great portent for all men. . . . About the so-called hydrogen bomb there has always been this one great question: "Is this possible?" This question will be answered if the projected test succeeds.[43]

Members of the panel also thought it paramount to distance the question of whether to proceed with the test from earlier decisions on the H-bomb and to stress that the decision on Mike might well be an irrevocable turning point—in effect, the last, best hope to stop an arms race that they viewed as likely to end in war.

In defense of its plea to postpone Mike, the panel noted that "much has changed since 1950." Members argued that the thermonuclear breakthrough by Teller and Ulam, which unlocked the secret of the H-bomb, had removed the fear that "Fuchs could have been of much help to the Russians in this field, since the information he could have supplied them has turned out in our experience to be misleading." There was also, as the panel knew, more recent intelligence on the status of the Soviet atomic energy program which tended to confirm that the Russians were not ahead of the United States.[44]

At the same time, some of the reasons advanced earlier for not building the H-bomb had assumed even greater salience. There still was no clear military rationale for the Super, the panel argued. In fact, H-bombs seemed likely to be more of a strategic advantage to the Russians—since it was the United States, not the Soviet Union, that had large cities vulnerable to destruction by superbombs. Further, the limited nature of the war in Korea had prompted American military leaders to ask for smaller and more discriminate—not larger and more powerful—bombs. "There is something odd in the prospect of a test which may be some ten times as powerful as any weapon we plan to produce for at least the next few years," the panel observed.

The panel also pointed out that should the Soviets prove uninterested in the test-ban—or should they agree to it and then violate the agreement—the United States could proceed in a matter of weeks with renewed testing of even more powerful atomic bombs and in a matter of months with the test of Mike. In the meantime, atomic bombs already in the American arsenal were not only much more powerful, but far more numerous than when Truman approved the all-out effort for the H-bomb. Like the Rabi-Fermi proposal, the "unique" feature of the standstill, Bush emphasized, was the ease of verification: "it separates the problem of limitation of armament from the problem of 'inspection.' "

Among the other practical reasons mentioned by the panel for not proceeding with Mike was the fact that "Soviet scientists will be able to derive from the test useful evidence as to the dimensions of the device." This information would include not only the radiation-implosion secret of the H-bomb but even what materials had gone into the device.[45]

But the panel's final argument for delaying Mike was nontechnical: "The test comes at a bad time." Exploding the world's first hydrogen bomb as the last act of the Truman presidency would send the wrong message to the world in general and the Russians in particular, the panel objected, and might also bind Truman's successor to an ineluctable cycle of building bigger and more fearsome weapons. Appealing to the president's concern with his place in history, members of the panel concluded that a postponement of the test "not only is desirable, but could become a decisive act of statesmanship."

To give balance to their presentation, the panel conceded that there was a powerful argument against postponement: "We need all the strength we can get" was, they agreed, a view both widespread and justified in the West following the Communist invasion of South Korea. But while acknowledging this and other counterarguments, the panel's sympathy was plainly with the standstill—and its concluding recommendation was unequivocal: "Let us postpone the test if such a decision can be understood, explained, and properly supported."

"The descent into the Maelstrom. . ."

Reaction in the government to the disarmament panel's secret proposal could not be divorced from the pressures of other, more public events that occupied Truman's attention. These included the costly and still-undecided war in Korea, where the president had steadfastly refused to rule out the possibility of using nuclear weapons to break the military deadlock.[46] Rising hysteria over alleged spies and Communists in the government was likewise manifested in the notorious loyalty hearings then being conducted by Wisconsin Senator Joseph McCarthy. Ironically, Truman's early attempt to defuse the internal security issue by dismissing it as a "red herring" only drew more attention to McCarthy's allegations. Acheson himself was caught up in the widening controversy when the secretary of state publicly defended a former aide, Alger Hiss, from charges of espionage and treason.[47]

There can be little doubt that both the tenuous international situation and domestic paranoia over "atom-spies" influenced the advice that Truman received on the nuclear standstill from his political and military advisers, and colored as well the president's own reaction to the idea.

There was also no letting up in the H-bomb lobby's crusade for the Super. In late March 1952—just before Bush approached Acheson with his proposal—the heads of all three military services had written to Robert Lovett, Johnson's replacement as defense secretary, raising once more the specter that the Soviets were ahead in the race for the H-bomb. The cause of their alarm was a Pentagon briefing that Edward Teller had given the previous day on probable Soviet progress toward the H-bomb, which Teller had combined with a renewed pitch for a second weapons laboratory. Wrote Dean in his journal of this briefing: "Arneson said he thinks Teller is trying to scare the daylights out of the people in [the Department of Defense] needlessly. . . . Teller has end-runned it again. He is taking the occasion to go off on the second lab question again." [48]

Teller also at this time briefed the National Security Council on the thermonuclear program, where he apparently made several key converts to the cause of the second laboratory. The physicist's briefing the previous week of Deputy Secretary of Defense William Foster on presumed Soviet progress toward an H-bomb prompted Foster to urge that the H-bomb program be broadened and intensified with the creation of another atomic lab. Although the second laboratory was opposed by both Dean and the GAC, Teller's wishes prevailed. But since the Livermore lab did not begin operations until July 1952, it would arrive on the scene too late to do anything more than analyze the test results of the Mike device, which was designed at Los Alamos.

Like the Super itself, the impetus behind the second lab was the fear that the Russians were winning the arms race. Concluded the memo that the service chiefs sent to Lovett that spring: "it is wholly possible that the Russians may be abreast of, or even ahead of, us in the development of thermonuclear weapons." [49]

Despite reawakened fears that the Russians were winning the race for the H-bomb, most of the president's political advisers refused to reject the standstill proposal outright. Acheson, for example, was sufficiently intrigued by the idea to ask Paul Nitze, head of the State Department's Policy Planning Staff, for his opinion in writing. Nitze was already well acquainted with the H-bomb controversy, as chief architect of the foreign policy review ordered by the president and ex officio member of Acheson's superbomb committee. Following Truman's January decision on the H-bomb, Nitze had originally proposed testing the superbomb while forgoing its production, until Truman's March decision for the all-out effort effectively ruled out that option.

In a June 9, 1952, memorandum to Acheson, Nitze worried about verification of the standstill. Without "some form of inspection and verification within the USSR," he wrote, "the United States could not be certain the Soviets were abiding by a test moratorium: The arms race would not end; it would merely be somewhat more concealed." Nonetheless, Nitze suggested that Truman might wish to raise privately the issue of postponing Mike with the two rival presidential candidates—Adlai Stevenson and Dwight Eisenhower, before the election. "If, as a result of such consultation, there is found to be a strong objection to the test prior to the beginning of the new President's term, it would be desirable to postpone the test," Nitze wrote.[50] Bush had meanwhile also received encouragement for the standstill from scientists like Hans Bethe.[51]

As the summer of 1952 began, however, pressures were mounting in Congress and at the Pentagon against any delay in testing the H-bomb. McMahon reportedly hinted to Gordon Arneson that he would seek Truman's impeachment if the president decided not to go ahead with Mike. That May, McMahon had written to the White House urging that Truman approve immediate and full-scale production of H-bombs if Mike proved successful. While confessing that he had his own misgivings about "these hideous weapons entering into the arsenals of the world," McMahon nonetheless thought that "overwhelming American superiority in H-bombs may well be the decisive means of keeping open the future for peace." Terminally ill with cancer, the Joint Committee on Atomic Energy chairman declared from his hospital bed that if he were the next president he would begin his term by building "thousands and thousands" of H-bombs.[52] A mid-August memorandum to Acheson from Arneson similarly warned of "very strong feelings evident in the Pentagon against delay." Lovett, in particular, was reportedly adamant that Mike go ahead as scheduled.[53]

Resisting these pressures, Acheson's Committee on the Super-bomb and the AEC that August unanimously recommended that Truman postpone Mike until after the election. Significantly, the standstill proposal had now become subordinate to the more immediate issue of delaying the test past election day, November 4. By the end of August, the president had yet to decide for or against a delay—but Truman hinted at his own feelings when he told Dean that he would certainly be pleased if technical reasons caused a postponement.[54]

With barely a month to go before the test, scientists as well as Truman's political advisers remained of two opinions on the timing of Mike. Following a two-hour briefing on the H-bomb by Teller, Nitze changed his mind and now urged no further delay. On September 9, Bethe wrote to Dean, asking the AEC chairman to intervene personally with the president to postpone the test.[55]

In a review of options requested by Acheson, Arneson reiterated that Mike "may well represent a point of no return," as the last opportunity to "avert the descent into the Maelstrom."[56] Indeed, as many scientists probably were aware, there was by now a political risk to being identified with the standstill. Members of the disarmament panel had already discretely informed Acheson that they were "disturbed about presenting their views on this matter formally." Oppenheimer—soon to be under attack by

Strauss, McMahon, and other members of the H-bomb lobby for alleged "foot-dragging" on the Super—was understandably reluctant to be seen as a prominent sponsor of the idea. Oppenheimer later claimed he "did nothing whatever about it" when Bush told him of talking to Acheson about the standstill proposal.[57]

As late as the beginning of October, Truman was still toying with the idea of postponing Mike, though he had told neither Stevenson nor Eisenhower of the decision he was facing. Finally, on October 9, Truman asked Lovett "to see to it that the situation develops in such a way that the test did not take place until after [the election]." According to Lovett, what the president desired was that "arrangements should be made for slowing up delivery of equipment or some other technical obstacle be found to prevent the test from taking place before the election." Truman "wanted this to be done without the generation of any official documents," Lovett noted.[58]

Some six days later, the president's emissary, AEC Commissioner Eugene Zuckert, flew to the H-bomb test site in the Pacific with orders to stop Mike. But after a last-minute telephone call from Dean, who relayed Zuckert's message that any delay in the test would cause subsequent problems for the entire thermonuclear program, Truman relented and allowed the countdown to continue. With the president's about-face, the last obstacle in the way of Mike—and the last hope for a nuclear standstill during the Truman administration—disappeared.[59]

The fact that not even an eleventh-hour order by Truman himself was able to slow the momentum behind Mike confirmed the accuracy of the GAC's warning that the H-bomb would come to have a life of its own. The test of the sixty-five-ton experimental device, nicknamed "the sausage," proceeded on schedule in the minutes leading up to dawn on November 1 in the Pacific—October 31 across the international dateline in Washington.

Mike's yield was equivalent to almost ten-and-a-half million tons of conventional explosive—powerful enough to dig a crater two miles wide and a half-mile deep out of the ocean floor and to return most of the coral atoll of Elugelab to the sea.[60] (As Teller had correctly predicted more than a year earlier at the George test, the islands around Eniwetok "would not be large enough for the next one.") Changes being made to the design of the device as late as the eve of the explosion suggest that the Mike test could not have taken place any earlier than it did, despite subsequent claims to the contrary by Teller and the H-bomb lobby.[61]

"Proceeding grimly at an ever more rapid pace. . ."

Reactions to the success of Mike varied widely among the scientists who had been involved in the lengthy controversy over the H-bomb. At Berkeley, Teller, Lawrence, and Alvarez were relieved when the magnitude of the explosion was confirmed by the campus seismograph. But across the country, at Princeton—where Oppenheimer and the members of the SAC/ODM were meeting—the response was ambivalent. Participants later described the mood of the committee as "gloomy" and "grim."[62]

One topic discussed at the Princeton meeting was whether the committee, which thus far had been virtually ignored by the Truman administration, should voluntarily disband. Although its members decided to continue to offer their services to the government in hopes that the next president might make better use of their advice, rumors also circulated at the meeting of new political troubles facing Oppenheimer, a foreboding sign of even greater troubles to come for the physicist.[63]

For Bush and others who supported the nuclear standstill, Mike represented a narrowly missed but nonetheless irretrievably lost opportunity—the closing of one last open door. In April 1954, during his testimony at Oppenheimer's security hearing, Bush would argue that Mike

> marked our entry into a very disagreeable kind of world. I felt strongly that that test ended the possibility of the only type of agreement that I thought was possible at that time, namely, an agreement to make no more tests. . . .
> I think history will show that was a turning point . . . when we entered into the grim world that we are entering right now, that those who pushed that thing through to a conclusion without making that attempt have a great deal to answer for.[64]

Because of Mike, it was with diminished hopes that the disarmament panel forwarded its report, "Armaments and American Policy," to the president in mid-November 1952, during Truman's final weeks in office.

Warning that the "contest in producing weapons of mass destruction is proceeding grimly at an ever more rapid pace," the report highlighted the panel's feeling that there was a new and urgent "need for candor about the arms race"—a need made even more pressing by the success of Mike. The panel urged Truman to inform the American public, perhaps as his final act in office, about the essential facts of the arms race that had yet to be disclosed—including "the character of major weapons, their expanding rate of production, and the enormous and important fact that they are possessed by both sides."[65]

On December 30, the top officials of the Truman administration, minus the president, gathered in Acheson's office to consider the disarmament panel's report. Having recently received a detailed briefing on the results of Mike, the civilian heads of the military services were uncharacteristically united in the opinion that "a weapon was in the offing which, in sufficient numbers, might have the power to destroy the world."[66]

With a unanimity born of fear, the service chiefs endorsed the panel's recommendation that Truman invite president-elect Eisenhower, and possibly also the leaders of Congress, to join him in issuing a frank report on the nature and direction of the nuclear arms race—one that would contain many of the same terrifying details that the president and the military leaders had just learned about Mike. "They felt," the heads of the services wrote, "that the public should have knowledge of this development in the hope that such awareness might make it possible for statesmen, by renewed efforts, to bring about effective international control of these and other weapons." Truman, who had already seen an earlier version of the panel's report, seemed receptive to its recommendation, even to the point of asking Air Force Secretary Thomas Finletter to draft such a statement, to be released on the last day of the year.[67]

Lovett, however, strongly opposed the panel's proposal for a candid description of the arms race by the president. Acheson acknowledged that he, too, was "very troubled indeed" by the idea, fearing that "a horrendous statement such as the one proposed without suggesting any solution to the situation would generate a sense of utter frustration and lead to public clamor that something be done, however foolish." He felt that "the American people probably already had enough information about thermonuclear developments."[68]

The objections raised by Acheson and Lovett prevailed over the appeals of Oppenheimer and the disarmament panel at the December 30 meeting. Finletter, at its end, volunteered that "the whole project should be scrapped." Instead, an alternative statement—one that would, in Acheson's words, "focus on the Kremlin as the culprit rather than the American people and the rest of the free world"—was unobtrusively incorporated into Truman's parting speech a week later, in which he only vaguely alluded to the H-bomb.[69] At Acheson's urging, Truman likewise rejected the disarmament panel's request that its classified report and recommendations be made public. The president's decision determined that the nuclear arms race would continue as it had begun—shrouded in secrecy.

II

*Fragile Hopes,
1953–1960:
The Impetus toward
Arms Control*

5

"Racing toward Catastrophe"

Atoms for Peace and War

With the successful test of the American hydrogen bomb, the attention of scientists and of the new president gradually turned from building to controlling the weapons of mass destruction. The opportunity for a nuclear standstill now past, Eisenhower expressed interest in another recommendation of Truman's disarmament panel: greater candor about the arms race.

"It doesn't do any good to run. . ."

Unlike Harry Truman, Dwight Eisenhower was well acquainted by the time of his inauguration with the dangerous world that science had called into being. Just a week after his election, Eisenhower was briefed on the Mike test in the course of a golf outing at an Augusta, Georgia, country club. At Truman's invitation, the president-elect and his choice as secretary of state, John Foster Dulles, visited the White House on November 18, 1952, to hear more about Mike. Together, Truman and Secretary of State Dean Acheson also briefed their successors on present and potential trouble spots, including Korea, Iran, and American relations with NATO. Earlier, Truman had taken Eisenhower aside in the Cabinet Room to talk over some issues that Truman considered especially sensitive—among which was the frightening and unexpected power of the H-bomb. The following day, AEC chairman Gordon Dean went to Eisenhower's suite at New York's Commodore Hotel to give the president-elect a more detailed briefing on the H-bomb test.[1]

Dean's information probably contributed to Eisenhower's feelings of ambivalence toward science and its practitioners. Since his days as a wartime commander, Eisenhower had seemingly been impressed more with the threat than the promise of technology. (In his memoirs, Vannevar Bush recounts briefing General Eisenhower on the German "wonder weapon," the V-1 buzz bomb, on the eve of the Normandy invasion. "You scare the hell out of me," Eisenhower admitted at the end of the briefing. "What do we do?" Bush recalled that he and Eisenhower agreed the simplest solution was to bomb the V-1 sites during the invasion, so that none of the weapons could be launched.)[2]

Eisenhower also never shared the average American's infatuation with gadgets. Accustomed to having a military aide or valet carry out everyday menial chores, he left the White House in 1961 reportedly unfamiliar with dial telephones.[3]

A casual conversation between Eisenhower and another Republican, Harold Stassen, a week before the inauguration reveals how deeply the president-elect was affected by the news of Mike. Stassen, reading a draft of Eisenhower's inaugural address, observed that its only reference to science— the observation that it "seems ready to confer upon us, as its final gift, the power to erase human life from this planet"—"tended to give the scientists a rough time." Eisenhower's response was unusually blunt: "Just listen to the stories of the hydrogen bomb. And it doesn't do any good to run. Some day we will get those boys up to tell us some of the facts of those things. They are terrifying."[4]

The secret briefings on Mike by Truman and Dean stayed with the new president. Fully a year after assuming office, Eisenhower admitted that he continued to "worry over people's seeming reluctance to recognize the threat of the hydrogen bomb." An aide claimed that throughout Eisenhower's first term the president frequently reminded him: "We've just got to let the American people know how terrible this thing is."[5]

"Our only hope. . ."

Eisenhower was probably cheered to learn, upon reading the disarmament panel's report a week or so after assuming office, that scientists shared his concern about the accelerating arms race. In mid-February, 1953, the president himself raised the subject of the panel's report in a meeting of the National Security Council. Noting that he had "a high opinion" of the report and its conclusions, Eisenhower said he wanted everyone in the room to be "thoroughly familiar" with it. But at least two of those present misread the reason for Eisenhower's enthusiasm. Vice President Richard Nixon mused that it might be possible "to make some kind of sensational offer on the disarmament side, which the Soviets would of course not accept, and which would therefore put them on the spot"—a suggestion promptly endorsed by Secretary of State Dulles, who added that "we had squeezed all the juice out of our last proposal."[6]

Only a week later, however, during another NSC discussion, Eisenhower voiced concern that the disarmament panel's report was another case of scientists interfering in politics. It seemed "strange" to him, Eisenhower acknowledged, "that two eminent scientists [Oppenheimer and Bush] had been put on the Panel and that they had immediately moved out of the scientific realm into the realms of policy and psychology." His experience as president of Columbia University had taught him, he said, that "most scientists concerned with atomic problems had no real grasp of the security issue." A better idea, he suggested, would have been for Truman to appoint two panels—one to discuss the scientific and technical issues and another to recommend specific political steps.[7]

Although Eisenhower also said on this occasion that he emphatically agreed with the report's appeal for "candor," and likewise its notion of "enoughness"—the view that the nuclear arms race was approaching a situation in which both sides would have sufficient weapons to destroy the other, no matter what steps either might take—he rejected one of the panel's most prominent recommendations. He was opposed, Eisenhower said, "at this stage to indicating to the American people anything about the size of our stockpile of weapons." Despite his comment about the need for separating scientists and policy, Eisenhower put Bush in charge of a new committee given responsibility for suggesting how best to carry out the recommendations in the disarmament panel's report. The president's decision seemed a tacit admission either that he felt science and policy had become inseparable or that scientists had become indispensable as advisers in the nuclear age.[8]

Three weeks later, Bush's report simply reiterated the disarmament panel's conclusion. There was, Bush argued, "much greater danger from lethargy on the people's part than from panic." The most important thing for the public to know about the arms race, he emphasized, was the fact that *"it's a 2-way affair."*[9]

More than two months after the president read the disarmament panel's report—and despite his early expression of interest in what some in the government had begun to call Operation Candor—the administration had yet to take any action on the panel's recommendations. On May 27, at the suggestion of Robert Cutler, Eisenhower's national security adviser, both Bush and Oppenheimer were called to an NSC meeting to discuss the report. There Oppenheimer described what was obviously a depressing trend: Whereas the United States had had no more than three atomic bombs in 1945, it now had almost a thousand, each one several times the power of the original. "Our only hope in facing this situation," Oppenheimer concluded, "was an informed and steady public—adding, for Eisenhower's benefit, "to explain to the people the nature of their dilemma it was necessary for the highest voice in the land to speak."[10]

Although Eisenhower said that "he certainly agreed in principle with Dr. Oppenheimer's recommendation in favor of candor," he also voiced concern "about the security aspect of the release. What facts could safely be revealed to the public?" Oppenheimer replied that the question of what information to release and when was essentially a political one, but that "he was sure that in general the policy of candor was several years overdue."

The real gap between the president and the physicist on the subject of candor became evident at the end of this meeting. The president "suggested that, in describing future U.S. weapons tests, the Atomic Energy Commission delete the word 'thermonuclear,' because it was quite possible that omission of this term would add to Russian confusion and ignorance of the status of our program." Oppenheimer diplomatically withheld comment— even though he certainly realized that while such a ploy might confuse the American public, it would hardly deceive the Russians.

"Until we have looked this tiger in the eye. . ."

Eisenhower's remarks to Oppenheimer showed that the president, as well as the public, remained ignorant of some fundamental facts about the arms race.

As the disarmament panel and Oppenheimer had pointed out, the original reason for the extraordinary secrecy surrounding the American nuclear stockpile—the fact that the atomic arsenal was pitifully small—no longer applied by 1953. Yet the cloak of government secrecy that had been drawn around the subject in 1945 persisted—amid efforts to pull it, if possible, even tighter.[11]

Concern with security had intensified following the unmasking of Fuchs and other espionage scandals, which had seriously damaged Truman's presidency. Lingering worry over with so-called atom spies was probably another reason the Truman administration's top-secret "Policy on Atomic Warfare" (NSC-30), which discouraged public discussion of U.S. nuclear weapons policy as potentially threatening to American security, was left unchanged during Eisenhower's first term.[12]

Nonetheless, in the summer of 1953, Eisenhower was still surprisingly receptive to the aims of Operation Candor. That July, the president confided to Dulles that his goal now went well beyond a frank accounting to the public of the destructiveness of hydrogen bombs; it also included "a carefully thought out program of speeches, national and international conferences, articles, and legislation." The alternative to candor about the bomb, Eisenhower hinted, was an arms race that "would either drive us to war—or into some form of dictatorial government."[13]

But in an NSC meeting at month's end, during which the president fretted over delays that were still hindering the project, Operation Candor encountered opposition from within Eisenhower's own inner circle when AEC Chairman Lewis Strauss voiced doubts about the wisdom of the enterprise.

Strauss actually held two important jobs in the new administration: The current chairman of the AEC had earlier been appointed special adviser to the president on atomic energy, a position Eisenhower created. Strauss was chosen for the AEC post, Cutler wrote to Eisenhower aide Sherman Adams, because what was needed for the role was "not a scientist or a lawyer but a practical business manager"—since, as Cutler noted, the AEC "is a very big business."[14]

In the July NSC meeting, Strauss objected "to the connotations of the word 'candor,'" he told the president, because of its suggestion that "this implied deception up to now." While Eisenhower agreed that "we should not beat our breasts and say, 'Look, we are candid,'" the president defended the initiative.[15]

Coincidentally, that same month, Oppenheimer—who, like Eisenhower, was becoming exasperated by the delays attending Operation Candor—tried on his own to compel the government to be more forthright about the bomb. Appearing in the July issue of *Foreign Affairs* was an article by the physicist, which had been approved for publication by the president, that contained many of the conclusions and recommendations in the secret disarmament panel report. Titled "Atomic Weapons and American Policy," Oppenheimer's article favored redirecting the nuclear arms race away from hugely destructive offensive weapons, like the H-bomb, to less powerful atomic weapons that might be used to stop a conventional invasion of Europe or even to shoot down enemy bombers headed for America. The article also echoed the disarmament panel's theme of "enoughness": "The very least we can say is that, looking ten years ahead, it is likely to be small comfort that the Soviet Union is four years behind us, and small comfort that they are only about half as big as we are."[16]

But the centerpiece of Oppenheimer's article was his plea that the government do more to inform the public about the bomb: "It is my opinion that we should all know—not precisely, but quantitatively and, above all, authoritatively—where we stand in these matters." As Oppenheimer warned, "until we have looked this tiger in the eye we shall be in the worst of all possible dangers, which is that we may back into him."

Ironically, the subsequent furor over Oppenheimer's public appeal may have done more to hinder than to help the cause of candor about the bomb—as well as adding to Oppenheimer's own subsequent troubles. But another and far more serious setback for that cause was the detection, the following month, of the first Soviet bomb test involving a thermonuclear component. As subsequent events determined, the news of the Russian bomb would prompt the first test of the Eisenhower administration's new policy of candor.

"We are now well ahead of the Soviets. . ."

On August 7, 1953, following what he described as "a restless and worried night," Strauss wrote to Eisenhower concerning prospective Soviet nuclear weapons developments. Strauss's biggest worry was the fact that the United

States had not detected a Soviet atomic test for nearly two years. He speculated that the Soviets had perfected nuclear weapons to the point where
additional testing was unnecessary; or, even worse, that they had devised a
means to test nuclear and perhaps even thermonuclear weapons while evading detection, perhaps by exploding the bombs either deep underground or
in the immense depths of Lake Baikal. "If that should be so," Strauss wrote,
"their latest test—1951—may have been of an essential component for their
H-bombs and it may have been satisfactory for that purpose. In that case,
the next test they make might very well be a test of an H-bomb."[17]

American detection of a Russian bomb test only five days later prompted Eisenhower to remark that Strauss "must have a pipe line into the Kremlin." The fourth nuclear test to occur in Stalin's Russia—hence Joe-4 in the
parlance of American intelligence experts—occurred in the early morning of
August 12 and was detected almost immediately by acoustic and seismic
sensors. That evening, planes of the Air Force's Long-Range Detection Program picked up the first fallout from the explosion.[18]

Verification that the explosion had involved fusion as well as fission
was made public in an announcement by Strauss on August 20. The AEC
chairman carefully described it as "an atomic test" of "both fission and
thermonuclear reactions," but not as an H-bomb. Nonetheless, American
reporters unwittingly abetted the Soviets' subsequent claim that Russia, and
not the United States, had built the world's first deliverable H-bomb.[19]

In fact, the bomb exploded by the Russians showed it was the United
States, not the Soviet Union, that was ahead in the arms race. As Strauss privately informed Eisenhower, the Soviet test had less than a third the explosive yield of Mike. Even more importantly, analysis of the fallout from Joe-4
suggested that the Russians had embarked upon the wrong road to the multimegaton Super.[20]

On August 21, Congressman Sterling Cole, the new chairman of the
Joint Committee on Atomic Energy, wrote to Eisenhower with the news that,
"thanks to [the work of American scientists], we are now well ahead of the
Soviets—both in fission weapons and in thermonuclear developments."[21]

In a press conference on October 8, the president referred to the Soviet
test as of "a weapon, or the forerunner of a weapon, of power far in excess
of the conventional types." But to Strauss's evident relief, Eisenhower shied
away from further candor. "We do not intend to disclose the details of our
strength in atomic weapons of any sort," he told reporters.[22]

"We don't want to scare the country to death. . ."

By fall 1953, Operation Candor was viewed by some in the Eisenhower
administration less as a policy of openness than as an opportunity for a propaganda ploy. Still, the spirit, at least, of the original initiative lived on in
the president, who now extended the idea to include greater openness in
America's dealings with Russia. On September 10, Eisenhower informed

Strauss of an idea that he "did not think anyone had yet thought of" for a cooperative approach to the Soviets.[23]

Eisenhower proposed that the United States and the Soviet Union each turn over to the United Nations a fixed amount of weapons-grade fissionable material "for peaceful use." In order to sell the idea to Strauss, the president suggested that the amount of plutonium and enriched uranium to be surrendered to the United Nations "could be fixed at a figure which we could handle from our stockpile, but which it would be difficult for the Soviets to match."[24]

Strauss acknowledged that Eisenhower's idea was "novel and might have value for propaganda purposes," but the AEC chairman questioned its effect on the arms race. As Strauss explained to the president, the advent of H-bombs meant that "the relative importance of a stockpile of *fissionable* material is reduced since it is only required as a primer while quite different substances, *not fissionable*, support the thermonuclear explosion."[25]

The president, nonetheless, refused to be put off. Several weeks earlier, while on vacation in the Colorado Rockies, Eisenhower had assigned speechwriter and confidant C. D. Jackson the task of drafting a national address on the new policy toward Russia that had grown out of Operation Candor. Eisenhower wanted the speech to "contain a tremendous lift for the world—for the hopes of men everywhere." Jackson thought the speech potentially "not only . . . the most important pronouncement ever made by a President of the United States, it could also save mankind."[26] Upon Eisenhower's instructions, the proposed conversion of weapons-grade fissionable material into fuel for civilian atomic power plants became the new focus for the speech, and for Operation Candor.

Within the White House, Operation Candor was redubbed "Operation Wheaties" when it became the subject of discussion at breakfast meetings with the president, and later "Atoms for Peace" when it was tied to Strauss's plan for extending the peaceful uses of nuclear energy to developing countries. The change in nomenclature would later seem particularly apt, since the evolution of "Candor" into "Wheaties" signaled the transformation of Eisenhower's sincere desire to slow the arms race into a Madison Avenue public relations gambit.[27]

Atoms for Peace received varying degrees of support from within the administration, but for reasons that did not necessarily coincide with the president's. Cutler, for example, rationalized that "this offer would be our last hope," because if the Russians rejected it "we would reconcile ourselves to life in an atomic world in which the Soviet threat would be ever present."[28] The Joint Chiefs, concerned that too much honesty might "leave the American public with a sense of endless burden, fear, and hopelessness," urged Eisenhower to downplay the destructiveness of nuclear war in his speech and to "be less specific in revealing the power of bombs now in our atomic stockpile."[29]

By late September, Eisenhower worried that continuing discussion of the speech both within the administration and outside—the result of leaks published by journalists Stewart and Joseph Alsop—"had taken the edge off the idea." He also was concerned that even toned down the passage dealing with the arms race might be too grim. "This leaves everybody dead on both sides, with no hope anywhere," Eisenhower complained to Jackson about one draft. "Can't we find some hope? We don't want to scare the country to death."[30] The president was also troubled that the speech might spark new and more insistent calls at home for greater defense spending—whereas his actual intent, Eisenhower told Strauss and Dulles, was "some hopeful alternative" to the arms race and a "fair offer" to the Soviets.[31]

"A blank wall. . ."

On the afternoon of December 8, 1953—more than a year after the disarmament panel made its first appeal for candor about the arms race to Truman—Eisenhower delivered his long-awaited Atoms for Peace speech before an enthusiastic United Nations General Assembly. But before the week was out, Russian representatives at the United Nations had rebuffed Atoms for Peace, offering in its place an even more ambitious and less realistic plan for "general and complete disarmament."[32] Under the weight of what Dulles called the Soviets' "peace offensive," the "hopeful alternative" to the arms race that Eisenhower had sought—and with it, Atoms for Peace—gradually collapsed. Following the Soviet rejection, Eisenhower and the NSC agreed in secret that, while they "would listen to any proposals which the USSR cared to submit on the control or abolition of nuclear weapons, we would not be drawn into any negotiations on this subject."[33]

Before Atoms for Peace would be officially abandoned, there was one final postscript to Operation Candor—one that cast an ominous shadow over the future of science advising in the Eisenhower administration. A few days prior to his speech at the United Nations, Eisenhower had called Strauss and other top administration officials into the Oval Office in response to an urgent appeal from Defense Secretary Charles Wilson. Because of information received from Wilson, Eisenhower announced, he was ordering that a "blank wall" be put between atomic secrets and Robert Oppenheimer, who was henceforth to be regarded as a potential security risk.

Earlier in the month, Eisenhower had confided to his diary the fact that the charges against Oppenheimer were nothing new; but they reminded him that someone very early in his term—he thought it was Strauss—had warned that Oppenheimer was not to be trusted. If Oppenheimer "is really a disloyal citizen," Eisenhower reflected in the diary, "then the damage he can do now as compared to what he has done in the past is like comparing a grain of sand to an ocean beach."[34]

On December 23, at Strauss's direction, Oppenheimer's security clearance was officially suspended and classified documents were removed from his office and his home at Princeton. Eisenhower's order made Oppenheimer, the ultimate insider among scientists advising the American government for more than a decade, an outsider virtually overnight.[35] It was only the beginning of a protracted ordeal for Oppenheimer—one that would over the next several years outrage many in the American scientific community and, in the process, alter relations between U.S. scientists and their government.

Strauss, who had virtually no scientific training and who made no secret of his deep and lasting enmity for Oppenheimer, henceforth replaced the physicist as the government's leading authority on atomic policy. Like the role of Groves, the "Atom General" of the Truman administration, the advice of the "Admiral"—as Strauss preferred to be called, in recognition of his wartime commission—went essentially unchallenged in the Eisenhower administration when it came to atomic energy.[36] The scientists on the GAC, who might logically have been expected to be Eisenhower's chief advisers on the bomb, remained, as a group and individually, silent in the face of the storm clouds gathering around Oppenheimer's career.

Isidor Rabi, who had replaced Oppenheimer as chairman of the GAC in the summer of 1952, was the most likely candidate to fill the unofficial post of science adviser to the president on the bomb—not only because of Rabi's membership on both the GAC and SAC/ODM, but also because of his long-standing personal acquaintance with Eisenhower. The two met when Eisenhower visited Columbia University, in 1947, prior to becoming the university's president. On that occasion, according to Rabi, Eisenhower had been impressed by his frankness. While president of Columbia, Eisenhower frequently called upon Rabi for advice.[37]

Rabi also shared Eisenhower's growing concern about the peril of nuclear weapons. Rabi was pleased to discover, during a visit to the Oval Office shortly after Ike's inauguration, that the president agreed with his view that the United States was at an inevitable disadvantage in a nuclear arms race—not only because it was more difficult to keep secrets in a democracy but also because modern weapons had diminished the importance of geographic isolation, historically the nation's principal safeguard against attack.[38]

But Rabi's teaching and research at Columbia left him neither the occasion nor the desire to serve full-time as a science adviser to the president.[39] Perhaps more to the point, there was still no such post to be filled. More than a decade after Szilard and Einstein's unorthodox appeal to Roosevelt on the atomic bomb, a direct link between the president and scientists advising the government had yet to be established. Meanwhile, Rabi and his colleagues on the GAC and SAC/ODM were content to remain in the background. Under the part-time stewardship of Caltech president Lee DuBridge, the latter group met on an irregular basis; its recommendations and deliberations were sent to the president through ODM director Arthur Flemming. Eisenhower had yet to call upon the twelve-member committee since assuming office.[40]

By both design and default, therefore, it was to Strauss and his scientists that Eisenhower turned for advice on the bomb. Strauss assumed this responsibility with alacrity and guarded it jealously. Indeed, except for Oppenheimer, he had never had a rival for the role. As the special adviser to the president on atomic energy, Strauss determined not only the kind of advice that Eisenhower would receive on nuclear weapons but also, to a large extent, the policies that followed from it.[41] Equally significant was the fact that the scientists whom Strauss picked as his advisers—alumni of the H-bomb lobby like Edward Teller, Ernest Lawrence and physicist-mathematician John von Neumann—fully shared Strauss's conservative view of the arms race and the Russians.[42]

With the declining influence of the GAC, Oppenheimer's eclipse, and SAC/ODM's passivity, Strauss and these scientists became de facto the first science advisers to Eisenhower.

"Unusual urgency. . ."

In February 1954, members of the Air Force's newly formed Strategic Missiles Evaluation Committee, also known as the Teapot panel, concluded that recent advances, which promised smaller and lighter H-bombs, would soon make it possible to use rockets to drop superbombs on targets an ocean away in a fraction of the time it took a bomber to fly the same distance. The implications for the arms race were revolutionary, von Neumann, chairman of the missile panel, informed Trevor Gardner, assistant secretary of the Air Force for research and development.[43]

The multimegaton H-bomb that was just entering the American nuclear stockpile weighed some twenty-one tons and was so unwieldy it could only be carried by the B-36, the nation's largest bomber. (In training flights, the plane would soar several hundred feet into the air when a mock-up of the huge bomb was released.)[44] Carrying only a single weapon apiece, the planes would take several hours to reach their targets in the Soviet Union and could be shot down en route by Russian defenders.

By contrast, the next generation of H-bombs, while of comparable yield to the current behemoth, would weigh less than a ton and might be smaller than the average American sedan, von Neumann told Gardner. Several such weapons could be carried to targets deep inside Russia by a single bomber. But the most important feature of the new miniaturized H-bomb—and one that justified bringing it to the president's attention—was the likelihood that it would fit atop the intercontinental-range rocket being developed for the Air Force.[45] Thus, the smaller, lighter H-bomb made possible what some were already calling the ultimate weapon: an H-bomb-tipped ballistic missile with intercontinental range. The ICBM, which did not require guidance from the ground and hence was immune to jamming, would hurtle to earth from space at speeds too fast to be intercepted.

Until the Teapot panel's report, the advent of the ICBM had seemed an unlikely prospect anytime soon. At a 1949 congressional hearing, Vannevar Bush had flatly predicted that intercontinental-range missiles would prove too costly and too inaccurate to be worth building "for a long period of time to come."[46] President Truman thought the ICBM so unpromising that he twice refused to spend the money appropriated by Congress for research on the missile.[47] Although the ICBM program was revived in early 1951, a year later von Neumann and the Air Force Scientific Advisory Board recommended that it be sacrificed in order to accelerate work on the nuclear-powered bomber.[48]

One reason for pessimism about the ICBM was the daunting array of technical difficulties that had to be overcome. Envisioned was a seven-engine, ten-story–high behemoth: the minimum-size rocket needed to loft a ten–thousand-pound atomic bomb a distance of five thousand miles.

Barely had the Second World War ended when the Air Force assigned the contract to build the first ICBM to Convair, where it became Project MX-774. Almost immediately, postwar fiscal constraints brought cutbacks in the program. Fundamental and seemingly insurmountable obstacles also confounded the missile's designers. For one thing, the most powerful turbopumps that could be fitted inside the thin metal skin of Convair's missile proved unable to feed fuel to the rocket's engines fast enough to maintain thrust. Later, company engineers discovered that the fuel itself, sloshing around inside the rocket during flight, would cause it to veer out of control. Nor was it known whether the ICBM's atomic warhead would survive its fiery reentry into the atmosphere.[49]

While work on the ICBM proceeded at an agonizingly slow pace, progress at the weapons laboratories was more rapid than had been expected. The success of Mike promised to make the accuracy of ICBMs less a concern, since an H-bomb could land two or three miles from the aiming point and still destroy most targets. In October 1953, von Neumann had briefed Air Force officials on the pending dramatic improvement in thermonuclear weapons. Two weeks later, the Air Force assembled the eleven-member Strategic Missiles Evaluation Committee (SMEC) under von Neumann's direction to assess the implications of this breakthrough.[50]

The Teapot panel concluded that henceforth the requirements for the ICBM could be "radically relaxed." The panel's scientists also believed that it might be possible to deploy the first of these missiles as early as 1960.[51]

The report of SMEC was given additional force by a concurrent RAND study on ballistic missiles, which was equally optimistic about the suddenly improved prospects for the ICBM. While the Teapot panel stopped short of urging an immediate crash effort to build ICBMs, it warned that a situation of "unusual urgency" might develop should Soviet progress in rocketry create "a compelling political and psychological reason for our own effort to proceed apace."[52]

"Nothing was out of control. . ."

Less than three weeks after von Neumann gave Gardner the SMEC's report, the first H-bomb warhead developed for the ICBM was successfully tested in the Pacific. Like Mike, the power of the bomb exploded on February 28, 1954—in a test code-named Bravo—surprised even the scientists who had built the device. Bravo's fifteen megatons was nearly twice the yield that its designers had predicted, and half again the power of Mike.[53]

But with Bravo there were other and even more disturbing surprises to come. As scientists who witnessed the test subsequently discovered, the bomb's greater than expected yield was accompanied by a larger than expected amount of radioactive fallout. Due to a last-minute wind shift and to the unprecedented heights reached by Bravo's mushroom-shaped cloud, the fallout was also carried many miles further downwind from the test area than had been the case in the Mike explosion.[54]

The intensely radioactive white ash that continued to fall from the sky far from and long after the Bravo test presented a new danger, hitherto little appreciated by the public. Hours after the test, some seventy-five miles from the site of the explosion and outside the test area perimeter, fallout from Bravo settled on the Japanese fishing boat *Fortunate Dragon*. By the time the boat returned to port in Japan two weeks later, all twenty-three crew members were suffering from radiation sickness; one sailor subsequently died. The incident sparked protests against atomic testing throughout the world.[55]

Because of Bravo, public apathy about the testing of nuclear weapons ended virtually overnight. Popular concern was given further impetus by Eisenhower's candid admission in a press conference some three weeks after the test that "this time something must have happened that we have never experienced before, and must have surprised and astonished the scientists."[56] While Strauss assured Secretary of State Dulles, in a telephone conversation, that Bravo had come as no surprise, that "nothing was out of control. Nothing devastated"—Dulles remained unconvinced.[57] (Strauss told others in the administration that he believed the *Fortunate Dragon* was actually a Soviet spy boat and that he had asked the CIA to investigate. An "eyes only" CIA report sent to Strauss on April 29 concluded that there was no evidence to support his theories that the *Fortunate Dragon* had carried spy gear or that the original boat had been sunk—"a substitute vessel having been offered for inspection.")[58]

The AEC chairman inadvertently compounded the administration's public relations problem by his ill-timed boast at the president's March 31 press conference that a single Bravo-sized bomb could destroy an entire city.

"Any city," he elaborated. Eisenhower visibly winced when Strauss, in response to a reporter's question, confirmed that this included New York.[59]

Strauss's press conference gaffe drew attention to the fact that, in late March, the AEC released a film of the 1952 Mike test featuring an H-bomb fireball dwarfing the superimposed skyline of New York City. The following month the administration, without fanfare, quietly withdrew the film from circulation.[60] Plainly, Strauss's prediction to Eisenhower that the public would "rejoice" at the success of Bravo had badly misjudged the public mood.

"The *dis*arming of atomic energy. . ."

Just as Bravo awakened public concern with radioactive fallout, it also brought Eisenhower's attention back to the disarmament panel's report and Atoms for Peace. In the wake of the test, the president reminded Strauss that upon being appointed to head the AEC he had been instructed that his "first assignment is to find some new approach to the *dis*arming of atomic energy." Although both his administration's "New Look" military policy and Dulles's "massive retaliation" doctrine were dependent upon nuclear weapons, Eisenhower's steadfast rejection of Strauss's repeated urgings that he witness a nuclear test seemed a sign of the president's growing unease with that reliance.[61]

Indeed, on April 7, Eisenhower announced at a press conference that the United States would neither build nor test any bombs larger than Bravo while he was president.[62] Later that month, Eisenhower secretly instructed Strauss to complete Operation Castle, the test series of which Bravo was a part, as soon as possible. When this series was finished, the president confided to Dulles, he was thinking of taking a step that many were then urging, namely, "a moratorium on all further experimentation whether with H-bombs or A-bombs."[63]

6

"An Age of Danger"

From the Killian Report to Sputnik

Worried about the long-term health peril of radioactive fallout, Eisenhower and Dulles in the spring of 1954 revived an idea originally proposed by scientists during the H-bomb debate but not discussed in government since the disarmament panel: a ban on nuclear testing. The goal of a nuclear test ban, however, had to contend with mounting fear of a Soviet surprise attack—inspired by recognition of the newly emerging ICBM threat and made more acute by chronic ignorance in the West about what was going on behind the Iron Curtain.

"Gazing into eternity. . ."

Part of the impetus for renewed interest in a nuclear test ban came, unexpectedly, from one of the AEC's most conservative commissioners: Thomas Murray. An engineer by training, Murray had been in charge of New York City's subway system during the Second World War. Murray claimed that his interest in nuclear power stemmed from the prediction of a physicist, in 1940, that the subways of the future would run on atoms instead of coal. Also a prominent Democrat, Murray had been appointed to the commission by Truman and had been at Eniwetok to witness Mike, where the super-bomb test left a lasting impression upon him. As he later wrote: "I . . . had a feeling I might be gazing into eternity, or into the gates of hell."[1]

Concerned as well that the Russians might learn the secret of the Super from tests like Mike, Murray shortly thereafter tried unsuccessfully to get Strauss and the AEC's other commissioners to support a bilateral moratorium on thermonuclear testing.[2] On March 14, 1954, some two weeks after Bravo, Murray appealed directly to Eisenhower by letter, asking that the president cancel or at least postpone the upcoming hydrogen bomb test in favor of an "Atomic Summit" of Soviet and American leaders: "The United States is far ahead of the USSR in the field of thermonuclear weapons," Murray assured Eisenhower. The fact that the United States had conducted a total of fifty-six nuclear weapons tests—compared with just four by the Soviets—"has given us a weapons technology that is highly advanced . . . so much so, that we could accept a delay of a year or more in testing weapons of yields greater than a hundred kilotons without our progress being greatly hampered."[3]

Instead of adding large multimegaton H-bombs like Mike and Bravo to the stockpile, Murray argued, Eisenhower should limit the American nuclear arsenal to "thousands and thousands" of small kiloton-yield weapons— an area in which the United States had conducted many more tests and hence would have a major and potentially lasting advantage over the Russians if testing were to be suspended.

Eisenhower was sufficiently intrigued with Murray's idea to seek the advice of Dulles and of Strauss—who was strongly and immediately opposed to Murray's suggestion. If the United States were indeed ahead in the arms race, Strauss argued, then the additional testing of big bombs, not a moratorium, was needed for the nation to maintain its lead. Dulles evidently shared Strauss's opinion. Some five days after receiving Murray's letter, the president curtly rejected both the "Atomic Summit" and the proposed moratorium. The flaw in the plan, Eisenhower wrote Murray, was that it relied upon cooperation from the Russians, "and experience has not provided any encouragement for that degree of reliance."[4]

Discouraged but undeterred, Murray raised the idea of a moratorium on thermonuclear tests again with Dulles the following December—pointing out "that it was possible to distinguish between atomic and thermonuclear explosions" and hence that such a ban "would be easily susceptible of independent verification." However, Murray's meeting with the secretary of state, according to Dulles's account, "lasted only five minutes because there was confusion about the appointment, and I had another engagement. . . . I thanked Mr. Murray for his ideas."[5]

Years later, in his memoirs, Murray would speculate that Eisenhower rejected his proposal for an H-bomb testing moratorium because the president had not understood that violations "could easily be detected by our own equipment which was already effectively operating." Wrote Murray: "I realized from the President's answer that the policy aspects of the proposed moratorium had not been clear to him."[6]

"The power of reason . . ."

Despite their rejection of Murray's proposed moratorium on nuclear testing, Eisenhower and Dulles began to explore the idea of a test ban on their own. On April 20, 1954—some two weeks after Indian Prime Minister Jawaharlal Nehru appealed to the United Nations for an "international standstill" on all nuclear weapons tests—Dulles confided to Henry Cabot Lodge, the U.S. representative to the United Nations, that he had "for some time been talking to the President and others about a moratorium on H-Bomb experiments. I think this is an area where we have a chance to get a big propaganda advantage—and perhaps results." Later that same day, Dulles also broached the subject with British diplomats, whom he found cautiously enthusiastic about the idea, perhaps because Great Britain had successfully tested its own atomic bomb two years earlier.[7]

At a National Security Council meeting in early May, Dulles proposed a formal interdepartmental study of a moratorium, noting that the tests of Operation Castle had "put us a lap ahead of the USSR." Strauss disagreed, pointing out that had the United States suspended testing before the thermonuclear breakthrough by Teller and Ulam, there might still be no American H-bomb. Eisenhower said that he had "a rather different view" of the moratorium than Strauss—namely, that "we could put [the Russians] on the spot if we accepted a moratorium. . . . Everybody seems to think that we're skunks, saber-rattlers and warmongers. We ought not to miss any chance to make clear our peaceful objectives." Against the objections of Strauss and Defense Secretary Charles Wilson—as well as those of the Joint Chiefs of Staff, who a week earlier had gone on record against a test moratorium—Eisenhower ordered that the study be carried out.[8]

Nonetheless, opposition to a moratorium endured and even increased. At a second NSC meeting that May, Strauss cited, among other objections, unspecified technical difficulties in policing such an agreement. He also suggested the possibility that "the propaganda ball might well be stolen from the U.S. by the USSR." In reply, Eisenhower reiterated that "he could perceive no final answer to the problem of nuclear warfare if both sides simply went ahead making bigger and better nuclear weapons. . . . Soon even little countries will have a stockpile of these bombs, and then we *will* be in a mess."[9] A few days later, Wilson raised the prospect that the Soviets might try to evade Western detection by testing their H-bombs "at some location outside the USSR, such as in the Antarctic."[10]

In the face of such high-level opposition, Dulles formally withdrew his support for a moratorium on June 23, at the third NSC meeting devoted to the topic. His decision was arrived at reluctantly—and "illustrated the power of reason against the power of will," Dulles said. Dulles explained that he had been convinced by Strauss that the Russians would be able to conceal the tests.

The AEC chairman had also meanwhile raised another argument

against a moratorium. Strauss claimed that because the United States still needed "a small megaton weapon for defense against hostile aircraft," no moratorium could begin until after January 1956, the earliest practical date for the testing of an atomic warhead for a new antiaircraft missile.[11] Strauss argued at the June 23 meeting that there was "something essentially illusory" in a moratorium that allowed both the United States and the Soviet Union to go on manufacturing nuclear weapons. "The real fallacy in this whole business, however, was the unenforceability of any agreement on the subject with the Russians," he protested.[12] After being assured by Strauss that the new nuclear-tipped antiaircraft missile would make it possible to defend American cities from attacking Soviet bombers, Eisenhower, too, finally relented on the subject of a moratorium—announcing that "in any event we were not going to stop conducting tests of atomic weapons, and that there was no reason to do so until some new alternative was in sight."

While the secret debate on the moratorium was raging at the top levels of government, another, more personal drama was unfolding in Washington. It, too, showed the remarkable extent of Strauss's influence at the White House.

In the spring of 1954, the "blank wall" that Eisenhower had earlier ordered put between Oppenheimer and atomic secrets was extended, at Strauss's instigation, to exclude Oppenheimer from any future advisory role in the government. That April, Eisenhower, at Strauss's urging, personally reviewed the voluminous files that the FBI and AEC had compiled on Oppenheimer, including Strauss's own thick dossier in support of his charge that Oppenheimer had deliberately slowed the development of the Super by as much as eighteen months.[13]

Still unconvinced of the truth behind Strauss's allegations, Eisenhower nevertheless agreed with the AEC chairman that the evidence against Oppenheimer was serious enough to warrant an investigation. His greatest concern with the Oppenheimer case, Eisenhower confided to press secretary Jim Hagerty, was "that all our scientists are not made out to be Reds." By approving the AEC's investigation of Oppenheimer, Eisenhower reasoned, he might be able to head off a threatened congressional hearing by Senator Joseph McCarthy into the government's alleged laxity in keeping atomic secrets.[14]

On June 29, some six weeks after it had begun, the AEC investigation into the loyalty of Oppenheimer ended with a four-to-one vote against reinstating the scientist's security clearance, which was due to expire in another month in any event. Concluding three weeks of hearings and three-quarters of a million words of testimony from both the accusers and defenders of Oppenheimer, a personnel review board headed by former Secretary of the Army Gordon Gray found the physicist guilty not of disloyalty but of "fundamental defects in his character." The only member of Gray's panel to express doubts about Oppenheimer's loyalty was Thomas Murray. Many of Oppenheimer's colleagues thought Teller's testimony had been especially damaging.[15]

Until this time, Eisenhower had been shielded by Strauss from any awareness of how the "Oppenheimer trial", as it became known, had split the American scientific community and alienated scientists from the government. Although the AEC's decision not to renew Oppenheimer's security clearance was interpreted by the physicist's peers as only the last step in a long and deliberate campaign to humiliate and silence one of the most outspoken among them, the fact that the president remained ignorant, even after the hearings, of the passions stirred up by the Oppenheimer case was evident in a note that Eisenhower sent to Strauss. The president inquired as to whether there was not another area, outside of atomic energy, where the famous scientist might continue to play a role. "Why do we not get Dr. Oppenheimer interested in desalting sea water?" Eisenhower naively asked Strauss.[16]

"The Soviet threat. . ."

Eisenhower's retreat on the moratorium in the spring of 1954 was only the first occasion when the president and Dulles were talked out of a test ban by Strauss. But there may have been another reason why the president thought it best to postpone talk of a test ban: reports of Soviet technological progress on another front.

That March, Chairman Lee DuBridge and other members of the Scientific Advisory Committee of the Office of Defense Mobilization briefed Eisenhower on the implications of the success of Operation Castle, which had just concluded in the Pacific. At one of the committee's rare personal meetings with the president, DuBridge told the president that the warhead for the American ICBM was almost ready to enter production.[17] But DuBridge also reported that in time the Russians could be expected to match America's technological prowess. Indeed, the prospect even existed, and had been given credence by a 1953 CIA report, that the Soviet Union was already ahead of the United States in rocketry, having moved on to the ICBM while America continued to devote its resources to building slower and more vulnerable strategic bombers.[18] (The CIA report—based upon interviews with German rocket scientists recently returned from Russia— speculated that the Russians would have an operational ballistic missile as soon as 1955, or by 1957 at the latest.)[19]

What this meant, DuBridge and the SAC's scientists pointed out to Eisenhower, was that soon, and for the first time in its history, the United States itself might become the target of a devastating surprise attack. Previously, the CIA believed that Russian agents smuggling atomic bombs into the United States were probably a more immediate threat than outright attack, since the Soviets' Tu-4 bombers lacked the range for any but one-way "suicide" raids on the United States. News of the Soviets' thermonuclear test in 1953 and the now seemingly-imminent prospect of Russian ICBMs fundamentally changed this calculation of risk.[20]

The importance of knowing just how far the Soviets had come toward matching—or perhaps even surpassing—the United States in military technology was clear to Eisenhower well before the visit of SAC's scientists to the Oval Office.

Very early in his first term, in fact, the president had complained to aides that the quality of U.S. intelligence on Russia was deficient in two respects: It failed to distinguish between Russian military capabilities and intentions, and it neglected to put what had come to be called "the Soviet threat" in proper perspective.[21]

CIA estimates made no attempt to measure Soviet capabilities—the quantity and quality of their bombers, ships, tanks, and troops—against corresponding American capabilities to arrive at an overall or "net" assessment, Eisenhower protested. Similarly, the agency's monthly National Intelligence Estimate simply stated how likely it was that the Russians would launch a surprise attack that month, based upon the location and readiness of their forces, giving little or no regard to whether it would be in the enemy's interest to initiate such an attack.

As a result, barely had he moved into the White House—the pictures were not yet on the walls, the carpet not yet down in the Oval Office, Eisenhower later recalled—when the military services began to bombard him with requests for more weapons, based upon the direst possible interpretation of the Soviet threat.[22]

His own experience as Allied supreme commander, Eisenhower told friends, caused him automatically to discount the military's claims of an imminent threat to the nation's security. Advised in April 1953 that the Truman administration had identified 1954 as the year of maximum danger for the United States, Eisenhower promptly responded, "we're not in a moment of danger, we're in an age of danger."[23]

Following the briefing by SAC/ODM, and in response to a specific recommendation from DuBridge and ODM director Flemming, Eisenhower decided to appoint an outside panel of scientists to study how the advent of H-bombs and the prospect of ICBMs would affect the nation's security and to recommend specific steps in response. The president also asked the panel to consider how technology, which had created the threat of surprise attack, might be employed to lessen that danger.[24]

"The dilemma of the total decision. . ."

In early April 1954, DuBridge asked James Killian, the president of MIT and a member of SAC/ODM, to head the panel that was to look at the role technology might play in addressing the problem of surprise attack. Specifically, Killian's panel was asked to suggest innovative ways to gather intelligence that could warn of a future Pearl Harbor and to recommend methods for increasing the nation's retaliatory striking power. The purpose of the study, Eisenhower informed Killian in a subsequent letter, would be to

advise the administration not only on the present state of the strategic balance between the Soviet Union and the United States, but also on whether
current military trends favored this country or its adversary.[25]

Killian was one of those to whom William Golden had turned in 1950 when
writing his report on a science adviser for the White House. Although
trained in business and engineering rather than the sciences, Killian had
earned something of a national reputation as a technical expert on military
matters, due in part to a 1948 *Atlantic* article he coauthored on the subject
of air defense. Two years later, he had taken part in Project Charles, an Air
Force-funded study at MIT on defending the nation against Russian
bombers. As Killian recognized, the unexpectedly early appearance of the
ICBM now threatened to make both the Charles study and its product, the
Distant-Early-Warning Line of radars and jet interceptors, obsolete.[26]

Ultimately more than forty scientists, engineers, and technicians would
take part in Killian's Technological Capabilities Panel (TCP), which was
divided into three subpanels dealing respectively with offense, defense, and
intelligence. Besides Killian and DuBridge, the membership of the panel's
steering committee, which oversaw the work of the subpanels, included
James Doolittle, hero of the wartime raid on Tokyo, and Edwin Land,
inventor of the Polaroid camera.[27]

The TCP's 175-page, top-secret report, "Meeting the Threat of Surprise
Attack," was formally presented to Eisenhower at a February 14, 1955,
meeting of the NSC specially convened for the occasion.[28]

The Killian report concluded that the arms race with Russia was likely
to have four distinct phases. During the first, or current, phase, lasting for
the next year or so, the United States would have a military advantage over
the Soviet Union but neither country could be sure of winning a nuclear war
by striking first. In the second phase, lasting perhaps from 1957 to 1960,
America "will have a very great offensive advantage relative to the USSR . . .
and will be less vulnerable than previously to surprise attack"—at least if
the nation adopted the corrective measures contained elsewhere in the
report.[29] In the third stage, the relative strategic advantage of the United
States would slip away as the Russians developed multimegaton hydrogen
bombs and the means for their delivery. Yet even "this would continue to be
a phase favorable to the U.S.," the scientists predicted. In the fourth and
final phase—indefinite in length, but perhaps no more than a decade
away—both sides would be so well armed that an "attack by either side
would result in mutual destruction."

Killian's panel was encouraged by the fact that the United States was
still significantly ahead in the nuclear arms race and urged Eisenhower to
approve a second, nontechnical study of "what diplomatic and political
policies" could be employed to exploit America's existing strategic superiority over Russia.

Among the specific measures the panel recommended as a response to the Soviet threat was accelerating work on a number of existing Pentagon projects, including research into more efficient jet fuels and speeded-up development of the nuclear-powered bomber, the antimissile missile, and a new antiaircraft missile with an atomic warhead. (The warhead for this last weapon—improbably named Ding-Dong, later to be retitled Genie—was already under development but had not yet been tested; Strauss had used the upcoming test as an argument against the test ban the previous year.)[30]

The panel recommended that the president assign the "highest national priority" both to building the ICBM and to developing an intermediate-range ballistic missile (IRBM), which promised to be easier to build than the bigger, longer-range missile and hence likely to be operational sooner. Basing IRBMs at sea, on either ships or submarines, would also reduce their vulnerability, the panel pointed out.

Following the panel's recommendations, Eisenhower in the next several months approved a crash effort to build two Air Force ICBMs, Atlas and Titan, and two IRBMs, the Army's Jupiter and the Air Force's Thor. The liquid-fueled Atlas was to be the nation's first operational intercontinental-range ballistic missile. Later, also in response to the TCP report, the president approved funds for a solid-fuel, submarine-launched ballistic missile—the Navy's Polaris.[31]

Noting that uncertainty about Russia's real military capabilities had been a constant frustration to them in preparing their report, the panel emphasized that the United States "*must* find ways to increase the number of hard facts upon which our intelligence estimates are based." The need to know more about the Soviet Union was central to what the experts, in the section of their report titled "Intelligence," termed "the dilemma of the total decision": the dilemma that the president would face if confronted with evidence of an imminent Soviet sneak attack. "The total decision must be made almost spontaneously, else it will be too late. Its consequences being total, it cannot be delegated."[32]

Killian and Land, the chief authors of the section of the report dealing with intelligence, considered recommendations in this area too sensitive to share with their colleagues on the panel—or even to mention in the top-secret summary of this section of their report. Instead, on Thanksgiving eve, 1954, Killian and Land personally briefed Eisenhower in the Oval Office on their ideas for avoiding the dilemma of the total decision. At Eisenhower's insistence, they deleted any reference to this meeting in their February briefing of the NSC.

"The mosquito. . ."

The solution that Killian and Land proposed to the problem of finding out what was going on behind the Iron Curtain was a jet-powered, ultrahigh-altitude "glider" capable of operating above Soviet air defenses. The prototype of such a plane—dubbed the Utility-2, or U-2—had already been built by Lockheed. The legendary designer of the U-2, Kelly Johnson, had suggested to the Air Force that it be used as a spy plane a year earlier, but his idea had been rejected.[33]

At the November meeting in the Oval Office, Land informed Eisenhower of the intelligence potential of high-resolution photographs taken from a fast-moving plane flying at a great height. Land had already approached a fellow inventor about the possibility of building a unique seven-aperture camera for the U-2. The two men calculated that the camera would make it possible to identify objects no bigger than several inches across in a 120-mile–wide swath of territory from pictures snapped more than ten miles up.[34]

As important as the U-2's reconnaissance capabilities was its ability to survive in the air above Russia. Even below its maximum operating altitude, Land told Eisenhower, the U-2 would be safe from Soviet jet interceptors and some 20,000 feet above the range of current Russian surface-to-air missiles.

At the conclusion of the White House meeting, Killian and Land asked Eisenhower to approve funds to build thirty of the planes they called "the mosquito"—the number they thought necessary to photograph all of Russia—at a cost of just over a million dollars apiece.[35] Eisenhower showed immediate enthusiasm for the U-2, Killian remembered. While Killian and Land were still in the Oval Office, the president ordered CIA Director Allen Dulles to enlist the Air Force's Trevor Gardner and Richard Bissell, director of the CIA's Clandestine Services branch, in support of the U-2 program, which the CIA would later code-name Project Aquatone.[36]

But Eisenhower also emphasized at this meeting that his approval for the secret overflights was conditional. At the president's order, planning for the flights was to be done jointly by the CIA and the Air Force's Strategic Air Command. Final approval for each ten-day "package" of flights would come from Eisenhower personally—and only after he had been briefed on the purpose of each mission, the actual course that the plane would follow, and the likelihood it could be brought down by Soviet air defenses. Of those present at the Oval Office meeting, only John Foster Dulles expressed a reservation—warning that "difficulties might arise out of these operations"—but even he "thought we could live through them."[37]

"Legitimate grounds for irritation. . ."

American overflights of the Soviet Union for intelligence purposes was hardly a new idea, as all at the Thanksgiving eve meeting were aware. As early as 1947, the Navy had begun sending unmanned balloons equipped with cameras and other instruments over Russia in an effort to find out what was going on behind the Iron Curtain. The balloons were carried over the Soviet Union by the prevailing winds and recovered when they reached the territory of friendly nations.[38]

While the balloons were able to penetrate deep within Russia, they were also subject to wind shifts and unpredictable atmospheric conditions and hence could not be relied on to photograph specific targets. Worse, when some of the balloons unexpectedly fell to earth in Russia, both the purpose and the capabilities of the project were compromised. Despite the decidedly mixed record of the Navy's balloon reconnaissance project, the Air Force, too, began sending camera-bearing balloons over Russia in January 1956 under a program known as Project Genetrix.[39]

Eisenhower had never shown much enthusiasm for the balloon program, but he reluctantly acceded to the military's persistent arguments that the overflights were necessary in order to identify strategic targets in Russia. When the Soviets lodged a diplomatic protest against the balloon intrusions in early February 1956—after putting the remains of one of the errant balloons on display in Moscow—the president ordered the overflights to cease, and so notified the Russians. In a meeting a few days later, Eisenhower openly criticized the overflight program before the Joint Chiefs, saying that "if these balloons had been sent over us, we might be talking about mobilizing." The balloons, Eisenhower complained, "gave more legitimate grounds for irritation than could be matched by the good obtained from them."[40]

In addition to the balloons, the Air Force and the Navy, with cooperation from the CIA and the National Security Agency, had begun sending specially equipped aircraft on flights along the borders of the Soviet Union as early as 1948. On occasion, the planes deliberately crossed into Soviet air space and penetrated hundreds of miles into Russia before dashing back to safety across the border.[41]

The purpose of such flights was to expose and identify Soviet air defenses by getting the defenders to activate their tracking and fire control radars—the precise location and frequencies of which could then be recorded by the intruding aircraft—and to photograph Soviet military installations. But the dangers and the drawbacks of these sporadic raids over so-called denied territory were obvious. The vast interior of Russia—including the most interesting targets from an intelligence perspective, remained out of range. Even more of a problem was the vulnerability of the planes and their pilots during such raids. Between 1952 and 1955, there were at least seven incidents where American planes flying over Russian territory were attacked by Soviet fighters, resulting in more than thirty U.S. airmen dead or missing. Just two weeks before the clandestine visit of Killian and Land to the Oval Office, the Russians had shot down an Air Force B-29 in Soviet air space near the Sea of Japan, killing one crewman.[42]

Beyond the human and material price of these overflights, Eisenhower worried that another casualty of such operations would be the prospect of better relations with the Soviet Union. But, despite these misgivings, the argument that the U-2 could avoid being shot down—and the urgency of learning more about Russia—prompted him to approve Aquatone.

"A peaceful land. . ."

In June 1955, the president received a report from another committee of experts. The Vulnerability Panel, headed by former New York Governor Nelson Rockefeller, had been asked to suggest ways to exploit Soviet weaknesses and to recommend proposals that Eisenhower might take to the summit with Russian leaders the following month in Geneva.[43]

Two ideas born of the Vulnerability Panel—a proposal for reciprocal overflights and a U.S.-Soviet exchange of blueprints of military installations—were promptly rejected at this summit by Soviet Premier Nikita Khrushchev, who called them "a bald espionage plot." Although the so-called Open Skies initiative failed to "open a tiny gate in the disarmament fence," as Eisenhower had hoped, the Russians' rejection of the offer nonetheless cleared the way for proceeding with the U-2 overflights.[44]

Even before the U-2 took to the air on its maiden flight over Russia on July 4, 1956, Open Skies had shown that Eisenhower was looking for some way to ensure that the spy plane would become an asset rather than a liability in U.S.-Soviet relations. The fact that Eisenhower insisted at the Thanksgiving eve Oval Office briefing that the U-2 program be run by the CIA and not the Air Force was, Killian thought, an indication of the president's concern that pinpointing targets for attack in the Soviet Union in the event of war—which might well increase Soviet fears of a surprise attack at the same time that it allayed such concerns in the United States—not be the plane's only mission.[45]

Shortly before the U-2's inaugural overflight, Eisenhower received a reminder that the secret missions over Russia were likely to be politically sensitive. At a late June 1956 meeting in Moscow with Air Force Chief of Staff General Nathan Twining, Soviet Marshall G. K. Zhukov complained that overflying of an adversary "leads not to strengthening good faith and removal of fear, but mistrust and fear, and also provides military material which threatens the security of peoples." (Twining later passed along to Eisenhower a bizarre variation on Open Skies proposed by Zhukov, whereby the United States and the Soviet Union would agree to fly unarmed bombers over each other's capital as a sign of mutual trust.)[46]

The first U-2 missions took the spy plane directly over Leningrad and Moscow. Killian was at an NSA listening post in West Germany when the U-2 took off from an Air Force base near Wiesbaden and headed over the Soviet Union. While CIA representatives with him expressed surprise and concern that the Russians were able to track the plane on their radar—the U-2 had gone undetected in previous test flights across the United States—Killian remembered the voices of Soviet air defense commanders as "flabbergasted and afraid."[47]

The quality of the photographs taken by the U-2 exceeded the expectations of even its promoters, and a mission over the Ukraine was flown the following week. At an Oval Office briefing on the July 4 mission attended by Bissell and Killian, Eisenhower expressed delight with the results and promptly approved the next set of overflights. But he also voiced concern about the future of the program and its possible effect upon Soviet-American relations. It was "his desire," Eisenhower told the group, that "the entire pattern be designed to cover all that is vital quickly." The president also reiterated that he "must be contacted before deep operations are initiated."[48]

Significantly, these first missions contradicted the image of Russia bristling with rockets and bombers. "It was a peaceful land," said one who saw the early U-2 photographs of the Soviet Union. As he had earlier in the case of the balloon overflights, Eisenhower mused what this country's reaction would be "if they were to do this to us." Thus, with Aquatone barely under way, Eisenhower was already having doubts about the wisdom of continuing the overflights. Eisenhower's staff secretary, Brigadier General Andrew Goodpaster, conveyed the president's reservations about the U-2 to Dulles and Bissell in a telephone conversation on July 10. Perhaps because the president was relieved to find that "the basis for concern on our part of surprise action is much less than when he approved the activity," Goodpaster noted, Eisenhower seemed "very close to a decision not to continue."[49]

But the U-2 overflights were proving too valuable to discontinue. In mid-October 1956, the CIA was tipped off to the developing Suez crisis when a U-2 flight over Malta discovered an unannounced buildup of Anglo-French forces there. Another U-2 flying over eastern Europe at this time witnessed Russian preparations to crush the Hungarian revolt. Khrushchev complained to the State Department about this particular mission, and Dulles telephoned Eisenhower to tell him "we are in trouble about these overflights."[50]

Because of the valuable intelligence the United States was getting from the U-2—which included targeting data on Soviet nuclear weapons installations, submarine pens, and missile testing sites—Project Aquatone was allowed to continue, although Eisenhower told Allen Dulles in mid-November that the flights were beginning to "cost more than we gain in the form of solid information." Accordingly, the president approved more flights over eastern Europe, "but not the deep one" over Russia, he told Bissell. The planes should also "stay as close to [the] border as possible," the president instructed the CIA.[51]

The following month, Eisenhower told John Foster Dulles that he was considering a "complete stoppage of the entire business." A few weeks later, however, plans were being made to send the planes once more over Russia.[52] Like the bewitched broom of the sorcerer's apprentice, Project Aquatone was assuming a life of its own.

"A vague, unproven danger. . ."

In the spring of 1955, the subject of the nuclear test ban had surfaced once again, this time at a five-nation disarmament conference in London—where Eisenhower's representative at the talks, Harold Stassen, the president's special assistant on disarmament, reported that the Russians seemed suddenly receptive to a temporary ban on thermonuclear testing.[53]

But the response of Ernest Lawrence and Edward Teller, scientists belonging to the Nuclear Task Force that Stassen had assembled for the conference, was strongly negative. (Worried that Stassen might prove too independent, Strauss had not only recommended Lawrence and Teller for the task force, but insisted that one accompany Stassen to London.)[54] On the basis of the AEC scientists' advice, and also because of a top-secret report that Stassen received at this time from the Livermore laboratory, which claimed it would be possible for the Russians to test nuclear weapons undetected, Stassen agreed to backpedal on the moratorium.[55]

That summer, the Russians began another ambitious new test series.[56] Analysis of the debris from a bomb tested on November 22, 1955, showed that the Soviets, too, now had a true Super.[57]

The question of banning nuclear tests did not come up again until the following April, when Adlai Stevenson, Eisenhower's opponent in the 1956 presidential election, introduced it as a campaign issue. Stevenson's proposal for a moratorium on nuclear testing was partly the inspiration of his own informal group of science advisers—physicists associated with the Federation of American Scientists. But another impetus may have been Thomas Murray's renewed crusade for a thermonuclear test ban. Murray had finally gone public with his own proposal earlier in the month, after one last secret appeal to Eisenhower, Strauss, and the Joint Committee on Atomic Energy had been rejected. (Believing that Murray, a Democrat, had been the inspiration for Stevenson's test-ban proposal, Strauss promptly ordered all of Murray's classified correspondence and memoranda on the subject recalled by the AEC.)[58]

This public discussion of the test ban as a campaign issue was short-lived, however, Stevenson subsequently undermined his own argument by criticizing Eisenhower for being "dilatory" in developing modern weapons like the ICBM. Thus, as the president pointed out, there was a "paradox" to Stevenson's stand against the H-bomb but for the missile—"because one without the other is rather useless."[59]

While Eisenhower in public continued to state that a test ban was unnecessary and might even endanger the nation's security, in private he began to explore the idea anew with his top advisers. At the end of August, Eisenhower wrote to Strauss to inquire about the feasibility of an end to nuclear testing—reminding the AEC chairman that he had "spoken to you several times about my hope that the need for atomic tests would gradually lift and possibly soon disappear."[60]

Eisenhower also noted in his letter to Strauss that the AEC was no longer the sole source of advice on the bomb. Isidor Rabi, who had stepped down from chairmanship of the GAC in July 1956 to replace DuBridge as head of SAC/ODM, had meanwhile informed Eisenhower that it was possible to temporarily stop nuclear testing, since the nation had a proven stockpile of modern bombs. Stassen, too, had recently expressed the hope that nuclear weapons development would soon progress to the point where the United States might be able to take the initiative in disarmament negotiations with a test-ban proposal.[61]

But Strauss was as unyielding as ever on the moratorium when he discussed the subject with the NSC and the president the following September. In May, during congressional hearings in which the possibility of a test ban was discussed, the AEC chairman had refused on security grounds even to talk about the measures that might be necessary to verify such a ban. Once again, Strauss's chief argument that fall was the difficulty of verifying a moratorium. Following what Goodpaster described as "spirited discussion," Eisenhower assented that "any stopping must be predicated upon an inspection plan." Lacking such a plan, consideration of a test ban was once more deferred.[62]

Growing popular concern with the health hazards of radioactive fallout from nuclear testing—the result of scientists' warnings about the effects of strontium-90 upon infants and children—soon propelled the test-ban issue back into the 1956 campaign debate. In October, a government press release defending Eisenhower's stand against the test moratorium cited the difficulty of verifying such a ban and concluded with the caveat: "This specific matter is manifestly not a subject for detailed public discussion—for obvious security reasons." Privately, Eisenhower instructed John Foster Dulles to make a State Department study of fallout and testing about to be released "so factual as to be uninteresting." In an effort to calm the test-ban controversy, Strauss unwittingly added fuel to the flames. Claiming that radiation from fallout was only "a vague, unproven danger to generations yet unborn," Strauss warned of "the more immediate and infinitely greater danger of defeat and perhaps obliteration at the hands of an enemy who possesses nuclear weapons of mass destruction."[63]

As the election neared, the AEC chairman, perhaps fearful that the president would change his stand on the moratorium under public pressure, intensified his campaign against the test ban. In late October, at the request of Strauss and Cutler, Eisenhower met with a dozen scientists who opposed the test ban. On election eve, the group's spokesmen—Teller and Lawrence—warned at a news conference that a moratorium would not be "self-enforcing," since "not all atmospheric tests can be detected with instruments."[64] Although the AEC's assurances did not still public concern about fallout, Eisenhower gave no outward sign of his own private sympathy with Stevenson's goal.

On the eve of his reelection, Eisenhower seemed to be entertaining second thoughts about the growing role of scientists in his administration. Thus, the president, Goodpaster wrote, smiled wistfully in observing during an October 9 press conference "that it seemed to him that every new survey of our problems by a scientific team seemed to result in recommendations that we undertake additional things. He rather wished we would find a team which would recommend programs which we could dispense with."[65]

By the end of his first term, on the of advice of scientists, Eisenhower had committed the country to a variety of new and expensive defense programs, foremost among which was an accelerated effort at missile building. Yet, despite increasing cost—the budget for Atlas alone rose from $14 million in 1954 to $161 million in 1955—the ICBM program had still to produce an operational missile.[66] Nor had it deflected the criticism of a Democratic Congress that Eisenhower was not spending enough on defense.

Nonetheless, by his actions Eisenhower now seemed a committed believer in the value of scientific advice—whether by choice or out of a feeling of necessity. Early in 1956, for example, Eisenhower had reaffirmed that faith by appointing Land a member and Killian head of the newly established and highly secretive President's Board of Consultants on Foreign Intelligence Activities.[67]

"Crucified on a cross of atoms. . ."

Following the brief flurry of interest during the election campaign, the test ban had once again begun to fade from view when an especially large number of Russian nuclear tests between January and April 1957 reawakened public concern. In the wake of these tests, in what was becoming a recurrent springtime ritual, at the beginning of June the Soviet Union proposed a two-to-three-year joint moratorium on testing. Unlike previous proposals, however, the Russians this time agreed "in principle" to on-site inspection by international authority.[68]

The Soviet offer prompted Eisenhower once again to ask Strauss whether the nation's nuclear arming had advanced to the point where a temporary ban on testing could be considered. On June 3, the president challenged the AEC chairman to show why testing needed to continue—since, as Eisenhower said, the country already had "a pretty darn fine arsenal of atomic weapons."[69]

Strauss strongly defended continued testing, repeating the argument that the nation needed a new interceptor missile to counter the emerging ICBM threat. The warhead for the antiballistic missile, or ABM, was to be tested in Operation Hardtack, scheduled for the coming year. Aware of the president's—and the public's—heightened concern about fallout that spring, the result of new Soviet and American tests, Strauss reassured Eisenhower that the bombs of Hardtack would produce less than one tenth the radioactivity created by Bravo. Despite Eisenhower's repeated protests that the tests and the weapons themselves cost too much, Strauss remained adamant on the need for more testing, and the meeting ended in a tense stalemate.[70]

Concerned that Eisenhower was no longer persuaded by his logic, Strauss urged Eisenhower to meet with the scientists of Stassen's Nuclear Task Force—Teller, Lawrence, and Livermore physicist Mark Mills—to hear some new arguments against the moratorium. A related purpose of the scientists' visit, Strauss informed the president, was to acquaint him with the progress made in Operation Plumbbob—the latest series of American nuclear tests, which had begun in April— and to hear about the tests planned for Operation Hardtack, which were aimed at development of a so-called clean bomb: a nuclear weapon that would produce almost no radioactive fallout.[71]

On June 20, the trio of scientists promoted the clean bomb at closed hearings before the Joint Committee on Atomic Energy. Their well-publicized claim, in a press conference immediately following, that it would be "a crime against humanity" for the United States to stop testing before the nation had developed nearly fallout-free nuclear weapons, prompted test-ban opponents in the Senate to urge that the president also meet with Lawrence and his colleagues.[72]

In the Oval Office some four days later, Lawrence boasted that the nuclear labs already knew "how to make virtually clean weapons down to small kiloton weapons." Teller told Eisenhower that the clean bomb would be ideal for countering a Soviet invasion of Europe and might be developed in six or seven years, but only if testing were allowed to continue. Another reason for continued tests, Teller claimed, was that Plumbbob had demonstrated the future promise of "peaceful nuclear explosions"—in which H-bombs could be set off in deep underground cavities, lined with steel and filled with water, to mine ore or to release oil trapped in rock. Nuclear explosions might also be used to alter the course of rivers, or "perhaps even modify the weather on a broad basis through changing the dust content of the air."[73] But Mills raised a troubling aside. Recent studies of how atomic bombs could be exploded in deep holes to generate electric power "had by chance illustrated a way in which a country could evade a test ban while carrying out thermonuclear testing."

The scientists' predictions about the clean bomb had the desired effect—Eisenhower once again backed away from the test ban. "No one could oppose the development program they had described," Eisenhower told his visitors at the end of the forty-minute meeting. The nation "could not permit itself to be 'crucified on a cross of atoms,' so to speak." The president even mused that "we may want the 'other fellow' to have clean weapons too—perhaps it is desirable to turn over our techniques to him." (Teller deferred comment on the president's suggestion until he was outside the Oval Office, whereupon he asked Goodpaster to tell Eisenhower that "our weapons incorporate other technological advances of great value that we don't wish to give to the Soviets." He was, Teller said, particularly worried by what might happen "if the Soviets secretly continued testing and developed clean bombs while the U.S. was left only with dirty bombs which we couldn't use because of world opinion.")[74]

In a conversation the following day, Eisenhower surprised Dulles with his enthusiasm for the clean bomb. But the president's remarks to his secretary of state, who had meanwhile also met privately with the scientists, revealed that Eisenhower either misinterpreted or failed to understand much of what he had been told about the clean bomb. The "real peaceful use of atomic science depends on their developing clean weapons," which he thought they could do in "four or five years," Eisenhower explained to Dulles.[75] On June 26, Eisenhower repeated for the press the same garbled version of the scientists' assurances he had given Dulles. Claiming that American nuclear weapons were already 96 percent fallout free, Eisenhower said that the experts had promised to produce "an absolutely clean bomb" within the next few years.[76]

The contradictions, scientific and otherwise, behind the president's claims of clean nuclear weapons were ridiculed at home and abroad. "How can you have a clean bomb to do dirty things?" asked Khrushchev rhetorically.[77] In America, scientists and reporters were equally puzzled. As *The New York Times* journalist James Reston noted, "An increasing number of the major foreign-policy issues facing the nation are now, at bottom, scientific and technological issues on which the President must be guided by scientists and technicians who themselves are deeply divided."[78] A White House reporter asked Eisenhower whether the clean-bomb controversy had caused him to consider appointing a full-time science adviser. Eisenhower responded that it "hadn't occurred [to him] to have one right in my office," but he promised to "think about it."[79]

"I am hearing many, many ideas. . ."

His "main dilemma," Eisenhower complained to Strauss late that summer, "is that of planning and carrying out extensive tests on the one hand while professing a readiness to suspend testing in a disarmament program on the other. From much of the world this paradoxical conduct may bring accusations of bad faith."[80] While telling Dulles that he was "sympathetic" to proposals for reducing the amount of fallout from the next series of nuclear tests, the president also worried that schedule changes necessary to reduce the threat of radioactivity from the tests might "wreck" the elaborate preparations for Operation Hardtack.[81]

Before Hardtack got under way, Eisenhower and the country received the first of several shocks from Russia. On August 26, 1957, Khrushchev publicly confirmed a fact already known to American intelligence—namely, that the Soviet Union, earlier in the month, had successfully flight-tested an intercontinental-range rocket.[82] The test meant that the Soviets were unquestionably ahead of the United States in the missile race. American efforts in rocketry had thus far fallen far short of the Soviets' success.

The previous April, two months after its first failure, the Air Force's Project Thor suffered another setback when an erroneous computer signal caused the destruction of the next rocket to be tested. A week later, the second test firing of an Army Jupiter IRBM ended in an explosion when the missile, after ninety-three seconds of flight, went out of control due to the sloshing of propellant in its tanks. On May 21, the third Thor IRBM blew up on its pad five minutes prior to the scheduled launch.[83]

Although the third Jupiter had a successful test flight ten days later, the same would not be true of the inaugural flight of the Air Force's Atlas on June 11. The flight began with the ICBM rising majestically from its test stand, but ended seconds later when a malfunctioning valve caused a booster engine to shut down and the missile had to be destroyed. In September, exactly a month after the Soviets' success, a second attempt at launching an Atlas ended in another spectacular fireball when one of the missile's main engines prematurely shut down.[84]

The fact that the Soviets were the first to successfully flight-test an ICBM was an acute embarrassment to the Eisenhower administration—even if the world did not yet know about either the long string of American failures or the single, unheralded success of Jupiter. But in terms of military implications, the Russian achievement was less threatening than it first appeared. Analysis of fallout from Soviet nuclear tests showed that Russian scientists had yet to match their American counterparts in shrinking the size of missile warheads. For that reason, the Soviets' ICBM was nearly twice the size of Atlas, which made it more cumbersome to move, harder to hide, and hence more vulnerable than the American ICBM.[85] But the Russian booster's size gave it an advantage in lifting power, with consequences that would soon become evident.

On October 4, 1957, the Soviet Union launched Sputnik I, the first artificial earth satellite. More than two years earlier, the Russians had announced that they would make the attempt; the United States, too, had pledged to launch a satellite as part of its contribution to the International Geophysical Year.[86] Indeed, the possibilities of using earth-orbiting satellites for scientific research, weather forecasting, and espionage had been recognized as early as 1946 in a RAND report.[87]

Subsequent efforts by the government to belittle the Russian accomplishment achieved the opposite of what was intended. When Defense Secretary Wilson dismissed Sputnik as "a neat scientific trick," his comments were widely interpreted as an attempt by the administration to cover up what was now widely perceived to be the nation's technological inadequacy.[88] Ignored in the reporting of Wilson's remarks was his point that the Soviets' lofting of a 184-pound package of instruments into space was still far short of what it would take to guide a two-ton thermonuclear warhead to a pinpoint location on the other side of the earth. (When Wilson left the administration three days later to resume a business career, his departure was popularly—but wrongly—thought to be a reaction to Sputnik. He was replaced at the Pentagon by former Proctor and Gamble president Neil McElroy.)[89]

While Eisenhower recognized that Sputnik was not a "technological Pearl Harbor," as one critic called it, the launching of the Russian satellite was for many Americans almost as serious a psychological blow. In response, four days after the Soviet coup, the president assembled his military advisers in the Oval Office and announced that he had decided to put both the ICBM and the IRBM programs on a "crash" basis.[90]

The furor caused by the Soviet ICBM and Sputnik, as well as the recent controversy over the clean bomb, focused public attention anew upon the kind, and the quality, of science advice reaching the president. Eisenhower seemed to acknowledge this fact at a press conference on October 9. "Suddenly all America seems to become scientist," he complained good-naturedly, "and I am hearing many, many ideas."[91]

7

"A Vested Interest in This Field"

The President's Science Advisory Committee and the Test Ban

The Soviet launching of Sputnik provided the necessary spur for Eisenhower to take the step that had been urged upon Truman at the time of the Korean war: appointment of a part-time science advisory committee led by a full-time science adviser having an office in the White House. The creation of the President's Science Advisory Committee (PSAC) provided Eisenhower a new source of technical advice on policy questions, apart from the partisan pleadings of Lewis Strauss. A nuclear test ban, which had been steadfastly resisted by Strauss and the AEC's scientists, quickly became the focus of PSAC's attention.

"Missing a sense of urgency. . ."

On October 15, 1957, in response to a recommendation from the National Academy of Sciences, Eisenhower called the fourteen members of the Office of Defense Mobilization's Science Advisory Committee to the Oval Office to discuss the future of science advice in the White House. The SAC/ODM meeting had been scheduled before Sputnik, but the Soviets' achievement gave the session an added purpose.

American science, the president worried, was being "outdistanced." Isidor Rabi, the first scientist to speak, said he agreed with Eisenhower that—in the absence of "vigorous action"—the United States might be passed by the Russians within a generation, just as America had "caught up with Europe and left Western Europe far behind."[1]

When Edwin Land complained that he and his colleagues "feel themselves isolated and alone" at a time when "the Russians attempt to inspire all of their people with science," Eisenhower countered that this was because the Soviets followed the undemocratic "practice of picking out the best minds and ruthlessly spurning the rest." In order to create a new scientific spirit within the context of a democracy, the president said, it was first necessary to instill "an attitude toward science similar to that held toward various kinds of athletics in his youth." Another speech, he conceded, simply "would not do the job."

Eisenhower had a mixed response to Rabi's suggestion that he appoint a scientist to act as his personal adviser. Every such appointment, Eisenhower protested, "simply adds to the burdens of the Presidency—but perhaps the individual could be a great help in getting the right point of view across." Rabi thought it essential "to get someone whom the President can live with easily (in the sense of working with him agreeably)," but who was also "completely sound scientifically." James Killian added that a committee of scientists working with a presidential science adviser "could be most helpful," although "in the short term," he agreed, "there is missing a sense of urgency and mission in the scientific community."

While the encounter between Eisenhower and SAC/ODM was amiable, one tense moment was a reminder of the strain created by Sputnik. When one member of the committee remarked, with regard to the ICBM, that appointment of a science adviser "could help the President not to forget such policy decisions," Eisenhower "interjected with vehemence," Goodpaster wrote, that he had not forgotten the urgency behind the ICBM—"those charged with the program had."

At meeting's end, Eisenhower promised to speak out soon on the need for a "proper attitude toward science," perhaps as early as his next press conference. He said he would rely on the scientists themselves to draw up the specifics on the kind of advisory committee they had in mind. Outside the Oval Office, the members of SAC/ODM picked Rabi, the most respected and experienced scientist among them, to draft a proposal.

"A complete, sudden reversal. . ."

On October 28, before he had finished the task assigned to him, Rabi informed Eisenhower in a top-secret "eyes only" memorandum of a way that scientists might be of immediate help in dispelling the shadow of fear cast over the country by Sputnik. What Rabi proposed was a "defensive missile system"—in effect, an impenetrable shield in space—against Soviet ICBMs.[2]

The inspiration for Rabi's idea was Hans Bethe's discovery of a hidden flaw in the design of Soviet nuclear warheads. Bethe uncovered the flaw in the routine analysis of fallout from Russian atomic tests. As Rabi explained, this design defect made the thermonuclear warhead of a Soviet ICBM theoretically vulnerable to "preinitiation" as it reentered the atmosphere in the final moments of flight. The result, Rabi informed Eisenhower, was that Soviet warheads could be made to explode prematurely, and harmlessly, in space if bombarded by neutrons from an exploding U.S. nuclear weapon at a critical point in their trajectory.

Rabi asked Eisenhower to approve "priority development of an emergency ICBM defense system of the kind described" and also to consider "the advisability of securing immediately a world-wide moratorium on nuclear explosions." While the Russians were apparently unaware of the flaw in their warheads, Rabi contended, with continued testing they "seem certain to discover the feature that they now lack."

Rabi's revelation was doubtless given even greater force by a classified report on the Soviet ICBM program that Allen Dulles sent to the president the same day. The secret CIA study estimated that the United States lagged behind the Soviet Union in rocketry by two to three years and predicted that the Russians would have a dozen ICBMs by the end of 1958, before either Atlas or Titan was operational. "The country is in a period of grave national emergency," Dulles warned Eisenhower.[3]

The following day, October 29, Eisenhower called Rabi and Strauss into the Oval Office to discuss the idea of an antimissile shield. Rabi's proposal promptly became the subject of a contentious encounter between the physicist and the AEC chairman. Strauss "was inclined to question some of the assumptions and conclusions" behind Rabi's proposal, he told Eisenhower—since "the Soviets can always steal our secrets." The exchange soon shifted from the space shield to the test ban. Rabi pointed out that an earlier opportunity to slow the arms race had been missed and urged that "as a matter of self-interest" the nation immediately propose a halt to all nuclear testing. It was, Rabi said, "a tragedy that we did not stop our tests before the Soviets tested their thermonuclear weapon in their last series."[4]

Rabi also used the occasion to comment on other advice that Eisenhower had received from the AEC's scientists, noting that "it had been a great mistake for the President to accept the views of Drs. Teller and Lawrence" in the controversy over clean bombs.

Eisenhower was surprised by Rabi's criticism of Teller and Lawrence, protesting that "he thought they were eminent in their field (as all agreed they were)." The president asked the physicist directly whether there was not mutual respect among the atomic scientists, Rabi and Teller included. "Rabi said simply that they had known each other for twenty years or more," Goodpaster wrote in the minutes.

The president's meeting with Strauss and Rabi ended inconclusively. Since calling an immediate halt to testing would "be making a complete, sudden reversal in our position," Eisenhower noted, it was "hard to see how we could do this in terms of our public opinion, and the opinion of our allies." But Rabi's proposed moratorium also had an undeniable attraction, Eisenhower acknowledged. "The President recalled that he had often said that if we are ahead of the Soviets in these matters, we should agree to stop in order to freeze our advantage." Resolving that "the first thing to do is to get the scientists of the various groups together and see how they resolve the matter," Eisenhower ordered National Security Adviser Gordon Gray and Strauss "to assemble the best scientific talent of their agencies to give further study to this matter."[5]

After Rabi left, the president asked Strauss to remain behind in the Oval Office for a personal discussion. Noting that "Dr. Rabi is a brilliant scientist and a friend of long standing," the president asked Strauss "to examine [Rabi's proposal] very thoroughly . . . from the standpoint of national risk and international purposes. . . . Sometimes these proposals have not been thought through, and must be modified when mature, experienced judgment in these broader matters is applied to them." In reply, Strauss admitted that, "Dr. Rabi and Dr. Teller have opposed each other very sharply over many years, for example with respect to the development of the hydrogen weapon."

While this brief debate over the creation of an "emergency ICBM defense" remained hidden from the public eye, its effect on Eisenhower may have been no less profound than that of Sputnik. The confrontation between Rabi and Strauss had finally awakened the president to the existence of a long and deep ideological split within the scientific community. "I learned that some of the mutual antagonisms among the scientists are so bitter as to make their working together almost an impossibility," Eisenhower wrote in his diary that day. "I was told that Dr. Rabi and some of his group are so antagonistic to Doctors Lawrence and Teller that communication between them is practically nil."[6]

"A program of action. . ."

A few days before meeting with Rabi and Strauss at the White House, the president had asked James Killian, a member of SAC/ODM since its inception, to take command of the newly created PSAC, which would be directly responsible for science advice in the White House. The creation of PSAC was in response to the October 15 discussion at the White House. Killian would be chairman of PSAC and also the first "special assistant to the president for science and technology," the official title to be given the president's science adviser.[7]

Eisenhower announced PSAC's creation and Killian's appointment in the course of a nationwide radio and television address on the evening of November 7, 1957, that stressed Killian's role as the president's newest adviser on defense. Warning that "we could fall behind—unless we now face up to certain pressing requirements and set out to meet them at once," the president detailed "a program of action" for making science once again a preeminent concern in the United States: "The first thing I have done is to make sure that the very best thought and advice that the scientific community can supply, heretofore provided to me on an informal basis, is now fully organized and formalized so that no gap can occur."[8]

The same afternoon as the president's speech to the nation, several of the scientists who would shortly become inaugural members of PSAC took part in a special White House briefing on the so-called Gaither Report.

The report was the product of the Security Resources Panel, a group of more than seventy scientists, civilian strategists, and defense consultants, headed by San Francisco attorney Rowan Gaither, president of the Ford Foundation, and electrical engineer Robert Sprague, president of Boston's Sprague Electric Company. The panel had been called together the previous April at the urging of the NSC and SAC/ODM to advise Eisenhower on the steps he should take to enhance military preparedness and to deter a nuclear war.[9]

The panel's conclusions were alarming and pessimistic. Moreover, the launching of the first Sputnik while the report was in preparation and of a second Soviet satellite, a half-ton capsule carrying a dog, only four days before the White House briefing gave the scientists' dire warnings a disturbing aura of plausibility.[10] Unlike Killian's Technological Capabilities Panel, which, two years earlier, had recommended specific but limited steps to improve national security, such as accelerating the IRBM program and building the U-2, the Gaither Report urged a massive and wholesale rearming of America—including a nationwide fallout-shelter program costing more than $20 billion, to prepare for the possibility of nuclear war.[11]

Eisenhower's initial reaction to the Gaither Report was polite but noncommittal. Secretary of State Dulles, on the other hand, attacked the report outright in a telephone conversation with the president shortly after the briefing. Dulles advised Eisenhower that the theoretical scenarios of a Soviet sneak attack depicted in the report "were so remote in practice that I doubted whether we would be justified in going to the extremes in the way of cost that alertness would require." While Eisenhower agreed with Dulles, his real concern, he said, was that the classified study would not remain secret for long—a prediction that proved prophetic.[12]

At the end of the November 7 briefing, the president asked a few of the scientists who had played a major part in the study to remain behind. Eisenhower confided to the group that he now realized he had asked the wrong question of the panel: "You can't have this kind of war," he told the stunned scientists. "There aren't enough bulldozers to scrape the bodies off the streets." Instead, the president said, he hoped to enlist the scientists' talents in pursuit of another goal: a nuclear test ban. "Everybody in the Pentagon is against it," Eisenhower complained.[13]

"No urgency on Mars. . ."

By mid-November, when he still had not heard from Rabi on the specifics of a science advisory committee, Eisenhower assigned the task of drafting PSAC's terms of reference to Killian. The description of the science adviser's duties that Killian sent to the president a month later highlighted, in the same words that Eisenhower had used in his November 7 speech, the need for PSAC to give "primary attention to the use of science and technology in relation to national security." Newspapers, taking their cue from Eisenhower's remark, had already dubbed Killian the administration's new "missile czar."[14]

Killian's draft specified that the science adviser's job would be full time, that PSAC would meet regularly, and that members would serve fixed terms on the committee—"the intent being to provide for a rotation of membership." PSAC would also draw upon the advice of additional outside scientists by appointing nonmember "consultants." A separate "checklist" that Killian appended to the document raised the possibility that Eisenhower might wish to create "a new Manhattan Project" to coordinate work on priority defense programs like the antiballistic missile and reconnaissance satellites.

Although the position of science adviser did not have cabinet status, Killian was entitled to attend cabinet and NSC meetings as a so-called backbencher. He resolved to make the most of this arrangement by sitting, whenever possible, in the president's direct line of vision.[15]

On December 1, Killian announced the names of those who would serve on PSAC. The fact that most of the scientists and engineers picked by Killian and subsequently approved by Eisenhower had experience in defense-related work suggests that, from the outset, the president and his science adviser expected PSAC to serve as a counterbalance to the AEC and the military. Of the twenty-three members and consultants to join PSAC, fourteen—including Rabi, Bethe, Killian, and Land—had previously served on SAC/ODM. David Beckler, who had been the secretary of SAC/ODM, assumed the same role in PSAC. Members of PSAC agreed to serve four-year terms.[16]

A week later, PSAC held the first of its scheduled monthly meetings in Room 159 of the old Executive Office Building adjacent to the White House—the same room in which, sixteen years earlier, Secretary of State Cordell Hull had received Japan's ambassadors on the eve of Pearl Harbor. Appropriately, this first meeting was dominated by discussion of the spy-satellite program and other steps the nation might take to avoid a devastating surprise attack. All agreed that the arms race, not the space race, should have the highest priority. While development of the antiballistic missile was "urgent," Beckler wrote in his minutes, there was "no urgency on Mars."[17]

But the space program did attract PSAC's attention in the following days. At a February 1958 cabinet meeting, Killian reported to the president that while there would probably be "some additional dramatic Soviet space developments, such as a shot at the moon, between now and the time we can catch up to them," there could no longer be any doubt as to the ultimate outcome of the space race. Because of America's superior technological capability, Killian said, the United States "will surpass the USSR—but it will take time."[18]

Shortly thereafter, Eisenhower announced to the nation that Killian would create a new PSAC panel to make recommendations for a national program of space exploration. Two of the space panel's recommendations promptly met with Eisenhower's approval—reconstituting the National Advisory Committee for Aeronautics as the National Aeronautics and Space Administration (NASA) and making space exploration a predominantly civilian enterprise. That March, PSAC released its first report to the public: a well-received primer on outer space.[19] However, the president rejected the space panel's advice that he avoid potential public relations disasters by conducting future satellite launches in secret.

In keeping with Eisenhower's goal of finding old programs to dispense with as well as new ones to pursue, PSAC's scientists recommended—and Eisenhower approved—cancellation of Project Vanguard, the Navy's troubled rocket program, whose effort the previous December to launch the nation's first satellite had ended in spectacular failure. Instead, Explorer I had been lofted into orbit by an Army Jupiter booster on January 31, 1958.[20]

Elsewhere, PSAC scientists were not so influential. Killian and his colleagues also advised the president to abandon the nuclear-powered aircraft program, and to give precedence to development of the Army Jupiter over the Air Force's Thor. Killian personally urged Eisenhower to reject a wide variety of "wild-blue-yonder proposals" from enthusiasts in the Air Force—some of whose ideas for placing bombs and other weapons in orbit betrayed, the science adviser wrote, "an extraordinary ignorance of Newtonian mechanics."[21] But following intense lobbying by the Air Force, most of these programs survived.[22]

On the other hand, PSAC successfully urged Eisenhower to keep one project that the Air Force had decided to cancel—the Titan II ICBM—by pointing out that the solid-fueled missile could be stored in protected underground silos and hence would be less vulnerable than Titan I to a surprise enemy attack. For the same reason, PSAC persuaded the president to accelerate development of the Navy's Polaris missile.[23]

"This terrible impasse. . ."

The test ban was another subject that rapidly attracted PSAC's attention. At the end of 1957, the Soviet Union had repeated its offer of a two-to-three-year moratorium on nuclear testing. On January 6, 1958, when the Russian proposal was discussed at a NSC meeting, Killian announced that PSAC had already begun to look into the feasibility of a test ban. With an enthusiastic endorsement from Eisenhower and Dulles, the NSC directed Killian to appoint an interagency group of scientists to study the question. Six days later, Eisenhower formally proposed to the Russians that scientists from both nations join that summer in "technical studies of the possibilities of verification and supervision" for a test ban.[24]

But on March 24, before the studies could get under way, the test ban came into direct conflict with the clean bomb—which the AEC was once again promoting—at a special two-hour meeting of Eisenhower and top administration officials.

In preparation for the meeting, Strauss had sent the president a lengthy memorandum, "The Case for Clean Nuclear Weapons," which played on the president's concern for world public opinion. "The new approach outlined below," it began, "could regain the initiative for the U.S. and place the USSR at a disadvantage, as did Atoms for Peace and the Open Skies proposals."[25] Among other arguments against the moratorium, Defense Secretary McElroy raised the prospect of weapons laboratories becoming ghost towns. Eisenhower responded that he "thought scientists, like other people, have a strong interest in avoiding nuclear war."[26] While the president yielded once more to pressure from the AEC and the Pentagon to continue testing, he nonetheless asked those in the room "to think about what could be done to get rid of this terrible impasse in which we now find ourselves with regard to disarmament."

Only four days after what had seemed a disappointing denouement for the test ban, Bethe, chairman of the eleven-member interagency panel that had investigated the verification question, briefed the president and the NSC on its findings. Bethe noted that while the relative advantage of a test ban to the United States was a question outside his panel's study, there could no longer be any doubt as to the technical *feasibility* of such a ban.

Bethe's panel concluded that verification of an end to nuclear testing would require instrumented stations at approximately seventy locations in Russia and China, as well as the right to conduct a yet to be determined number of overflights and on-site inspections to investigate suspicious or unexplained events. By such means, Bethe claimed, the United States could reliably detect clandestine tests as small as one kiloton in yield—whether the bomb was exploded in the atmosphere, underwater, or on the surface of the earth. While conceding that it might still be possible to conceal underground tests of bombs as large as twenty kilotons, the panel concluded that the Russians would need to test bombs of even higher yield if they hoped to make significant improvements in their arsenal.[27]

Although some on the panel and on PSAC had hoped that Bethe's report might be finished in time to avert the next series of American nuclear tests, most, including Bethe, agreed that it was both "undesirable and practically not feasible" to suspend testing before the beginning of Hardtack, whose first test—code-named Yucca—was only a few weeks away.[28]

In early April—after the Russians had concluded their own most recent series of nuclear tests and renewed their moratorium offer—Eisenhower asked PSAC, the AEC, the Pentagon, and the State Department to make their final recommendations on a test ban before the end of the month.[29]

"This view will receive real attention. . ."

Recognizing both the potential significance of the advice PSAC had been asked to provide as well as the political sensitivity of its assignment, Killian elected to hold the committee's next monthly meeting at Ramey Air Force Base in Puerto Rico, away from the distractions of Washington, during the weekend of April 8–10, 1958. Not surprisingly, the test ban dominated the three days of discussion at Ramey.

From the outset, Killian warned its members that PSAC would face intense opposition from within the government if it took a strong stand in support of the test ban, since both the AEC and the Defense Department wanted "an absolute (not relative) advantage" over Russia. Rabi shared Killian's pessimism about winning over the opponents of a test ban: "They are saying, regardless of what [the] other side develops we cannot afford not to have more light weight or cleaner weapons." Herbert Scoville, assistant director of the CIA's scientific intelligence branch, cautioned that bureaucratic positions on the test ban were already so deeply entrenched that no amount of scientific evidence was likely to change anyone's mind.

Rabi, urging a test ban, argued along with Bethe that it should be only a starting point for subsequent steps toward real nuclear disarmament—since a ban "as such never meant anything [except] as a step towards something else." Bethe affirmed that the test ban was "an innocent place to start."[30]

In a vote that Saturday—the first and apparently only vote by PSAC in its history—all but one of the two dozen scientists at Ramey favored a resolution urging Eisenhower to pursue the test ban as an attainable short-term goal, separate from the long-running but thus far fruitless quest for disarmament. Only former Livermore director Herbert York abstained from the vote. As York later told Killian, he felt that "the whole matter of a nuclear test ban was largely political, and that therefore it was not entirely proper for a science advisory group to be making recommendations about whether it should be done and whether it would be to our net advantage."[31] The following day, however, York changed his mind, making the vote in support of the test ban unanimous. As York explained to Killian, Wiesner had meanwhile persuaded him "that whether or not a science-oriented group was the ideal forum, it was the only forum that had any chance of doing the right thing."[32] Because PSAC would be the first organization in the government to support the test ban, Killian told the group, "this view will receive real attention."[33]

On Sunday, PSAC was still split over whether to recommend that Eisenhower take the initiative on the test ban by canceling Operation Hardtack, by far the largest and most ambitious series of American tests to date, now less than three weeks away.

Scheduled for testing in Hardtack was a 200-kiloton warhead for the Navy's new Polaris missile. The test, if successful, would make it possible for the United States to deploy a significant portion of its nuclear deterrent in deep-diving submarines virtually immune from Soviet attack. Also to be tested was a version of the much-touted clean bomb. Finally, added to Hardtack at the last minute was Operation Argus—a series of high-altitude nuclear explosions designed to test not only a new concept for intercepting ICBMs but also the Russians' ability to detect clandestine tests in outer space.[34]

As Bethe pointed out at Ramey, any ban that began with a unilateral renunciation of testing by the United States, just after Russia had completed its own test series, would have virtually no chance of being accepted by the rest of the government. Ultimately, Killian and Bethe persuaded PSAC that recommending the cancelation of Hardtack would be unwise, if only on political grounds.

"His scientists . . ."

Killian presented PSAC's report on the test ban to the president on April 17—noting, according to Goodpaster, "that this is a controversial subject on which the observations of his group are limited to technical aspects only and must be balanced against other considerations." This disclaimer aside, Killian outlined PSAC's position in favor of the test ban. An agreement with the Russians to stop all nuclear testing after the completion of Hardtack in August 1958 "would be to our over-all advantage," he argued. "Cessation of testing, in the judgment of the group, would leave the United States in a position of technical advantage for a few years, which will otherwise be lost."[35]

While acknowledging this meant that nuclear testing might end before the country had perfected a warhead for its antiballistic missile, Killian pointed out that the ABM faced even more significant technical hurdles, whereas the United States already had "warheads which could serve satisfactorily, although perhaps not with the ultimate in efficiency."[36]

Eisenhower told Killian that he was impressed with the reasoned and dispassionate case that PSAC made for an end to nuclear testing—adding that "he had never been too much impressed or completely convinced by the views expressed by Drs. Teller, Lawrence and Mills that we must continue testing of nuclear weapons." But Killian thought the change in thinking at the White House best illustrated by the fact that Eisenhower now referred to PSAC's members as "*his* scientists."[37]

The president lost little time in acting on PSAC's endorsement of the test ban. On April 20, Eisenhower sent Khrushchev a letter, drafted by Dulles, repeating his proposal for a Soviet-American technical study on the feasibility of verifying a permanent test ban. Some twelve days later, the Soviet premier accepted the president's offer. Although both Strauss and McElroy voiced strident objections that they had not been informed about the letter to Khrushchev—and the Joint Chiefs, in an April 30 memorandum, advised Eisenhower that a test ban "will be to the distinct disadvantage of the United States"—the chorus of protests this time was ignored at the White House. In another exchange of correspondence between the two leaders early in May, Eisenhower and Khrushchev agreed to begin technical talks on the test ban in Geneva that summer.[38]

"The right to elect and select. . ."

In the weeks following the Ramey meeting, PSAC's influence at the White House continued to grow. The start of technical talks between Soviet and American scientists at Geneva also coincided with the departure of one of the test ban's most vocal opponents in the Eisenhower administration. In late June, Strauss resigned as chairman of the AEC to return to private life and the world of business.[39] Strauss's replacement at was John McCone, a California businessman who likewise vigorously opposed the test ban. Moreover, before leaving the government, Strauss took steps to ensure, through his appointments to the GAC, that nuclear testing advocates would continue to have a prominent voice in the administration.

Thus, it was at Strauss's urging that Ernest Lawrence was included among the Committee of Experts, the delegation of scientists picked by Killian and PSAC to represent the United States at Geneva. (Teller had been the AEC chairman's first choice, but opposition from within the government forced Strauss to withdraw his name.) In addition to Lawrence, PSAC physicists Robert Bacher and James Fisk joined fifteen experts from other U.S. government agencies, as well as scientists from Britain, Canada, and France, to make up the Western delegation to the Conference of Experts.[40]

On June 18, preparatory to the start of the Geneva talks, PSAC met again with the president. Bethe reported that the effort to develop fallout-free nuclear weapons was encountering new snags. Tests of the clean bomb had been "too ambitious," Bethe reported, and "tried to make bombs cleaner than was justified." There was, he said, a "limit on the amount of cleanliness that can be achieved."[41]

The meeting also included discussion of a concern that Eisenhower had expressed more than once since Sputnik: the growing influence of science and scientists in his administration. The increase in the number and importance of scientists, Eisenhower thought, might eventually make it necessary "to have the right to elect and select some of these people." The previous March, Eisenhower had complained to Republican leaders that when scientists got before television cameras they were prone to become "excited . . . and to say the damnedest things."[42] However, Killian's worry was that PSAC had shown too little, not too much, initiative. The day before, the science adviser had called PSAC together to ask, "Has the Science Advisory Committee become too conservative? Are there bold imaginative projects we should be encouraging?"[43]

"The weight of argument. . ."

By early August, Killian's reports of progress in the Geneva technical talks gave Eisenhower new reason to hope for progress on the test ban. If "full technical agreement is reached," the president told his science adviser, "the weight of argument [for the test ban] would be very great."[44]

But some ten days later, Eisenhower received a reminder of how far from unanimity the scientific community was on putting an end to nuclear testing. McCone had brought Teller and Los Alamos laboratory director Norris Bradbury to the White House to brief the president on the results of Hardtack I, which had only one more test to go. The discovery of a hitherto unrecognized "blackout" effect from high-altitude nuclear explosions called for more tests, Bradbury and Teller argued. Hardtack had also demonstrated the potential for "very small devices," Teller told Eisenhower.[45] The president, however, this time refused to yield to pressure from the AEC's scientists to continue testing. He "recognized," Eisenhower said, "that the new thermonuclear weapons are tremendously powerful; however, they are not, in many ways, as powerful as is world opinion today in obliging the United States to follow certain lines of policy."[46]

A few days later, McCone was similarly unsuccessful in persuading Eisenhower to exclude "peaceful nuclear explosions" from a test ban.[47] That same day, Eisenhower was briefed by Fisk on the Conference of Experts' report. While the details were yet to be ironed out, Fisk admitted, Western and Soviet scientists had agreed at Geneva that "a workable and effective control system to detect violations of an agreement on the worldwide suspension of nuclear weapons' tests is technically feasible." The conference concluded that Bethe's proposed network of seventy inspection stations, together with an unspecified number of periodic on-site investigations, would be able to verify such a ban.[48]

Before the month of August was out, Eisenhower had announced a one-year moratorium on American nuclear tests beginning at the end of October and proposed to Khrushchev that negotiations start in the fall on a permanent test ban—an offer that the Soviet leader promptly accepted. By summer's end, a Committee of Principals—consisting of the secretaries of state and defense and the heads of the AEC, CIA, and PSAC—was appointed to prepare the American negotiating position at Geneva.[49]

"If you want disarmament. . ."

In order to complete the ongoing round of nuclear tests in time to meet the October 31, 1958, moratorium deadline, testing in the Pacific and at the

Nevada test site accelerated to a nearly frenetic pace. The press dubbed Operation Hardtack II, as it was officially known, "Operation Deadline" after some seven tests were carried out in two days at the end of October—including a pair of underground explosions in the Nevada desert that unexpectedly broke through the earth's surface, releasing a small amount of radioactivity into the air.[50]

Once the moratorium was in effect, PSAC urged Eisenhower to press the Russians for negotiations that would lead to a permanent halt to nuclear testing. In a meeting with the president on November 18, Killian reaffirmed the committee's unanimous view that a test ban was both verifiable and in the nation's best interest—even though it might slow or even stop the development of nuclear weapons: "The feeling of the group was summed up by the statement that if you want disarmament, you must be willing to give something up; this would make an excellent first step." There was also a veiled admonition in Killian's reminder: "If one looks back over the history of United States and Soviet weapons development, one has to conclude that a test cessation at an earlier date would have left the U.S. in a position of much greater relative military advantage."[51]

PSAC continued to bolster its argument for the test ban in a succession of reports to the president. In early November, Killian reported to Eisenhower that analysis of the results of Operation Argus, the nuclear tests carried out over the South Atlantic during the summer and early fall of 1958, showed that the idea of creating an antimissile *cordon sanitaire* above the earth by nuclear explosions remained chimerical. The twin facts that the experiment had not worked and that the Russians had detected the secret U.S. tests were additional arguments for the test ban, Killian pointed out.[52]

In mid-December, the report of PSAC's ABM panel concluded that the difficulties being encountered in developing an antimissile missile likewise bolstered the case for the test ban. American warheads, the panel reported, were currently lighter-weight and more efficient than Soviet warheads, allowing U.S. ICBMs to make better use of decoys to foil antimissile defenses. Should nuclear testing be allowed to continue, however, "there is no reason now to foresee, for the Soviets, any less sophistication in warhead design in 1964-65 than we foresee for ourselves."[53]

PSAC also urged Eisenhower to stand fast against two alternatives to a comprehensive test ban that were being discussed elsewhere in the administration and in Congress. The first was a "threshold" ban that would allow the testing of bombs up to a certain yield; the second, a partial ban that would permit nuclear testing to continue underground. In the case of the threshold ban, Killian advised the president not to "scuttle" the prospects for a complete end to nuclear testing just to keep alive the hope of developing more efficient bombs with lower yields. Similarly, while a ban that allowed testing to go on underground "would avoid the political problems of fallout," Killian noted, "it was unanimously felt that this is strictly a propaganda step and not a basic issue at all."[54]

"Highly dismaying news. . ."

But while Killian and PSAC argued for the test ban at the White House, opposition to a ban was being rallied both inside and outside the Eisenhower administration. *Our Nuclear Future,* a book by Edward Teller and RAND physicist Albert Latter, argued that verification of an end to nuclear testing was virtually impossible: "It is almost certain that in the competition between prohibition and bootlegging, the bootlegger will win."[55] Far more serious, however, was the secret assault that Teller and Latter mounted against the ban behind closed doors.

Earlier, Killian had asked scientists at Los Alamos and Livermore to prepare a report for PSAC on how a prolonged halt to testing might affect the development of nuclear weapons. Los Alamos director Bradbury subsequently reported that his laboratory, while unenthusiastic about indefinite suspension of testing, had no overwhelming objections to a temporary ban. But the verdict from Livermore—where Teller had recently been appointed director—was altogether different.

Latter told in a 1985 interview how scientists at the laboratory, at Teller's urging, devised "some wild schemes" for cheating on a test ban. Among the ideas proposed for foiling detection of clandestine tests was exploding the bomb inside a giant egg-shaped structure strong enough to contain the force of the nuclear blast; another scheme would have employed an enormous collapsed "lung" for the same purpose. In order to hide secret tests in outer space, Teller and his colleagues proposed orbiting a gargantuan shield that would mask the telltale x-rays of a nuclear explosion from earthbound observers. Perhaps the most ingenuous idea was to set a bomb off directly underneath a mountain with parabola-shaped sides—the effect of which would be to reflect the shock waves of the blast straight down to the center of the earth. But this and other ideas were subsequently rejected as either impractical or prohibitively expensive. The would-be inventor belatedly realized, Latter said, that parabolic-sided mountains do not occur in nature.[56]

Finally, in early January 1959, on the eve of the briefing that Teller and Latter were to give Killian and members of PSAC's test-ban panel at Livermore, Latter and Teller recognized a plausible way for cheaters on a ban to evade detection. Latter's scheme for evasion involved exploding the bomb in a huge excavated cave or chamber deep underground, where the shock wave from the explosion would be effectively muffled, or "decoupled," from the surrounding earth. By such means yields as high as 300 kilotons might be made to appear very much smaller, and the seismic signal from less powerful explosions might not be detected at all.[57] The possibility that underground nuclear tests might escape detection by decoupling had been anticipated in Bethe's March 1958 PSAC report, but it had been dismissed there as unrealistic. At the Livermore briefing, decoupling gained a new life.[58]

Virtually coincident with discovery of what became known as the "'Latter hole' theory" was another major technical setback for the test ban. Experts analyzing the results of tests in Plumbbob and Hardtack II uncovered evidence that the Conference of Experts had overestimated the strength of seismic signals from underground nuclear explosions. These same experts discovered that it was also more difficult than previously calculated to distinguish underground tests from earthquakes. Seismologists looking at the revised data concluded that effective verification of a comprehensive test ban might require a tenfold increase in the number of instrumented stations and a corresponding rise in the number of overflights and on-site inspections needed to monitor such an agreement.[59]

Together with the decoupling argument, these discoveries were "highly dismaying news for the American delegation" at Geneva, Killian confided to PSAC—particularly since they seemed to call into question the fundamental soundness of the detection system that had been proposed by the scientists. On January 5, Killian informed the president that new information necessitated a major change in the U.S. negotiating position at Geneva.

With the nearly overnight change in U.S. terms at Geneva—which now demanded 650 rather than 70 inspection stations, and other, much more intrusive measures—Eisenhower worried aloud about a "loss of confidence" in American intentions.[60] As Eisenhower predicted, efforts to represent the change merely as the result of a "refinement of analysis" failed to convince the Russians. The chief U.S. representative at the talks, Ambassador James Wadsworth, informed Washington that the sudden shift in American terms had "resulted in the most violent reaction imaginable" from the Soviets. The furor over the changes, Wadsworth later noted, "spread a pall over the negotiations from which they never completely recovered."

The fact that "we have now raised our technical estimates on nuclear detection capabilities" made the United States appear guilty of bad faith, Dulles told Eisenhower in a mid-January meeting. "All present agreed that this . . . had put us in a bad spot," Goodpaster acknowledged. A subsequent American effort to resolve the dispute over decoupling was promptly rejected by the Russians.[61]

"Draw back from our original efforts. . ."

That winter, discouraged by the stalemate on underground tests, Eisenhower was forced to retreat from the comprehensive test ban. In late February 1959, the president called Killian into the Oval Office to discuss the possibility of a threshold test ban. Although PSAC had unanimously rejected a threshold ban just a few months earlier, Killian now stated that a compromise was necessary—since decoupling threatened to "invalidate the threshold concept."[62]

Moreover, even though a subsequent PSAC study concluded that decoupling was less a threat to verification than had been represented at the Livermore briefing, the technical obstacles to a test ban remained formidable nonetheless. For example, a report on decoupling forwarded to Killian by PSAC physicist Lloyd Berkner in March concluded that the number of instrumented stations needed to monitor a test ban on Russian soil was now estimated at 180—far fewer than the 650 the United States demanded after the second look at the Hardtack data, but far more than the 70 originally asked for, and certainly well above the "handful" to which the Russians had informally agreed.[63]

These difficulties inspired a new caution on PSAC's, and especially Killian's, part. In mid-March, when Killian raised the question of whether PSAC should make new recommendations to the president in the area of arms control, only Wiesner—probably the most outspoken advocate of the test ban on the committee—spoke up to say that he thought it important that PSAC "establish a vested interest in this field."[64]

At a Camp David meeting between Eisenhower and British Prime Minister Harold Macmillan later in the month, Killian—confessing that his "heart was not in it"—presented what he called "a clear and fair statement" of the technical obstacles standing in the way of a comprehensive test ban. What he feared most, Killian admitted, was "a fatal error" in verification standards that might allow the Russians, by testing secretly, to make rapid progress in developing nuclear weaponry. Concern with verification had ultimately caused the science adviser to drop the idea of a threshold test ban. Killian now advised the president and Macmillan to "draw back from our original efforts [and] settle for some more limited form of test agreements," such as a ban on all but underground nuclear testing.[65]

On April 12, the president, following Killian's advice, offered Khrushchev a choice between a limited or a total test ban, provided the Russians were willing to accept the U.S. plan for on-site inspection. Ten days later, the Soviet leader flatly rejected a comprehensive test ban under American terms, but left open the possibility of a limited ban.[66]

The possibility of a compromise was explored further that May when Eisenhower endorsed a British proposal for an annual quota of on-site inspections. However, McCone argued once again that effective verification was nearly impossible—citing Killian's own estimate that as many as 1,000 to 1,500 "suspicious" seismic events were detected in Russia yearly, whereas the British proposal allowed only 25 to 50 annual inspections.[67] Conceding that he was "not of course personally in a position to decide what is scientifically reasonable," Eisenhower yielded to the AEC chairman. At a cabinet meeting a month later, the president acknowledged that he was "getting somewhat pessimistic about the whole activity in Geneva. The political as well as the nuclear test negotiations seem to be getting nowhere."[68]

"Glad to join in the process. . ."

Eisenhower's frustration with the setbacks in the test-ban negotiations was becoming palpable that spring. If "scientists can help to show concrete ways to make progress on arms control, he will be most grateful and glad to join in the process," the president told Killian in exasperation.[69]

While the test-ban talks remained stalemated, PSAC was able to be more helpful with some of the president's other concerns, including the rapid growth of the country's nuclear arsenal and the need for unbiased technical advice on weapons procurement. The previous fall, when the Army lobbied for a major increase in the number of tactical nuclear weapons, Eisenhower cited PSAC scientists in resisting the appeal, pointing out that "the three scientists who had visited him the day before (Drs. Land, Purcell, and Killian) had shown less enthusiasm than he has heard at other times in this area."[70]

Despite the existence of PSAC, however, many in and out of government still feared that not enough was being done to represent the interests of science in the Eisenhower administration and to ensure that the right type of scientific advice reached the government.

In the immediate aftermath of Sputnik, Congress briefly discussed creating a Department of Science to oversee federally funded research—until the success of PSAC rendered the discussion moot. Concern with Russian space spectaculars and the trouble-plagued American ICBM program had inspired Defense Secretary McElroy to approve, in the fall of 1958, a major reorganization of the Department of Defense, establishing an Advanced Research Projects Agency (ARPA) to oversee the Pentagon's antimissile and space programs. The following February, also as part of the 1958 Defense Reorganization Act, ARPA was put under the Office of the Director of Defense Research and Engineering (DDR&E), which was created to reduce competition and wasteful duplication in defense-related research among the military services.[71] The civilian head of DDR&E was, in effect, the science adviser to the secretary of defense and was also expected to serve as a counterbalance to the influence of the Defense Science Board—the Pentagon advisory panel established in 1956, whose members were drawn from defense contractors and universities engaged in government-funded research.[72]

In theory, DDR&E represented a potential rival to PSAC. But Eisenhower's choice of former Livermore laboratory director Herbert York to head the new office avoided such conflict in practice. Having previously served both on PSAC and as chief scientist at ARPA, York sympathized with Eisenhower's desire to eliminate wasteful projects from the defense budget. Within weeks of assuming his post at the Pentagon, in fact, York and DDR&E had joined Killian and PSAC in challenging the continued funding of two favored Air Force projects: the B-70 bomber and aircraft nuclear propulsion.[73]

"Boring from within . . ."

As the stalemate in the Geneva talks threatened to continue into the new year, Killian, too, was becoming exasperated with test-ban opponents. According to the science adviser's memoirs, one such scientist frankly admitted that his "technical" opposition to the ban was politically inspired: "Dr. [Albert] Latter said to me in casual conversation that whatever advances might be made in detection technology, the West Coast group led by Teller would find a technical way to circumvent or discredit them."[74]

Perhaps in part because of this frustration, Killian announced in late May 1959 that he would resign the post of science adviser that summer.[75] Just two days before leaving the government, Killian beat back another attempt by McCone to persuade the president to abandon the moratorium.[76]

Eisenhower picked George Kistiakowsky, PSAC's foremost expert on the problem-plagued American missile program, to replace Killian. (Killian later thought it unfortunate that one of his final meetings with the president as head of PSAC was for the purpose of briefing Eisenhower on the latest failures in the ICBM program. All five previous tests of the Atlas had ended in failure due to broken fuel lines and excessive vibration, and the missile testing program had been suspended while the problems were being corrected.)[77]

Kistiakowsky spent July 15, 1959, his first day as science adviser, dealing with issues far removed from the troubled missile program. According to the detailed diary he kept while at the White House, among "Kisty's" first tasks were to assign radio-frequency bands for astronomers and to mediate a dispute between the Army and NASA over which would have the authority to shoot monkeys into space.[78] By that afternoon, however, Kistiakowsky was already wrapped up in the technical minutiae of the test ban. He complained that Killian's ready acceptance "of the weak evidence of the Bacher panel"—the latest PSAC study, which concluded that it would be possible to conceal underground tests from on-site inspectors—had already "tied my hands a bit" on what he could recommend to the president about the talks in Geneva.[79]

Unlike Killian, Kistiakowsky did not hesitate to challenge the technical arguments used to undermine the test ban. The "notion of evasion through Latter holes is completely nonsensical," he wrote in his diary on July 28. "These things are too uncertain and too costly for any national program of evasion to be based on them." Kistiakowsky nonetheless realized that the test-ban debate had little to do with scientific method or rules of evidence. There was, he wrote, a "political impossibility of ratification of a treaty in the face of the theoretical possibility of the Latter hole."[80]

While Kistiakowsky was ready to promote the test ban, he was reluctant to risk a confrontation with McCone by attacking arguments against the ban in the AEC chairman's presence. McCone "does not think much of 'scientists,'" and was "feeling thwarted by PSAC," Kistiakowsky noted in his diary. Consequently, the science adviser arranged a private meeting with Eisenhower to discuss the test ban.[81]

In early August, acting, apparently, upon his new science adviser's recommendation, Eisenhower announced that he would extend the testing moratorium scheduled to expire at the end of October to the start of the new year. The president's announcement provoked a "wild reaction," Kistiakowsky noted, from both the AEC and the Defense Department—which just two days before had urged Eisenhower to resume nuclear testing immediately. Indeed, McCone retaliated in subsequent weeks by charging—falsely—that PSAC was responsible for leaking the results of the secret Argus tests to the press.[82]

It was also evidently on Kistiakowsky's advice that Eisenhower changed his mind that fall about a total ban on nuclear testing. Kistiakowsky was thus "elated," he wrote in his diary, when the president announced, in the course of a Veterans' Day cabinet meeting, that an end to atmospheric testing would not be enough—that the ban should extend to testing underground and in space. "This is a tremendous change from the attitude which prevailed recently that really all we can do is to seek disengagement from the comprehensive treaty concept and try for an atmospheric ban," Kistiakowsky wrote in his diary that evening. "I guess 'boring from within,' which I have been doing the last couple of months, has finally borne some fruit." But he remained concerned, Kistiakowsky admitted, about "how long this decision will stand—since Defense will unquestionably hit the roof when it learns of it."[83]

"The incredible morass of indecision . . ."

This time, it was the lack of progress in the negotiations at Geneva during the coming months rather than Pentagon opposition that caused Eisenhower to once again rethink his support for a comprehensive test ban. During a Cabinet meeting in Augusta a few days after Christmas, the president declared himself both angry and "amazed" at the virulence of the Soviets' latest denunciation of the U.S. offer. At year's end, Eisenhower announced that while the United States was no longer bound by the terms of the moratorium, he would nonetheless "not resume nuclear weapons tests without announcing our intention in advance."[84]

With the start of the new year, following further attacks on PSAC by McCone—who accused "scientists of having gotten us into the mess we are in now, politically," Kistiakowsky wrote—the science adviser urged Eisenhower to retreat from the comprehensive test ban in favor of a threshold test ban. As Kistiakowsky told the president, recent experiments at the

Nevada test site indicated that it was possible to reliably detect underground explosions having yields down to 20 kilotons (equivalent to a magnitude of 4.75 on the Richter earthquake scale). By accepting a threshold test ban, the country could "disregard the potential evasion of monitoring by means of far outer-space tests or underground tests using big Latter holes, and toss the hot potato back to the Soviets."

In Kistiakowsky's view, political realities, not technical facts, had finally doomed the comprehensive test ban. He reached his decision, the science adviser acknowledged, having become "convinced that a comprehensive treaty would not be ratified by the Senate since AEC, DOD, and Teller will all testify in opposition."[85] The threshold plan also promised to extricate the administration from "the incredible morass of indecision in which we have been for several months," Kistiakowsky wrote. The stalled test-ban talks had left the president "obviously tired and impatient with the whole subject . . . it was almost impossible to conclude what he wished to be done."[86]

"The missile gap doesn't look to be very serious. . ."

While the Geneva talks remained "utterly inconclusive" by early 1960, one bright spot on the horizon was the improving picture the administration had of the so-called missile gap—thanks to the U-2.

Kistiakowsky learned the truth about the missile gap only two days after being sworn in as science adviser when he was briefed on the U-2 program by CIA Deputy Director Richard Bissell. Until then, Kistiakowsky, like many in the administration, had subscribed to the theory that the Soviets were far ahead in the missile race.[87]

However, because the U-2 and its discoveries remained among the most closely held secrets in the government, neither Kistiakowsky nor Eisenhower was able to share the good news about the missile gap with the American public. In a private letter to "Swede" Hazlett, his friend of long standing, written in the weeks after Sputnik, Eisenhower had hinted at the burden of knowing things about the Russians that he could not reveal: "In the matters that currently seem to be disturbing the country so much, you can understand that there are many things that I don't dare allude to publicly, yet some of them would do much to allay the fears of our own people."[88]

The U-2 photographs were both spectacular and mysterious. An early overflight accidentally discovered the Soviets' missile test center at Tyuratam, but no tangible evidence of the mounting hordes of Russian ICBMs claimed by Khrushchev (and originally predicted by the CIA) was uncovered. Official projections of Soviet missile strength had continued to climb after Sputnik.[89]

Evidence that a missile gap existed and was growing—but in America's favor—began to accumulate in the fall of 1959 as the hundreds of Russian ICBMs projected in earlier intelligence estimates failed to appear in U-2 photographs. In October 1959, the Pentagon's National Evaluation Group agreed for the first time with the lower figures for Soviet missiles now cited by the CIA's National Intelligence Estimate.[90] As Kistiakowsky wrote in his diary at this time, "the Soviets are ahead of us in propulsion, but that is all." Regarding both numbers and capabilities, "we are almost even with them, although their missiles are probably more reliable in terms of launching, but not as accurate."[91]

While Eisenhower was unwilling to let the truth be known about the missile gap outside a small circle in his administration, it plainly influenced his negotiating stance toward the Russians, as well as his response to domestic critics who continued to warn of a missile-bristling Soviet Union. Kistiakowsky later wrote of how, in the midst of a November 1959 briefing on "the growing threat from the USSR," Eisenhower "quite suddenly stopped his usual doodling, raised a hand, and said: 'Please enter a minority report of one.'"[92]

A CIA briefing by Allen Dulles in early January 1960 provided the most detailed picture yet of the Russian missile program. "For the first time," Kistiakowsky wrote in his diary, "this estimate was based not on capabilities but on probable plans because there is no evidence that the Soviets are engaged in any crash ICBM program and hence obviously are not using their full capability. . . . In fact the missile gap doesn't look to be very serious. . . ."[93]

The following month, Eisenhower proposed an end to nuclear testing in the atmosphere and a ban on underground tests above the 4.75 threshold. The president acknowledged that it would still be theoretically possible for the United States and Russia to test in deep space, but his proposal called for a new joint effort by Soviet and American scientists to devise detection techniques that would allow a complete ban on nuclear testing.

The fact that the United States would be able to continue nuclear testing underground under the terms of this latest proposal softened domestic opposition to the test ban. In a March meeting with the president, even McCone gave grudging approval to a threshold agreement—since it would, he reminded the president, allow U.S. nuclear weapons development to proceed virtually unhindered.[94]

This sudden and surprising upturn in the Geneva negotiations prompted an equally quick reaction from die-hard test-ban opponents outside the administration. That spring, Edward Teller testified before the Joint Committee on Atomic Energy that the Russians could and would cheat on a threshold ban. While protesting the interference of the "goddamn committee," Eisenhower nonetheless yielded to its request that he meet once more with the controversial physicist. On April 26, Teller told the president and the cabinet that the United States as well as Russia could violate the proposed Geneva agreement with impunity.[95]

Despite such opposition, Eisenhower resolved that the test ban would be prominent among the issues to be discussed with Khrushchev when he met with the Soviet leader at the Paris summit in early May.[96]

"We scientists had failed him. . ."

The approach of the Paris summit—and the fact that the test ban would likely be a major focus of the discussions there—drew attention anew to the military strength of the Soviet Union.

Ironically, the more that was known about Soviet military capabilities, the more uneasy American intelligence experts became about remaining uncertainties. Thus, while U.S. photo interpreters searched in vain for the rockets that Khrushchev had boasted his nation was turning out "like sausages," requests for additional U-2 overflights grew.

In private, senior Air Force officials broadly hinted that the Russians had been successful in hiding their missiles from the prying eye of the U-2.[97] As these skeptics pointed out, vast areas of Russia behind the Urals remained beyond the range of the spy plane. Parts of European Russia, rumored to hide secret missile sites and air bases, remained shrouded in cloud cover for much of the year and thus had yet to be photographed by the U-2. At the same time, Project Corona, the CIA's spy satellite program, had suffered setback after setback since the failed effort to launch Discoverer I in January 1959.[98]

Consequently, even as Eisenhower was again considering an indefinite suspension of the overflights in the spring of 1960, there were those in the CIA and Air Force urging him to approve new U-2 missions. What the president had assumed would be the last overflight of Russia to take place before the Paris summit was successfully carried out on April 9. Barely had the plane landed, however, before Eisenhower was being pressured to approve yet another U-2 mission—this time to investigate reports of an ICBM complex near Sverdlovsk.[99]

The shooting down on May 1, 1960, of the U-2 piloted by Francis Gary Powers finally put an end to the flights of the spy plane over Russia—and thus accomplished in a single stroke what Eisenhower had repeatedly tried but failed to do for several years.[100] The price, however, was to be the collapse of the summit in which Eisenhower had invested his last waning hopes for progress toward a test ban.

Recriminations and regret for the failed summit cast a wide net. By mid-May, when it was clear that Khrushchev would not meet with Eisenhower because of the U-2 incident, Eisenhower vented his frustrations in a comment to Goodpaster: "The President said that the intelligence people, he thought, had failed to recognize the emotional, even pathological, reaction of the Russians regarding their frontiers."

Kistiakowsky was stunned to learn that Eisenhower also held the scientists who had recommended the U-2 program at least indirectly responsible for the collapse of the Paris summit. Meeting alone with Eisenhower in the Oval Office on an unrelated matter shortly after the shootdown, Kistiakowsky was surprised when the president, "referring to the U-2, [said] that we scientists had failed him." When the science adviser attempted to defend his colleagues and PSAC—noting that "scientists had consistently warned about the U-2 eventually being shot down"—Eisenhower "flared up," Kistiakowsky wrote in his diary, and "ended very sadly that he saw nothing worthwhile left for him to do now until the end of his presidency."[101]

"The captive of a scientific-technological elite. . ."

Eisenhower's anger had abated by the time of his final meeting with PSAC, on January 12, when he acknowledged his "deep sense of obligation" to the committee. The president, according to Goodpaster, also "noted that more and more he has tended to put scientific advice into more and more subjects of national policy. He thought this body holds great influence in our federal system." His gratitude, the president told the scientists, was "not only for the work they have done, which he finds most impressive, and valuable, but for the stimulation of thought he gains and the broadening and deepening of his own understanding." Eisenhower said that he was "deeply hopeful" that PSAC would be continued into the Kennedy administration—which, he feared, had already shown a tendency toward "centralized dictation and [an] attitude of omniscience."[102]

Acting as a kind of informal liaison between the incoming and outgoing administrations, Jerome Wiesner offered his own postmortem at this meeting on Eisenhower's greatest disappointment: the failure of his administration to ban nuclear testing. Wiesner attributed that failure to the absence of a lobby or an effective advocate for disarmament in the White House. Eisenhower agreed, suggesting as a possible solution a "first secretary of government," who would meet with each agency every day specifically to discuss the progress the administration was making toward peace.[103]

Some five days after his valedictory to PSAC, Eisenhower gave a further indication of his feeling that science and scientists had played a mixed role in his administration. In his televised farewell address, Eisenhower warned against "the acquisition of unwarranted influence, whether sought or unsought, by the military-industrial-complex." In virtually the same breath, Eisenhower also pointed to the "danger that public policy could itself become the captive of a scientific-technological elite."[104]

PSAC members subsequently disagreed over the exact meaning of the president's celebrated dual warning. There could be no doubt, however, about the government's increased reliance on scientists as advisers as a result of Eisenhower's presidency. In the realm of arms control in particular, PSAC had established, as Wiesner had hoped, a vested interest. This reliance and that interest were, as much as progress toward the test ban, part of Eisenhower's—and PSAC's—legacy for the next administration.

III

Guarded Futures, 1961–1988: The Perils and Promises of New Technology

8

"Where a Fresh Start Is Badly Needed"

Politics and Science in the Kennedy Administration

S cience advising during the thousand-day presidency of John Kennedy represented a considerable contrast—both in style and substance—to the Eisenhower administration. While many of the issues that would dominate the Kennedy administration, such as the nuclear test ban, were inherited from Eisenhower, the approach of the next president and his science advisor would be distinctively new.

"An enthusiast for a single approach. . ."

The impatient, self-confident attitude of the new administration was evident even before Kennedy took office. During the traditional inaugural-eve briefing that the president gave the president-elect, in the Oval Office on January 19, 1961, the subject of the test ban arose only once in the course of the hour-and-a quarter session—when Eisenhower asked Kennedy if he wished to discuss the prospects at Geneva. Kennedy summarily declined Eisenhower's offer. He had, Kennedy said, already been briefed on the Russians and Geneva.[1]

Kistiakowsky shared Eisenhower's concern about Kennedy's youth and inexperience, particularly since the new president had yet to announce his choice of a science adviser. Some four days after the election, Kistiakowsky had written to Paul Nitze—a foremost Eisenhower critic, and Kennedy's representative on the transition team—complaining that the new administration still had not picked someone to head PSAC. Kistiakowsky thought the omission showed that "the selection of a science adviser was not considered to have a top priority" with Kennedy.[2]

In his letter to Nitze, the departing science adviser suggested four candidates for the post, all past or current members of PSAC: William O. Baker, Harvey Brooks, Edward Purcell, and Jerome Wiesner. Since Wiesner had served as Kennedy's de facto science adviser during the campaign, Kistiakowsky was doubtless aware that the electrical engineer from MIT was likely to be the president's choice. Perhaps also mindful that Wiesner had been an outspoken advocate of the test ban, Kistiakowsky cautioned Nitze about Wiesner's "tendency to become an enthusiast for a single approach."

An expert on early warning radar, Wiesner joined the Army's Scientific Advisory Board in 1956 and served as well on SAC/ODM before joining PSAC in the spring of 1958. It was while at MIT's Radiation Laboratory that Wiesner became a personal friend and adviser to the young senator from Massachusetts. In 1960, while Wiesner was still officially a member of Eisenhower's PSAC, Kennedy asked him to serve as a campaign adviser for scientific and technological matters—an unprecedented arrangement to which Eisenhower and Kistiakowsky acceded, somewhat to Wiesner's surprise.[3]

As Kistiakowsky alluded in his letter to Nitze, Wiesner considered arms control, particularly the nuclear test ban, a high-priority item for PSAC. In December 1959, Wiesner had been the first to propose a ban on missile flight-testing as a way to curb the arms race. Such a ban, which encountered adamant opposition in the Pentagon, was premature, Kistiakowsky decided.[4] Subsequently, Wiesner made enemies in Congress by speaking out against development of the so-called neutron bomb, which members of the Joint Committee on Atomic Energy were promoting as an argument for resuming nuclear testing.[5]

Kennedy formally announced Wiesner's appointment as science adviser in February 1961. Warning the president that there would inevitably be opposition to the appointment because of his liberal political views and reputation as an arms control enthusiast, Wiesner claims that Kennedy waved his concern aside with the comment, "Why the hell do you think I'm asking you to do this?"[6]

The new science adviser immediately sought—and received—assurances from Kennedy that PSAC's tradition of political independence would continue in the new administration. Kennedy also readily assented to Wiesner's recommendation that current members of the committee be allowed to serve out their four-year terms. Kennedy likewise allowed Wiesner to select the scientists to replace four PSAC members whose terms were about to expire.[7]

Kennedy was quick to turn to his scientists for advice. Indeed, as his administration began, the president faced a backlog of technical issues demanding prompt attention. Among them: what priority to give to the space race (and whether to launch a manned mission to the moon); whether to lend federal support for a new, ambitious plan to explore and map the ocean floor; and what to do about the unrestricted use of pesticides—which, as science was only beginning to recognize, were slowly poisoning the oceans and the land.⁸ PSAC already had a number of these and other issues under study.

A report that Wiesner sent to the president in early July 1961 showed the wide diversity of PSAC's interests and concerns. The list included desalinization, the nation's industrial development, the future of the West Virginia coal industry, environmental health, domestic air traffic control, and the exploration of outer space.⁹ The subject of space exploration, in fact, presented an early opportunity for PSAC to prove its independence—and, in the process, to demonstrate the sometimes fine line it trod between science and politics.

"Cheapest, safest, and first. . ."

A month before he was sworn in as science adviser, Wiesner had already begun an ad hoc study of the rationale behind manned space flight. The findings of the so-called Wiesner Report, given to Kennedy eleven days before the inauguration, were forthright and controversial. PSAC's Space Panel, which included Edwin Land and Edward Purcell, argued against putting men either in earth orbit or on the moon. Outer space, Purcell wrote in the panel's report, could be explored "cheapest, safest, and first" by instrumented probes.¹⁰ The report concluded, with emphasis, that *"A crash program aimed at placing a man into orbit at the earliest possible time cannot be justified solely on scientific or technical grounds."*

The PSAC report was another reflection of the science adviser's own jaundiced view of manned exploration of space. A year earlier, Wiesner had reintroduced the idea of a missile flight-testing ban in the hope that it might "get the United States out of the space race, which otherwise will continue to be a serious source of embarrassment and frustration."¹¹ The Space Panel's recommendations also stood in conspicuous contrast to the avid urgings of the Space Council headed by Vice President Lyndon Johnson, who championed the intensive exploration of space by American astronauts.

Kennedy found neither Wiesner's report nor Purcell's logic persuasive and decided to go ahead with Projects Mercury and Gemini, for man-in-orbit. "I don't think anyone is suggesting that their views are necessarily in every case the right views," Kennedy observed of the PSAC report in a press conference on January 25.¹²

The new president likewise gave priority to politics over science in deciding to proceed with Project Apollo—the program to put an American on the moon before the end of the decade. As skeptics and critics pointed out, Kennedy's announcement in late May of his decision to approve Apollo closely followed not only the Soviets' successful launching of the first man into orbit but also the failed Bay of Pigs invasion of Cuba.[13]

Kennedy's Apollo decision prompted a split in the ranks of PSAC— whose members urged Wiesner in vain to try to talk Kennedy out of the lunar landing. Instead, the science adviser and the president arrived at a *modus vivendi* over Project Apollo, Wiesner claims: "Henceforth, he never called it science; and I never opposed it once he made the decision."[14]

"Undue weight. . ."

With the exception of what priority should be given the space race, the president and PSAC shared remarkably similar views. The White House also enjoyed vital support from the Pentagon's chief scientists, whom Kennedy appointed upon Wiesner's recommendation. That spring, Caltech physicist Harold Brown replaced Herbert York as Director of Defense Research and Engineering; York's former deputy at DDR&E, physicist Jack Ruina, became the new head of the Advanced Research Projects Agency.[15]

Like Eisenhower and Kistiakowsky, Kennedy and Wiesner were eager to find old Pentagon programs to cancel in the interests of economy, a goal they shared with Kennedy's energetic secretary of defense, Robert McNamara. Due in part to the united front presented by the administration's science advisers, Kennedy and McNamara were able to succeed in areas where their predecessors had failed—canceling long-standing and previously sacrosanct Pentagon projects like the B-70 and the nuclear-powered bomber, for example, while at the same time accelerating the development of less vulnerable deterrent forces, like the Polaris submarine-launched ballistic missile.[16]

The nuclear test ban, however, remained foremost in the president's mind. Early on in the administration, McNamara and Deputy Defense Secretary Roswell Gilpatric began meeting with Wiesner twice monthly to discuss progress in verification and other scientific issues related to the ban. One of Kennedy's first acts as president had been to ask the Russians to postpone the resumption of test-ban talks in Geneva from early February to late March, in order to allow time for a reassessment of the U.S. negotiating position.

By choosing John McCloy, a prominent Republican banker and former Eisenhower envoy, to head this reassessment, the new president was quick to show that the emphasis at Geneva henceforth would be on practical politics, not narrow technicalities. Kennedy instructed McCloy, his special assistant for disarmament, to suggest specific American concessions that might facilitate progress in the negotiations. Acknowledging the importance of scientific advice, McCloy appointed past and present PSAC members to the fourteen-member Ad Hoc Panel on the Technical Capabilities and Implications of the Geneva System, and chose James Fisk, Bell Labs president and a founding member of both SAC/ODM and PSAC, to head both this panel and the U.S. technical team about to return to Geneva.[17]

In another move meant to disarm test-ban opponents, Kennedy that February expanded the membership of the Committee of Principals, the top policy-making group on arms control. Henceforth, the committee's permanent roster would include the chairman of the Joint Chiefs—who, during Eisenhower's presidency, had been one of the most effective opponents of a test ban.[18]

Kennedy's choice to head the Atomic Energy Commission—Glenn Seaborg, the Nobel Prize-winning chemist and former chancellor at Berkeley—proved a marked contrast to Seaborg's predecessor, John McCone, on the test-ban issue. At their first meeting, Kennedy informed Seaborg of his feeling that McCone's efforts in the area of the test ban had been "insufficient." Early in Seaborg's tenure, the AEC chairman advised Kennedy against giving "undue weight" to the opinions of the nuclear laboratories, which still steadfastly opposed a test ban.[19]

In order to further strengthen his hand in Washington as well as in Geneva, Kennedy brought together in early March a number of the foremost congressional opponents of a test ban, including the entire membership of the JCAE, to acquaint them with the new U.S. position before it was presented at Geneva. Kennedy assured the senators and congressmen that a test-ban treaty was not an end in itself, but could be the beginning of a long-overdue thaw in the cold war—one that might eventually yield results in other areas, notably Berlin and Laos.[20]

"It does matter that we test. . ."

Predictably, the efforts by Kennedy and Wiesner to negotiate a permanent end to nuclear testing revived slumbering opposition to the test ban.

In early April, the Air Force forwarded to Kennedy a secret RAND study, "Some New Considerations Concerning the Nuclear Test-ban," which concluded that there were "new aspects of the nuclear problem that say, in sum: it does matter that we test."[21] The RAND report had been reviewed and approved by a panel of experts picked by the Air Force, including that service's chief scientist, David Griggs; Edward Teller; and Livermore physicist John Foster.

Among the new arguments given for the resumption of nuclear testing was the claim by the Air Force's panel that the present moratorium "is holding up our own [ABM] program" by making it impossible to test the warhead for the missile in space. The panel also cited the need to develop more "discriminate" nuclear weapons, like the neutron bomb, for tactical use in the event of a war in Western Europe, and the importance of Project Plowshare, a program originating at Livermore for the peaceful use of nuclear explosives.[22] In their own subsequent report, PSAC and Wiesner methodically countered the claims made by the Air Force's panel and contained in the RAND report.[23]

At a meeting with Kennedy on April 22, McNamara confirmed the military's desire to resume testing immediately in order to make further yield-to-weight improvements in existing weapons and to develop a new warhead for the ABM. Nonetheless, McNamara advised the president that, in his personal view, neither argument made a compelling case for abandoning the moratorium.[24]

One of the strongest voices in favor of renewed testing that spring came once again from Congress—specifically, from members of the JCAE.[25] Furthermore, a Gallup poll in July showed that popular sentiment, too, had shifted since the fallout scare of the late 1950s: A clear majority of the public now favored the resumption of nuclear testing.[26]

Following a disputatious summit meeting between Kennedy and Khrushchev in Vienna in June, and the Russians' subsequent threat to abandon the postwar Allied settlement on Berlin—a crisis that culminated in the building of the Berlin Wall that August—Kennedy was understandably reluctant to consider any new concessions at Geneva, where negotiations remained at a deadlock over the Soviets' insistence upon the right to veto on-site inspections.[27]

Still, in the midst of these setbacks to his diplomacy, and with pressures growing to resume testing, Kennedy refused to order Seaborg to begin preparations for the resumption of nuclear testing. Such a step would have signaled to the world that the administration was moving in a direction away from Geneva and toward the ultimate collapse of the test-ban talks. Instead, the president turned once again to PSAC, with a renewed request that its members try to remove the technical obstacles in the way of a test ban.

"Any decisions in the near future. . ."

The charge that the Russians were already violating the testing moratorium was one of those obstacles, and an obvious challenge to the possibility of a permanent test ban. Although three separate studies conducted between 1959 and 1961 by the CIA's chief scientist, Herbert Scoville, had been unable to find any evidence for the Air Force's persistent claim that the Soviets were cheating, the studies had not put an end to the allegation—even within the CIA itself. In 1960, CIA director McCone had branded the doubts Herbert York expressed about purported Soviet violations "practically treasonous."[28]

In June 1961, Kennedy appointed a nine-member panel, headed by Stanford physicist Wolfgang Panofsky, to look into the question of Soviet cheating and other issues affecting the viability of a test ban. In 1958, Panofsky had chaired the Technical Working Group in Geneva, which dealt with the problem of detecting nuclear tests conducted in outer space. Panofsky had looked not only at the technical feasibility of testing in space but

also at its cost relative to its effectiveness. His panel calculated that the liabilities of conducting secret nuclear tests in deep space, or behind the sun or
moon, were likely to be out of all proportion to the results gained.[29]

Panofsky's new panel came to a similar conclusion about the likelihood
of Soviet violations. Not only was the Air Force's case "unproven," Panofsky concluded, but the greater the level of Soviet cheating, the greater the
likelihood that such cheating would be discovered. The panel used similar
logic in countering another argument for the resumption of nuclear testing—the need to develop an effective defense against ballistic missiles—by
pointing out that the proposed American ABM (dubbed Nike-Zeus) would
be far more expensive to build than the countermeasures the Soviets could
use to defeat it.[30]

But the most striking finding of the Panofsky Report was its frank
admission that the question of whether to resume testing ultimately depended on considerations outside the scope of any scientific study. At the heart
of Kennedy's decision, it argued, was a question that only the president
could decide: whether U.S. nuclear strategy should continue to be based on
deterrence or whether it should seek overwhelming superiority that might
make it possible to win a nuclear war by landing the first blow. "Therefore,
any decisions in the near future concerning the resumption of nuclear testing
can be governed primarily by non-technical considerations," Panofsky reasoned. The physicist personally presented his report to the president at a
White House meeting on the future of the moratorium on August 8.[31]

Kennedy evidently found Panofsky's message persuasive, for two days
later the president announced that the chief U.S. negotiator in the test-ban
talks, Ambassador Arthur Dean, would shortly return to Geneva. Dean's
instructions from Kennedy were to investigate the possibility of a threshold
ban, which would not require numerous intrusive inspections. But before
the talks could resume, the Soviet Union's announcement that it intended to
resume unrestricted nuclear testing abruptly put an end to hopes for
progress in the negotiations.[32]

"Diminish danger. . ."

The fact that the Russians resumed nuclear testing at the beginning of
September, only two days after Khrushchev's announcement, was proof of
premeditation in the Kremlin's decision to violate the moratorium. Accordingly, the resumption of Russian testing prompted an outcry in the United
States against Soviet duplicity. As Teller and other test-ban opponents pointed out, the CIA's failure to warn of the moratorium's end in advance hardly
inspired confidence in its ability to detect test-ban violations.[33]

For Wiesner and many PSAC scientists, the fact that the Soviets had
unilaterally decided to resume atmospheric testing did not necessarily mean
that it was in the best interests of the United States to follow suit. Moreover,
PSAC's technical arguments in favor of restraint were supported by political

considerations already evident to Kennedy.[34] In hastily convened meetings at the White House, Wiesner and NSC aide Carl Kaysen urged Kennedy to delay the resumption of testing by the United States—in part so that the administration might reap the maximum political benefit for showing restraint in the face of Soviet provocation.[35]

The president's reluctance to approve the immediate resumption of nuclear testing also reflected a long-standing concern about the health hazards of radioactive fallout—a topic that had often been discussed by Kennedy and Wiesner.[36] Abbreviated notes that the president jotted down on White House stationary during a briefing on the arms race testified to this concern: "We have been the leader. Soviets have dragged their feet. *Diminish danger. Fallout—radiation. Children.*"[37]

Nor had Kennedy, even at this late date, altogether abandoned hope of reinstating the moratorium. That, at least, seemed the aim of the surprise proposal that Kennedy and British Prime Minister Harold Macmillan made to Khrushchev in early September, calling for "an immediate atmospheric test-ban with no inspection." Kennedy and Macmillan wrote a personal note to the Soviet leader, urging him not to explode any more multimegaton bombs in the atmosphere "because of the amount of fallout that would be occasioned thereby."[38]

When Khrushchev failed to respond to the Anglo-American initiative by the September 9 deadline—instead, in the interim the Russians exploded three more bombs above ground—Kennedy still declined to order the resumption of atmospheric testing. Kennedy's decision had the wholehearted support of PSAC and Wiesner, who arranged for Kennedy to meet with Teller, believing that the president should also hear the opposing point of view. Teller urged the president not only to resume unrestricted testing immediately but to embark upon construction of a nationwide system of shelters to protect the U.S. population from nuclear attack.[39]

Yielding to mounting public and congressional pressure, Kennedy had announced on September 5 that the first American nuclear test in almost three years—an underground explosion of 2.5 kilotons, code-named Antler—would take place in midmonth. But he still refused to give the go-ahead for atmospheric tests.[40]

The incentive for the United States to resume unrestricted testing increased overnight when the Soviets exploded a mammoth 58-megaton bomb on October 30. Press reaction in the United States to the Russian test gave credence to reports of a Soviet "superbomb," rumored to be the "spectacular new device" that Senator Henry Jackson had warned Kennedy the Russians might be developing.[41]

Advised by Seaborg that it would be difficult—perhaps even impossible—to keep preparations for the resumption of atmospheric nuclear testing a secret, Kennedy announced in early November that the United States was planning to resume unrestricted testing over the Pacific in the coming months.[42] In order to maintain a close watch over the U.S. testing program, the president appointed Wiesner, Seaborg, and Brown members of a new oversight panel, the Committee on Atmospheric Testing. Whereas Eisenhower had required only that the AEC obtain his permission for a particular series of tests, Kennedy now demanded that the commission get his approval for each of the tests it planned to carry out.[43]

"The Russians might have drawn even. . ."

In addition to the political fallout created by the giant Russian bomb, the headlong nature of the new Soviet testing program, which exploded fifty bombs in almost as many days, reopened the debate over the relative position of the two sides in the nuclear arms race. Analysis of airborne debris from the tests seemed to substantiate PSAC's prediction that continued testing would allow for major Soviet gains. In a meeting with the president on November 20, Wiesner reported that the Soviets had made significant yield-to-weight improvements in their weapons. It was PSAC's "tentative conclusion . . . that the Russians might have drawn even with or passed us in some aspects of thermonuclear weapons."[44]

The renewed Soviet testing program had also very nearly reversed the negotiating positions at Geneva. Once the Russians had completed their own test series they were willing to discuss a ban on atmospheric testing; but the United States, which would not be able to stage its first above-ground test for another six months, was suddenly reluctant to agree to the atmospheric testing ban that Kennedy and Macmillan had proposed in September.

Wiesner was now almost alone in the administration in arguing against the resumption of nuclear testing. His attempt to make a case for unilateral restraint—on the grounds that "the key issue was not whether the United States was equivalent to the Soviet Union in every aspect but whether it was missing anything it needed for its security"—found no support at a Committee of Principals meeting on November 22.[45]

"Complemented, rather than competed with. . ."

While PSAC focused on the test ban, scientists working for the Pentagon—in DDR&E and the Advanced Research Projects Agency—turned their attention to technical concerns that would in the days to come cast a much larger political shadow. One of these was the nation's antimissile program.

In late 1958, while serving on PSAC's antiballistic missile panel, Jack Ruina had recommended that research be continued on the Army's ABM, Nike-Zeus, but that actual deployment of the system be deferred until major problems were resolved.[46] Several of the high-altitude American tests postponed because of the moratorium had been meant to investigate promising new approaches for an antimissile defense. One experiment proposed by ARPA's ABM research program—Project Defender—would test the feasibility of using high-energy x-rays from a nuclear explosion to physically dent and deform enemy warheads in midflight, causing them to burn up on reentry.[47]

The resumption of nuclear testing reopened the ABM debate, with the Army once again urging the Kennedy administration to deploy Nike-Zeus. Eager to ensure that the president listen to both sides on the ABM, Wiesner prevailed upon Kennedy to meet with ARPA-head Ruina—who briefed Kennedy at the presidential compound in Hyannisport, Massachusetts, on Thanksgiving eve, 1961. Ruina argued that an effective ABM was still a long way from deployment, pointing out that neither of the two upgraded versions of Nike-Zeus then under consideration offered much hope for defending American cities. At the end of Ruina's briefing, Kennedy and McNamara decided to indefinitely defer the deployment of Nike-Zeus in favor of research into a new concept for the antiballistic missile, known as Nike-X.[48]

Also adding their voice to ARPA's on the test ban and the antiballistic missile at this time were scientists of the State Department's newly founded Arms Control and Disarmament Agency (ACDA). Established in September 1961, ACDA's work was specifically directed at improving verification techniques and removing some of the long-standing technical obstacles to progress in Geneva. PSAC scientists—including Kistiakowsky—had played a major role in the creation of ACDA. Moreover, since many of the agency's new recruits—including its chief scientist, physical chemist George Rathjens—were borrowed from PSAC and ARPA, ACDA's studies "complemented, rather than competed with" the work of its predecessors in the White House and the Pentagon, in Rathjens' view.[49]

In the spring of 1962, PSAC was given wider responsibility when Kennedy established by executive order, at Wiesner's prompting, an Office of Science and Technology (OST) within the White House. The president's action was in part a response to a recent study by Harvard political scientist Richard Neustadt on the organization of the presidency. According to PSAC Secretary David Beckler, the purpose of OST was to reduce the number of people on the White House staff and to bring the process of science advising closer to the president's inner circle.[50] However, the fact that the science adviser, in addition to being the head of PSAC, was now also the director of OST meant the loss of some autonomy in Wiesner's subsequent view. Thus, whereas the special assistant to the president for science and technology was not required to testify before Congress on account of executive privilege, henceforth the science adviser, as head of OST, enjoyed no such immunity.[51]

"An absolute requirement. . ."

In late April 1962, the United States resumed atmospheric testing with an ABM-related test, code-named Adobe, which was part of the AEC's Operation Dominic. One of forty tests approved by the Committee on Atmospheric Testing out of forty-nine requested by the AEC, Adobe was the first American nuclear explosion carried out above ground since October 1958.[52]

Up to the final days before Adobe, PSAC and Wiesner had continued to urge the president not to resume atmospheric testing. In mid-December 1961, Wiesner wrote to Kennedy arguing that the United States would probably not be giving up much by refusing to test in the atmosphere. DDR&E Director Harold Brown made the same point in a letter to the president a week later, in which he noted that the "strongest arguments" for the resumption of testing concerned weapons-effects experiments related to the antiballistic missile, but "most of what needs to be learned can be discovered by underground tests."[53]

At the end of the month, others were urging Kennedy to cancel Dominic. Just before Christmas, Prime Minister Macmillan also tried but failed to talk the president into postponing the entire Dominic series at a summit meeting in Bermuda. On December 29, Kennedy aide Arthur Schlesinger argued in a memorandum to the president that "the political benefits to not resuming testing would outweigh the military losses." Schlesinger and presidential confidant Theodore Sorensen reportedly worked on a draft of an undelivered speech in which Kennedy would announce a decision to forgo atmospheric testing as an act of unilateral restraint.[54]

Even after the decision to resume underground testing had been made, not all in the administration abandoned hope for a return to the moratorium. In early 1962, Brown and McNamara sent the president a DDR&E report— "The U.S.-U.S.S.R. Military Balance With and Without a Test-ban"—that argued for reinstating the moratorium. Even a temporary end to testing, the report claimed, would have a positive effect on the nuclear arms race, in that technical uncertainties would remain on both sides: "U.S. and Soviet efforts to understand the currently not-well-understood effects of nuclear weapons on communications and radar systems would be severely hampered [whereas] development of anti-missile systems would be slowed somewhat but would not be prevented."[55]

As late as February 1962, when Kennedy called together his key advisers to discuss whether to make another try in Geneva before resuming testing, he was still looking for a way to cancel, or at least postpone, Dominic. "What Kennedy seemed to hope for was some eleventh-hour agreement with the Russians that would make testing unnecessary," Seaborg writes. However, facing more pressure from the AEC, the military, and the public, the president announced in a televised speech that March that the United States would resume atmospheric testing.[56]

Nonetheless, Kennedy evidently had not abandoned hope that the moratorium might be quickly reinstated and testing once again suspended. The test-ban talks began again in mid-March in Geneva, this time under the auspices of the United Nations' Eighteen-Nation Disarmament Committee. At preparatory White House meetings earlier in the month, Kennedy had asked his scientists to suggest minor technical concessions sufficient to jar the negotiations off dead center—but not so significant as to jeopardize American interests or to draw fire at home. Wiesner reported that the Project Vela detection program being developed by ARPA and PSAC scientists—with vital help from the British—had recently made impressive gains in distinguishing between underground explosions and earthquakes. Still, he conceded, there seemed little prospect of further narrowing the gap between the United States and Russia on verification steps anytime soon.[57]

To be sure, that gap had closed substantially since technical talks between Soviet and American experts began under Eisenhower. Initially, the Russians balked at allowing even instrumented stations on their territory, whereas the United States was demanding as many as one hundred intrusive on-site inspections annually. But progress in bringing the two sides closer together had since stalled. For more than a year, the numbers on each side had not changed: The United States was demanding between ten and twenty on-site inspections, while the Soviet Union was unwilling to grant more than two or three. In March 1962, when a new Soviet proposal in Geneva called for a completely uninspected ban, the possibility of agreement diminished further. A PSAC panel that Wiesner hurriedly convened to study the latest Russian offer advised Kennedy emphatically that *"onsite inspection is an absolute requirement for any system."*[58]

"The situation doesn't look any more hopeful. . ."

Kennedy remained stubbornly unwilling to give up hope for the negotiations, even after the Soviets announced a second series of atmospheric tests that June. But in an ironic and wholly unintended way, the resumption of U.S. nuclear testing itself provided part of the impetus needed for a breakthrough in the Geneva test-ban talks.

Thus, AEC scientists were surprised and unsettled by the results of one of the nuclear tests carried out in Operation Dominic.[59] Code-named Starfish Prime, this experiment, specifically designed to help in developing an antiballistic missile, was meant to gauge the effects on communications and radar of a 1.4-megaton explosion 250 miles above the earth. Starfish's electromagnetic pulse unexpectedly shorted out electrical circuits in Hawaii some 800 miles away and damaged the electronics of an orbiting satellite. (At least one U.S. physicist privately worried that such high-altitude tests might alter the earth's magnetic field—an effect, he feared, that would doom many species of migratory birds to extinction.) The AEC's belated realization that Starfish had taken place while a Soviet cosmonaut was in orbit prompted Kennedy to ask for an immediate investigation by PSAC. The committee concluded that, while the cosmonaut was safe, future such testing could threaten spacefarers and might even imperil NASA's plans to put a man on the moon. While relieved to learn that Starfish had caused no permanent damage, the president was said to be "extremely upset" at the AEC's oversight. Kennedy and McNamara decided not to proceed with a third and more powerful test, Urraca, which would have exploded the largest bomb of the series at the greatest height, some 750 miles above Johnston island in the Pacific.[60]

There were also other, more peaceful, developments that provided a spur to renewed efforts in Geneva. In July, Arms Control and Disarmament Agency Director William Foster reported to Kennedy that recent progress by ACDA scientists promised to make verification of a test ban easier, including "achievement of a long-range seismic detection capability which will make it possible to detect events in the USSR from stations outside that country." This new technology promised to reduce by three quarters the number of instrumented stations and so-called "black boxes" necessary to police a test ban, making verification much less intrusive. A second piece of good news was the related discovery that it was less difficult than previously thought to distinguish between earthquakes and underground nuclear explosions in Russia.[61]

Still, these technical improvements fell far short of a breakthrough in verification, as Foster and Wiesner were quick to admit to Kennedy. Moreover, domestic politics muted even the cautious enthusiasm that this good news had generated. When, on the basis of Foster's report, Ambassador Dean announced in Geneva that it might no longer be necessary for the Soviets to agree to instrumented stations on their soil, test-ban foes in Congress protested that the president was granting unilateral concessions to the Soviets—forcing Kennedy to issue a prompt "correction" of the U.S. position.[62]

Although compelled to remain publicly circumspect about the improving prospects in Geneva, Kennedy was encouraged by the progress reports from ACDA and PSAC. That August he decided to drop the number of onsite inspections from twelve to eight—while confiding to Foster that six would be the administration's "rock-bottom number." Lest a leak to the newspapers subsequently rule out further modifications to the U.S. position, Kennedy forbade any number to be written down in planning papers.[63]

However, on August 20, a report to Kennedy from Wiesner—whom the president had meanwhile sent to Geneva to explore the possibility of a diplomatic breakthrough—dashed hopes once again. The "situation," Wiesner wrote, "doesn't look any more hopeful seen first-hand than it does when viewed through cables and newspapers."[64]

"Time might be running out. . ."

As 1962 came to a close, it was probably neither the disturbing results of Starfish nor the encouraging news about verification that most influenced the future of the test-ban talks, but rather a subtly changed attitude on the part of the president toward the Geneva negotiations. As Kennedy began to observe with increasing frequency that fall, "time might be running out" on the test ban. The president's science advisers not only shared Kennedy's new sense of urgency toward the test-ban talks, they were to some extent its inspiration and cause.

Specifically, Wiesner and Kennedy now implicitly accepted what Killian and Kistiakowsky had only belatedly conveyed to Eisenhower and the latter had perhaps been too reluctant to grasp—namely, the fact that science and technology offered no final unchallengeable answer to every technical argument that could be raised against the test ban.

As early as the first meeting of Kennedy's Committee of Principals, in March 1961, Wiesner had emphasized two practical points that were often lost sight of in subsequent discussions of the test ban—"that a *single* clandestine Soviet test would not significantly change the power balance, and that . . . a series of tests could hardly go undetected."[65] Meanwhile, Panofsky's investigation of charges of Soviet cheating had similarly concluded that the likelihood of detecting a Russian violation of the moratorium increased in direct proportion to the instances of cheating. Thus, even if there were only a 5 percent chance of detecting a particular test, Panofsky reasoned, the odds of detecting one test in a series of twenty clandestine explosions approached near certainty.

At the heart of this new pragmatism was a growing appreciation by Kennedy of a point that Wiesner and PSAC argued was paramount—the fact that national security represented a balancing of risks in which the test ban might be a less dangerous course than a continuing, unrestricted arms race. As Kennedy admitted in a July 1962 speech, there could be no technical guarantee that the Russians would not try to cheat, or that a clandestine test might go undetected. But such risks, he argued, "pale in comparison to those of the spiralling arms race and a collision course toward war."[66]

The Cuban missile crisis of October 1962 unquestionably propelled the president further along this line of thought. In the aftermath of the showdown over Cuba, where nuclear war seemed only narrowly averted, there was a redoubling of efforts by Kennedy, McNamara, and Wiesner on behalf of the test ban.[67] But it was a less obvious concern—the growing U.S. fear of a nuclear-armed China—that played the vital role in sustaining the momentum of the test ban talks.

Early in 1963, the CIA warned that China was about to become the world's next nuclear power. Satellite photography revealed preparations for an atomic test being made near Lop Nor in isolated northwestern China. The CIA's experts predicted that the test might even occur before the end of the year.[68]

At a January 21, 1963 meeting of the National Security Council, ACDA Director Foster urged Kennedy to tell the world what he had already confided to Foster privately—that the president wanted the test ban primarily "for its impact on the arms race and on Communist China. . . ." The following day, Kennedy conceded that "if the nuclear test-ban includes only the Russians and the U.S., it is not worth very much." His hope, the president said, was to include the French and the Chinese in any agreement.[69] At a Committee of Principals meeting on February 1, Kennedy reiterated that a major reason for the test ban was to keep China from getting the bomb.[70]

Another spur to the test-ban talks was a Pentagon report that Kennedy received from McNamara the following month, which stated that even an end to testing by the United States and Russia would not be enough to stop the eventual spread of nuclear weapons around the world. The report described the end of testing by the superpowers as "a necessary, but not a sufficient condition for keeping the number of nuclear countries small"—a number that might otherwise include eight more countries by the end of the decade, it warned.[71]

The Pentagon also predicted that a partial test ban which allowed underground experiments by the United States and Russia would only "legitimize this activity" in the eyes of states aspiring to become nuclear powers. In order to truly have a hope of stopping the proliferation of nuclear weapons, the United States, the Soviet Union, "and others, would probably have to employ stronger incentives and sanctions than [have] seriously been considered so far." But the report failed to specify what such steps were or how they might be carried out.

"Hard to find a way out. . ."

Momentum toward a Soviet-American test-ban agreement continued to build that spring—in part because the Kennedy administration seemed resolved not to let esoteric technical arguments on verification, which had stalled the talks in the past, become once again a major obstacle to progress.

In fact, it was no longer the limits of detection technology but rather the fear of domestic political opposition to any concessions that seemed to be restricting American flexibility in Geneva. In the spring of 1963, Kennedy told members of Congress that even if seven to eight on-site inspections were no longer technically necessary to discover Russian cheating, that number might still be needed to ensure Senate ratification of a test-ban treaty. Wiesner—who privately urged Kennedy to reduce the U.S. demand to five inspections—was told by the president that any further reduction would almost certainly face implacable opposition from the Joint Committee on Atomic Energy.[72]

The science adviser reluctantly conceded that politics, not technology, had imbued the number of on-site inspections with a "magic" of their own. Even though there was virtually unanimous agreement among the experts that the rationale behind seven inspections was not only ambiguous, but to some extent even arbitrary, there could be no backing down from that number. A private conversation with Soviet Ambassador Anatoly Dobrynin had convinced Wiesner, he admitted in a report to Kennedy in early May, "that both sides were now so frozen publicly [on the number of inspections] that it would be hard to find a way out of the present impasse."[73]

Curiously, virtually ignored in all the talk about on-site inspections was the fact that the guidelines for even a single inspection had never been worked out fully within the Kennedy administration—much less between the United States and the Soviet Union. Wiesner doubted that the Soviets would ever agree to the "unbelievable expedition" that some American experts had in mind. In his view—and that of PSAC's—it was the fear of the consequences of detection, not the number of on-site inspections, that would be the real deterrent to cheating on a test ban.[74]

"The most dangerous man in the government. . ."

The sudden revival of activity in Geneva naturally focused attention on those who had helped to bring about the most recent round of negotiations. In a speech on the Senate floor that February, one of the most outspoken opponents of the test ban, Connecticut Senator Thomas Dodd, blamed PSAC for persuading Kennedy to give up the neutron bomb in the interests of the ban. As the debate over the test ban heated up in Congress, Wiesner himself also became the target of attack. Missouri Senator Stuart Symington reportedly warned Kennedy that his science adviser was "the most dangerous man in the government."[75]

To be sure, Wiesner had—for better or worse—become closely linked with Kennedy's cause, in the matter of the test ban especially. The science adviser's growing prominence in the pending congressional fight over the test ban reflected his close relations with the president and his equally high standing with Kennedy's top aides. On those occasions when he "lost an argument [with Kennedy]," Wiesner remembered, "it was quickly taken up again by Kaysen or Bundy."[76]

Nonetheless, the final push for the test ban in the late spring and early summer of 1963 was the result of Kennedy's own bold initiative. The president took the first step in this direction in late April when, at Macmillan's urging, he proposed to Khrushchev that the West send "very senior representatives" to Russia to discuss removing the remaining obstacles to a test ban. Khrushchev's acceptance of Kennedy's offer two weeks later paved the way for the visit of the president's personal emissary—former New York Governor Averell Harriman—to Moscow in mid-July.[77]

But even before Harriman's mission to Moscow got under way, the president's June 10 speech at American University's commencement exercises anticipated the coming breakthrough in the negotiations. In his address, Kennedy characterized Geneva as a place "where the end is in sight, yet where a fresh start is badly needed." To prepare the ground for the negotiations, the president announced that the United States would conduct no more nuclear tests so long as Russia exercised similar restraint. In a little-noticed passage near the end of the speech, Kennedy also warned of the dangers of nuclear proliferation.[78]

As momentum continued to gather on behalf of the test ban, the pace of the opposition likewise quickened. Throughout the spring, the Joint Committee on Atomic Energy and the House Armed Services Committee—whose chairman, John Stennis, was a determined opponent of the test ban—conducted congressional hearings meant to cast doubt on the ability of the United States to verify a test-ban treaty with Russia. Antiban scientists like Edward Teller and John Foster were among the key witnesses testifying against a treaty. In June, Teller delivered an impassioned plea to reject the test ban at a breakfast meeting attended by nearly a hundred members of Congress.[79]

As Kennedy and Wiesner recognized, the opposition of Teller and other scientists to the test ban was having a significant effect inside as well as outside Congress. Only four days after his American University speech, Kennedy presided over a Committee of Principals meeting at which McNamara and Rusk warned that it would be impossible to enlist the support of the Joint Chiefs of Staff for a test-ban treaty so long as scientists like Teller and Foster were advising them, in private sessions at the Pentagon, that continued testing was necessary to correct alleged defects in America's nuclear weapons. "Such statements were inaccurate and had to be refuted on the record," McNamara protested.[80]

In an effort to broker this controversy—and to assure domestic support for a test-ban treaty—Wiesner arranged a meeting of the president with Teller and Foster. The result was a fragile consensus, Wiesner believed, and a unanimity that proved to be not only short-lived but was probably always more apparent than real. In any event, Teller's support for even a partial test ban proved transitory.[81]

By the middle of the summer, there were increasing signs that opposition from Congress, the Joint Chiefs, and the nuclear labs to a comprehensive ban on nuclear testing was forcing the administration to consider limiting its goal to a partial test ban that would continue to allow underground testing. A compromise appeared inevitable when conservatives in Congress confidentially advised Kennedy that he would have to abandon his objective of a total test ban if he expected to receive support for a partial test-ban treaty.[82]

The major political advantage of a partial test ban, Kennedy and Wiesner both recognized, was that it rendered moot the unending technical wrangle over seismic verification and on-site inspection. But a limited ban would still allow the development of future nuclear weapons. As PSAC had earlier informed the president, a partial test ban would not have a significant effect upon the arms race.[83]

Ultimately, it was Khrushchev, not Kennedy, who made the choice between a limited or a comprehensive test ban. Yielding, Wiesner believes, to domestic pressures similar to those facing Kennedy, Khrushchev announced on July 2 that the Soviet Union was ready to prohibit nuclear testing every-where but underground. Two weeks later, when Harriman arrived in Moscow to begin twelve days of negotiations—with overtures aimed at extending the talks to include a total test ban—the Soviet leader stood fast.[84]

Hastened, perhaps, by this mutual retreat on the comprehensive test ban, the negotiations in Moscow on a limited ban moved quickly to a conclusion. A draft treaty was initialed on July 25 and signed by Secretary of State Dean Rusk and Khrushchev at a formal ceremony in the Kremlin on August 5.[85]

"The overwhelming majority of informed scientists. . ."

The signing of the 1963 Limited Test-ban Treaty marked the culmination, if not quite the fulfillment, of a six-year effort by PSAC and three science advisers. The signing of the treaty heralded, as well, the beginning of a subtle but fundamental change in the relationship between the president and his scientists. It was no longer as passive advisers but as spokesmen and public advocates that Wiesner, PSAC, and PSAC's alumni lobbied the Senate on behalf of the test ban in ratification hearings that summer. Not since 1946, and the triumphant battle of the "reluctant lobby" for legislation guarantee-ing civilian control of atomic energy, had scientists played such an impor-tant role in Congress.

Kennedy acknowledged the vital importance of the scientists' support by asking Norman Cousins, a leader in the Citizens' Committee for a Nuclear Test-Ban, to persuade Killian and Kistiakowsky to speak in favor of the treaty before the Senate. (Previously, virtually every scientist appearing before Congress had testified against the test ban.) In July, scientists outside the gov-ernment, urged on by Wiesner, issued a press release claiming that "the risk of continuing the arms race without a test-ban treaty is considerably more than the risk that such a treaty might be violated by secret testing."[86]

By summer's end, the ratification hearings before Senator William Ful-bright's Foreign Relations Committee had evolved into a public showdown between pro- and antiban scientists. Despite what Kennedy and Wiesner thought had been an earlier promise of support, Edward Teller opposed the partial test-ban treaty in testimony on August 20.[87] In order to counter Teller, Wiesner paraded a host of distinguished proban scientists before the Senate. In addition to Killian and Kistiakowsky, these included Harold Brown, Herbert York, Glenn Seaborg, and Los Alamos Director Norris Bradbury.

The highlight of Wiesner's—and PSAC's—public relations campaign for the test ban was an August 24 press release featuring an endorsement of the treaty by some thirty-five Nobel laureates.[88] In a final effort, PSAC issued a statement directly refuting claims made by Teller and John Foster in the course of their testimony; it was sent to the Senate on September 10 by National Security Adviser McGeorge Bundy, who wrote Kennedy: "The statement can be used as additional evidence that Dr. Teller is speaking not for the scientific community, but rather against the position taken by the overwhelming majority of informed scientists."[89]

When Fulbright's committee endorsed the limited test-ban treaty by a vote of sixteen to one, the fight moved outside Congress—with a television appearance in early September on "Meet the Press" by Teller, who also spoke against the treaty later the same month at the National Press Club.[90] But even Teller—aptly described during the Senate hearings as "the leading opponent of the treaty"—acknowledged at one point in his Senate testimony that opposition to the limited test-ban treaty was now a doomed rearguard action; at best, a delaying tactic. When the Senate ratified the Limited Test-ban Treaty on September 24, PSAC scientists rejoiced in their long-awaited and oft-delayed vindication.[91]

"The hard decision. . ."

While proud of the role they had played in helping to shepherd the test-ban treaty through the Senate, Wiesner and PSAC were nonetheless disappointed that they and the administration fell short of their goal of a total prohibition on nuclear testing. Many would eventually come to regard the comprehensive test ban as a significant missed opportunity—a view that Wiesner thought Kennedy also shared.[92] Wiesner believed that Kennedy hoped to follow up this limited success with an agreement for a comprehensive test ban in his second term. For the science adviser, as for PSAC, the tragedy in Dallas that November—and Khrushchev's ouster a year later—did not end these hopes so much as defer them to a later agenda.

As Kistiakowsky predicted, Wiesner had broken with the precedent of the "neutral" science adviser and established a new tradition of political activism on the part of PSAC. For his part, Kennedy recognized that on those occasions where politics and science meet—as in the test ban—complex problems may defy technical solutions. The president acknowledged this fact in a speech at the National Academy of Sciences shortly before his death. There he observed that the failure of scientists to "unite in their recommendations to makers of policy [was] only partly because of scientific disagreements. It is even more because the big issues often go beyond the possibilities of exact scientific determination. . . . In the end, the hard decisions inescapably involve imponderables of intuition, prudence, and judgment."[93]

9

"A Nation Cannot Be Built with Gadgets"

Johnson, Hornig, and the Vietnam War

T he hope and expectation of Wiesner and PSAC that the Limited Test-ban Treaty would be carried further in the Johnson administration to include a ban on all nuclear testing was soon disappointed. Thus, Lyndon Johnson's interest in the peaceful applications of science was, if not less ambitious, at least much closer to home. From the outset, science advising in the new administration centered on attaining the Great Society that Johnson proclaimed upon being elected president.

"When the president wants advice. . ."

A few weeks before John Kennedy was assassinated, Wiesner reminded the president of his desire to return to MIT. Wiesner had originally planned to be in the administration for only a few years, but Kennedy persuaded him to stay on until the end of the first term. Upon Wiesner's recommendation, Kennedy had already picked Donald Hornig to be the next science adviser.[1]

A Harvard-trained physical chemist, Hornig had worked at wartime Los Alamos on the trigger mechanism for the plutonium implosion bomb. In 1960, while a professor at Princeton University, Hornig was appointed a member of PSAC and the following year served on Wiesner's Space Panel—where he learned firsthand the responsibilities of a science adviser to the president. Informed by an aide on *Air Force One* that Kennedy wanted his opinion on a NASA project, Hornig said he would submit a written report after the plane landed—to which the aide retorted that Kennedy wanted Hornig's opinion immediately, adding: "When the president wants advice, you had better give him advice."[2]

Shortly after Lyndon Johnson's inauguration in January 1964, Hornig was officially confirmed by the Senate as director of the Office of Science and Technology. The switch from Wiesner to Hornig, like the transition from Kennedy to Johnson, was sudden and dramatic, and the differences between the two men were soon apparent. Press accounts during Kennedy's term described Wiesner as the government's "science czar"; no such status would be accorded Hornig.

Whereas Kennedy had had a natural scientific curiosity and felt at ease with scientists Johnson harbored a lifelong distrust of intellectuals—the "Harvards," he called the braintrust inherited from Kennedy. With the notable exception of Glenn Seaborg, who stayed on as AEC chairman, Johnson's relations with scientists remained distant.[3]

There was another reason why Johnson early on regarded PSAC and its scientists with a certain measure of distrust, if not disdain. While Johnson served in the Senate, and later as vice president, PSAC had opposed some of his pet projects—most notably, the lunar landing mission. "Scientists were a nuisance to him in Apollo," Hornig observed. Wiesner thought the fact that he and other scientists had flocked to Kennedy rather than to Johnson in the early stages of the 1960 presidential campaign also "left some scars." The result, Wiesner said, was that Hornig "had to carry the burden of Johnson's alienation from the scientists."[4]

A forewarning of this alienation had been evident, Hornig thought, shortly after Kennedy's election, when Johnson was appointed head of the Space Council and Edwin Land had attempted to give the vice president the same sort of "pep talk" he had given Eisenhower in 1957. Unlike Eisenhower's enthusiastic response to Land's impromptu lecture, Johnson merely "listened in stony silence," Hornig recalls.[5]

Another example of early conflict between Johnson and scientists concerned Project Rover—a joint effort by NASA and the AEC to build a nuclear -powered rocket engine—long opposed by PSAC. Although Rover was plagued by technical problems and cost overruns, the project remained in Kennedy's budget due, in part, to Johnson's lobbying. Nonetheless, shortly after becoming president, Johnson decided to cut funding substantially for the project. Asked why he was suddenly willing to abandon Rover after so many years of support, Johnson answered—"with," Wiesner said, "an ashamed look on his face—'Because I'm president now.'"[6]

"What science can do for grandma. . ."

Despite his suspicion of intellectuals, Johnson plainly owed a debt of gratitude to PSAC's alumni—particularly Wiesner, York, and Kistiakowsky, who had been the organizing force behind "Scientists and Engineers for Johnson" during the 1964 campaign.[7] In return, Johnson earned the early respect of the majority of the nation's scientists by awarding Robert Oppenheimer the Enrico Fermi Medal in a White House ceremony shortly after becoming president.[8]

Within months of assuming office, however, Johnson's relationship with Hornig became more formal and distant. While Johnson at first continued the tradition of meeting regularly with his science adviser and occasionally with the full membership of PSAC, these sessions increasingly became mere progress reports on the committee's long-term projects. Although Hornig submitted a total of 113 memoranda and reports to Johnson between 1964 and 1968, only a handful of these resulted in action.[9]

The new president also lacked Kennedy's personal rapport with PSAC. "Meetings with Johnson tended to be more like audiences," Hornig recalls. Harvey Brooks, a PSAC member since the Eisenhower administration, thought that Johnson "never really listened to PSAC. Even when PSAC was briefing Johnson, you always felt that he was just sitting there waiting, composing his next speech." Paul Doty, who had joined Kennedy's PSAC, remembered how Johnson once kept the entire committee waiting more than half an hour for a scheduled meeting while he sat alone in the Oval Office.[10]

Excluded from the innermost councils of government, Hornig turned to others in the administration—particularly Defense Secretary Robert McNamara, with whom the science adviser and DDR&E head Harold Brown met twice monthly to discuss military matters and questions related to arms control. As a result, McNamara, not Johnson, became the real audience for PSAC.

As defense secretary, McNamara was also the man to whom the president turned in matters affecting the nation's security. When a breakdown of the northeastern power grid plunged New York City and much of the East coast into darkness on November 9, 1965, for example, Johnson's first call was to McNamara, who then contacted Hornig. The science adviser subsequently telephoned an explanation of the blackout's cause to Johnson at his Texas ranch.[11]

Earlier that year, a telephoned request from the president to Hornig at home led to an all-night series of calls between the science adviser and PSAC's scientists, who together drafted the terms for a joint Japanese-American study program on the diseases of the Pacific Basin before the scheduled arrival of Japan's prime minister the following morning. Johnson was sufficiently pleased with this last-minute arrangement to repeat the performance when the president of Korea visited Washington in 1966.[12]

Johnson and Hornig together planned a major shift in the focus of science advice. Whereas the emphasis of Hornig's predecessors had been on technical issues relating to national security, such as the test ban, Johnson and his science adviser put greater emphasis on applying technology to solving domestic problems—on "what science could do for grandma," as the president said.[13] As a result, during Johnson's first two years, PSAC undertook studies that resulted in reports on the use of nuclear energy in desalting water for irrigation, and on the timely prediction of earthquakes.[14]

Johnson was equally eager to reap the maximum political benefit from OST. "For $18 billion per year," Hornig said the president told him, "there ought to be something to say at least once a week." Johnson repeatedly encouraged his science adviser to make science more newsworthy—ignoring Hornig's protest that science, and scientists, were unsuited to public relations work. "We gave it a try and never submitted anything," Hornig said of Johnson's request for a weekly press release.[15]

"A pointed brush-off. . ."

When the president did not seek their advice, some of PSAC's alumni decided to express their views in another forum. Several of those who played a major role in the test-ban debate during the Kennedy years continued to be outspoken on the subject of the nuclear arms race.

In October 1964, Wiesner and York broke the unwritten rule against former PSAC members speaking out in public concerning a subject on which they had offered advice to the president with an article on the test ban in *Scientific American*. The article attracted attention not so much because of its advocacy of a comprehensive test ban as for its authors' claim that the "clearly predictable course of the arms race is a steady open spiral downward into oblivion." So that there would be no doubt about their views on the arms race, York and Wiesner underscored their conclusion: *"It is our considered professional judgment that this dilemma has no technical solution."*[16]

The message itself probably seemed unremarkable to the public. But as a colleague told York and Wiesner, while virtually every scientist he knew shared their view, they were the first with the courage to put it in italics. The fact that its authors were the former science adviser to President Kennedy and the former chief scientist in the Pentagon provoked criticism of York and Wiesner both within and outside the government, and ultimately prompted a rebuttal in *Scientific American* from antiban physicist Eugene Wigner.[17]

Ironically, it was not the publicly expressed views of York and Wiesner on the comprehensive test ban but a private letter that Kistiakowsky and Wiesner wrote to the president a year later on the subject of Vietnam which brought PSAC's "old guard" for the first time into open conflict with the Johnson administration. The letter proved to be the opening shot of a long and damaging war for both Johnson and his scientists.[18]

In the late fall of 1965, worried by systematic U.S. bombing of North

Vietnam and the first substantial commitment of American ground troops to South Vietnam, Wiesner and Kistiakowsky urged Johnson to reverse the escalating involvement there. Their appeal went unacknowledged—even after they reminded the president that they had served on a science advisory panel to him during his 1964 campaign. "We got what amounted very much to a brush-off," Kistiakowsky later observed. "A pointed brush-off," amended Wiesner.[19]

Kistiakowsky's disillusionment with the Johnson administration had actually begun earlier that year when the president cavalierly ignored the recommendations of the President's Task Force on Preventing the Spread of Nuclear Weapons, on which Kistiakowsky had served. Since the panel's recommendations conflicted with the administration's NATO policy—and because Johnson's political nemesis, Robert Kennedy, had recently adopted the nonproliferation issue—the report of the task force was disregarded by Johnson and later suppressed. Writes Seaborg of the nonproliferation panel in his memoirs: "It was simply consigned to oblivion, and the work of the government in the committee's subject area went forward as though the report had never been written. The time and conscientious effort of distinguished private citizens and a superbly qualified government staff were thus essentially thrown away."[20]

Early in 1966, as escalation of the Vietnam War continued, Wiesner wrote a second letter—this time in conjunction with Roger Fisher of the Harvard Law School—addressing it to Vice President Hubert Humphrey for delivery to Johnson. This second letter, too, received no reply, although "the vice president caught a lot of hell for delivering it," Wiesner recalls. His brief letter-writing campaign left him convinced, Wiesner said, that Johnson was unreachable on Vietnam.[21] In contrast, near the end of his thousand days in office, President Kennedy had turned to Wiesner and PSAC for ideas on Vietnam. But PSAC had been able to offer little in the way of useful advice by the time of the assassination.

Hornig had similar trouble capturing the president's attention. During a January 1966 meeting with Johnson, Hornig—concerned that he and PSAC were becoming almost superfluous in the government—suggested that PSAC help the president win the Vietnam War. Specifically, what Hornig proposed was the creation of a special ad hoc "Vietnam Panel."[22] Later that year, along with the newly formed Vietnam Panel, PSAC's Strategic Military Panel was augmented by several specialized offshoots having relevance to Vietnam—including panels dealing with military aircraft, antisubmarine warfare, and biological and chemical warfare.

Independent of PSAC and Hornig, former Livermore physicist John Foster, who replaced Harold Brown as head of DDR&E in 1965, tried to enlist scientists at the national laboratories, as well as at various think tanks under contract to the Pentagon, into helping with the war effort. In January 1966, Foster and the Defense Science Board proposed the creation of a technical think tank specifically for Vietnam, to be located on a Navy ship anchored off Saigon, where PSAC and other government-funded scientists might go "for perhaps a year at a time." While nothing came of Foster's proposal, it illustrated the high hopes some experts entertained for how science and technology might make a difference in the war.[23]

"We were all conspicuously unsuccessful. . ."

Early proposals for using technology to win the Vietnam War seemed limited only by the imaginations of their inventors. Among the ideas to come from the RAND Corporation, for example, was using flash powder to temporarily blind Viet Cong insurgents traveling supply trails at night. Another, aimed at denying the enemy the cover of darkness, proposed hanging luminescent plastic strips from trees outside villages thought to be likely targets for attack. A far more ambitious scheme for achieving the same effect would have placed giant foil-covered balloons in stationary orbit above Vietnam in order to reflect perpetual sunlight on the jungle below.[24]

Other inventions of the time included chemicals that would turn mud into a jellylike substance to render roads impassible and a "superweed" that would grow so quickly and become so dense as to make the jungle virtually impenetrable. (On an opposite tack was a "superweed-killer," or defoliant, to remove the jungle canopy under which the enemy hid, which proved more practical.) In the fall of 1966, Operation Popeye was initiated—a secret program involving cloud seeding and attempts at weather modification to make the annual monsoons come earlier and stay longer and thereby impede the transport of enemy supplies to the south.[25]

With few exceptions, most early proposals for using advanced technology in Vietnam were either unfeasible from the outset or subsequently disappointing when tried in the field. Thus, a plan for training explosives-laden pigeons to land on North Vietnamese supply trucks went awry when the birds were unable to distinguish friendly from enemy vehicles.[26] A miniature radar and computer for calculating the location of mortar fire, developed by Los Alamos scientists specifically for Vietnam, worked well in the New Mexican desert but proved unsuited for use in the jungle. "We were all conspicuously unsuccessful," former director Norris Bradbury observed of his laboratory's efforts on behalf of the war.[27] Even those efforts initially considered "successes"—such as defoliation—had adverse side effects, the consequences of which would later become apparent.

"Battle of the barrier. . ."

By early 1966, when it was obvious that their appeals to Johnson had been ignored, Wiesner and other PSAC alumni tried another, altogether different approach to de-escalating the war. One of the instigators of this effort was MIT physicist Jerrold Zacharias, who had served on the original SAC/ODM and on PSAC from 1961 to 1964. Zacharias and others of the so-called Cambridge mafia—including Wiesner, Kaysen, and Kistiakowsky—decided that their next appeal would be to McNamara.[28]

While technology might not be able to win the war in Southeast Asia, Wiesner and the Cambridge group argued, it might at least bring about a military stalemate that could lead to peace. In a January 1966 letter to McNamara aide and confidant John McNaughton, these scientists proposed an anti-infiltration barrier—stretching across the demilitarized zone separating North and South Vietnam—to serve as an alternative to bombing of the North.[29] McNamara, who was becoming increasingly skeptical of Air Force claims about the effectiveness of the bombing, was sufficiently intrigued by the barrier idea to meet with Zacharias that March.

The following month, McNamara proposed that the Cambridge group conduct its own study of "technical possibilities in relation to our military operations in Vietnam."[30] Because of the growing antiwar mood on college campuses around the country, Zacharias and his colleagues decided that the usual university affiliation for the top-secret, Pentagon-sponsored study might be unwise. Instead, they proposed that the study be done in cooperation with the Jasons—a group of some forty young physicists who met in secret session each summer to consider defense-related problems for the Pentagon.

The Jasons had their roots in a secret 1958 Pentagon-funded undertaking known as Project 137, an attempt by the Defense Department to attract new talent to the study of military problems. The group was formally brought together for the first time the following year at Los Alamos under the auspices of the Pentagon's Institute for Defense Analyses (IDA), and given the code name Project Sunrise. (The moniker Jason, which the scientists themselves selected, apparently derived from the Greek temple appearing on IDA's logo.) Since 1959, the Jasons had met every summer, usually at a college campus on the east or west coast.[31]

As early as 1961, the subject of Vietnam was a focus of controversy among the Jasons. Some three years later, there was still no agreement on the contribution that scientists might make to the war, and by 1965 Vietnam had moved far down the Jasons' agenda.[32]

Spurred by the first major commitment of American troops, however, the 1966 Jason agenda included a discussion of how to cut the Ho Chi Minh Trail, the main supply artery for the insurgents. The meeting had already been scheduled when Zacharias suggested that his group and the Jasons conduct a joint study of the barrier idea.

The Jasons and Zacharias subsequently agreed to hold two separate sets of meetings, which the leaders of both groups and as many of the Jasons as possible would attend. "Jason East"—actually Zacharias and his Cambridge associates—met at Dana Hall, a private girls' school in Wellesley, Massachusetts; "Jason West" gathered at the Santa Barbara campus of the University of California. Later, the main figures in each group met at Dana Hall to compare results and prepare a single report to be sent to McNamara.[33]

There was general agreement that the joint study, to begin in mid-June 1966, would focus on three specific technical issues in addition to the barrier: the military effectiveness of American bombing of North Vietnam; the reliability of U.S. intelligence statistics on enemy infiltration and casualties; and the use of electronics in the war.[34]

At preliminary sessions with the defense secretary that spring, the Cambridge group and the Jasons learned that McNamara's doubts about the air war and the "body count" had steadily grown. As an alternative to the bombing, McNamara suggested a crude mechanical barrier across the Ho Chi Minh Trail—consisting of chain-link fence, barbed wire, guard towers, and a defoliated no man's land—similar to that originally envisioned by Zacharias. However, estimates were that it might take up to four divisions of ground troops to protect those building the barrier. The Jasons countered with a plan for a much more advanced "anti-infiltration fence," utilizing remote sensors to identify troops and vehicles.[35]

From the outset, relations between the Jasons and the Cambridge group were far from harmonious.[36] The Jasons' "electronic barrier" provoked the most controversy, with disagreement focusing not only on the nature of the barrier but also on its fundamental purpose, according to Gordon MacDonald, a Jason member and senior IDA official. At the heart of the dispute was the question of whether the barrier was primarily intended to be an argument against the bombing or a technological wonder that would help win the war.[37] Thus, behind the seemingly technical argument over whether the "fence" across the demilitarized zone should be a physical or an electronic barrier ran a deeper and more fundamental split among the scientists. "There were," MacDonald recalls, "different views of what was wanted. The Cambridge group wanted a paper that would justify stopping the bombing of North Vietnam. To the Jasons, the study was just a way to look at technical means of hindering supplies going to South Vietnam."[38]

But on other issues, including the effectiveness of the bombing, the Cambridge group and the Jasons were in full agreement. The opening sentence of their joint report for IDA, which was completed at the end of August, confirmed McNamara's worst suspicions: "As of July 1966 the U.S. bombing of North Vietnam (NVN) had had no measurable direct effect on Hanoi's ability to mount and support military operations in the South at the current level." The IDA report went on to charge that the bombing might even be having the opposite of the intended effect—in that it "clearly strengthened popular support of the regime by engendering patriotic and nationalistic enthusiasm to resist the attacks."[39]

The authors of the study were equally pessimistic about the ultimate outcome of the ground war. Since the statistics used to measure progress in Vietnam were highly unreliable, they wrote, "there is currently no adequate basis for predicting the levels of U.S. military effort that would be required to achieve the stated objectives—indeed, there is no firm basis for determining if there is any feasible level of effort that would achieve these objectives."

On the matter of the barrier, the Jasons' viewpoint ultimately prevailed. The IDA study endorsed a high-tech electronic marvel—a far more elaborate, more sophisticated, and more expensive version of the simple fence that McNamara and the Cambridge group originally had in mind. The electronic barrier would have two parts: an array of very sensitive air-dropped sensors meant to pinpoint enemy troop and truck concentrations for immediate destruction by bombing or artillery, and small camouflaged mines—also sown by aircraft along jungle trails—intended to kill or incapacitate enemy soldiers. Zacharias' group, "the elder scientists who were much more politically aware," in MacDonald's words, had opposed giving the Air Force any major role in the barrier for fear that the military would dominate the project.

Not only the technology but also the purpose of the barrier had been subtly, if substantially, transformed. No longer envisioned merely as a tactical innovation or an adjunct to the war effort, the barrier was now promoted as a surrogate for both ground troops and bombing, to be built and maintained at an annual cost judged between $800 million and $1 billion.[40] Novel technologies and futuristic weapons—including remote-controlled helicopters and bomb-dropping drones—would in time be developed to deal with countermeasures, the report predicted, in what was described as a fluid and never-ending "battle of the barrier."[41]

By contrast, the doubts of the Cambridge group remained unaddressed and unresolved. "We were very uncertain of the feasibility of this scheme," Kistiakowsky claimed several years later. "There was a very heated internal debate in August whether we should even present the plan to Mr. McNamara."[42] Nonetheless, the electronic barrier received the endorsement of both DDR&E and PSAC following a briefing of Foster and Hornig at Wellesley, and the report was sent to McNamara at the end of August.

The new barrier concept was explained in detail to the defense secretary on September 7, 1966, in an informal meeting at Zacharias' Cape Cod home.[43] McNamara was "apparently strongly and favorably impressed" with the idea, according to a classified Pentagon history of the project.[44] At the conclusion of the meeting, the Cambridge/Jason study group on Vietnam was officially dissolved, its recommendations having been accepted.

Some eight days later, McNamara ordered DDR&E to establish a Pentagon task force to implement the erecting of the electronic barrier. In a compromise between Zacharias' group and the military, it was agreed that while the task force would be headed by Army Lieutenant General Alfred Starbird, Kistiakowsky and several Jasons would also be members. To ensure that work on the barrier remained, in McNamara's words, "high-priority, top secret, and low profile," the task force was assigned the misleading title "Defense Communications Planning Group."

"The McNamara Line. . ."

What was already known, among the Jasons at least, as "the McNamara Line" was destined not to remain secret long. In July 1967, during a trial of barrier technology at Elgin Air Force Base in Florida, more than five thousand "button bomblets"—tiny packets of explosives designed to make a loud noise for benefit of the sensors when stepped on, but not to wound— were accidentally washed onto neighboring beaches by a freak storm, prompting press speculation that they were part of a secret Pentagon project connected with Vietnam.[45] On September 7, 1967, exactly a year after he had given approval to the barrier, McNamara called a news conference to officially announce the project.[46]

Even before the barrier became fully operational in late 1967, under the code name Operation Igloo White, some of its designers began to discover for themselves how prescient were the objections raised at the Dana Hall meetings. As members of the Cambridge group had predicted, the purpose of the barrier was subtly transformed or, as some believed, sabotaged by the Air Force. Once the McNamara Line was in place, the Air Force—which had initially opposed the project, fearing it might divert resources from the air war—used Igloo White to justify an increase in the bombing campaign, claiming that the sensors allowed them to identify more targets on the ground. Thus, as Zacharias had warned, the Air Force came to regard the McNamara Line as an adjunct—not an alternative—to the bombing. Vehement objections by Zacharias and Kistiakowsky were ignored by the military. Feeling that he and his colleagues were being used by the Pentagon to justify a course of action they found odious, Kistiakowsky resigned in protest from Starbird's task force.[47]

The barrier also sowed seeds of discord between the Jasons and the rest of the American scientific community, and even among the Jasons themselves. One Jason who had taken part in the Dana Hall study, but who had since left the group, denounced the scientists' alliance with the Defense Department as immoral in a lengthy letter to IDA's MacDonald. "Vietnam had now become such a divisive subject that no one wanted to touch it," he later observed.[48] Arguments over U.S. conduct in Vietnam and the contribution of scientists to the war destroyed the collegiality of the Jasons' summer studies and made individual members the target of criticism at scientific conferences in the United States and overseas.[49]

The technical performance of the barrier, as well, ultimately disappointed all but its most ardent supporters. Although electronic sensors played a significant role in repulsing the North Vietnamese attack on the Marine garrison at Khe Sahn in January 1968, elsewhere the McNamara Line failed to live up to expectations. Even after Igloo White was expanded the following April to include the "use of electronic sensors in a wide range of tactical applications," according to a Pentagon history of the project, the barrier neither reduced the bombing of the North nor appreciably slowed the infiltration of North Vietnamese troops and their supplies into South Vietnam.[50]

By spring 1968, the man for whom the barrier had been named was preparing to leave the Pentagon—in part because of his disillusionment over Vietnam but also under pressure from Johnson, who had become annoyed with McNamara's doubts about the effectiveness of the bombing and his growing pessimism on the war. In the meanwhile, the barrier had developed a life of its own; Igloo White was not stricken from the military budget until March 1969, and the Defense Communications Planning Group was not formally disbanded until June 1972.[51]

"Stay away from Vietnam. . ."

Belatedly, and somewhat hesitantly, Hornig and PSAC had also ventured further into the Vietnam quagmire in 1966, shortly after McNamara was briefed on the electronic barrier. Wiesner believed that PSAC's interest in the war was spurred by the intervention of the Cambridge "outsiders."[52] Hornig, on the other hand, claims that until then the message to PSAC from those around Johnson had been, "Stay away from Vietnam."[53]

The president might also have been reluctant to approach scientists for help on Vietnam because many of Hornig's colleagues outside the government had joined the ranks of protesters against the war. In January 1966, some twenty-nine distinguished scientists from universities in the Boston area had signed a statement protesting the government's use of crop-destroying chemicals in Vietnam.[54] Whether by design or default, Johnson remained isolated from the advice of the scientists in the White House—even on what were essentially technical judgments. Despite the profound effect that the 1966 Cambridge/Jason study had on McNamara, for example, there is no evidence that Johnson was ever formally briefed on its findings.

Like the Jasons, PSAC's scientists, too, were quickly disabused of the notion that technology promised a light at the end of the tunnel in Vietnam. In mid-March 1967, PSAC reported to Johnson that it was looking into technological improvements in helicopters, body armor, infantry weapons, booby-trap detectors, and methods for rescuing downed pilots in the jungle.[55] But following a two-week summer seminar at Falmouth on Cape Cod, members of PSAC's Ground Warfare Panel, chaired by Stanford physicist Sidney Drell, had come to the conclusion "that technology played only a peripheral role in pacification as compared to the social, administrative, and policy problems that existed within the South Vietnamese government and between the U.S. and the [South Vietnamese] government."[56] Its Military Aircraft Panel similarly reported to PSAC at this time that "technology can contribute to political and economic growth of the country, but we do not believe that [it can] substitute for effective government organization and honest political programs." The panel concluded succinctly: "A nation cannot be built with gadgets."[57]

Despite this progressive disillusionment, there remained a genuine reluctance on PSAC's part to challenge administration policy in Vietnam. A July 1966 report by the Military Aircraft Panel on the effectiveness of air power in Vietnam ended with a tepid observation on what seemed an implicit indictment of the bombing campaign: "We were concerned that so many of the criteria by which progress is being measured relate to magnitude of effort and reflect little consideration of the actual effect achieved."[58]

Indeed, Hornig's reluctance to confront Johnson on Vietnam became an increasingly contentious issue within PSAC itself. Some committee members who urged the science adviser to point out the folly of the war to the president and his political advisers blamed Hornig's reticence on fear of suffering the fate of the messenger bearing bad news. Hornig, on the other hand, defended his caution as mere prudence—and as necessary lest he and PSAC lose whatever influence they might still have with the president.[59]

In ways that were subtle and some that were not, Vietnam had already undermined Hornig's always precarious relationship with Johnson. The science adviser thought it significant that after 1966 he was no longer invited to the traditional year-end budget review and barbecue held at the president's Texas ranch. Hornig also subsequently confessed to feeling caught between his obligation to serve the president and his duty to represent the views of PSAC's members. As both the war and domestic opposition to it escalated, that conflict became increasingly evident.

"Some trepidation. . ."

The use of nonlethal gases in Vietnam was another issue that forced Hornig to walk a tightrope between Johnson and the nation's scientific community. In 1964, Hornig had defended the administration's use of defoliants in Vietnam against protests by the Federation of American Scientists. By 1967, reportedly after prodding by PSAC members, Hornig himself delivered a petition to Johnson signed by five thousand scientists protesting the government's use of defoliants and incapacitating gases in Vietnam.[60]

PSAC and Hornig unwittingly found themselves in the eye of the storm over the use of gas in the war. A PSAC-initiated study of the possible long-term health effects of exposure to tear gas, inspired by Vietnam, assumed unexpected domestic significance when antiwar demonstrators were being tear-gassed on American campuses. "You couldn't very well make a formal argument that what you would use on your own people at home might be criminal when used against others," Hornig recalls. Not surprisingly, the science adviser did not wish to exacerbate his problems with the president over Vietnam by appearing to side with antiwar protesters.[61]

Hornig's position between the president and the protesters came to resemble Johnson's own dilemma in Vietnam—in that both men felt they could neither resolve their predicament nor abandon it. He remained at his post, Hornig claims, because Johnson repeatedly threatened to put OST under the authority of the Bureau of the Budget, or even to dissolve it and PSAC outright if the science adviser resigned.[62] Hornig, like Johnson, decided to temporize—in this case, searching for a middle ground between the president and the nation's scientific community.

In February 1967, on the same day he delivered the petition against defoliation to Johnson, Hornig wrote a memorandum to the president urging him to "make a statement that we have a 'no first use' policy with regard to chemical and biological warfare, with the exception of riot gases and herbicides." Johnson's pointed refusal to issue such a statement outraged scientists, who directed their anger at Hornig. At the same time, the president was reportedly furious with his science adviser for delivering the petition and writing the memorandum.[63]

By the end of the year, the president's stock with the nation's scientists had sunk so low that Johnson warned Hornig he might not participate, as customary, in the annual ceremony awarding the National Medals of Science—lest one of the recipients "take the occasion to make a scene at the White House." Johnson did, in fact, present the medals, although there remained "some trepidation" throughout the ceremony, Hornig recalls. On another occasion, when one of the scientists he had recommended for membership on a PSAC technical panel "delivered a fierce denunciation of the president and his works from the steps of a university library," Hornig withdrew the man's name from consideration for the post.[64]

"The most pessimistic view yet. . ."

Despite the disappointment of the electronic barrier, McNamara shared with an increasing number of PSAC members the conviction that government scientists might still be of help in ending, if not winning, the Vietnam War. In the latter half of 1967, McNamara asked both IDA and PSAC to report on the effectiveness of the bombing of North Vietnam. McNamara's request coincided with a suggestion from the ad hoc Vietnam Panel that PSAC conduct a comprehensive, interagency review of the bombing which—unlike the 1966 Cambridge-Jason study—would go directly to the president.[65]

Many PSAC members welcomed this opportunity to take a fresh look at the air war, viewing it as a way to strengthen their case against further escalation of the conflict. "By then, there was also a perception that Johnson might be amenable to giving up the bombing," Hornig remembers. The purpose of this latest study, he said, was to give McNamara the "intellectual ammunition to stop the bombing."[66]

McNamara apparently intended to use the new study of the air war as a justification for de-escalating—or at least redirecting—the current bombing effort. According to MacDonald, who chaired the IDA study, what most distinguished the 1967 report from that of the previous year was McNamara's insistence that its focus be broadened to include not only the effectiveness of the air war but also other alternatives: "There were no limits to what could be looked at: the mining of harbors; coastal bombardment by ships; weather modification; chemical warfare."[67]

The IDA study was completed in early fall 1967 and immediately briefed to McNamara—where "it struck a resonant chord," MacDonald claims. Some three volumes in length, the top-secret report was subsequently described by the Pentagon's history of decision making on Vietnam as "probably the most categorical rejection of bombing as a tool of our policy in Southeast Asia to be made before or since by an official or semi-official group."[68] The fact that its authors were unable to see how any amount of bombing in Vietnam might be militarily decisive made it "by far the most pessimistic view yet," MacDonald confirmed. "It made a strong case against the effectiveness—and the potential effectiveness—of the bombing. It said it was unlikely you could make a dent."[69]

The findings of the so-called MacDonald Report were confirmed by PSAC's own bombing study at this time, based largely on information presented in CIA reports and briefings.[70] PSAC members agreed that Hornig should personally present the bad news to Johnson. Hornig's briefing of the president in early January 1968 finally prompted the dramatic confrontation that the science adviser had long labored to avoid.[71]

Both McDonald's report and the PSAC study also figured in what became the administration's final review of its Vietnam policy. In March 1968, following North Vietnam's Tet offensive, the pessimistic assessment of the future of the war by a distinguished assembly of senior political advisers—officially called the Senior Advisory Group, but informally known as "the wise men"—was based in part on the conclusion of both studies that the conflict could not be won from the air.[72] Further, on March 23, when Johnson's speech writer and confidant Harry MacPherson wrote a memorandum to the president urging him to call a temporary halt to the bombing, MacPherson cited the conclusion of the MacDonald Report in support of his recommendation. A week later, MacPherson drafted the portion of Johnson's televised address to the nation simultaneously announcing a halt to the bombing and the president's decision not to seek reelection.[73]

"The poison of Vietnam. . ."

In spite of Hornig's efforts, what the science adviser aptly described as "the poison of Vietnam" inevitably spilled over into PSAC's other dealings with the administration. A case in point was the continuing debate within the government over the ABM.[74]

In 1961, Kennedy and McNamara had narrowly decided against an ABM deployment on the advice of Wiesner and ARPA's Jack Ruina. Since then, the ABM decision had returned several times and in various guises to confront the secretary of defense. Despite improvements in ABM technology, McNamara's reasons for not proceeding with deployment of the weapon remained the same and were preeminently technical in nature. Among them, Ruina notes, was the difficulty of distinguishing between real missile warheads and decoys; the fact that the ABM's radars could be "blinded" by the blackout effect of the first nuclear explosion; and the still unsolved problem of "defending the defense" against being overwhelmed by sheer numbers.[75]

Still, by January 1964, Ruina was worried "that after many years of research and development on missile defense both powers must now be at the point of deciding on deployment." He and Jason Murray Gell-Mann wrote a four-page paper for a Pugwash meeting in India, providing a new argument against the weapon. This time Ruina and Gell-Mann focused not on the technical faults of the ABM but on the fundamental strategic problem of defending against a missile attack.[76]

In their paper, Ruina and Gell-Mann raised the disquieting prospect that even after both sides had spent billions on an ABM, the

> net result would be that the strategic balance would still be maintained but in a much less obvious manner than originally. . . . Population centres would still be vulnerable and populations would still in essence be kept as hostages. Therefore, no substantial gain will have been achieved by either side and yet the cost to each side would be great and the added dangers significant.[77]

As both men were well aware, their case seemed to contradict both military custom and common sense: "Traditionally, one thinks of defensive steps as being reasonable, unaggressive and stabilizing measures," they wrote. The paper's conclusion "that deployment of a ballistic missile defense system may not be desirable [would seem] perhaps surprising to many," the authors accurately predicted.[78]

The paper might have been ignored altogether were it not for a sympathetic response from NSC deputy Carl Kaysen. Furthermore, Ruina and Gell-Mann's argument was given a statistical foundation in a Pentagon study sent to McNamara that same month by DDR&E director Harold Brown. The DDR&E report, on the future of the nation's nuclear strategy but not the ABM per se, expressed doubt that the United States could escape destruction in a nuclear war occurring during the next decade—irrespective of what steps the Pentagon might take.[79]

"The dam was about to burst. . ."

Pressure from Congress and the Pentagon to deploy an ABM remained constant, the discouraging words from PSAC and ARPA notwithstanding. Early in 1964, on the advice of McNamara, Johnson resisted another appeal by the Joint Chiefs of Staff to begin deploying Nike-X, the latest version of the ABM. To buttress his case against the ABM, the defense secretary reportedly sent Johnson the January DDR&E study and reminded him as well of PSAC's consistent pessimism on the subject of missile defense.[80]

Since the early 1960s, PSAC's Strategic Military Panel had met with DDR&E scientists to review the progress of ARPA's ABM research program, Project Defender. "Every year the panel listened to the Pentagon— and every year we wrote a report that advised against ABM," recalled Hans Bethe, who participated in several of the annual reviews.[81] In 1965, on the advice of PSAC, McNamara again advised Johnson to defer Nike-X deployment—this time indefinitely.[82]

But pressure the following year from the Joint Chiefs and Congress forced the ABM issue open anew. In part, the pressure stemmed from official confirmation by the Soviets of what American reconnaissance satellites had been secretly observing for some time—namely, that the Russians were building their own defense against missiles. Thus, in late spring 1966, Congress voted funds to begin Nike-X deployment, even though McNamara had not requested the money and despite the fact that the defense secretary announced he would refuse to spend it on ABM deployment.[83]

Until this time, and on essentially technical questions that were less politically sensitive (such as whether to proceed with development of a supersonic transport plane), Johnson had been willing to defer to McNamara's judgment.[84] But on the issue of defending the nation against a Soviet missile attack—where Johnson had reason to suspect the Republicans of reviving the specter of an "ABM gap" in time for the 1968 election—the president began to move toward a break with McNamara.

In November 1966, Johnson and McNamara held the first of a series of meetings to discuss the ABM and other outstanding defense issues. A month later, in the third and last of these meetings, Johnson conditionally accepted McNamara's offer of a compromise on the ABM. Defying the Joint Chiefs' unanimous recommendation for immediate deployment, Johnson deferred a commitment to Nike-X until after the Russians had been approached about negotiating limits on the nuclear arms race. It was McNamara's hope that these talks might yet make it possible to head off the ABM.

To further support his case against the ABM, the following month McNamara arranged for the president to meet with Hornig and his predecessors as science adviser, along with the former and present directors of DDR&E and the Joint Chiefs of Staff, who remained advocates of deployment. The timing of the meeting was "critical," Hornig remembers, since the budget for the next fiscal year was about to be finalized and "the dam was about to burst" in Congress on the ABM.[85]

Just before the White House meeting, McNamara polled the scientists individually on a proposed alternative to Nike-X—a limited or "austere" ABM deployment capable only of defending against an attack from China, not Russia.[86] He found little support for the so-called anti-Chinese ABM. Assembling in Hornig's PSAC office before trooping over to the White House, the scientists unanimously reaffirmed that they opposed deploying any ABM.[87]

At the Oval Office on January 4, following an endorsement of Nike-X by Army General Earle Wheeler, chairman of the Joint Chiefs of Staff, each of the four science advisers and former DDR&E director Herbert York gave five-minute explanations of why they opposed the ABM. Secretary of the Air Force Harold Brown and DDR&E director John Foster were also present, but remained silent. "In order to avoid possible embarrassment," McNamara told the president he would summarize the anti-ABM views of the two current members of the administration.[88]

Most, if not all, of the scientists at the White House that day left evidently believing that their unanimous stand against the ABM was likely to be the final word on the matter. The meeting was "a successful holding action," in Hornig's view.[89]

"PSAC was not asked for advice. . ."

The letter Johnson sent to Soviet leader Aleksei Kosygin some three weeks after his meeting with the scientists, proposing talks aimed at curbing the nuclear arms race, not only fulfilled the president's half of the bargain with McNamara but also seemed an implicit acceptance of the scientists' point of view. "If we should feel compelled to make such major increases in our strategic weapons capabilities, I have no doubt that you would in turn feel under compulsion to do likewise," Johnson acknowledged.[90] Those who had been at the Oval Office meeting on the ABM were further encouraged when Kosygin agreed to meet with Johnson in the coming weeks to talk about placing limits on the arms race.

But it was not until the following June that the two leaders finally met—in Glassboro, New Jersey, chosen because of its location midway between the Russians' U.N. mission in New York and Washington, D.C. There, despite earnest protestations by McNamara and Johnson that the United States would, if necessary, build new offensive weapons to overwhelm Russian antimissile defenses, Kosygin proved unwilling to abandon the Soviet ABM. Several weeks later, in a tacit acknowledgment of the stalemate at Glassboro, Johnson persuaded McNamara to make good on his half of the bargain by agreeing to proceed with ABM deployment.[91]

But McNamara resisted actually taking that step for several more months. Finally, in a mid-September 1967 speech before an assembly of newspaper editors in San Francisco, he announced the administration's decision to deploy Sentinel, the limited "anti-Chinese" ABM that the scientists had earlier rejected. The defense secretary also stated his determination to make Sentinel the most "austere" ABM possible.[92]

McNamara's announcement stunned those scientists who believed that the ABM issue had been settled at the Oval Office meeting. Wiesner, for example, professed "shock" at McNamara's announcement.[93] Kistiakowsky protested in a telegram to a prominent ABM foe in Congress that McNamara's speech "might have given unintentionally the impression that I endorse immediate start of the deployment of [the] Sentinel thin ABM system." Hans Bethe, who had long been a consultant to PSAC's Strategic Military Panel, which had advised in vain against deploying the ABM, later observed of McNamara's announcement: "It was one time PSAC was not asked for advice."[94]

For PSAC members, Johnson's decision to proceed with the ABM, despite their unanimous advice to the contrary, represented a watershed in relations with the president on a par with Truman's H-bomb decision. Thus, many thought Johnson's ABM decision a vivid sign of the president's disregard for scientists' advice.[95]

The feeling that they had been ignored—or, worse, betrayed—by Johnson and McNamara on the ABM remained strong even among those scientists who recognized that the "austere" ABM defense was perhaps the best that could be expected from an impossible political situation.

Wiesner—hardly a stranger to the rough etiquette of Washington politics—cited his disappointment over Johnson's decision as the reason he "went public" with his opposition to Sentinel in a speech in Santa Barbara shortly after McNamara's announcement.[96] The administration's ABM was not so much "anti-Chinese" as "anti-Republican," other PSAC members quipped. Indeed, Johnson's decision the following year not to seek another term as president underscored for PSAC's scientists just how unnecessary the ABM decision had been, and undoubtedly added to their frustration at being ignored.

Ultimately, like Vietnam, the public ABM debate had a divisive effect upon both PSAC and the American scientific community. ABM opponents within PSAC were accused by colleagues outside the government of remaining silent too long. Hornig came under fire from both sides for refusing to take a public stand on the ABM and for not insisting upon congressional hearings on the weapon.[97] In March 1968, when Bethe and Richard Garwin published an anti-ABM article in *Scientific American*, Secretary of the Army Stanley Resor wrote an internal Pentagon memorandum promising "all practical assistance" to any Defense Department scientist interested in countering the charges against Sentinel.[98]

Wiesner's speech and the article by Bethe and Garwin also raised the question of how far former PSAC members should go in criticizing a policy of the government on which they had offered contrary advice. None of those who publicly opposed the ABM was currently a member of PSAC. Wiesner had resigned in 1964; Garwin left a year later when his term expired; and Bethe had not been a member of the committee since 1959. Yet

Wiesner, as other former science advisers, remained a PSAC "consultant-at-large," and both Garwin and Bethe were occasionally retained by the committee as consultants on specific projects, including periodic studies of the ABM. Hornig later thought the phenomenon of former PSAC members speaking out in public regarding a subject on which they had earlier advised the president "a kind of sea change" in PSAC's relations with the president; one that "raised the question of whether members of PSAC were servants of the president—or would go off like some kind of unguided missile."[99]

In subsequent months, other PSAC and DDR&E alumni spoke out publicly against the ABM on their own or joined members of Congress in opposing the weapon. That July, for example, York, Kistiakowsky, Wiesner, and Bethe sent telegrams to the Senate urging that the deployment of Sentinel be delayed "for a year or more," and that the ABM debate be reopened in congressional hearings.[100]

"Hard to attract the president's attention. . ."

Partly as a result of the ABM and Vietnam, the camaraderie and collegiality that distinguished early relations between PSAC and the Pentagon had largely disappeared by the end of the Johnson administration. Moreover, the Pentagon had by this time essentially supplanted PSAC as the main source of scientific advice on defense issues—as the electronic barrier and Johnson's 1967 ABM decision showed. With McNamara's departure from the Pentagon in the spring of 1968, the president's scientists also lost their only real audience in the Johnson administration and their most valuable ally of the past seven years. As Kistiakowsky complained in a letter to *The New York Times* that May, PSAC's role had been "largely taken over by professional military scientists and those in the aerospace industry and thinktanks."[101] "It was hard to attract the president's attention in the last year," Hornig acknowledged.[102]

With the approach of the 1968 presidential election, the polarization in the country at large over Sentinel and the war in Vietnam was reflected as well within the ranks of PSAC—one of whose members accused his colleagues of using the committee's monthly meetings to lobby on behalf of Democratic candidate Hubert Humphrey, who had taken a stand against the ABM.[103]

But, in fact, a number of the president's scientists were already looking beyond Vietnam and the ABM to the cardinal choices facing the next administration. For these scientists the fact that "technical issues [concerning] the proposed strategic arms limitation talks with the Soviets" were among the items listed in PSAC's October 1968 "Status Report" to Johnson seemed a testament to their earlier efforts, as well as a sign of hope for the future.[104]

10

"No Longer as Adviser but as Citizen"

The Crisis of Science Advising under Nixon and Ford

During the Nixon years, scientists working for the Pentagon almost completely supplanted the civilian advisory role of PSAC. Just as Robert McNamara proved to be the real audience for science advice under President Johnson, National Security Adviser Henry Kissinger was the member of the Nixon administration most interested in scientific advice on topics ranging from arms control to the development of new and more sophisticated weaponry.

"Very sensible and, in fact, enlightened. . ."

Richard Nixon's relations with scientists, like Lyndon Johnson's, usually contained an element of tension. Although President Eisenhower in 1954 credited Vice President Nixon with discouraging Senator Joseph McCarthy from using the Oppenheimer hearings to attack all American atomic scientists, many scientists remained distrustful of Nixon—and suspicious of his motives.

During a visit to the vice president's office in December 1959, for example, Kistiakowsky was surprised to find Nixon expressing views on the nuclear test ban that were "very sensible and, in fact, enlightened." Later, however, Kistiakowsky reflected on the motive behind the call to Nixon's office: "Another reason the vice-president may have had for asking me to his senate office was that on this particular day a herd of photographers were taking pictures of him during all of his activities, and we were duly photographed together and filmed, while both us spoke animatedly." As Kistiakowsky suspected, the picture was later used to promote Nixon's 1960 presidential campaign. "I was not invited again to the office of the vice-president," Kistiakowsky noted in his diary.[1]

The ambivalence that scientists felt toward Nixon while he was vice president carried over into PSAC's relationship with Nixon as president. One PSAC member later characterized Nixon's attitude toward the committee's scientists as "schizophrenic."[2]

PSAC scientists nonetheless respected—if only grudgingly—Nixon's legendary political acumen. Even after his supposed "retirement" from politics following his unsuccessful 1962 bid to become California's governor, Nixon made a point of staying in touch with prominent Republicans in the nation's scientific community—among them, physical chemist William O. Baker, then vice president for research at Bell Laboratories, whom Nixon consulted before running in the 1968 presidential race. During the 1968 campaign, Nixon called for a renewed national effort in peaceful scientific research— the same spirited, if ill-defined, plea that he had made during his first run for the presidency.[3]

Indeed, Nixon acted with almost unprecedented promptness in appointing physicist Lee DuBridge to the post of science adviser on December 3, only a month after winning the election. Nixon's move allayed the fear of PSAC's liberal members that he might pick an archconservative like test-ban opponent Willard Libby and seemed encouraging evidence that there was substance behind the image of the "new Nixon." It also seemed auspicious that the choice of DuBridge was announced at the same time as another key appointment, that of Harvard politics professor Henry Kissinger to be the president's national security adviser.

"The Long incident. . ."

DuBridge was head of the wartime radiation laboratory at MIT and then chairman of SAC/ODM in the Eisenhower administration, resigning just a year before the creation of PSAC. As Nixon pointed out when announcing DuBridge's appointment, he had known the scientist some twenty-two years; when Nixon first ran for Congress from southern California, DuBridge was president of Caltech.[4]

DuBridge, who was sixty-eight when he became Nixon's science adviser, accepted the post with the understanding that he would serve no more than two years. Nonetheless, he looked forward to the position with excitement and anticipation, inspired by candidate Nixon's public promise to improve the strained relationship between the White House and the nation's scientists.[5] DuBridge announced that his first goal as science adviser would be to narrow the gap between the scientific community and the government—a gap that was rapidly becoming a chasm because of the war in Vietnam.

Initially, DuBridge seemed to be making progress toward his goal. In early February 1969, Nixon and DuBridge announced a $10 million increase in funding for the National Science Foundation, the budget for which had lost ground to inflation during Johnson's presidency. Although in percentage terms financial support for basic scientific research did not increase until later in the Nixon administration, the president's announcement was taken by scientists as at least a symbolic move in the right direction.[6]

Yet a hint of the trouble to come was evident even before DuBridge was officially confirmed—when he was pointedly not included among the members of Nixon's inner circle called to the president-elect's suite in New York City's Pierre Hotel to draft position papers on various issues during the transition. A few months later, Nixon also rejected DuBridge's choice of Cornell chemist Franklin Long, formerly a PSAC member and assistant head of the Arms Control and Disarmament Agency, to be director of the NSF. Nixon had let it be known that his veto was prompted by Long's opposition to the ABM program. After news of the incident elicited a popular outcry in the nation's scientific community, the president withdrew his objection to Long, but the latter subsequently declined the post because of the controversy.[7]

In retrospect, what became known as the "Long incident" was a warning to scientists—not only of the trouble to come on the ABM but also of the importance that Nixon and his staff attached to the political views of nominees. The episode seriously damaged the reputation for nonpartisanship that Nixon hoped to establish with the scientific community, and further alienated the president from scientists. As an editorial in *Science* noted, Nixon's treatment of Long accomplished virtually overnight what it had taken President Johnson several years and a war to do.[8]

It was also soon apparent that the new president, like his predecessor, failed to share PSAC's priorities and concerns. Beset, like Johnson, by scientists protesting the government's policies in Vietnam, Nixon made it plain that he intended DuBridge and his scientists to restrict their advice to the domestic realm. With the exception of a PSAC report on chemical and biological weaponry—which reportedly played a role in Nixon's 1969 decision to halt manufacture of such weapons by the United States—PSAC's advice on military matters was rarely sought by the president.[9] Instead, the administration assigned the weapons-acquisition studies that had previously been within the purview of PSAC to DDR&E and the Advanced Research Projects Agency.

PSAC's members were perhaps most disappointed that arms control did not receive a higher priority in the Nixon administration. The Soviet-American Strategic Arms Limitation Talks—which had gotten off to a false start under Johnson and which many PSAC holdovers hoped would be a primary focus of the Nixon administration—were twenty-eighth in line among the national security study memoranda that Kissinger ordered prepared before the inauguration.[10] Instead, it was to the ABM that Nixon and Kissinger first turned their attention.

"Capable of an objective view. . ."

In early February 1969, Nixon Defense Secretary Melvin Laird unwittingly inaugurated the next round of the missile-defense debate by announcing that deployment of Sentinel was to be suspended pending a month-long review of the entire ABM program. Laird made it plain that public protests against the ABM had made the review necessary. Unnerved by the prospect of having nuclear-armed missiles in close proximity—the so-called bombs-in-the-backyard issue—a growing number of ABM opponents had organized protests in cities identified by the Army as possible sites for Sentinel. Even Senator Chet Holifield, conservative chairman of the Joint Committee on Atomic Energy, announced in mid-February that he would oppose Army plans to build an ABM base near his home in southern California.[11]

Nixon's decision on Sentinel underscored the fact that the ABM debate was now on grounds no longer so much technical as political. Laird assigned the task of reviewing the options for the ABM to Deputy Defense Secretary David Packard and DDR&E's John Foster rather than to DuBridge and PSAC—almost certainly because PSAC's anti-ABM views were already well known.[12]

The report that Foster and Packard sent to Nixon and Kissinger in late February recommended that Sentinel be abandoned in favor of a new ABM, which would use components of the old system to offer a limited or "thin" defense of cities—but which had as its primary goal the far less ambitious and more manageable defense of the nation's land-based ICBM force. On March 14, Nixon announced that he would seek additional funding from Congress for the new ABM, dubbed Safeguard.[13]

For the first time in the long history of the ABM debate, PSAC and its scientists had not even been consulted by the government on Safeguard. In making his decision, Nixon announced that he had relied for advice on Packard and Foster and on recommendations from Kissinger's NSC staff. As Foster subsequently acknowledged, he and Packard had also virtually ignored PSAC and its experts in their study.[14]

The two Pentagon officials did not meet with DuBridge and representatives from PSAC's Strategic Military Panel regarding the study's findings until February 26—when the finished report was about to be sent to the White House.[15] It was not until some three days after the announcement of the president's decision to deploy Safeguard that Foster briefed the full membership of PSAC on the weapon.[16]

The fact that the Nixon administration made its decision on the ABM in almost total isolation from scientists outside the Pentagon was reported

by *The Washington Post* on the same day as Nixon's Safeguard announcement, in a leak that was said to have infuriated the president.[17]

A week before the Safeguard decision, the opposition of PSAC's alumni
to the ABM had become a matter of public record in Senate hearings. To
the administration's chagrin, the hearings before Senator William Ful-
bright's Foreign Relations Committee featured a parade of former science
advisers and PSAC consultants who voiced their opposition to the ABM.[18]

Testifying at the opening session of the hearings, James Killian urged
the Nixon administration to create an ad hoc committee of experts, modeled upon his Technical Capabilities Panel, to make recommendations on
the ABM.[19] Kistiakowsky warned that even a limited ABM system "would
be open ended" and "could lead to a continuously expanding system, which
would obviously be a stimulus to a heightened arms race."[20] After Jerome
Wiesner and Donald Hornig expressed similarly negative views on Sentinel,
one senator declared that he was "unable to find a former Presidential science adviser who advocates the deployment of the ABM system."[21]

Herbert York, Hans Bethe, George Rathjens, and Jack Ruina also testified on the technical flaws of the ABM and its potentially destabilizing effect
on the arms race. When, near the scheduled end of the hearings, Nixon
announced his decision for Safeguard, anti-ABM senators ordered the sessions expanded to include testimony on the new ABM system.[22]

The discord between scientists and the administration concerning the ABM
inevitably spilled over as well into PSAC. Like Hornig on Vietnam,
DuBridge increasingly found himself caught between his colleagues on
PSAC and the president on matters related to the ABM. In a last-ditch effort
to salvage some scientific support for Safeguard, the White House on March
17 released a letter signed by DuBridge that defended Nixon's ABM decision. Prior to making the letter public, DuBridge had tried but failed to persuade others on PSAC to sign his statement congratulating Nixon "on the
excellent decision you have made and the clear and thoughtful way in which
you presented it."[23] Although DuBridge later excused the letter as a rushed
effort that had not been carefully thought out by the administration, both
he and the document drew fire from scientists around the country, adding to
the building tension between the science adviser and PSAC.[24]

The ABM controversy also angered Kissinger, who had earlier
expressed doubts to Nixon about PSAC's political allegiance to the administration.[25] The damage that scientists' opposition caused the ABM program
was obvious to both men in late summer 1969, when the Senate approved
Safeguard's initial appropriation by the narrow margin of one vote.

The following spring, when the Senate conducted hearings into the second
phase of Safeguard, former PSAC scientists again played a starring role,
challenging both the feasibility and the desirability of an ABM defense. Senators again questioned the impartiality of the advice the president was

receiving on the ABM, pointing as evidence of the Pentagon's pro-Safeguard bias to a new Defense Department study of the ABM known as the O'Neill Report.[26] The fact that the declassified report was leaked to the press before it could be introduced as evidence at the Senate hearings increased Nixon's suspicions of PSAC's scientists, who were now accused of openly allying with Safeguard's political opponents.[27]

The Nixon administration ultimately won the Safeguard battle, but barely. In mid-August 1970, a final effort to restrict funding for the program was defeated in a fifty-two to forty-seven Senate vote. The narrowness of this margin, and the residual ill-feeling that the battle caused at the White House and among the nation's scientific community, made it a Pyrrhic victory at best for the administration—whose final selling point for Safeguard had been as a mere "bargaining chip" in the Strategic Arms Limitation Talks. As one senator noted during the ABM hearings, the bias shown in Pentagon studies of Safeguard caused him to wonder "whether the [Defense] Department is capable of an objective view of these matters." Another ABM critic argued after the hearings that "the question is whether [DDR&E] and Secretary Laird are right or the overwhelming proportion of the scientific community of the country is right."[28]

Ultimately, both sides lost credibility in the ABM battle: the administration because of the obvious bias of the Pentagon studies; the scientists for being suspected of leaks that proved damaging to Safeguard. The debate also raised questions about PSAC's future in the Nixon administration. For PSAC's scientists, the fight over the ABM seemed proof that Nixon looked to his scientists less for advice than for approval.

"Just about at a point of no return. . ."

While the attention of senators, scientists, and the public was centered on the ABM, the momentum behind another weapon—multiple independently targetable reentry vehicles (MIRV)—was growing.[29] Even before it was first flight tested, MIRV enjoyed the support of a powerful, if unlikely, political alliance consisting of the Air Force, private industry, anti-ABM scientists, and Congress. Because, initially, there was so little debate on MIRV—and perhaps also because he was notoriously uninterested in the technical details of arms control and modern weaponry—Nixon gave most of the responsibility for early decisions on MIRV to his national security adviser.[30]

Eager to educate himself about the complexities of nuclear strategy and modern weapons, Kissinger appointed his own informal panel of scientist advisers within a few weeks of joining the administration. Among them were current PSAC members and consultants who opposed Safeguard, including Sidney Drell, Wolfgang Panofsky, Richard Garwin, and Jack Ruina. Kissinger asked a former Harvard colleague—biochemist Paul Doty, a member of Kennedy's PSAC—to chair the panel. The "Doty group," as it became known, began meeting regularly with the national security adviser on an average of once a month.[31] Kissinger's arrangement with the Doty group was unique in the Nixon administration—many of whose members looked upon scientists as the enemy—but it was also one that essentially excluded the science adviser and PSAC.

The future of MIRV and its implications for the arms limitation talks was an immediate topic of the Doty group's interest and concern, with Ruina being perhaps the first to point out that MIRV held hidden dangers.[32] As early as 1964, Ruina had written to the Advanced Research Projects Agency warning that MIRV—which had initially seemed merely a cost-effective way to counter the Soviet ABM—threatened to upset the delicate strategic balance by giving the side that struck first a potentially decisive advantage. In the letter, Ruina urged that "a systematic study of the implications of MIRV . . . for the U.S. and S.U. arsenals ought to be undertaken."[33]

Although no such study was carried out, an undercurrent of concern about MIRV had nonetheless developed within the American scientific community by the end of the Johnson years—due in part to Ruina's warning.[34] As a member of the General Advisory Committee on Arms Control and Disarmament in the Nixon administration, Ruina also gradually persuaded others on the committee that MIRV might actually prove to be more of a liability than an asset to the United States. Thus, if both the United States and the Soviet Union had MIRVs, the fact that the bigger Russian rockets could carry heavier payloads than their American counterparts would disproportionately benefit the Soviets, Ruina pointed out.[35] Furthermore, MIRV seemed likely to imperil the Strategic Arms Limitation Talks about to get under way. In early August 1968, shortly before the inaugural test flight of the U.S. MIRV, a coalition of anti-MIRV senators and Pentagon officials, backed by newspaper editorials and a petition sent to the Defense Department by concerned scientists, vainly urged that the test be postponed.[36]

Following the success of this first flight-test, Ruina and others in the Doty group still hoped to slow, or even stop, the administration's headlong rush toward MIRV. Many more successful trials would be necessary before the weapon could be considered operational, and estimates were that it would be mid-1971 before MIRV could be deployed.[37]

In the spring of 1969, anti-MIRV forces gained a powerful political ally in Massachusetts Senator Edward Brooke. That April, Brooke met with Nixon to add his voice to those urging at least a temporary halt to MIRV testing. When another MIRV trial in late May—the first of a final round of flight tests—showed that his direct appeal had been rebuffed, Brooke sponsored a resolution calling for a moratorium on future MIRV tests that was subsequently approved by nearly half the Senate.[38]

Public appeals that the administration stop or at least delay MIRV testing were echoed in the Doty group's private meetings with Kissinger.[39] In an urgent proposal sent to Kissinger that June, Ruina and George Rathjens warned that the United States was "just about at a point of no return" with MIRV. If the present pace of testing continued, they wrote, it would soon be too late to avoid U.S. deployment—to be followed in time by Soviet deployment of the weapon. They also pointed out that the Russians were already known to be conducting tests of an ICBM with multiple, nonindependently targetable warheads.[40]

Rathjens and Ruina urged Kissinger to adopt one of two new approaches to MIRV: either an immediate announcement of a unilateral moratorium on flight testing, which the United States would then invite the Russians to join; or "waiting until the Strategic Arms Limitation Talks to deal with the problem as a matter of high priority." In the case of a MIRV moratorium, they argued, the United States could rely on reconnaissance satellites and other sources of intelligence to monitor Soviet compliance. But, whichever option was chosen, quick action by the administration was critical, Ruina and Rathjens emphasized: "Even if a moratorium should perhaps be the first order of Strategic Arms Limitation Talks business it may be too late. Failure to achieve a MIRV moratorium may well foreordain those talks to failure."[41]

Neither Nixon nor Kissinger was persuaded by the arguments for a unilateral MIRV test ban, though Kissinger was reportedly willing to consider linking a ban on MIRV flight testing with progress in SALT. The deployment of MIRV, Kissinger assured Brooke in mid-August, was not "inevitable."[42]

To Brooke, Kissinger argued that U.S. support for a moratorium on MIRV testing hinged on the resolution of two technical issues: First was whether, as the Pentagon argued, the Russians were already testing a weapon equivalent to MIRV in accuracy; second was whether the United States could, as the Doty group contended, reliably detect Soviet violations of a MIRV test ban. Beginning in the spring and continuing throughout the summer of 1969, the debate over these two questions raged behind closed doors in Washington, with scientific opinion in the administration remaining strongly divided.[43]

But to several members of the Doty group, Kissinger's decision to exclude them from the interagency "MIRV Panel" he had established to investigate Soviet progress toward the weapon, and his appointment of a former deputy director of DDR&E to mediate the dispute over the verifiability of a moratorium, effectively doomed the chances for stopping MIRV in any case.[44] Evidently Kissinger had decided the previous spring that he would rather seek a limit on ABM, in view of the "Pentagon's strong stand in favor of MIRV," according to one chronicler of the MIRV decision.[45] Disregarding arguments by the CIA as well as the Doty group, Nixon and Kissinger sided with Foster and the Pentagon in concluding both that the Russians were already testing a "MIRV equivalent" and that a ban on flight testing would not be verifiable.[46] As it had in the case of the ABM, the Nixon administration chose to ignore PSAC in making its decision for MIRV.

"Enormously difficult, perhaps impossible. . ."

By the end of 1969, most opponents of the hydra-headed weapon conceded that it was probably too late to stop MIRV—which continued to be omitted from the agenda of the Strategic Arms Limitation Talks, where American diplomats were specifically enjoined by Nixon from even discussing the possibility of putting restraints on the development or deployment of the weapon.[47]

Nonetheless, as late as January 1970, Garwin was still involved in analyzing the details of a "proposed MIRV moratorium."[48] That March, the GAC on Arms Control and Disarmament, prodded once again by Ruina, likewise urged that MIRV flight testing be stopped. In April, Rathjens wrote to Kissinger again, this time urging that the first MIRVed ICBM, which was about to become operational, "be modified to accommodate a single warhead, or better still cancelled."[49]

Rathjens' renewed plea was, like his first, simply ignored by the administration; little more than two months later what was probably the final opportunity to stop MIRV disappeared with scant notice. On June 19, 1970, exactly a year after Nixon had promised Brooke he would consider a MIRV flight-testing ban, the Air Force deployed the first MIRVed Minuteman. A few weeks later, the Navy tested the first MIRVed submarine-launched ballistic missile.[50] In July 1971, Garwin, at a meeting in Washington with three other weapons experts, conceded that a Soviet-American agreement aimed at restricting MIRV deployment would now be "enormously difficult, perhaps impossible."[51]

The Doty group, although never formally dissolved, simply faded out of existence—apparently with the mutual and tacit consent both of its members as well as of their sponsor—during the early 1970s.[52] Among the reasons for its demise was the fact that Kissinger had meanwhile become Nixon's secretary of state. This new responsibility—coincident with his intimate involvement in the diplomatic opening to China and revived negotiations to end the Vietnam War—left Kissinger "too busy," Doty said, to consult with the scientists.[53]

But other members of the Doty group questioned whether Kissinger had ever intended to listen to their advice. Despite repeated requests, for example, Kissinger never delivered on his promise to arrange briefings for the group on the Strategic Arms Limitation Talks. As Panofsky noted of Kissinger: "He didn't want the scientists to be a formal advisory group or to get too much power."[54] The possibility that they had been used by Kissinger to impart a false aura of scientific objectivity to the administration's deliberations on the ABM and MIRV was acknowledged by several members of the group.[55] Other critics have pointed to the ABM and MIRV decisions as evidence that Kissinger used his consultations with scientists to justify actions they in fact opposed.[56]

Kissinger, for his part, subsequently justified his failure to heed or even to consult PSAC directly about the ABM and MIRV on the grounds that "the process [of advising] was becoming chaotic. For the president to make a decision we had to offer him some general concepts related to our national strategy, rather than make him arbitrate excruciatingly technical controversies."[57]

"Shunted aside. . ."

DuBridge and the members of PSAC were likewise almost entirely ignored by Nixon during the debate over MIRV and the Strategic Arms Limitation Talks. Most notably, the president's science adviser was not included on Kissinger's influential Verification Panel, which provided technical guidance for the talks.[58] Nonetheless—despite the fact that its advice was neither heeded nor sought by the White House—PSAC continued on its own to investigate technical developments related to the ABM, MIRV, and SALT.

PSAC's monthly status reports also reflected the increasing preoccupation of the committee, and the country, with Vietnam. Its February 1969 Status Report noted that a joint report on the war by PSAC and its Ground Warfare Panel had been forwarded to General William Westmoreland, the American commander in Vietnam. The following October, DuBridge released a public statement on behalf of the administration announcing that use of the defoliant Agent Orange in Vietnam would henceforth be restricted, and PSAC's ad hoc Vietnam Panel listened to a classified briefing by strategist Herman Kahn on the performance thus far of Nixon's policy of "Vietnamization." In November, the panel met with former CIA analyst Robert Komer—then director of the administration's Operation Phoenix—to discuss "Phase III Vietnamization."[59]

As Vietnamization began to allow for the withdrawal of American troops, PSAC's interest shifted to future guerrilla wars. Despite, or perhaps because of, the disappointments of the McNamara Line, PSAC's Ground Warfare Panel met for two days in early March 1970 to consider new ideas for an "automated battlefield," as well as "unconventional vehicle propulsion." Following the spread of the war into Cambodia that spring, the Vietnam Panel decided to look at the possibility of "Vietnamizing the Laotian interdiction campaign." However, PSAC continued to have little direct impact on the war in Southeast Asia.[60]

In August 1970, DuBridge announced his resignation, citing age as his principle reason for leaving the government. But the real cause of DuBridge's early departure had more to do with politics at the White House. For many months the decline of the science adviser's importance had become increasingly evident. Originally, DuBridge had held almost weekly audiences with Nixon; now the science adviser could count on seeing the president only on ceremonial occasions, such as Nixon's annual meeting with PSAC. Discursive five-page memoranda that DuBridge continued to send to Nixon were now, confirmed one White House staffer, routinely "shunted aside."[61] Despite the fact that DuBridge had originally planned to stay at his post for two years, he told friends early in 1970 that he would leave the government that summer.[62]

DuBridge blamed not Nixon, but the staffers on the president's Domestic Council—in particular, the aides dubbed the "German shepherds" by the press, Robert Haldeman and John Ehrlichman—for his trouble at the White House. The conflict between the science adviser and Nixon's political advisers had led earlier that year to a showdown over a series of PSAC recommendations on the environment. Since then, DuBridge considered Haldeman and Ehrlichman a major cause of the impasse between the president and PSAC.[63]

Even before DuBridge's departure, the Nixon administration had consulted with a number of senior scientists, including William O. Baker of Bell Laboratories, about a replacement. Nixon's announcement, at his annual meeting with PSAC in September, that he had chosen an electrical engineer, Edward David, as the next science adviser reportedly took not only PSAC but even DuBridge by surprise.[64]

"A practical man. . ."

The choice of David—a forty-five-year-old computer specialist from Bell Laboratories, described by Baker as possessing "the skills of synthesis" and as "a bridge between generations"—seemed designed to smooth relations between Nixon's staffers and PSAC. Although he had never served on the committee itself, David had been a consultant on several PSAC panels. Nonetheless, coming from the world of industry rather than that of academe, David was considered by most of the committee an "outsider." As if to stress that point, Nixon referred to David as "a practical man" no fewer than three times in the brief news conference announcing the appointment.[65]

True to his image, and in contrast to DuBridge, David held no illusions about having close contact with Nixon or much direct influence on administration policies. (The science adviser jokingly referred to his approach as "David's Law: In a closed system such as the White House, influence is conserved.")[66] David also demonstrated a greater degree of political savvy when, as one of his first acts in office, he announced that the Office of Science and Technology would establish closer contacts with the Office of Management and Budget, whose director, George Shultz, had been one of DuBridge's most influential critics in the Nixon administration.[67] When he received petitions from Nobel Prize-winning scientists protesting administration policy in Vietnam, David simply put them in the White House mail bag—instead of hand delivering the letters to the president, as had Hornig and DuBridge. Although a political conservative, David also maintained ties with PSAC's traditionally liberal alumni.[68]

David's pragmatism was equally evident in his readiness to compromise. When, in the spring of 1971, political pressures from Congress and elsewhere led the Nixon administration to propose a multibillion dollar "war on cancer," David supported the program even though he disagreed with its "crusade-like" approach.[69] His knack for compromise also allowed David to reinstate two Apollo lunar missions that were to have been canceled by the administration—but he was unsuccessful in persuading Nixon to pursue a scaled-back, less expensive space shuttle program.[70]

David's practical, businesslike approach seemed to portend a change for the better in the committee's relations with Nixon—as was evident, for example, in the fact that David was invited to meetings of Kissinger's SALT Verification Panel, from which DuBridge had been excluded.[71]

David's appointment was also a notable exception to a growing trend in the administration: the filling of key advisory posts with political appointees. When David Packard resigned as deputy defense secretary in 1971, his replacement was William Clements, a leader in the newly established Committee to Re-Elect the President. Shortly thereafter, Clements—claiming that the military had been lax in pursuing new technological developments—replaced DDR&E head John Foster and likewise fired the director of the Advanced Research Projects Agency, filling those posts with his own men. Clements also subsequently appointed new heads of the research and development branches of the Army and Navy.[72]

With the approach of the 1972 campaign, the brief "honeymoon" between Nixon and PSAC that seemed the result of David's appointment came to an abrupt end. In a move that seemed a further downgrading of the science adviser's role, Nixon that September appointed William Magruder special consultant to the president on technology. The newly created post put Magruder, an engineer and former Lockheed test pilot, in direct competition with David for the attention of the White House. Soon thereafter Nixon picked Magruder to take over the New Technologies Opportunity Program that had been initiated by David and OST as part of their effort to find commercial applications for recent scientific and technological advances.[73]

Distrust and the effects of partisan politics were increasingly evident in White House relations with PSAC. Commissioned by David to calculate the cost of research into high-energy particle physics, Panofsky and a colleague were not allowed to meet with the science adviser in private to present their report, as was customary. Instead, a White House staffer was present to take notes on everything that was said.[74] By the fall of 1972, rumors began to circulate that Nixon intended to abolish PSAC upon his reelection. During the presidential campaign, there was also speculation, which David dismissed, that he would be replaced after Nixon's expected victory.[75]

By his own measure, David's record of accomplishments by the end of Nixon's first term was mixed. As science adviser he was no more successful than his predecessors in persuading the president to take decisive action to stop the spread of nuclear weapons. When he tried to talk to Nixon about nuclear proliferation, David said, he found the president preoccupied with "Vietnam, SALT, and China."[76] David was also unsuccessful in opposing the joint Apollo-Soyuz mission—the rendezvous in space of American astronauts and Soviet cosmonauts scheduled for July 1975—on the grounds that the project cost too much and ran the risk of disaster. Thus, Nixon and Kissinger, who reportedly looked upon the mission as a tangible symbol of the administration's policy of detente, overruled David's objections.[77] On the other hand, David secured the president's approval for a $100 million increase in the NSF's budget, long promised by Nixon.[78]

Indeed, in contrast to the early skepticism with which the nation's scientific community had greeted his appointment, David received generally high marks from critics at the end of nearly three years in office. One former skeptic, writing in *Science,* conceded with perhaps a hint of surprise that David's record in the White House was "not too bad."[79] Said another scientist in his defense: "David is the only thing around to remind Nixon that there *is* a scientific community."[80]

"No longer as adviser but as citizen. . ."

The episode that led to PSAC's demise and the abolition of the post of science adviser traced its origins to the early 1960s and the debate over the supersonic transport, the SST. But its consequences would be felt long after David—and Nixon—were gone from the government.

The controversy over the American SST program began in September 1963, when President Kennedy committed the nation to developing by decade's end "a commercially successful supersonic transport superior to that being built in any other country in the world." Launched at almost the same time as Project Apollo, the SST program soon proved to be, ironically, a more difficult undertaking. Thus, the difficulties with the SST concerned not unproven technology but the less malleable constraints imposed by politics and money.[81]

For all the SST's vaunted technological sophistication, the chief problem vexing the program was simple noise—specifically, sonic booms caused by the shock wave created as the plane flew faster than the speed of sound. The Federal Aviation Administration experts' prediction, in a 1966 letter to McNamara, that "it may be unrealistic to assume that the proposed [SST] will be acceptable to the public in domestic operation" proved to be a prophetic understatement.[82]

By April 1967, when the Johnson administration picked Boeing to manufacture a prototype SST, another study—this one headed by a former airline executive—found there were other "important unknowns" concerning the project. These included whether the SST would be too noisy at takeoff, too big for existing runways, and too inefficient to compete with subsonic airplanes already in service.[83] But the public's concern about the SST's sonic boom remained the greatest obstacle to its development. As was the case with the ABM, a large part of the opposition to the SST came from individuals worried about the impact on their daily lives.[84]

Until the Nixon administration, PSAC had played only a small role in the controversy over the SST, whose most avid supporters were to be found in private industry. But early in 1969, Nixon asked the Department of Transportation to create an interagency SST Review Committee—its members to include DuBridge as well as representatives from the Interior Department, the Pentagon, and the Council of Economic Advisers. Shortly thereafter, DuBridge, with Nixon's permission, created a parallel "ad hoc SST Review Committee" within the Office of Science and Technology, placing at its head PSAC physicist Richard Garwin.[85]

While both reports proved to be critical of the SST, the chairman of the interagency study, Undersecretary of Transportation James Beggs, tried to accentuate the positive about the airplane in a summary he prepared for Nixon in mid-March. The report by the Garwin panel, on the other hand, not only was much more direct in its criticism of the SST program—citing still unresolved questions about noise, commercial viability, and unknown environmental effects—but also went so far as to recommend outright cancellation of the project.[86]

Ignoring the recommendation contained in the Garwin report, Nixon announced at a press conference in September 1969 that his decision was "to go ahead" with the SST.[87] Furthermore, the administration refused to release the text of the Beggs committee's report or any portion of the study spearheaded by Garwin. As a result, the focus of criticism by SST opponents shifted from the airplane itself to Nixon's apparent muzzling of his scientific advisers.[88]

While the Garwin report continued to be withheld from the public and Congress on the president's order, its chief author decided that there was nothing to prevent him from giving his own opinion on the SST as an independent scientist.[89]

Garwin had raised the question of the propriety of a current PSAC member speaking out against administration policy just three days after Nixon's SST decision when he sent a letter to all the SST panel members expressing his views on dissent.[90] "I believe," Garwin wrote, "that the communication in any administration, and in particular in the present one, is sufficiently poor, and the need for education of responsible officials so great, that it is unwise for high-level advisers on publicly-known issues to restrict their advice to one person."[91]

While always careful to note that the opinions he expressed were his alone, and not those either of PSAC or of the SST panel whose report he had helped to write, Garwin's testimony before the Senate and House left little doubt about where he stood on the SST. Drawing from a briefcase bulging with charts and tables—none of which, he took pains to point out, was evidence borrowed from the PSAC SST panel—Garwin spoke of the technological and economic compromises that had gradually transformed the SST into a behemoth that would cost several times original estimates, be too big to use existing runways, and make as much noise at takeoff as fifty 747s, though able to carry only a fraction of the passengers of a single jumbo jet.[92]

Garwin further claimed that the government was guilty of withholding or misrepresenting information on the SST, charging that the data given Congress by the administration was "less than adequate, and in many cases distorted." Magruder, the administration's spokesman, countercharged that "the weight of scientific opinion" contradicted Garwin's predictions of environmental damage from the SST, and accused the PSAC physicist of committing "technical mischief" in his testimony on SST noise.[93]

Despite the furor raised by Garwin's anti-SST testimony, Congress in early 1970 voted funds for the project for another year. But opposition to the SST was not quelled. That summer the influential Federation of American Scientists took a stand against continuing with the SST. Another blow came in September, when a consortium of distinguished economists added its voice to those speaking out against the plane. Six months later, Congress voted to stop funding for the SST. By the time the Garwin report was released to Congress—in August 1971, almost two years after Nixon had given the order to go ahead—the question of building the SST had become moot.[94]

Garwin's decision to act, as he wrote, "no longer as adviser but as citizen," touched off a firestorm of controversy within the administration—a controversy that quickly spread to PSAC, whose members were divided on the appropriateness of Garwin's action. Several former science advisers were critical of Garwin for "going public" against the SST. DuBridge, for example, blamed his colleague's "extracurricular activities," in part, for PSAC's subsequent fate. Hornig considered Garwin's action "entirely out of line," believing that the physicist should have resigned from PSAC before going public with his dissent.[95] Other PSAC members agreed that Garwin should either have refused the invitation to testify before the House Appropriations Committee or at least have resigned from PSAC prior to testifying.

But Garwin also had his supporters in PSAC. Two of those who served with him on the Doty group and on the Strategic Military Panel, Panofsky and Drell, came to their colleague's defense. As Panofsky argued, the fact that a scientist was a current PSAC member should not preclude him or her from advising those outside the committee or the White House—on the premise that "you cannot get good advice if the president owns your opinion before all possible fora." While agreeing that it "was one of those delicate areas where one can never feel at ease or comfortable," Drell said that it is not only possible but also sometimes necessary for PSAC members to "walk a tightrope"—so long as "you don't use on the outside what you've learned on the inside."[96]

While there was similar ambivalence concerning the so-called Garwin incident within the scientific community, the White House reaction to Garwin's dissent was clear: PSAC and its scientists were now regarded as a political liability. "Who in the hell do those science bastards think they are?" asked one White House staffer. "Who needs this bunch of vipers in our nest?" was the response of another. Yet a third member of the White House staff pointedly declared that he now regarded the post of science adviser as "an anomaly."[97] There was one issue, though, that both PSAC and its enemies in the Nixon administration agreed on in the wake of the Garwin incident: As Garwin had argued in a September 1970 letter to David, the "question of what PSAC should be and what it should work on currently needs review."[98]

"Rabi, times have changed. . ."

Nixon's reelection in November 1972 provided the occasion for the move that had been rumored for several months and that some White House staffers felt was long overdue. In what was termed a "restructuring" of his administration, Nixon announced that both OST and PSAC would be abolished outright and that the functions of the science adviser would be transferred to the director of the NSF, H. Guyford Stever. Nixon also made plain that Stever's duties would be considerably more circumscribed than those of the president's science adviser and would not include, for example, any responsibility for advising on matters relating to national security.[99]

For most of its members, PSAC's demise came with little or no direct warning. (Apparently only David was apprised of the approaching storm.)[100] The committee learned of its fate in January 1973 at what turned out to be PSAC's final meeting, when members were told that the resignations they had submitted—as part of the pro forma ritual at the end of any president's term—were, in this case, going to be accepted. Ironically, one of the topics scheduled for discussion that day was how PSAC might improve its relations with the president. When Rabi spoke out about the need for PSAC to take a more active role, DuBridge—who, like Rabi, continued to attend PSAC meetings as a consultant-at-large—interjected, "Rabi, times have changed."[101] Stever, arriving late to the meeting, found its members already filing out of the room. "We've been fired," one told him.[102]

There were—as many PSAC members subsequently conceded—a multitude of possible reasons for Nixon's decision, among which the Garwin incident seemed, in retrospect, only the proximate cause. Stever thought that PSAC had had the fatal misfortune of becoming branded "anti-business."[103] David, on the other hand, believed that PSAC had probably sealed its doom by continuing to offer unbidden advice on defense issues like the ABM and by the scientific community's opposition to administration policy in Vietnam.[104] Whatever the reason, by abolishing PSAC and the post of science adviser, Nixon precluded any future demonstrations of independence by White House scientists.

Contrary to the fear expressed by a *Science* editorial in the wake of Nixon's action that science advising would henceforth be the domain of "young Republican lawyers," a substitute for OST soon grew up in the Nixon administration. Less than a week after the committee's dissolution, Stever and the president's new budget director, Roy Ash, agreed to create a Science and Technology Policy Office (STPO) within the White House to assume some of the functions of the now defunct OST.[105]

Although STPO, like its predecessor, would be able in theory to initiate studies on its own, in reality its independence was severely proscribed. The charter for the new organization, for example, dictated that it would tender advice on military matters only "when requested" by the Pentagon or the National Security Council. The fact that both the Defense Department and the NSC had science advisers of their own meant that in practice there would be little demand for the new agency.[106]

With the exception of Soviet-American scientific exchanges and a good-will visit of his own to Moscow in December 1973, Stever's main responsibility was to advise on domestic concerns—such as improving industrial productivity and agricultural crop yields—and to preside at ceremonial occasions. Although Stever anticipated, in the wake of the fall 1973 Arab oil embargo, that he and the NSF's newly created Office of Energy Policy might be able to play an important role for the president and the country, this was preempted by Nixon's appointment of an "energy czar" and the creation of the Energy Research and Development Agency.[107] Stever's few meetings with Nixon focused on the continuation of the Soviet-American scientific contacts that David had initiated while science adviser.[108] By late spring 1973, with the unraveling of the story behind the Watergate break-in, Stever found the president "extremely preoccupied" with the scandal and later that year feared that Nixon might even be "breaking under the strain." The White House, in any event, had long since ceased being interested in science advice.[109]

"No hope for this idea. . ."

At a gathering in Cambridge of former science advisers shortly after PSAC was dissolved, a majority agreed with Kistiakowsky that the return of a PSAC-like entity to the White House would probably have to await the end of the Nixon administration. "There was agreement that as long as Nixon was president, there was no hope for this idea," Stever recalled.[110]

With Nixon's resignation in August 1974, however, and the swearing in of Gerald Ford, hopes were suddenly raised that both PSAC and OST might be reconstituted. As vice president, Ford had been approached by Stever, William O. Baker, Edward David, and James Killian about reviving PSAC once the government was no longer immobilized by the Watergate scandal. In June 1974, a blue ribbon panel organized by the National Academy of Sciences and chaired by Killian recommended the reappointment of a presidential science adviser. Only a week after his inauguration, in fact, Ford informed Stever that he wished to talk about restoring a science advising apparatus to the White House "in the near future."[111]

But the restoration of PSAC proved to be a more difficult undertaking than either Stever or Ford imagined. When Stever next met with the president, that fall, Ford had decided that in order to quiet fears of a revival of an "imperial presidency" any replacement for PSAC should be established by an act of Congress rather than by executive order.[112] Moreover, as both Stever and Ford were well aware, Congress—reacting to what it regarded as presidential deception over the ABM, MIRV, and the SST—had meanwhile created its own science advisory apparatus for the legislative branch.

Several months before the abolition of PSAC, Congress had tacitly acknowledged both the increasing importance of technical advice and the declining significance of the science advising apparatus in the White House by passing legislation to establish the Office of Technology Assessment. OTA was to provide the legislature with "early indications of the probable beneficial and adverse impacts of the applications of technology."[113] Although theoretically limited to providing information to the members of Congress and to assessing the impact of technology, rather than advising on the broad subject of science, OTA was still, intentionally or not, a partial surrogate for OST and PSAC. The vital difference was that the new agency was created to serve Congress, not the president. OTA also contracted out the studies requested by legislators to scientists at universities and think tanks, much as PSAC had relied upon outside consultants.[114] An early concern of both Ford and Stever was that OTA might step across the narrow divide separating science advice from "technology assessment."[115]

The quest to put a scientist back in the White House hit other snags—most notably, a delay in the confirmation of Ford's vice president, Nelson Rockefeller, with whom Stever was to have worked out details for PSAC's replacement. Accordingly, it was not until the summer of 1975 that the Ford administration proposed to Congress the creation of a surrogate for OST within the executive branch. The director of the new office would be appointed by the president and confirmed by the Senate and thus would become, in effect, the president's science adviser.[116]

The proposed legislation became the subject of heated partisan debate between Democrats and Republicans over which party would have the credit for returning a scientist to the White House. Consequently, it was not until another year had passed that a rudimentary science advising apparatus was reestablished in the executive branch with the creation, in May 1976, of the Office of Science and Technology Policy. Although OSTP was destined to be only a pale shadow of OST, the story of its origins showed the degree to which science advising had become a political issue.

While there was no attempt under the terms of the legislation passed in 1976 to reestablish PSAC per se, Ford implicitly agreed to entertain that possibility in the future by establishing a presidential commission on science and technology, to be chaired by William O. Baker and Simon Ramo, a pioneering aerospace scientist and member of the National Science Board. Thus, one purpose of the Baker-Ramo commission was to explore what might be done to restore a permanent science advisory presence in the White House.[117]

The question of whether PSAC should be reconstituted became an issue as well in the 1976 presidential contest when the claim was made by backers of Ford's opponent, Jimmy Carter, that the three years since the abolition of PSAC had shown the perils of a presidency lacking a science adviser. As Killian and Wiesner had predicted at the 1973 Cambridge meeting of PSAC alumni, the result of PSAC's demise was less a legacy of mistakes made than of opportunities missed and dangers unrealized.

In PSAC's absence, for example, the former members of the Strategic Military Panel, who were among the nation's most knowledgeable experts on defense, played little or no part in the major revision of American nuclear strategy that took place under the direction of Defense Secretary James Schlesinger in 1973.[118] Later that same year, when heavy losses by Israeli tanks and aircraft in the so-called Yom Kippur war surprised Pentagon commanders, former members of PSAC's Ground Warfare Panel pointed to the existence of a classified study, carried out under their auspices several years earlier. The report had predicted that cheap and lightweight antitank and antiaircraft missiles would soon threaten the ascendancy of such weapons on the battlefield. The fact that the Pentagon was caught unaware by these technological developments seemed tacit affirmation, these experts argued, that the government would continue to ignore its scientists at its own peril.[119]

Another kind of technological surprise was the nation's vulnerability to the oil embargo imposed by Arab states in retaliation for American support of Israel in the 1973 war. Earlier, DuBridge and David had independently warned the president of the country's dangerous dependence on foreign oil.[120]

With the approach of the 1976 election, Kistiakowsky and others among PSAC's alumni went so far as to blame not only the "energy crisis" but even unnecessary concern over the outbreak of a swine flu epidemic on the failure of Nixon and Ford to heed the counsel of scientists.[121]

11

"We Want You to Know of Our Judgment"

Science and Conflict in the Carter Administration

Those hoping, in 1976, for an immediate return to what they regarded as the "golden age" of science in the White House were forced to acknowledge that times had indeed changed—and that substantial obstacles now lay in their path. Significant resistance to recreating PSAC came not only from Congress but also from the potential rivals of PSAC within the executive branch itself, where the fear existed that an active and resurgent group of scientists with direct access to the president might threaten the status quo established since PSAC's demise.

"Lacking a counterbalance. . ."

The election of Jimmy Carter in 1976 inspired hopes among PSAC's liberal alumni for a revival of the influence and prestige that scientists enjoyed in the Eisenhower and Kennedy years. The new occupant of the White House seemed a kindred spirit. Carter was the first president since Herbert Hoover with an engineering degree and the only president to be familiar with the technology of nuclear power. Moreover, in the course of his presidential campaign, Carter had spoken earnestly about reducing the number of nuclear weapons—and even eliminating them altogether. This new optimism was reflected, for example, in a *Science* article published two weeks before

Carter's inauguration, which listed Wiesner, Panofsky, and PSAC veteran Lewis Branscomb (then a vice president and chief scientist for IBM) as the three top candidates being considered for the position of science adviser.[1]

But the ebullient mood began to dim in the days and weeks after Carter's inauguration as the post of science adviser remained unfilled. Carter's tardiness in choosing a scientist contrasted with the practice of his predecessors—all of whom had picked a science adviser by the time they assumed office.

Wiesner thought the delay in choosing a science adviser less worrisome than early evidence of the type of adviser the Carter administration was seeking: "I tried to persuade the Carter people that the most important single issue that the science adviser had to advise the president on was the national security issue. But Carter had a bunch of illusions and so did the people around him. He thought he was an engineer." When Wiesner urged the White House to make defense part of the science adviser's role, he said he was rebuffed by a presidential aide— who claimed that Carter wanted his science adviser to do "everything but defense," since "the president understands military things."

Almost certainly another reason for Carter's decision to restrict the role of the science adviser was his recently announced choice of Harold Brown to be defense secretary. Wiesner's prediction that the former director of the Livermore weapons laboratory, secretary of the Air Force, and head of DDR&E was going to have neither the time nor the inclination while defense secretary to also act as Carter's science adviser was, he said, genially dismissed at the White House—as was Wiesner's prediction "that Brown is going to be in kind of a lonesome position, since if he tries to do what Carter wants he's going to be in trouble with the Joint Chiefs of Staff." But without an active and independent science adviser, Wiesner warned, the Carter administration would be "lacking a counterbalance" to the military.[2]

"A long-shot candidate. . ."

Carter's private thoughts on the role of the science adviser were revealed when he invited Frank Press to the Oval Office some three weeks after the inauguration. Describing Brown as his "physics adviser," Carter reportedly explained to Press that he was seeking "another kind of scientist" to serve as science adviser.[3]

Press and Brown came from strikingly similar backgrounds. The two were graduate students together at Columbia, later going on to Caltech, where Press taught and Brown became president.[4] When he received the summons from Carter, Press was a senior professor at MIT, a fifty-two-year-old geophysicist and seismologist who, in 1963, had been the only scientist in the American delegation sent to Moscow to work out the final details of the nuclear test-ban treaty. Press had also written a position paper on earthquake prediction for Carter during the presidential campaign.[5] But according to *Science,* he had always been considered "a long-shot candidate" for the post of science adviser.[6]

Press was quick to recognize the new exigencies of science advising in the wake of PSAC's demise. During testimony at his Senate confirmation hearings, for example, he volunteered an understanding that the science adviser "does operate in a political world and that his work is the work of the government primarily, not the work of science itself."[7] Press also vowed to strive for close relations between the Office of Science and Technology Policy and the Office of Management and Budget, which had not been a priority with most of his predecessors in PSAC. While he had no intention of attempting to revive PSAC per se, Press said, he hoped to call upon "PSAC-like" ad hoc committees of scientists from outside the government—particularly since Carter had informed him that the administration intended to run "a lean White House" and expected Press to do the same with OSTP.[8]

But the fact that Press would not be officially sworn in as science adviser until May 1977 was another constraint upon his influence in the White House. Ironically, the delay was occasioned in part by Carter's desire to have a highly visible swearing-in ceremony for his science adviser. Accordingly, Press joined the administration too late to have much impact on the initial planning for dealing with several major issues, including the American negotiating position in the second round of the Strategic Arms Limitation Talks. But in Press's view, this was an area already "well along and well handled" and hence one where "OSTP could add little of value."[9]

Instead, Harold Brown would serve as the Carter administration's primary consultant on matters relating to arms control and defense. Brown played a central role in Carter's decision, announced at the end of June, to cancel production of the B-1 strategic bomber. The defense secretary-designate had deliberately sidestepped an opportunity to endorse the bomber in his confirmation hearings. Shortly after assuming office, Brown decided that two other weapons then under development by the United States—cruise missiles and the B-2 "Stealth" bomber—looked like better investments than the B-1.[10]

Carter acknowledged Brown's role in the B-1 decision when he wrote in his private journal that the defense secretary had "been very courageous to recommend that the B-1 not be built."[11] As Wiesner predicted, the political outcry that greeted Carter's B-1 decision promptly made both the president and his secretary of defense appear "lonesome" figures in their own administration.

Despite Carter's comment about relying on Brown as his technical adviser in matters relating to national security, the president turned to his science adviser-designate for advice on one particular military decision even before Press's confirmation: the question of whether to proceed with development of an antisatellite weapon (ASAT). Press, like Brown, regarded the development of ASATs as a dangerous trend in the arms race, since they could be used to destroy the satellites that both sides—but especially the United States—depended on for warning of a nuclear attack. Accordingly, the president had raised the possibility of a ban on ASATs in a February 1977 letter to Soviet leader Leonid Brezhnev.[12]

In order to investigate the ASAT question, Press asked for and received Carter's permission to appoint a series of ad hoc PSAC-like panels in the spring of 1977. The first was to assess the comparative standing of Soviet and American technologies in computers, nuclear weapons, outer space, and high-energy lasers. Others dealt with nuclear nonproliferation, biological warfare, and military communications. As a result of these studies, Carter was able to announce early in his term that the United States enjoyed a substantial technological lead over the Soviet Union.[13]

Press's office was also an early source of advice on a technical question that would have a long and tortuous history: where and how to base the MX, the nation's next-generation ICBM. For that purpose, Press convened a "Missile Vulnerability Panel" to examine the claim—being made with increasing stridency by critics of Carter's plans to cut the defense budget—that the nation's land-based ICBM force faced an imminent "window of vulnerability," during which time it would be open to destruction by a Russian missile attack. Press asked the panel, as its first assignment, to investigate the feasibility of a recent Air Force proposal for countering the Soviet threat by putting the MX in long covered trenches in the American Southwest.[14]

In a report to the president that summer, Press's panel pointed out that a trench-basing scheme would make it difficult, if not impossible, for Soviet satellites to verify compliance with limitations on the MX in a SALT II treaty—a fact reportedly behind Carter's decisions in the fall to reject Air Force plans for immediate deployment of the missile in trenches and to cut $100 million from the MX program.[15]

Beyond the question of missile vulnerability and the MX, the science adviser warned of an even greater potential threat facing the nation—and the world. In one of his earliest memoranda to Carter, Press noted the scientific community's growing concern over the possible warming of the planet caused by the "greenhouse effect." The burning of fossil fuels and worldwide deforestation threatened to double the amount of carbon dioxide in the earth's atmosphere by the next century, bringing about a significant rise in temperatures, Press reported. However, because of the political sensitivity of the greenhouse effect—specifically, its potentially drastic effects upon industries worldwide—the issue only became the subject of further study.[16]

More effective was the testimony of Press and an OSTP staff member before the Senate that November in favor of an administration-sponsored bill that would put controls on "gene splicing," or recombinant DNA research.[17] Also recognizing the critical role that basic scientific research plays in identifying promising developments and future threats, Press joined in successfully urging Carter to allocate an additional $100 million for federally funded research, to be divided on the basis of merit among competing proposals from government agencies. Press as well organized a series of meetings to promote cooperation among the federal government, universities, and private enterprise in the area of industrial innovation.[18]

But it was because of the revival in mid-1977 of the controversy over a comprehensive test ban that science advising in the Carter administration faced its first major challenge.

"Environment of distrust. . ."

For nearly fifteen years, since the signing of the Limited Test-ban Treaty in 1963, hopes of halting the testing of all nuclear weapons had been deferred, despite the argument of PSAC scientists that a comprehensive test ban (CTB) represented the next logical step in arms control. In their view, the CTB might induce other nations to sign the Treaty on the Nonproliferation of Nuclear Weapons, which had been agreed to by the superpowers in 1968, but which almost a dozen other countries capable of developing nuclear weapons had yet to endorse.[19] Moreover, CTB advocates argued that only a complete ban on testing could rule out development of new nuclear weapons by the United States and the Soviet Union.

Since 1963, too, there had been dramatic progress toward removing the major technical obstacle to a CTB: the difficulty of detecting small underground nuclear explosions. Because of advances in seismic detection, geologists believed that it was possible to reliably detect—and to distinguish from earthquakes—even "decoupled" underground nuclear explosions of a magnitude down to a few kilotons. As a result, the earlier technical squabbles over decoupling and seismic verification had lost their salience in the test-ban debate.

Furthermore, it was now recognized that the previous often great disparity between American and Soviet estimates of nuclear test yields—which had contributed, Press said, to the "environment of distrust" between the United States and Russia—was the result not of subterfuge and duplicity but of the radically different geology of the superpowers' respective test sites. (Seismic signals created by an exploding bomb traveled much further and stronger through the hard granite common at Soviet test sites like Semipalatinsk, scientists had discovered, than through the porous alluvial tuff predominant at the Nevada Test Site.)[20]

But improved detection techniques were only part of the reason for the revival of interest in a CTB. Changing politics also played a major role. Carter assigned priority to the CTB in a so-called Presidential Review Memorandum, PRM-16, during his first weeks in office. Progress toward a CTB also seemed a priority of the Soviets, who raised the question of a total ban on nuclear testing early in Carter's term.[21]

Significantly, even after the SALT negotiations temporarily bogged down in the spring of 1977—when the Soviets rejected outright a hastily made proposal by the administration for "deep cuts" in strategic offensive missiles—interest in the CTB did not diminish. Negotiations for a comprehensive test-ban treaty among Soviet, American, and British negotiators were begun at Geneva that fall. At the end of several months, both sides had offered concessions on such previously insurmountable issues as on-site inspections and the right to conduct peaceful nuclear explosions.[22]

In order to facilitate progress toward the CTB, Press created another PSAC-like committee in early 1978 to advise Carter on how an end to nuclear testing might affect American security. Press's CTB panel included several PSAC or ARPA alumni: Panofsky, York, and Ruina, among them. Reportedly at the insistence of Department of Energy Chairman James Schlesinger—the most prominent opponent of the CTB in the administration—the directors of the Los Alamos and Livermore national laboratories, Harold Agnew and Roger Batzel, were made ex officio members of the panel. While finding that verification of a comprehensive test ban no longer presented a major problem, scientists on Press's panel soon discovered a new obstacle in the way of the treaty: the argument by Agnew and Batzel that the United States needed to continue testing in order to guarantee the reliability of the nation's nuclear stockpile.[23]

The stockpile reliability argument had been made by opponents of a total test ban as early as 1963, when the CTB had first seemed a possibility, and it was raised again during Senate hearings in 1971 by Defense Department officials opposed to reviving the CTB.[24] In the winter of 1977–1978, when unexpectedly rapid progress in CTB negotiations seemed to increase the likelihood of a treaty banning nuclear tests, the question of stockpile reliability became the dominant technical argument used by critics of the treaty.[25]

The dispute over stockpile reliability that raged in the CTB panel meetings during the winter and early spring of 1978 was both highly technical and highly classified; as such, it lay beyond the understanding, or even the awareness, of the public. Ultimately, treaty supporters—conceding that a total test ban of infinite duration would create legitimate doubts about stockpile reliability—suggested a compromise, which the panel adopted. In its report to Press and Carter, the CTB panel suggested a test ban of five years' duration, after which time both sides would be free to reassess the agreement.[26]

In May 1978, Carter announced that his administration's goal was now a limited-duration five-year CTB treaty. Although the president's retreat meant that the CTB would be more a moratorium than a test ban, even so the idea came under attack from the Pentagon, the Department of Energy, and two of its earlier sponsors—Agnew and Batzel—who wrote a still-classified letter to Press reportedly urging, as an alternative, either a permanent treaty allowing low-yield testing or a shorter-duration moratorium on all testing.[27]

"All or nothing. . ."

In an effort to resolve the dispute over the CTB within his administration, Carter agreed the following month to a suggestion from Schlesinger that he meet with the interested parties in the debate over stockpile reliability. On the afternoon of June 15, 1978, Schlesinger, Press, Agnew, Batzel, Brown, and deputy National Security Adviser David Aaron assembled in the Cabinet Room for a scheduled fifteen-minute meeting with Carter that actually lasted more than an hour.[28]

Agnew, the most vocal participant, asserted that continued testing was integral to the work of the national laboratories, on the grounds that "if you're in the nuclear business, then testing is part of the nuclear business." Supported by Batzel, Agnew urged a compromise—a 5–10-kiloton threshold on nuclear testing instead of an absolute ban. Aaron vigorously opposed Agnew's idea of a partial ban, taking the position that a CTB treaty should be, in Brown's words, "all or nothing." Press, by his own account, remained silent at the meeting by design; he had earlier expressed his views to the president in private. Moreover, as Press admitted, he was also aware of Carter's concern with "the political base that the laboratory directors had in Congress and [the president's] sensitivity not to alienate a fragile base of support for SALT II ratification."[29]

Ultimately, Carter yielded to the CTB's opponents—retreating from the figure of five years to advocacy of a three-year test ban. Agnew subsequently claimed that he and Batzel had "turned Carter around" on the CTB. But both Brown and Press agreed that the president's concern with gaining support for SALT II from the laboratories and the Senate was probably the determining factor in Carter's retreat on the CTB.[30]

Privately, several members of Press's CTB panel criticized Carter for meeting with the chief opponents of the test ban without inviting pro-CTB scientists to counter their arguments. Ruina, for one, ridiculed the notion that Carter's technical background was sufficient to allow him to act as his own science adviser: "Here's two guys who know all about nuclear testing arguing with the president, who only took a year's course at Union College in nuclear power plants. No judge would do that. He should have heard the entire panel and listened to both sides."[31]

For Ruina and others on the CTB panel, Carter's meeting with Agnew and Batzel marked a graphic illustration of the pitfalls awaiting a president in the absence of PSAC. At the Cabinet Room meeting there had been neither an alternate source of technical advice nor a counterbalance to the laboratories and the military. Members of the CTB panel, pointing to Carter's relative inexperience, also argued that the president made a tactical mistake by not insisting on a pledge of support from the laboratory directors for the limited-duration treaty in exchange for his retreat on the CTB, as Robert McNamara had done with the Joint Chiefs during the fight for the Limited Test-ban Treaty.[32]

"Technologically competent but implacably hostile. . ."

The debate over the CTB subsequently shifted to Congress, where the comprehensive test ban became the focus of two days of hearings before a House Armed Services subcommittee in mid-August 1978.

At these hearings, attacks on the CTB from within the administration continued. Physicist Donald Kerr—then assistant secretary of energy for defense and subsequently Agnew's successor as head of the Los Alamos laboratory—testified that a total test ban of even limited duration "would inevitably result in a steady decline of our confidence in the reliability of our nuclear deterrent . . . and risk a steadily growing asymmetry between U.S. and Soviet military forces."[33] When the White House later wrote a letter to the Department of Energy censuring Kerr for breaking with the president's policy, Schlesinger reportedly sent the letter on to Kerr with an accompanying note of congratulations.[34]

Scientists who supported the CTB attempted to rally support for the treaty both in the White House and among the public. That summer, two such advocates—Richard Garwin and Carson Mark—joined Norris Bradbury, Agnew's predecessor at Los Alamos, in appealing to Carter not to abandon the comprehensive test ban. "As individuals long involved in the conception, design, manufacture, test, and maintenance of many of the United States' nuclear and thermonuclear weapons," they wrote in a letter drafted by Garwin, "we want you to know of our judgment on a question which has assumed considerable prominence in connection with the Comprehensive Test Ban Treaty." The letter, also subsequently signed by Hans Bethe, went on to argue that nonnuclear testing and other methods would "provide continuing assurance for as long as may be desired of the operability of the nuclear weapons stockpile."[35] Garwin and his colleagues simultaneously sent copies of their letter to the president, to sympathizers in Congress, and to the Federation of American Scientists.[36]

When Senator Edward Kennedy introduced Garwin's letter into the *Congressional Record* two days later, it provoked an immediate outcry from CTB opponents. Thus, the effect of the letter was to extend the technical controversy over stockpile reliability for the first time beyond the administration to Congress and the public. In reply, opponents of the CTB in Congress subsequently produced letters from Agnew, Batzel, and former Livermore director Michael May in defense of continued proof testing.[37]

Perhaps understandably, the conflicting technical claims about stockpile reliability prompted Congress to complain of outright bafflement. "The principal problem," wrote a member of the House Armed Services Committee, which looked at the question, "is the nonexistence of a body of opinion which is both informed and unbiased." House members and senators, he protested, were caught between "the Nation's nuclear weapons bureaucracy"—"technologically competent but implacably hostile to any form of effective arms control"—and "the Nation's arms control bureaucracy, which to my mind has not exorcised all the objections raised by the treaty opponents." As a way of resolving the dilemma, House members proposed that Carter appoint a presidential commission composed exclusively of Nobel prize-winning American physicists to review the evidence on proof testing.[38]

Lacking an honest and independent broker of the controversy, Congress, too, failed to reach a consensus on proof testing. Instead, the House recommended a compromise on the CTB, urging Carter to seek a 10-kiloton threshold test ban.[39] But this proposal, as well, fell on deaf ears, since Carter had by this time already decided to deemphasize the CTB in favor of SALT II. In September, during a meeting at the White House, the president told Soviet Foreign Minister Andrei Gromyko that both sides should focus on SALT II "first, followed by a comprehensive test-ban agreement."[40]

Both Press and Brown later argued that the president's decision to chose SALT II over the CTB seemed at the time a prudent political judgment. But as a result, the comprehensive test ban never got the endorsement that its supporters had hoped—and, indeed, expected—from Carter's defense secretary and the president's science adviser.[41]

Press's decision not to speak out more forcefully on behalf of the test ban stemmed in part from his recognition of Carter's sensitivity to the political strength of CTB opponents in Congress. But it also originated in Press's own doubts about the wisdom of an indefinite ban on nuclear testing and the fact that stockpile reliability was a subject outside his technical domain.[42]

As defense secretary and as the president's acknowledged "physics adviser," Brown would logically have been the best administration spokesman for the CTB. Furthermore, as a former director at Livermore and a weapons designer in his own right, Brown's assurances on the question of stockpile reliability would surely have been considered authoritative. But Brown, like Press, seemed at best ambivalent about the merits of the comprehensive test ban. His reticence may have reflected as well "residual allegiances" to the national laboratories, thought one member of the CTB panel.[43]

"The shell game. . ."

Before the Senate would consider SALT II, Carter and his national security adviser, Zbigniew Brzezinski, felt that they had to resolve another outstanding technical issue—the fate of the MX missile.[44] Because of the need to garner support for SALT II, there was no longer any serious debate within the administration about whether to build the missile. Instead, the major decision facing Carter was which of two versions of the MX to build, and where to put it. Those most concerned with redressing what they claimed was the strategic imbalance caused by the Russians' continuing military buildup supported the larger version of the highly accurate, ten-warhead ICBM; those who worried more about the future survivability of the MX—and whether the missile could be fit into the framework of SALT II—were advocates of the smaller version, which could be carried by airplanes or missile-firing submarines.

Whereas the original Air Force proposal to base the missile in trenches had been abandoned, in part as the result of the report by OSTP's Missile Vulnerability Panel, the panel could find no support in the government for its recommendation that the MX be carried on specially built airplanes stationed at bases around the country.[45]

Moreover, following the OSTP report, an updated CIA assessment of Soviet missile tests had prompted Brown to reopen the MX question within the Pentagon in the fall of 1977. By year's end, a Defense Science Board panel headed by Livermore's Michael May was considering a mobile land-basing scheme. Early in 1978, an Air Force-sponsored panel endorsed a similar plan.[46]

To make sure that OSTP was not left out of the controversy, Press created a second Missile Vulnerability Panel, with new members, to look specifically at the question of MX basing. The new panel recommended that at least some of the projected force of two hundred MXs be carried aboard airplanes until a land-basing scheme could be found that was both verifiable and offered permanent protection for the missile.[47] Facing conflicting recommendations from Press, who favored the air-launched MX, and Brown, who urged land basing for the missile, Carter chose to defer a decision on deployment.[48]

The revived MX debate inadvertently demonstrated the limitations of what Press called OSTP's "PSAC-like" committees. Neither Missile Vulnerability Panel had the authority to present its advice and recommendations directly to the president. Furthermore, neither panel sought nor was given authority by Press to investigate the broader implications of strategic vulnerability. Yet both panels' members realized that it was difficult, if not impossible, to consider MX basing apart from the more fundamental questions of arms control and nuclear strategy—which remained the almost exclusive preserve of the Pentagon.

What turned out to be the final MX-basing study in the Carter administration was carried out that November, at the president's request, by the Pentagon's William Perry—the mathematician he and Brown had picked to be undersecretary of defense for research and engineering (the new title for DDR&E.)[49] In his report, given to the president some six months later, Perry effectively shot down the idea of air basing the MX by concluding that it might cost as much as $10 billion more than land basing. In the wake of Perry's report, attention shifted again to the ground-based mode favored by Brown, which was given the official title "multiple protective shelters" (MPS)—but was popularly known as the "shell game."[50]

"Political rather than technological grounds. . ."

In the spring of 1979, Brown chaired a series of three meetings of top administration officials given responsibility for deciding the fate of the MX. Out of these meetings came a recommendation for a so-called racetrack-basing scheme, whereby the two hundred MXs would be moved among some five thousand hardened shelters in a ten thousand square-mile area of the southwestern desert via a specially constructed railroad.[51]

A decision to build the bigger of the two versions of the MX under consideration effectively guaranteed that the missile would be based on land, since the bigger MX would be too large to fit into existing submarines or be carried aloft by airplanes. Brzezinski was reportedly the decisive advocate for the bigger missile—for reasons that were, he later acknowledged, more "geopolitical" than technical, reflecting his concern not only for SALT II, but also for how the MX decision would be viewed by the Russians.[52]

Press, although still in favor of air basing, chose not to present his case to Carter personally, a decision the science adviser would later regret.[53] Brown sided with the Defense Department and with Brzezinski's geopolitical arguments.[54] In early June, at the end of two climactic National Security Council meetings on the MX, the president agreed to proceed with the bigger land-based MX—later confiding his doubts about the decision to his private journal.[55]

To Carter, the MX decision was an admittedly flawed resolution to an unresolved political and technological problem. Despite earnest pronouncements at the start of his presidency about reducing the number of nuclear weapons, his choice on the MX had had the opposite effect. "Whatever the argument," wrote one chronicler of the MX decision, "the fact was that the allegedly dovish Carter administration, with the concurrence of virtually all its important members except CIA director Stansfield Turner and science adviser Frank Press, had gone ahead and approved the biggest addition to the American nuclear arsenal since the MIRVing program of the early seventies."[56]

Those who had advised Carter unanimously affirmed that domestic and international political considerations underlay the president's decision on the MX. As Perry subsequently observed with respect to the MX, "geopolitical arguments outweighed the technical arguments."[57] Brown believed this to be the case not only in the MX decision but in the other cardinal choices made by the Carter administration: "The technical arguments on both (or all) sides of each of those issues were less weighty than the political ones."[58] The fact that the MX—like "most of the national security issues" of the Carter administration—was "decided on political rather than technological grounds, [represented] a deliberate choice and judgment of this particular President," claimed Press.[59]

In the aftermath of the MX decision, opponents of the missile faulted not only the president's choice but also the advisory process that led up to it. As former PSAC consultant Herbert Scoville pointed out, the many and various studies of the MX carried out in the Carter administration had been limited to highly technical analyses of possible modes of deployment, while the larger question of whether the missile should be built at all never received the hearing it deserved.[60]

The MX and its racetrack also came under immediate attack in Congress—where critics objected not only to the missile's cost and its impact on the environment but also to the destabilizing effect the MX might have on the arms race.[61] Clearly unable to affect events within the White House, Garwin and Drell, both of whom had served as consultants to either OSTP or the Defense Department on the MX, publicly disparaged the racetrack-basing plan as "clumsy" and "vulnerable" in comments to the press.[62]

In February 1979, in testimony before the House Armed Services Committee, Garwin proposed what he and Drell claimed was a practical alternative to the MX: putting at least some of the nation's Minuteman ICBM force on board a fleet of small, specially designed diesel-powered submarines that would patrol the deep waters along America's coastline.[63]

The origins of the basing scheme, which Garwin and Drell nicknamed SUM (for "shallow underwater mobile"), were in a mid-1960s Pentagon study; the two had revived the concept at a 1978 meeting of the Jasons. Garwin had also promoted SUM while serving on Press's first Missile Vulnerability Panel and later as a member of a panel dealing specifically with the MX; Drell had pursued it as chairman of another Pentagon-funded study of ICBM vulnerability in 1978. When the administration announced its decision for the big MX in June 1979, Garwin and Drell pointed out that SUM's submarines could carry the new missile in lieu of Minuteman.[64]

In correspondence that fall with senior Pentagon officials and Senate opponents of the MX—who subsequently introduced the letters into the *Congressional Record*—Garwin and Drell responded to the technical arguments and objections to SUM raised by Perry and Air Force representatives. Garwin's frustration grew on learning that opposition to SUM in the Defense Department was based not upon technical grounds but on the same geopolitical and psychological considerations that had led to the bigger MX—specifically, the Pentagon's insistence on having a land-based missile and Brown's argument that abandoning the land-based MX would concede "an important perceptual advantage to the Soviets, a dangerously misleading signal."[65]

Stymied in their approach to the Pentagon, and believing that the Senate would be too slow to stop the racetrack, Garwin and Drell arranged through a sympathetic congressman to brief Brzezinski on the advantages of SUM in early February 1980. But what the two considered their last chance to stop MX and the racetrack disappeared later that year, during Carter's reelection campaign, when criticisms of the administration's foreign and military policies caused Brzezinski to renege on his promise to arrange a similar briefing for the president. Already under attack for his decision on the B-1 and the neutron bomb, Carter was understandably reluctant to reopen the MX debate, whatever the technical merits of the case.[66]

"More research was necessary. . ."

There were other, and more subtle, ways that political considerations showed their dominance over scientific judgment in the Carter administration. For example, concern with maintaining the reputation of the United States as a reliable supplier of fuel for nuclear reactors took precedence over action to discourage nuclear proliferation when the Carter administration decided to continue selling enriched uranium to India—despite evidence that the Indians had, contrary to their assurances, used reprocessed spent reactor fuel for the nuclear device they exploded in 1974.[67] Press and OSTP reluctantly endorsed the argument of the State Department and the Department of Energy that the United States had a better chance of influencing the international nuclear regime by selling India the enriched uranium than by quixotic attempts at stopping the spread of nuclear weapons.[68]

Science was also sometimes used as a tool—or a weapon—of diplomacy in the Carter administration. When Brzezinski learned of Press's plans to lead an American scientific delegation to China in the summer of 1979 as part of an exchange agreement, the national security adviser changed the scheduling of the visit so that it would take place immediately following a similar trip by Press to Russia. The close timing of the China visit would "really send a powerful signal" to the Russians, Brzezinski wrote in his personal journal.[69] Carter later canceled Press's visit to the Soviet Union to protest the Russians' handling of political dissidents; the trip to China took place on schedule.[70]

One area in which Press and OSTP expected to play a larger role—that of technical adviser on energy policy—was preempted by the Office of Energy Research of the Department of Energy, which Carter established shortly after assuming office. Except for the so-called energy summit—which took place in early July 1979 at Camp David, and to which the president invited a large number of experts and advisers, including Jerome Wiesner—OSTP was rarely called upon to advise on an issue of increasing concern to many of its scientists.[71]

Nonetheless, on numerous other occasions Carter depended on Press and OSTP for technical advice or to broker a dispute between rival government agencies. In one instance, the science adviser was called upon to adjudicate a feud between the Defense Department and the CIA over reconnaissance satellites.[72] OSTP also investigated at Carter's request the March 1979 nuclear reactor accident at Pennsylvania's Three Mile Island. A mysterious flash of light observed by a Vela satellite over the south Atlantic in September 1979—which some outside scientists speculated was the clandestine test of an atomic bomb by Israel or South Africa—was likewise looked into by a government-sponsored panel of experts. (OSTP consultants concluded that the cause of the light flash, while "technically indeterminate," was probably not a secret nuclear test.) Press's scientists were, as well, able to allay concern about a series of loud booms heard along the east coast of the United States the previous year. The booms, OSTP reported, were caused by aircraft flying at supersonic speed rather than by "unusual geophysical sources."[73]

OSTP was likewise involved in discussions on what to do about Cosmos 954, a nuclear-powered Soviet ocean-surveillance satellite that fell to earth in January 1978. Since the satellite's orbit carried it over the eastern seaboard of the United States, some consideration was given to "shooting it down, or to vaporizing it in outer space," according to David Aaron. The radioactive debris of Cosmos 954 ultimately landed harmlessly in the Canadian Arctic, but "another thirty minutes and it would have come down over New Jersey," Aaron said.[74]

Press and OSTP played a major advisory role, as well, on issues related to health policy, the civilian uses of space, the environment, and America's eroding economic and technological "competitiveness" with other nations.[75]

But, increasingly, the public's perception of science advising in the Carter administration was dominated not by OSTP but by advisory groups in other government agencies and in other branches of the government. Major studies of Three Mile Island, MX basing, and the potential effects of nuclear war, for example, were carried out and made public during Carter's term by the Office of Technology Assessment. Indeed, the fact that Senate opponents of the MX turned to OTA, the Library of Congress, and the Congressional Research Service for advice on alternatives to the racetrack in 1979 showed the extent to which Congress had developed its own independent source of technical advice.[76]

Moreover, the growing role that such organizations and the General Accounting Office played in interpreting scientific issues for Congress and the public suggested that an increasing number of technical issues were simply too controversial for the White House. Thus, while one of Press's earliest memoranda to the president had warned about the long-term danger to the earth of the "greenhouse effect," recognition of the domestic political and economic consequences of restricting the use of fossil fuels—as well as Carter's own subsequent and short-lived synthetic fuels initiative—prevented any but minimal steps from being taken toward dealing with the problem.[77] The phenomenon of "acid rain"—another environmental danger that threatened similarly catastrophic results—finally began to receive attention near the end of the Carter administration, where it immediately became the subject of a heated but inconclusive debate. "The consensus within the administration was that more research was necessary," Press acknowledged.[78]

The impending end of Carter's presidency prompted renewal calls for reconstituting PSAC from, among others, William Golden, author of the 1950 report that led to the original Science Advisory Committee. "Rising international tensions, growing domestic problems, and the approaching election," Golden editorialized in *Science,* made such a step "particularly timely. . . . Reestablishment of the PSAC would benefit the nation, strengthen the presidency, gratify Congress, and encourage the scientific and technological communities."[79]

12

"The President Doesn't Care about Wavelengths"

The Reagan Revolution and the Origins of SDI

On March 23, 1983, Ronald Reagan announced what was by far the most controversial of the cardinal choices of his presidency—a Strategic Defense Initiative with the revolutionary aim of rendering nuclear weapons obsolete. The story behind the origins of SDI—or "Star Wars," as it became known—is not only richly illustrative of Reagan's faith in science and technology, but it also brings together in a single focus many of the disparate themes in the relationship between presidents and scientists over the previous forty years.

"Teller knew about this. . ."

Ronald Reagan proved no more inclined than Jimmy Carter to return a scientist to a position of prominence in the White House. The delay in filling the post of science adviser especially disappointed Reagan's preinauguration Task Force on Science and Technology, headed by William O. Baker and Simon Ramo.[1] In their "Transition Report for Science and Engineering," submitted to the president-elect in December 1980, Baker and Ramo did not recommend the reestablishment of a President's Science Advisory Committee, believing PSAC's liberal reputation would make it politically anathema to the administration. Instead, they urged revitalizing the Office of Science and

Technology Policy through "strong and creative" ties to the budget office along with a "strong emphasis upon applied science" as opposed to basic research.[2] While Reagan seemed "amenable" to their argument that science should have a strengthened and more visible presence in the White House, Baker recalled, the report produced no visible results. The following February, when the last of the administration's appointments were announced, "there wasn't anything about a science adviser," Baker noted.[3]

Some three months into Reagan's term there was still no scientist in the White House—a fact that was due in part to the president's apparent lack of interest but also to the continuing split between the government and members of the scientific community. As many as a dozen candidates, including at least two members of the transition task force, had turned down the job of science adviser, citing age, career, or "personal reasons." One prospective nominee reportedly refused the position twice, fearful of being caught in an unwinnable battle between the president on one side and his colleagues in the scientific community on the other.[4]

Meanwhile, the administration toyed briefly with the idea of dispensing with OSTP and a science adviser altogether. Budget Director David Stockman reportedly told one visitor to his office that if OSTP could not be abolished outright, its staff would at least be cut to a minimum and moved as far from the White House as possible. "We know what we want to do," he quoted Stockman as saying, "and they'll only give us contrary advice."[5]

When Ramo and Baker discovered in March 1981 that there were still no funds for OSTP in the administration's budget, they went to Vice President George Bush, who promised to personally bring the matter to Reagan's attention. But it was Edward Teller, rather than Baker, Ramo, or Bush, who played the decisive role in picking a science adviser, according to Baker: "Bush went back to Ronald Reagan, and the people around Reagan suggested that Teller knew about this."[6]

"A mixture of surprise and unease. . ."

Reagan had gotten to know Teller in 1967, when the physicist gave the newly elected governor of California a guided tour of the weapons laboratory at Livermore.[7] The two had been in occasional contact since then, generally over defense issues. Reagan's rise to national prominence contrasted sharply with Teller's declining influence in Washington during the Carter administration—an eclipse that culminated in Carter's abolition of the President's Foreign Intelligence Advisory Board, which Teller had served as a long-time member.

Reagan's election in 1980 proved especially propitious for Teller. Earlier that year, while a senior research fellow at Stanford's Hoover Institution, Teller had contributed an essay on new military technologies to a volume intended as a blueprint for the Reagan administration.[8] Subsequently, the controversial physicist was picked to serve on the Baker-Ramo Task Force, as well as on the President's Foreign Intelligence Advisory Board when it was reconstituted early in Reagan's term.

Teller's candidate for science adviser was a forty-one-year-old protégé—George Keyworth, then head of the physics division at Los Alamos. In a 1986 interview, Keyworth acknowledged the central role that Teller played in his appointment: "Bluntly, the reason I was in that office is because Edward first proposed me, and the president very much admires Edward."[9]

Reagan's announcement in May 1981 that Keyworth would be his science adviser "drew a mixture of surprise and unease from the scientific establishment," reported *Science,* which also noted that Keyworth was "virtually unknown outside his field."[10] Ironically, while Keyworth's detractors cited his inexperience as a weakness, supporters claimed it as a strength. Arguing that "all he doesn't have is 20 years' membership in the club," Harold Agnew defended Keyworth on the grounds that "defense will be the thrust of this administration, and somebody who has the respect of the people in the defense labs is needed. For the past four years, you have had a geologist in charge, and the defense community has suffered."[11]

Keyworth soon made it plain that his interpretation of the role of science adviser differed dramatically from that of his predecessors—telling the OSTP staff, for example, that they should consider themselves "the president's slaves."[12] During his first weeks in office, Keyworth further demonstrated his loyalty to the administration by supporting the massive military buildup announced by Reagan's secretary of defense, Caspar Weinberger. The new science adviser also publicly defended the administration's decision to dramatically reduce federal funds for basic scientific research and to cut the National Science Foundation's budget by one fourth. (Later, however, Keyworth privately beat back Stockman's efforts to trim federal spending for scientific research by 10 percent as "nonessential" and campaigned successfully behind the scenes to restore much of the funding cut from the research budget.)[13] In another controversial move, Keyworth outraged life scientists around the country when he refused to take a stand during his confirmation hearings on whether the fundamentalist religious doctrine of "creationism" should be taught alongside evolution in public schools.[14]

Although Keyworth's announcement in December 1981 of the establishment of a fifteen-member White House Science Council (WHSC), to meet with him monthly on technical issues, briefly raised the expectations of outside scientists for better contact between the president and the scientific community, the hope expressed by *Science* that WHSC might become a "pared down PSAC" was quickly dispelled when Keyworth explained that the sole purpose of the new committee would be to advise him, not the president.[15] WHSC members would not meet with the president to offer advice, nor was the science adviser under any obligation to acquaint Reagan with their views. When critics charged that some of those Keyworth picked to serve on WHSC—Edward Teller and Harold Agnew, in particular—were hardly representative of attitudes in the scientific community, the science adviser responded that it was "of little value to the Administration, at least in policy advisory positions, to have people who do not share the Administration's view."[16]

"The question of . . . adequate scientific advice. . ."

In the fall of 1981, the Reagan administration became embroiled in its first political and scientific controversy when the State Department charged that the Russians were experimenting with chemical warfare in Southeast Asia and Afghanistan, in violation of international law.

Suspicion of Russian involvement in chemical warfare actually predated Reagan's presidency. During the late 1970s, the Carter administration had investigated allegations that the Soviet Union was supplying chemical and/or biological weapons to its Communist allies in Laos and Cambodia—possibly even deploying the lethal agents from helicopters and airplanes. But it was not until September 1981 that Reagan's secretary of state, Alexander Haig, announced that U.S. Army chemists had found "physical evidence" linking the mysterious illness and deaths of villagers in the war zone with the use of mycotoxins—a yellowish, sporelike nerve poison made from fungal mold. Since the manufacture and effective use of such a sophisticated poison exceeded the capabilities of indigenous forces in the area, Haig's claim pointed the finger of suspicion at the Russians.[17]

Haig based his charge on an analysis undertaken the previous summer by an interagency committee chaired by Richard Burt, a senior State Department official. Although Burt's committee included representatives from the Pentagon, the National Security Council, the CIA, the Defense Intelligence Agency, the Arms Control and Disarmament Agency, and even the Office of Management and Budget, neither OSTP nor Keyworth—who had just been confirmed as science adviser—was asked to take part. Not only was there an absence of independent scientific representation, but politics weighed heavily on the committee—which early came under pressure from House members eager to show Russian complicity in the poisonings in the wake of the Soviet invasion of Afghanistan. Politics also came into play in the announcement of the committee's findings. Thus, Haig's revelation concerning "yellow rain" was made in Berlin, where demonstrators were then protesting American plans to deploy new intermediate-range nuclear missiles in Europe.[18]

Initially, the American government's claim that the Soviets were responsible for yellow rain went virtually unchallenged. So seemingly persuasive was the evidence marshaled at congressional hearings in November that only one witness, Harvard biochemist Matthew Meselson, expressed doubts. As Meselson pointed out, the government's charge that "these mycotoxins are not native to warm climates" was contradicted by published reports documenting naturally occurring outbreaks of such poisonings in

Japan and India during the summer months. The fact that the Army and the small number of outside scientists it consulted had overlooked this fact raised "the question of whether the government availed itself of adequate scientific advice in its initial public assessment of the evidence," Meselson testified.[19]

Nonetheless, the doubts Meselson expressed were all but ignored in the outcry over the alleged Soviet involvement in chemical warfare. Nearly a year after Haig's announcement, even *Science* was giving credence to the State Department's claims. Late in 1982, Reagan administration officials pointed to what they claimed was "conclusive" proof of chemical warfare in Southeast Asia to support their contention that the Soviets were using similar methods in Afghanistan—where two Russian gas masks supposedly contaminated by mycotoxins were said to have been recently recovered from the battlefield.[20]

It was not until nearly two years after Haig's revelation, at the end of May 1983, that an alternate explanation for yellow rain was ventured by Meselson and a Yale entomologist. Both men were struck by the similarities between the government's yellow rain samples and pollen-filled bee droppings, which routinely fouled cars in nearby faculty parking lots. Further, several of the cases of illness and death said to have been caused by yellow rain, Meselson and other researchers noted, closely matched the symptoms of diseases endemic to Southeast Asia.[21] Earlier, in his 1982 testimony to Congress, Meselson had speculated that suspected victims of yellow rain in Laos and Cambodia might actually be suffering from the long-term effects of herbicides used by the United States during the Vietnam War.[22]

Subsequent attempts by the State Department to refute Meselson's claims as politically motivated—he was, in fact, a long-time and outspoken advocate of banning biological and chemical weapons—drew attention instead to flaws in the government's research. As subsequent articles in *The New York Times* and *Atlantic* magazine pointed out, neither the Army's experts nor the handful of outside scientists whom the administration consulted had bothered to look at what else besides mycotoxins the samples contained. Moreover, the government's experts had deviated from routine scientific procedure by neglecting to repeat critical tests and to submit their findings to independent review before announcing the results.[23]

Less explicable—or excusable—than the government's failure to follow the scientific method, these critics claimed, was the administration's attack on Meselson and others who challenged the validity of the State Department's chemical warfare hypothesis. By sticking blindly to its yellow rain theory, despite mounting scientific evidence to the contrary, the administration "succeeded in embarrassing itself and American science," charged one reporter.[24] Beyond "shoddy" research and "erroneous scientific reasoning," he argued, the incident seemed a troubling example of an attempt to bend scientific facts to fit a political premise.[25]

"A tar baby. . ."

It was not yellow rain but precipitation of an altogether different sort, falling much closer to home, that began to occupy the attention of an increasing number of scientists outside the government during Reagan's first term.

In the final year of the Carter administration, science adviser Frank Press had enlisted the participation of scientists and representatives from industry, universities, and charitable foundations in an Advisory Committee on Oceans and International Environmental and Scientific Affairs. Among other things, the committee looked at the increasing acidification of lakes and streams, caused by airborne pollutants injected into the atmosphere from smokestack industries in the midwestern United States and later deposited by rainfall throughout the Northeast.[26] In June 1980, Congress approved an interagency Task Force on Acid Precipitation, with representatives from the Agriculture and Energy departments and the National Oceanic and Atmospheric Administration, to look at the long-term effect that acid deposition might have on fisheries and wildlife.[27]

Although both Press's panel and the interagency task force continued their work into the Reagan administration, a growing number of outside scientists complained that neither the new president nor Congress was sufficiently concerned about "acid rain." In January 1982, the first report of the task force noted only that the problem required further study.[28] Congressional hearings on the causes and effects of acid rain, both that year and the next, prompted calls for further research—but never any concrete measures aimed at solving the problem or lessening its impact.[29]

As both Press and Keyworth recognized, acid rain was only partially a scientific dilemma. A major reason for the Reagan administration's inaction was the potential economic costs of treating the problem. Thus, far more intractable than any technological challenge was resolving the political conflicts that any solution was likely to engender. In Congress, the simplest and seemingly most efficacious technical solution proposed by representatives of eastern states—limiting the amount of high-sulfur coal burned by power plants and industries—was bitterly opposed by representatives of the southern, western, and midwestern states in which the coal was mined or the polluting industries were located. John Gibbons, Director of the Office of Technology Assessment, which had studied the problem of acid rain since 1981, considered the issue "a tar baby" because of its political ramifications.[30]

Following the Reagan administration's refusal to abide by Congress's 1982 recommendation that it fund additional research into the causes and prevention of acid rain, the National Research Council of the National Academy of Sciences undertook its own investigation, completing a comprehensive study of the phenomenon in June 1983. While the NRC report did not recommend any specific action to alleviate the problem, its conclusion that the overwhelming proportion of air-borne pollutants was man-made seemed to many scientists a tacit argument for government-imposed restrictions upon the industries causing the pollution.[31]

By the time of the National Academy's report, acid rain had also become a subject of considerable disagreement within the Reagan administration. Two days before the release of the report, physicist William Nierenberg, chairman of an OSTP review panel on acid rain, announced that he had Keyworth's permission to expand his study beyond the causes of the problem to include possible solutions. Originally, Nierenberg—who had served on Reagan's transition task force and was author of a Carter administration report on the greenhouse effect—had been asked only to review the scientific findings of an American-Canadian report on acid rain. However, arguing in a preliminary report that "actions have to be taken despite incomplete knowledge," Nierenberg's activist stance on acid rain provoked a storm of controversy in the government.[32]

When Nierenberg's study, with its plea for action, was released in 1984, Keyworth was caught in a crossfire. On the one hand, scientists and House members who were urging the president to take steps to curb acid rain accused Keyworth of deliberately delaying release of Nierenberg's report until after a key House vote on legislation aimed at controlling sulfur dioxide emissions. On the other hand, an administration official—who described Nierenberg's study as a "catastrophe, which careened from embarrassment to embarrassment"—specifically blamed Keyworth for the sudden pressure to do something about acid rain; the science adviser, he said, had been "full of assurances that this wouldn't happen when the study got underway."[33]

"Substantial political and technical miscalculation. . ."

Acid rain was only one of a growing number of issues on which Keyworth found himself on the losing side in a power struggle within the administration. The science adviser also came under fire for his stand on the seemingly endless wrangle over basing the MX.

During the 1980 campaign, Reagan had castigated Carter's choice of the racetrack basing mode for the MX as "unworkable," too costly, and a needless sacrifice of western lands. Even before Reagan assumed office, public and congressional opposition to the racetrack had effectively killed the idea. But a politically acceptable solution to the pending vulnerability of American ICBMs continued to elude scientists and strategists.[34] Late in 1981, a study by the Office of Technology Assessment reaffirmed that none of the five basing modes that "appear feasible and offer reasonable prospects of providing survivability [was] . . . likely to provide a substantial number of survivable MX missiles much before the end of this decade."[35] Notwithstanding that fact, Reagan and Defense Secretary Caspar Weinberger had already decided to make the MX the centerpiece of the administration's much-touted "strategic modernization" program.

Keyworth's background certainly qualified him to play a major role on the MX. Making some sense of MX basing was, in fact, "the first priority" assigned him in the Reagan administration, Keyworth said. Preparation of a new basing study was, as well, one of the earliest tasks that Keyworth gave the newly created White House Science Council.[36]

But by the time the WHSC study was undertaken, there was already a cacophony of advice on the MX reaching the president. In the spring of 1981, Weinberger had created a Defense Science Board panel under the direction of Berkeley physicist Charles Townes—a member of PSAC during the Johnson and Nixon administrations—to review the MX-basing options for the Pentagon.[37] Townes's report, given to Weinberger that July, failed to resolve the MX dilemma. Conceding that he was unable to come up with any better ideas on basing the missile, Townes recommended that the administration take another look at the racetrack as well as at two other previously proposed solutions to ICBM vulnerability.[38]

That fall, beset by conflicting opinion on where and how to base the MX, Reagan announced an interim decision on the missile. According to a plan worked out in Weinberger's office, between one third and one half of the first hundred MXs would be put into existing ICBM silos that had been "superhardened" to withstand the effects of a nearby nuclear blast.[39]

Within days, however, the president's decision came under fire in Congress—attacked on the grounds that it promised to do little if anything to close the impending "window of vulnerability" facing American ICBMs. Other critics branded the administration's choice "witless [and] a product of substantial technical and political miscalculation" when it was discovered that many of the silos proposed as temporary shelters for the MX were in regions of the country geologically unsuited for superhardening and that no technical experts had attended the meeting at which the president made his decision on the MX.[40]

"Doctor Densepack. . ."

Responding to this criticism of its interim MX decision, the Reagan administration called for a subsequent, second look at MX basing by a reconstituted Townes panel. The second Townes panel fared little better than the first, although this time its members endorsed a novel idea for basing the missile. (Two members of the second panel argued in vain that the administration should simply abandon the MX.) In a proposal that seemed a reversal of earlier logic—officially known as closely spaced basing, but unofficially dubbed Densepack—the second Townes panel recommended clustering the MXs so closely together that Soviet missiles targeted against them would encounter the phenomenon of "fratricide," whereby subsequently arriving warheads are destroyed by the debris and electromagnetic disturbances created by prior nuclear detonations.[41]

Several members of the panel reportedly expressed reservations about Densepack, and even Townes himself confided his doubts about the plan in a classified letter to Weinberger. Nonetheless, in late November 1982, the Reagan administration announced that it would rely on a combination of superhardening and Densepack to protect the MX from destruction.[42] That winter, Keyworth enthusiastically defended Densepack in congressional hearings. But Keyworth's testimony may only "have added to the confusion," said one observer. "Congress tried to sort through the technical aspects of [Densepack], but ultimately gave up," noted *Science*.[43] Keyworth's efforts earned him the title "Doctor Densepack" in the administration, prompting charges by scientists outside the government that the science adviser was acting more as a salesman for, than an adviser to, the president.[44]

Following lukewarm support for Densepack even from the Joint Chiefs of Staff, the Reagan administration was "absolutely stymied on the MX" by the winter of 1982–1983, Keyworth admitted, when the president created a third and final blue ribbon panel to study the problem of ICBM vulnerability. The report of the Scowcroft Commission, too, seemed to tacitly confirm that land basing of ICBMs had reached a technological dead end by recommending that the MX be put into existing silos until such time as it could be replaced by a new force of smaller, mobile, single-warhead missiles dubbed Midgetman.[45]

"A lead balloon. . ."

Keyworth's identification with the Densepack fiasco bore an unexpected cost for the science adviser, in terms both of his political influence within the administration and his credibility with his peers in the scientific community. In addition, another, less publicized incident at this time further undermined Keyworth's tenuous standing in the Reagan administration.

During the summer of 1982, Keyworth and Stockman had joined in a rare alliance against NASA's efforts to gain approval for construction of a permanent, earth-orbiting space station. Stockman's concern with the multibillion dollar project was strictly fiscal; Keyworth's opposition was pragmatic. He had "yet to see competitive, well-thought-out plans not only for what [the space station] would look like but what it would do," Keyworth said. The science adviser questioned not only the feasibility but also the need for the project—disparaging it as "a motel in the sky" and even potentially "a lead balloon."[46]

Stockman and Keyworth's opposition to what the latter termed a "carefully organized campaign" by NASA for the space station earned them the political enmity of some powerful figures in the administration. As a result, when an interagency committee was established under the direction of the National Security Council to advise the president on space policy, its members included representatives from virtually every government agency with an interest in the subject except OSTP and OMB.[47] Keyworth's negative judgment on the space station was eventually overridden by the president, who expressed enthusiasm for the project. But Keyworth's futile opposition to the space station would be remembered by the science adviser's foes in Washington.

"Technological enthusiasts. . ."

The final frontier was the arena for yet another confrontation involving the science adviser—in what would prove to be Keyworth's most controversial role. On March 23, 1983, Ronald Reagan announced in a televised address his Strategic Defense Initiative, the ultimate purpose of which, the president said, was to intercept enemy missiles in flight and thereby "to give us the means of rendering these nuclear weapons impotent and obsolete."[48] Within days, SDI became the most bitterly contested technical controversy in a generation.

SDI may have had its earliest origin in Reagan's 1967 visit to the Livermore laboratory, which introduced him to new ideas for strategic defense. More than a decade later, Reagan received an update on the subject during a campaign stop at the North American Air Defense Command (NORAD) in Colorado.[49] Reportedly, what most impressed Reagan during his NORAD tour was the fact that the United States, while able to track objects as small as a lost glove in orbit, remained powerless to stop Soviet missiles from landing on its territory.[50]

In the days immediately following Reagan's visit to NORAD, Martin Anderson—a Hoover Institution economist and domestic adviser to the Reagan campaign—drafted a memorandum for the candidate urging him to revive the long-deferred dream of an effective defense against ballistic missiles. "Of course, there is the question of feasibility, especially with the development of multiple entry warheads," Anderson acknowledged in his memorandum, "but there have apparently been striking advances in missile technology during the past decade or so that would make such a system technically possible."[51] The 1980 Republican platform embraced Anderson's theme in urging development of "more modern ABM technologies."[52]

During its last two years, and in response to technological advances, the Carter administration had dramatically increased the Pentagon research effort on high-tech defensive weaponry, including lasers and directed-energy weapons.[53] But few scientists familiar with such exotic technology were optimistic that it would yield an effective antiballistic missile defense anytime soon. In December 1978, for example, Richard Garwin and Wolfgang Panofsky publicly challenged Harold Agnew's claim that new defensive weapons might soon make nuclear deterrence "obsolete."[54]

In the Reagan administration, preeminent among those whom one critic called the "technological enthusiasts" for strategic defense were Edward Teller and retired Army Lieutenant General Daniel Graham, a former head of the Defense Intelligence Agency who had also been one of Reagan's 1976 campaign advisers.[55] But Graham and Teller embraced fundamentally different concepts of strategic defense. Graham believed that modernized versions of so-called killer satellites and other schemes conceived by the Air Force in the late 1950s and early 1960s could provide an effective defense against enemy missiles as early as the 1990s.[56] Teller, on the other hand, favored the more exotic speed-of-light weaponry being developed at Livermore—including such "third-generation" nuclear directed-energy weapons as the bomb-pumped x-ray laser, known at the laboratory by the code name Excalibur.[57]

In addition, a third approach to strategic defense was being urged on Congress at this time by the so-called laser lobby, headed by Wyoming Senator Malcolm Wallop and his legislative aide, Angelo Codevilla. The laser lobby favored prompt deployment of space-based chemical lasers—said by Wallop and Codevilla to be capable of destroying enemy rockets and their warheads in the early stages of flight.[58]

Despite the differences in their approach, Teller, Graham, and Wallop all shared a common ambition: to persuade the president to commit the nation to a defense against ballistic missiles. The result was three separate, if concerted, lobbying efforts by the main proponents of strategic defense.[59]

During the administration's first year, Graham personally briefed Reagan, Weinberger, Keyworth, and others on the ideas that his organization, High Frontier, had for a nonnuclear space-based defense.[60]

Only a few days after Reagan's 1981 inauguration, Teller and a Livermore protégé, physicist Lowell Wood, began briefing congressional and military leaders on progress the laboratory was making in developing the nuclear-pumped x-ray laser. In January 1982, members of the president's "Kitchen Cabinet" gave Reagan the results of a year-long study begun under the auspices of the conservative Heritage Foundation, on which Teller had worked, urging the president to launch the nation on a "Manhattan Project-like" effort to develop the weaponry necessary to protect it from nuclear attack. The following September—after protesting on a nationally televised talk show that his views on defense were being withheld from Reagan—Teller was granted the personal audience with the president he had long sought for the purpose of promoting Excalibur.[61]

As early as 1979, Wallop and Codevilla sent Reagan a draft of an article on space-based defense they had written for the journal *Strategic Review*, which the candidate reportedly returned with comments and annotations.[62] By 1982, Wallop and his allies had also opened up a second front for strategic defense—in Congress. That spring and summer the so-called laser wars raged between House advocates of accelerated research into short-wavelength weapons (like the nuclear-pumped Excalibur) and Senate supporters, including Wallop, of prompt deployment of less exotic, longer-wavelength chemical lasers.[63]

The enthusiasts for strategic defense went virtually unchallenged in the Reagan administration. Early skeptics of space-based defense, like Garwin and Panofsky, gradually found themselves excluded from the circle of scientists consulted by the White House.[64]

According to Keyworth, the president was sympathetic to the general idea of strategic defense, but remained oblivious to technical details: "He knows exactly where he wants to go, but couldn't care less about how to get there. . . . The president doesn't care about wavelengths and things like that." Publicly, Reagan had likened the Soviet-American strategic stalemate to a "Mexican standoff," with each antagonist holding a gun pointed at the other's head. In a private conversation on "the eroding trend of strategic stability," Keyworth said, the president confessed the subject "sent shivers up his spine."[65]

Keyworth, on the other hand, was inclined to protest the conflicting and exaggerated claims being made on behalf of strategic defense. Despite his relationship with Teller, it was Keyworth who discouraged a meeting between his mentor and the president, believing Excalibur fundamentally unsuited for strategic defense as well as technologically "premature." Keyworth agreed with Teller, however, that Graham's concept of a conventional space-based defense would be too vulnerable, and the science adviser was equally critical of the laser lobby. In the fall of 1981, Keyworth had chastised a gathering of aerospace executives for encouraging the belief that a space-based laser defense was just on the horizon.

Complaining on this occasion that he was spending up to three quarters of his time trying to "rebuff these advocates," Keyworth also admitted to being "fundamentally frightened" by the potential effect that strategic defense might have on the nuclear balance.[66] The chief scientist in the Pentagon, USDR&E Director Richard DeLauer, likewise admitted to "feeling pressure" from the advocates of strategic defense. Despite the fact that DeLauer, before joining the Pentagon, had worked for TRW on the very laser being championed by Wallop and Codevilla, he, like Keyworth, remained highly skeptical of the claims being made by the laser lobby.[67]

"A new strategic vision. . ."

In addition to these lobbying efforts, there was, by late 1982, another source of pressure on the Reagan administration to do something about strategic defense: growing public concern about the nuclear arms race.

Indicative of this concern was the fact that more than a half million demonstrators rallied in June 1982 in New York's Central Park to urge a halt to the production and testing of nuclear weapons. Less than two months later, a resolution expressing support for such a nuclear "freeze" failed to pass the House by only two votes. By year's end, a synod of Roman Catholic bishops was engaged in drafting what would become a highly publicized letter calling for an international prohibition on the manufacture and use of nuclear weapons.[69]

With the start of 1983, disillusionment and discontent with the nation's nuclear strategy extended even to the inner circles of the Pentagon—where Chief of Naval Operations Admiral James Watkins had begun urging that the nation consider putting a greater emphasis upon defense. Previously, Reagan had asked the Pentagon to reconsider the problem of defending the entire nation against missile attack, but the idea was reportedly greeted with little enthusiasm by Defense Secretary Weinberger.[70]

Watkins and the Joint Chiefs decided to make the question of defense the focus of their next regularly scheduled meeting with the president. On February 11, the chiefs and their chairman, Army General John Vessey, advised Reagan that the nation and the administration required a "new strategic vision." Although strategic defense was reportedly only one of five options that Vessey and Watkins offered as a foundation for this new vision, Reagan embraced the idea with enthusiasm after he asked each of the chiefs, in turn, whether they would support the change. (Coincidentally, the need to dispel the administration's "hawkish" public image, and to bring an end to the mutual hostage relationship with Russia, had become a frequent topic of discussion between Reagan and his close friends and advisers.)[71] The president assigned the task of giving shape to the new strategic vision to Deputy National Security Adviser Robert McFarlane, for whom strategic defense was also a developing concern.[72]

In mid-March, during a weekend retreat at Camp David, Reagan decided that he would announce the administration's new vision during a televised speech planned for later in the month. Originally, the speech was to have focused on the nature of the Soviet threat and the need for increased defense spending. At the president's orders, McFarlane, along with three members of his National Security Council staff, began drafting an addendum on strategic defense that would become known as the Insert.[73]

Reagan's science adviser did not learn of the president's plans until Saturday morning, March 19—only four days before the scheduled speech—when McFarlane called Keyworth into his office to read him a draft of the Insert and to pose a question that Reagan had raised during his weekend stay at Camp David: "Is now a good time to renew our efforts in strategic defense?"[74]

Keyworth later acknowledged that the president's inquiry surprised—even "stunned"—him. Just two months earlier, Keyworth had received, and forwarded to the White House, the results of a year-long investigation by a special White House Science Council panel, headed by physicist and WHSC member Edward Frieman. The panel's report focused on how certain new technologies, including various types of lasers, might affect the administration's strategic modernization program as well as strategic defense.[75] It echoed the doubts and reservations about space-based defense that had been expressed in an earlier study by OSTP's Assistant Director for National Security and Space, Victor Reis.[76]

Even after Teller—who was made, at his insistence, an ex officio member of Frieman's panel—persuaded the group to take a second look at Excalibur, the WHSC scientists refused to amend their negative assessment of the x-ray laser's potential as a weapon.[77] Indeed, only in the area of the emerging technology of adaptive optics—in which deformable or so-called rubber mirrors are used to compensate for the distortion of light as it passes through the atmosphere—did Frieman's report express any optimism at all about the use of lasers for defense.[78] Aside from what was almost literally this single ray of hope, nothing in the report gave encouragement to the belief that science or technology offered a short-term solution to the irreducible nuclear dilemma.

Consequently, when he forwarded the report to Meese and the White House shortly after receiving it, Keyworth "never even raised the strategic defense issue with the president," he said. Nor had the subject come up at the March 18 meeting of WHSC, the day before Keyworth's summons to McFarlane's office.[79]

Mindful, however, of the importance of being a "team player"—and doubtless aware, too, of enemies he had already made in the administration—Keyworth decided on March 19 to dodge McFarlane's question. Reportedly assured by McFarlane that only "a research program" was envisioned and that it would not proceed without the science adviser's blessing, Keyworth spoke not about the feasibility of strategic defense per se but about the promising technology of adaptive optics detailed in Frieman's report. Keyworth's second thoughts about the magnitude and direction of the president's initiative were laid to rest by McFarlane and his deputy, John Poindexter, during a second visit of the science adviser to McFarlane's office later that afternoon.[80]

"Forces . . . so major. . ."

On the evening of March 19, Keyworth met with Victor Reis to solicit the latter's support for strategic defense. "This is a political decision, not a technical one, and in political things you and I are not experts," Keyworth reportedly told Reis in defense of the president's plan. But Reis remained unpersuaded of the feasibility of the space-based defense at the center of Reagan's vision. Relying on lasers to shoot down ballistic missiles was like expecting laetrile to cure cancer, Reis told Keyworth.[81]

Keyworth also made frantic efforts that weekend to reconvene WHSC to discuss strategic defense. Shown a copy of the Insert at the hurriedly convened meeting in Keyworth's office on Sunday, few, if any, were inclined toward Keyworth's conversion, and several members expressed amazement at what the president was proposing. "I almost fell out of my chair when I saw it," said Frieman.[82] An alternative version of the Insert, drafted by Keyworth and Reis at their March 19 meeting, which would have made strategic defense the subject of a revived and expanded study by the Scowcroft Commission, was abandoned as the depth of Reagan's commitment became clear. "There was no mistaking the president's vision," recalled Solomon Buchsbaum, a Bell Labs physicist and WHSC member to whom Keyworth also turned for advice on the Insert.[83] "There were," Frieman agreed, "forces at work that were so major . . . that there was just no way any individual was going to stop this thing dead in its tracks."[84]

On Sunday, March 20, Keyworth was asked by McFarlane to brief Vessey and the Joint Chiefs on the president's forthcoming speech. On Monday morning, Keyworth attended a special Oval Office meeting on the Insert. "If there's one thing I do not mean by this, gentlemen," Keyworth said the president had pointedly reminded those at the meeting as they filed out, "it is some kind of a string of terminal defenses around this country."

Any doubt as to whether Keyworth shared the president's vision had vanished by Tuesday morning, March 22, when the science adviser was asked to take part in drafting the final version of the Insert, which was to focus on Reagan's goal of a total defense against ballistic missiles. Ultimately, only minor changes were made in the speech to placate Secretary of State George Shultz, who was worried about the feasibility of the president's initiative, and Assistant Secretary of Defense Richard Perle, who was concerned that NATO would protest being left out of SDI and that the Soviets would see it as primarily offensive in nature. Reportedly, Perle appealed to Keyworth, in vain, to "fall on his sword" or resign in protest against SDI.[85]

Instead, having overcome his initial doubts about the president's vision, Keyworth became the administration's most fervent spokesman for SDI. On Wednesday afternoon, a few hours before Reagan's address to the nation, Keyworth and Frieman apprised DeLauer and his deputy at the Pentagon, as well as George Shultz at the State Department, of what the president was about to say. That evening, following a reception and dinner, Keyworth listened to the announcement of SDI in the company of twelve prominent scientists who had been invited to the White House at the suggestion of Meese and Reagan.[86]

For each of the scientists at the White House, as for the nation in general, Reagan's announcement came as a complete surprise. Even Teller was caught unawares by the message of the Insert.[87]

"Something deeply troubling. . ."

In the weeks and months that followed Reagan's March 23 speech, the only constituency to whom Reagan had specifically appealed—namely, members of "the scientific community in our country, those who gave us nuclear weapons"—not only failed to share the president's vision but became the most vociferous critics of SDI.

Jerome Wiesner told *Science* that the president's speech was "really a declaration of a new arms race."[88] Wolfgang Panofsky thought Reagan's vision "spiritually troubling."[89] Hans Bethe argued that while exotic technologies like the x-ray laser remained a promising subject for laboratory research, they were far too weak a reed on which to base the nation's security. Of Excalibur, he observed, "Physics I quite believe in, but I'm a little doubtful about the engineering, and more than doubtful about the system."[90]

In the coming days, several other prominent PSAC or DDR&E alumni—including Isidor Rabi, Lee DuBridge, and Herbert York—expressed similar reservations about the technical feasibility or the strategic desirability of "Star Wars." SDI critic Richard Garwin argued in a *New York Times* Op-Ed piece that the system seemed just as well suited to an offensive role—as a way of "mopping up" the ragged remnants of the Soviets' ballistic missile force after an American first strike—a possibility that surely must have occurred to the Russians, if not to the president, Garwin pointed out.[91]

Beyond the technical question of whether "Star Wars" could be made to work, and the strategic one of whether it might endanger more than it would protect, George Rathjens and Jack Ruina voiced another concern: "What troubles us is less the expenditure of a billion dollars a year on research than holding out a vision of hope—the hope of an infallible defense—that is virtually impossible to achieve." There was, Rathjens and Ruina argued, "something deeply troubling about an advisory team that can encourage the President to raise such hopes."[92]

"Hardball days. . ."

The controversy into which SDI was born continued throughout its life in the Reagan administration. Critics charged that the unfounded technical optimism which had inspired SDI also acted to sustain it. By fall 1983, three separate government-funded panels had studied the feasibility of SDI and sent reports to the White House—but their detailed findings remained classified, and summaries made available to the public were subject to conflicting interpretation.[93] Subsequent independent studies by the Federation of American Scientists and the American Physical Society challenged these official reports, casting doubt on the possibility of achieving even modest SDI objectives.[94]

Because of Keyworth's self-admitted role as "cheerleader" for the program, criticism of "Star Wars" was increasingly directed at the science adviser himself, who was accused of letting political expediency triumph over scientific judgment. Ironically, Keyworth's fervent support for the program came under attack even by some within the Reagan administration—including Reagan's domestic adviser and chief of staff Michael Deaver, who blamed the science adviser for the fact that SDI had "come up to bite the president," Keyworth said.[95]

Certainly Keyworth's outspoken defense of SDI was increasingly at odds with the dominant opinion in the nation's scientific community. Rather than trying to close the gap between the administration and the nation's scientists over SDI, moreover, Keyworth's public statements seemed almost calculated to make that rift grow wider. The science adviser's "appearances in the press have sparked resentment" within the scientific community, noted a December 1984 *Science* article.[96] Keyworth responded to this criticism with an ill-advised attack on the media:"We're trying to build up America, and the press is trying to tear down America," he told reporters.[97] By the second anniversary of Reagan's SDI announcement, relations between the science adviser and the scientific community were under more strain than at any time since their nadir in the closing days of the Nixon administration.

Indeed, since the fall of 1984, things had gone from bad to worse for the science adviser. The director of the Federation of American Scientists blamed Keyworth for having "totally squandered" the prestige and credibility of the president's science adviser inherited from PSAC. *Science* branded administration cuts in the National Science Foundation budget for social science research and statistical studies as "not merely ill-informed attempts at exorcizing nonessentials, but punitive and politically motivated." Later that year, Keyworth's enemies in the White House were responsible for a rumor that the science adviser was about to be fired and the Office of Science and Technology Policy abolished.[98] While successful in dispelling the rumor, Keyworth himself acknowledged to an interviewer in December, "These are hardball days."[99]

Having weathered the efforts to fire him, Keyworth made plans of his own to leave the Reagan administration, in late November 1985, to found a Washington, D.C., consulting firm. But Keyworth's departure would hardly mean an end to the controversy over SDI—or over science advising. Once again the position of science adviser was turned down by several of the most qualified candidates, until Keyworth's former deputy at OSTP, John McTague, a physical chemist with a background in industry as well as academe, agreed to serve in that role until a permanent replacement was found.

At the end of an unexpectedly long interregnum, McTague, too, quit the administration in June 1986; shortly afterward it was announced that OSTP's budget and staff would be cut by a quarter in fiscal 1987. "What is not functioning well is the position of Science Adviser," McTague candidly told an interviewer upon leaving the White House. "There are not good personal relations with the West Wing."[100] In the fall of 1986, McTague was replaced by William Graham, a former NASA administrator and electrical engineer. But Graham's appointment, too, provoked controversy. At his confirmation hearings, the charge was made that Graham's appointment had been made conditional on his willingness to endorse SDI.[101]

"We need to do something. . ."

Like "Star Wars," science advising itself was facing an uncertain future at the end of Reagan's presidency—where one unintended effect of OSTP's decline in importance was the increased activity and influence of other advisory bodies in the government. In particular, this meant greater visibility and autonomy for the congressional Office of Technology Assessment.

But partisan politics and the unending rivalry of Congress and the White House necessarily limited the effectiveness of OTA, too, as a source of objective scientific advice and as a watchdog against the abuse of power by the executive. Following the release of a preliminary OTA study that cast doubt on the feasibility of SDI, the Pentagon demanded that the controversial report be withdrawn. A second, more comprehensive OTA review of SDI in 1985 drew fire from the Department of Energy, which accused its authors of leaking classified information. These pressures caused the OTA director to acknowledge, in a 1986 interview, that his agency might be reluctant in the future to look at such sensitive topics and could become more circumspect about publishing its findings.[102]

Another side effect of the decline of OSTP was the involvement for the first time of private groups and even individuals in arranging high-level scientific exchanges aimed at breaking the deadlock in superpower arms negotiations.[103]

To those who remembered PSAC, the failures and limitations of science advising during the Reagan years demonstrated a greater need than ever to return a formal but revitalized science advisory apparatus to the White House. Critics pointed to the 1986 Challenger disaster, the government's delay in facing up to the AIDS crisis, and the continuing decline of American industrial competitiveness as evidence of the urgent need for a change in the way that science advice reached the president.[104]

For MIT's Jerome Wiesner and Kosta Tsipis, "Star Wars" remained the foremost symbol of what was wrong with science advising. "This decision was confirmation, if any more were needed, that the president is getting very poor advice," the two editorialized in *The New York Times*.[105] But even some administration supporters conceded that presidential science advising had reached a new low during the Reagan years.

Indeed, the need to restore and revise the process of presidential science advising was acknowledged by one who had become the target of much of that criticism. Shortly before leaving his post in the Reagan administration, Keyworth conceded that "the time has come when we need to take a hard look at how science and technology is managed . . . we have reached the point where we need to do something."[106]

CONCLUSION

Speaking the Truth to Power
The Future of Presidential Science Advising

Over the almost fifty years that separated Franklin Roosevelt's decision to develop the atomic bomb from Ronald Reagan's SDI announcement, the world was transformed. Yet during this time presidential science advising seemed only to travel full circle. In 1983, as in 1939, a decision that would have far-reaching consequences was made by a president acting upon the advice of a handful of individuals, operating in secret, following little discussion and no open debate. What had happened, in the interim, to the advisory apparatus that was created to avoid arbitrary and ill-founded judgments and to ensure that all sides of a technical question received fair hearing? And what has happened since?

The decline of presidential science advising would continue into the next two administrations. As president, George Bush announced that he intended to revitalize a science presence in the White House. Bush's choice of Yale physicist Allen Bromley was applauded by the scientific community and Congress alike.[1] Just as important, the status of "assistant to the president" was restored to the position of science adviser in the Bush administration, making that post theoretically equal in authority with that of the president's national security adviser. This elevation of the role of the science adviser moved the position both symbolically and physically closer to the president.[2]

Another substantive change was the creation by Bush and Bromley of the President's Council of Advisers on Science and Technology (PCAST). Unlike the White House Science Council established during the Reagan administration, which had responsibility only for advising the science adviser, PCAST resembled PSAC in that it was intended to directly advise the president, by means of regularly scheduled meetings.[3]

But Bush and Bromley continued the trend of earlier administrations away from PSAC in their almost exclusive emphasis upon domestic issues—among them science education, industrial competitiveness, and the allocation of resources between "big" and "little" science.[4] The fact that the inaugural twelve-member PCAST included a professor of international agriculture, a cardiologist, a population biologist, a geneticist, and an economist demonstrated not only the ecumenical nature of the new organization but its focus upon issues close to home as well. The end of the Cold War late in Bush's term reinforced this emphasis upon domestic policy. Bromley himself reaffirmed the narrower role of PCAST by declaring that his primary job would be that of an "honest broker" rather than an advocate at the White House.[5]

In practice, science—and scientists—became even further submerged in the Bush presidency. Whereas only nine days elapsed between the creation of PSAC in 1957 and the committee's first meeting with Eisenhower, it was a full nine months before Bromley could introduce PCAST's members to Bush—a delay the science adviser attributed, in part, to the thicket of legal regulations and conflict-of-interest considerations that had grown up during the intervening years.[6] Bromley voiced similar frustration at the scientific community's criticism of him and OSTP for failing to lobby harder to increase funding for basic research and, likewise, at Congress's emphasis upon winning short-term "trophies" for individual districts at the expense of long-term investment in science and technology.[7]

But some of the disappointment that Bromley encountered on the job was doubtless the result of the limited role that he and the members of PCAST defined for themselves. Thus, although Bush's PCAST looked at the problem of nuclear proliferation after the Cold War, its Panel on Science, Technology, and National Security defined support for industrial competitiveness as "the single most important contribution science and technology can make to national security over the long term."[8] Tellingly, Bromley himself later lamented not forwarding to the president a draft report by PCAST on a matter that obviously involved the making of cardinal choices: world population growth and its social and environmental consequences. His reticence, Bromley confessed, was due to the "political atmosphere" surrounding the topic at the time.[9]

There were, as well, signs of more fundamental change in the perception of science, and science advice, from the early days of PSAC. As in the case of "megascience" projects like the international space station and the Superconducting Supercollider, it was increasingly difficult to make a persuasive argument—even among scientists—for the benefit of large-scale projects linked to basic research in a time of declining resources and shrinking budgets, especially when such projects lacked the emotional impetus of Sputnik or the national security imperatives of the Cold War.[10]

From outward appearances, the administration of William Jefferson Clinton stood ready to take up that challenge. Not only was "change" the watchword in the election campaign of the forty-eight-year-old Clinton, but the president's pick of a well-respected insider as science adviser, former OTA director Jack Gibbons, seemed intended to send a signal that pragmatism would be more important than ideology in Clinton's administration.[11] Like Bromley, Gibbons was given the title of assistant to the president and, as such, held seats on the National Security Council, the Domestic Policy Council, and the National Economic Council. Gibbons's prompt confirmation by the Senate likewise seemed a harbinger of quick action on the new president's agenda.

But the obstacles and delays that had afflicted Bush and Bromley survived to bedevil their successors. It took seven months for OSTP's four associate directors to be nominated and confirmed, and twice as long as it had during the Bush administration—eighteen months—for Clinton and Gibbons to create their own version of PCAST.[12]

Expanding from 12 to 18 members—six of them women—Clinton's PCAST also reflected an ethnic diversity in keeping with the president's campaign pledge to create an administration that looked more like America.[13] Initially, PCAST's focus was upon issues that its members felt had received too little attention in previous administrations—among them energy, health care, and the environment.[14] Vice President Albert Gore's particular interests in the computer technology of the Internet and the problem of global climate change created, in effect, a special constituency for science advice.[15]

Indeed, a wholly new innovation—the National Science and Technology Council—grew out of the "reinventing government" initiative championed by Gore and Clinton in the fall of 1993.[16] A Cabinet-level committee chaired by the president, NSTC was intended to coordinate science research and development projects across 22 federal agencies and departments.[17] Among the cooperative projects it promoted would be a "clean car" initiative to build a less-polluting vehicle in the near future and the "civilianization" of the Pentagon's highly accurate, space-based Global Positioning System (GPS).[18]

Early in 1995, the return of a Republican majority in Congress prompted calls for eliminating science- and technology-related offices in NASA, the Environmental Protection Agency, and the departments of Commerce and Energy.[19] The Republican ascendancy also led to proposed cuts of up to 35 percent in civilian science research and to the abolition of the Office of Technology Assessment that fall.[20] Although touted as a cost-cutting measure, the elimination of OTA seemed to many of the agency's longtime supporters more a politically inspired reprisal than a case of budget trimming.[21]

As a result of both the "reinventing government" initiative and Republican-imposed "downsizing," Clinton's OSTP by 1996 was three-quarters the size of the office under Bromley and Bush but had twice the workload, in Gibbons's estimation. In April 1998, the sixty-nine-year-old Gibbons stepped down as science adviser. He was replaced by Neal Lane, a physicist and former director of the National Science Foundation.[22]

The foremost concerns to confront Lane would be those inherited from Clinton's first term. They were also the cardinal choices likely to challenge the next administration at the start of a new century: the proliferation of weapons of mass destruction in a unsettled international environment, gradual but unprecedented changes in the global climate caused by industrialization, and population growth outdistancing the ability of nations to cope with the expanding numbers.

Principally, these are issues of international rather than national security, since they are of global scope, and their solution likely lies as much in the realm of science and technology as in politics. Nor is every vista of the future necessarily bleak. The so-called information revolution accelerated the decline of dictatorial regimes in eastern Europe and contributed to the collapse of the Soviet Union. The advent of high-resolution commercial observation satellites now promises to make a world of secrets transparent to any organization or individual with a computer and a credit card.[23] Since the United States is the only remaining superpower at the end of the millennium, however, this country and its leaders are likely to bear a disproportionate responsibility for the cardinal choices that will be made well into the next century.

At the same time, steps toward a solution may be made more difficult by an emerging antiscience and even antirational bias in public opinion.[24] Much of this attitude seems the inevitable result of the skepticism and bewilderment engendered by media attention to "junk science"—the conflicting claims and counterclaims put forward almost daily for new health cures, miracle diets, and so forth. But politics also plays a role. Repeated attempts were made in Congress during the Clinton administration to eliminate funding for research into climate change on the grounds that such research—including the study of global warming induced by carbon dioxide emissions—was inherently antithetical to business.[25]

In the years since the publication of C. P. Snow's *Science and Government,* the two worlds of science and government have in some ways become more disparate, and have moved even further apart. Where they of necessity must come together is in the making of policy. Here, as elsewhere, the past may be the most useful guide to the future.

Behind the steady decline of presidential science advising since PSAC has been a progressive loss of faith in the process by both sides: by scientists in the ability of the government to make proper choices based upon the evidence, rather than partisan pressures, and by presidents in the capacity of scientists to give objective advice, uncolored by personal views. Among presidents and scientists alike, this loss of faith has been reflected in the changing attitude of each toward the other. Certainly there seems, today, something strikingly outdated about the attitude expressed in Robert Oppenheimer's June 1945 report to the Interim Committee that "we, as scientific men, have no proprietary rights" and "no claim to special competence." Less than five years later, Oppenheimer himself abandoned this precept when he and others on the AEC's General Advisory Committee urged the government, on ethical grounds, not to proceed with development of the hydrogen bomb.

Barely a decade after President Truman's H-bomb decision, Jerome Wiesner—about to become President Kennedy's science adviser—proclaimed that PSAC's scientists had "a vested interest" in arms control. By the time of the Nixon administration, Wiesner and other former science advisers were openly challenging a variety of the president's policies on both technical and nontechnical grounds. It is perhaps not surprising that no president since Eisenhower has spoken of "his scientists."

The principal cause of this mutual disillusionment has been the politicalization of presidential science advising. Presidents and scientists alike bear some responsibility for the result.

Historical instances in which scientists have, for partisan reasons, taken sides on an issue provide a basis for the suspicion in government that experts use technical arguments to mask advocacy. In other cases, presidents in their eagerness to further a particular policy have misrepresented or willfully ignored the findings of experts. The trend toward encouraging the president's scientist to act as an advocate as well as an adviser in the administration that he or she serves has likewise blurred the role of the science adviser. It reached its nadir in the notion that the president's science advisers are also necessarily the president's slaves.

The history of science advising from the discovery of atomic fission to the end of the Cold War suggests that the question "Who advises?" is hardly less important than that of "Who governs?" In the immediate aftermath of PSAC's demise, various proposals were put forward for reestablishing a science advisory apparatus in the White House, among which were a Cabinet-level "Department of Science," a "troika" of science advisers modeled after the President's Council of Economic Advisers, and even a "science court."[26]

Today, none of the alternatives to PSAC proposed more than two decades ago seems adequate to the task of providing sound scientific counsel to the president. Moreover, subsequent experience suggests that both science and government have outstripped the original conception of PSAC. Even if the growth of real and prospective rivals in the government had not created insurmountable barriers to PSAC's return, it would appear unlikely that even a reconstituted PSAC could ever have anything like the prestige—or the influence—of the original.[27]

While some of the changes made in the science advisory apparatus since then—including the creation of PCAST—have had the effect of restoring an active science presence at the White House, additional reforms should be considered for the future.

Foremost, the president's science adviser and OSTP should reassert for themselves a significant role in advising on scientific matters affecting the nation's security, broadly defined. Clinton's PCAST moved in this direction by providing advice to the National Security Council on technical issues concerning the Comprehensive Test Ban Treaty and the worldwide proliferation of nuclear weapons. The science adviser should assume the role of arbitrator or referee whenever intragovernmental disputes arise over issues like environmental degradation by pollution or climate change from global warming.[28] Not only on domestic disputes but on larger issues as well, he or she should indeed play the part of an honest—but nonetheless active and engaged—broker.

Given the complexity of modern technological issues, the president's science adviser might wish to assign the task of reviewing the evidence behind controversial questions like climate change to an external blue-ribbon committee—on the model of Killian's 1954 Technical Capabilities Panel. To avoid the grandstanding and "agenda creep" that characterized the 1957 Gaither study, such a panel should be composed of technical experts rather than special pleaders chosen for the sake of political balance. To ensure finding the best possible talent, the panel's members should have the opportunity to present their findings directly to the president and the National Security Council. The end of the Cold War has, moreover, made it possible to recognize other, hitherto little-appreciated dangers—including environmental threats from ozone depletion and even the threat of an Earth-asteroid collision—that are properly the subject of study by such blue-ribbon panels.

While it would hardly be realistic to expect the dismantling of the science advisory offices of other government agencies, which have grown in influence since PSAC's demise, a strong science presence in the White House provides the equivalent of a medical second opinion on the cardinal choices facing the government. In that role it would once again serve as a needed counterbalance to more parochial interests. Like the original PSAC, the president's scientist should always be the sponsor—and, if need be, the defender—of good ideas that otherwise lack a bureaucratic constituency in the administration. Conversely, he or she should have responsibility for casting a critical eye upon government programs that, for partisan or other reasons, have heretofore received uncritical support.

Science advisers should also be allowed to define a broad mandate in their studies for the president—one that may legitimately question, for example, not only whether a weapon has achieved a certain technical capability but whether that capability, or that weapon, is needed at all. As the protracted saga of the MX missile demonstrated, little value will be attached to even highly informed technical judgments if they seem divorced from political reality and common sense. Some fifteen years after Reagan's announcement of SDI, an effective defensive against ballistic missiles was in fact no closer to realization. Instead, missile defense had become a battleground for the rival military services and favored contractors.[29] As such, it was once again an arena where an honest broker was needed. Not only arms procurement but the opposite problem—weapons of mass destruction proliferating to rogue states and even terrorists—is another area where the president's scientists should be encouraged to reestablish a vested interest.

In the meanwhile, tensions that have traditionally existed between the office of the science adviser and other White House agencies—specifically, the Office of Management and Budget—are likely to persist. In PSAC's day, establishment of a White House staff position shared between the offices of the national security adviser and the science adviser was an effective step toward recognizing mutual interests. Such a shared position was reestablished in the Clinton administration. One should likewise be considered between OMB and OSTP as a help in defusing perennial conflicts over budget matters.

The multiplicity of organizations in the government offering science advice suggests that new efforts at oversight and coordination may be necessary to avoid duplication of effort. The revival in the Bush administration of "fix-it"—the Federal Coordinating Council for Science, Engineering, and Technology (FCCSET)—and Clinton's creation of the National Science and Technology Council are both models for future coordination of the crosscutting work of various agencies, which will become necessary for allocating increasingly scarce resources.[30]

Science for policy, rather than policy for science, should continue to be the main focus of the president's science adviser. The direction of peacetime scientific research, along with the degree of federal support it receives, properly remains the purview of the National Science Foundation.

The rapid pace of technological change has created a greater need than ever for what Jerome Wiesner called "horizon scanning." The elimination of the Office of Technology Assessment, which used to perform the function for Congress, has exacerbated this need. Ideally, horizon scanning would not only provide warning of impending threats, but also anticipate and promote promising new technologies. Given the importance of the latter to the future, horizon scanning might be made the subject of semiannual reports to the president.

Reintroducing a forum for science advice in the White House will be of little advantage, of course, if the science adviser does not enjoy the president's confidence. The degree of trust between the president and the "first scientist" will always have a significant bearing on the effectiveness of both. Vannevar Bush's observation about science advice to the president in the 1940s—that its value depends not only upon who the science adviser is but who the president is, and how well they get along together—applies today as it did in the past, and will continue to do so in the future. In this connection, William Golden's original definition of the qualities to be sought in a science adviser remains generally apt: "He must be extraordinarily competent both technically, in order to comprehend the major programs and integrate them in his mind, and administratively, in order to avoid distraction by seductive details or special pleaders."[31]

Traditionally, the science adviser has been perceived as serving two masters—the president and the scientific community. While these two constituencies are not always in competition, when they do come into conflict the science adviser's first loyalty is to the president. In the event that the science adviser feels that such loyalty comes at the expense of the nation's best interests, resignation should precede protest. Yet, while recognizing that he or she is, as Kistiakowsky wrote, "first and foremost . . . a servant of the President," the scientists advising the White House should under no circumstances be considered the president's slaves, since that implies a willingness to sacrifice the very independence of judgment that makes their advice valuable.

In order to maintain a reputation for objectivity—which is, arguably, the most important asset the science adviser brings to the government—he or she should deliberately remain somewhat apart from the political fray, and the president needs to respect that separation. Although science advisers have in the past been effective salesmen for particular policies, the long-term cost has been to the credibility of the office. Ideally, the science adviser will enjoy the support and confidence not only of the president but of the scientific community. In any event, he or she must be of sufficient professional stature to risk being, on occasion, the bearer of bad news to either or both camps. While science advisers may be faulted for advice that is incorrect or misguided, they should not have to fear being pilloried for unpopular views.

Inevitably, tensions will occasionally arise between the president's need for confidential advice and the public's right to know, especially in matters affecting the nation's security. On such occasions, the president's scientists have a responsibility to regard their counsel—and, indeed, all their dealings with the White House—as privileged and confidential; such is the price that advisers pay for their right to speak the truth to power.

Leo Szilard's idealistic notion of a scientific *Bund* aside, presidents should realize that scientists are rarely likely to speak with one voice. Conversely, it is important for scientist-advisers to recognize that on those occasions when their voice is lost among the cacophony at the White House, they should not then seek a wider forum. While science advisers have, moreover, the same right as any citizen to support or oppose a policy on ethical grounds, it is true, as one PSAC alumnus has observed, that opinions based on moral considerations constitute advice from scientists rather than scientific advice.[32]

It is the duty of the science adviser both to draw the president's attention to promising or threatening new developments in science and to warn against what C. P. Snow described as "the euphoria of gadgets": overly optimistic schemes based upon unsubstantiated claims.[33] The president thus needs to know not only what is scientifically and technologically feasible, but also what is reasonable—for which information he will depend upon those whom Eisenhower called the government's only disinterested source of advice. In practice, the science adviser should help the president strike a balance between the administration's political objectives and scientific reality. In the past, disregarding one or the other has resulted in wasted resources and confusion over the nation's priorities.

Finally, prominent among the science adviser's tasks, as Wiesner suggested, is "to explore all the options—even the ones he doesn't like."[34] Yet the past fifty years of presidential science advising offer numerous examples of serious alternatives that were not fully explored, not adequately understood, and sometimes not even presented to the president. Making sure that the president is aware of and understands the alternatives—and, insofar as possible, their potential consequences—is perhaps the science adviser's premier responsibility when advising on the making of cardinal choices.

The contradiction inherent in a democracy of a handful of individuals with specialized knowledge giving secret counsel on what are potentially life-and-death decisions is, of course, not unique to the present era. As long ago as 1912, Woodrow Wilson warned that the country might be headed toward what he called, forebodingly, "a government of experts."[35] Almost a half-century after Wilson, a similar concern inspired President Eisenhower's warning about public policy becoming the captive of a "scientific-technological elite."

In 1960, the same year that Eisenhower's issued his celebrated warning, C. P. Snow wrote that "the results of the lack of communication between scientists and nonscientists . . . is worth examining. A good deal of the future may spring from it."[36] Snow's prediction proved prescient, and we live today with the consequences. Seen in retrospect, miscalculations and missed opportunities have always attended the making of cardinal choices—which, by their very nature, will continue to have the potential for both great good and enormous harm.

"Perhaps what is required more than advice," observed President Johnson's science adviser Donald Hornig, reflecting on the history of PSAC in 1980, "is a communications channel between the world of science and technology and that of politics."[37] For almost two decades, PSAC and the president's science adviser provided such a channel. Before then, and since, recognition of the need for science advice at the White House has usually been the result of a sudden, desperate crisis. The original recommendation for a science adviser, for example, came about as a result of the outbreak of war in Korea. The shock of Sputnik led directly to the charter creating PSAC, barely six weeks later. The Strategic Defense Initiative had its origins in the hope of putting an end to an unstable balance of terror.

Cardinal choices currently facing the nation and the world involve controversial scientific and technical issues: climate change, overpopulation, diminishing resources, the proliferation of weapons of mass destruction. Such issues are perhaps less dramatic than those of the Cold War, but their consequences are certainly no less dire. In the future, as in the past, making the proper choices will depend upon both the willingness and the ability of the two disparate worlds of science and government to work together toward a common purpose. Because of the unique position they occupy between those two worlds, the president's scientists are those best qualified by both knowledge and access to bridge that gap.

Appendixes

Einstein-Szilard Letter to President Roosevelt

August 2, 1939

Albert Einstein
Old Grove Rd.
Nassau Point
Peconic, Long Island
August 2nd, 1939

F. D. Roosevelt
President of the United States
White House
Washington, D.C.

Sir:

Some recent work by E. Fermi and L. Szilard, which has been communicated to me in manuscript, leads me to expect that the element uranium may be turned into a new and important source of energy in the immediate future. Certain aspects of the situation which has arisen seem to call for watchfulness and, if necessary, quick action on the part of the Administration. I believe therefore that it is my duty to bring to your attention the following facts and recommendations:

In the course of the last four months it has been made probable—through the work of Joliot in France as well as Fermi and Szilard in America—that it may become possible to set up a nuclear chain reaction in a large mass of uranium by which vast amounts of power and large quantities of new radium-like elements would be generated. Now it appears almost certain that this could be achieved in the immediate future.

This new phenomenon would also lead to the construction of bombs, and it is conceivable—though much less certain—that extremely powerful bombs of a new type may thus be constructed. A single bomb of this type, carried by boat and exploded in a port, might very well destroy the whole port together with some of the surrounding territory. However, such bombs might very well prove to be too heavy for transportation by air.

The United States has only very poor ores of uranium in moderate quantities. There is some good ore in Canada and the former Czechoslovakia, while the most important source of uranium is the Belgian Congo.

In view of this situation you may think it desirable to have some permanent contact maintained between the Administration and the group of physicists working on chain reactions in America. One possible way of achieving this might be for you to entrust with this task a person who has your confidence and who could perhaps serve in an inofficial capacity. His task might comprise the following:

a) to approach Government Departments, keep them informed of the further development, and put forward recommendations for Government action, giving particular attention to the problem of securing a supply of uranium ore for the United States;

b) to speed up the experimental work, which is at present being carried on within the limits of the budgets of University laboratories, by providing funds, if such funds be required, through his contacts with private persons who are willing to make contributions for this cause, and perhaps also by obtaining the co-operation of industrial laboratories which have the necessary equipment.

I understand that Germany has actually stopped the sale of uranium from the Czechoslovakian mines which she has taken over. That she should have taken such early action might perhaps be understood on the ground that the son of the German Under-Secretary of State, von Weizsäcker, is attached to the Kaiser-Wilhelm-Institut in Berlin where some of the American work on uranium is now being repeated.

Yours very truly,
A. Einstein

SOURCE: Spencer R. Weart and Gertrud Weiss Szilard, *Leo Szilard: His Version of the Facts* (Cambridge, Mass: MIT Press, 1978), pp. 94–95.

APPENDIX B

Fermi-Rabi Letter to the AEC

October 30, 1949

An Opinion on the Development of the "Super"

A decision on the proposal that an all-out effort be undertaken for the development of the "Super" cannot in our opinion be separated from considerations of broad national policy. A weapon like the "Super" is only an advantage when its energy release is from 100–1,000 times greater than that of ordinary atomic bombs. The area of destruction therefore would run from 150 to approximately 1,000 square miles or more.

Necessarily such a weapon goes far beyond any military objective and enters the range of very great natural catastrophes. By its very nature it cannot be confined to a military objective but becomes a weapon which in practical effect is almost one of genocide.

It is clear that the use of such a weapon cannot be justified on any ethical ground which gives a human being a certain individuality and dignity even if he happens to be a resident of an enemy country. It is evident to us that this would be the view of peoples in their countries. Its use would put the United States in a bad moral position relative to the peoples of the world.

Any postwar situation resulting from such a weapon would leave unresolvable enmities for generations. A desirable peace cannot come from such an inhuman application of force. The postwar problems would dwarf the problems which confront us at present.

The application of this weapon with the consequent great release of radioactivity would have results unforeseeable at present, but would certainly render large areas unfit for habitation for long periods of time.

The fact that no limits exist to the destructiveness of this weapon makes its very existence and the knowledge of its construction a danger to humanity as a whole. It is necessarily an evil thing considered in any light.

For these reasons we believe it important for the President of the United States to tell the American public, and the world, that we think it wrong on fundamental ethical principles to initiate a program of development of such a weapon. At the same time, it would be appropriate to invite the nations of the world to join us in a solemn pledge not to proceed in the development or construction of weapons of this category. If such a pledge were accepted even without control machinery, it appears highly probable that an advanced stage of development leading to a test by another power could be detected by available physical means. Furthermore, we have in our possession, on our stockpile of atomic bombs, the means for adequate "military" retaliation for the production or use of "super."

E. Fermi
I. I. Rabi

SOURCE: U. S. Department of Energy Archives, Washington, D.C.

APPENDIX C

The Golden Report

December 18, 1950

MEMORANDUM FOR THE PRESIDENT

SUBJECT: Mobilization of Science for War: A Scientific Adviser to the President

SUMMARY

I. Recommendation:

This memorandum recommends the prompt appointment of an out-standing scientific leader as Scientific Adviser to the President. His functions would be:

To inform himself and keep informed on all scientific research and development programs of military significance within the several independent Government departments so engaged.

To plan for and stand ready promptly to initiate a civilian Scientific Research Agency, roughly comparable to the Office of Scientific Research and Development (OSRD) of World War II.

To be available to give the President independent and comprehensive advice on scientific matters, inside and outside the Government, particularly those of military significance.

II. Reasons:

Two principal considerations lead to the recommendation that a Scientific Adviser to the President be appointed at this time:

More than ten independent departments and agencies of the Government are now conducting significant research and development programs of actual or potential military value. Their obligations for these purposes approximated $1,300,000,000 in FY 1950 (somewhat over 50% by the Department of Defense) and will be much greater in FY 1952. The procurement programs, for which research is the first step, will be many times these sums. Each of these agencies reports separately to the President. There is need for centralization of knowledge of all these scientific programs in one independent and technically competent individual to whom the President can turn for advice.

The office of Scientific Research and Development in World War II, and other civilian organizations in prior wars, were responsible for highly valuable technical advances outside of military channels. The proximity fuse, micro-wave radar, and the initiation of work on the atom bomb are notable examples. There will again be need for such a civilian scientific research agency, to supplement the work of the military and other established organizations through exploitation of research areas not suitable for them and to provide uninhibited working conditions for a limited number of leading scientific minds on radical and unorthodox ideas.

Plans for such as OSRD-type "Scientific Research Agency" should be developed promptly and the agency itself should be established in a modest way as soon as the first appropriate projects are selected, evolving thereafter in accordance with opportunity and the then prevailing degree of urgency. The Scientific Adviser to the President, with his competence and comprehensive knowledge, would be ideally qualified to plan the Scientific Research Agency and to discern opportunities for its initial projects and specific scientists to undertake them. At the time of the actual establishment of the Scientific Research Agency [a] decision would be made as to whether the Scientific Adviser would undertake to head its operating organization or whether another man should be called in for this function, leaving the former in his purely advisory capacity.

SOURCE: Papers of William Golden, Library of Congress, Washington, D.C.

APPENDIX D

The Disarmament Panel's Proposal for a Nuclear "Standstill"
Fall 1952

Memorandum by the Panel of Consultants on Disarmament

TOP SECRET   [WASHINGTON, undated.]

THE TIMING OF THE THERMONUCLEAR TEST

INTRODUCTION

As members of the Panel of Consultants on Disarmament, we have been attempting to reach useful conclusions about problems of American policy with regard to the limitation and control of armaments. Early in our work, as a part of a review of the development of armaments, our attention was called to the plan to test a thermonuclear device in November of this year. As we have continued to explore the problem of finding a way to work toward a moderation of the present arms race, we have become increasingly convinced that the projected test may be an event of considerable import for the future. We have found many considerations which argue for a postponement of this test until its full and future implications can be dealt with by the next Administration; we have also found that there are a number of considerations, some of them clearly important, which weigh against such a postponement. This account attempts to spell out and assess these varying considerations, and to state our own balance of feeling, which is that if certain important conditions can be met, it would be wise to postpone the scheduled test until 1953.

In reaching our conclusions, we have proceeded from a primary concern with the relevance of this test to the whole range of questions affecting the limitation and control of armaments; this was the only proper course for a Panel of Consultants on Disarmament. Moreover, we have not undertaken any comprehensive study of the whole range of opinion and judgment that exists in the government; our assignment has been to consult with the Secretary of State and officers of his Department. But the problem of armaments is not a narrow one, and we have been forced to consider questions which are the primary concern of professional soldiers and others. This overlap we fear is inevitable. Our judgments may be right or wrong, but we have not been able to disentangle ourselves from these problems. Unless he examines the character of weapons and the meaning of negotiations, one can hardly have sensible ideas as to how negotiations about weapons can be made useful.

The account which follows falls into five sections. Section I explains why we think this test of a thermonuclear device is so important, and why we think that so many new elements have appeared since thermonuclear development was first ordered in 1950 that the present plan to test a weapon in November is in itself a determinable event which deserves all the care and study that are given to major new problems. Section II suggests some of the disadvantages which we think may result from holding this test on schedule. Section II [III] deals with the possible advantages of postponing the test. Section IV is concerned with the disadvantages of postponement; we discuss some which seem to us not persuasive, and some which seem to us highly important. Section V presents our mixed conclusions.

I. THE PLAN FOR A THERMONUCLEAR TEST CALLS FOR A NEW DECISION
A. *Character of the Test*

A test of a thermonuclear device is planned by the United States Government for the month of November, 1952. This device is the product of many years of study, culminating in two and a half years of intensive technical effort which began after the Government's decision in 1950 to proceed with the development of a thermonuclear weapon. Great technical advances have been made in this period through a combination of good luck, great skill, and high dedication. This first test may not work, but among leading students of the problem there is now very little doubt that the scientists concerned are on the right track.

If this test is successful, it will have an explosive power one hundred to one thousand times as great as that of the atomic bomb used at Hiroshima. It will thus be something more than one more in a series of scientific tests. It will be impossible to conceal the fact that this event has taken place, and very difficult to conceal the fact that it is an event of great portent for all men.

The device which is to be tested is not a weapon; it is very heavy and it needs much mothering. In its present form it could not be delivered by any ordinary military means. But the fact that it is not a weapon is important only in terms of time; if the device works, there will be thermonuclear weapons in a very few years, and compared to this test, the test of the eventual weapon will be a discounted anticlimax. About the so-called hydrogen bomb there has always been this one great question: "Is this possible?" This question will be answered if the projected test succeeds.

The test, then, will be a great event if it succeeds. Any such event, in the normal course of administration, is carefully studied by those in authority in order to be sure that it is managed in the best possible way. In the case of this test, however, there is naturally a disposition to believe that the basic decision is past, on the ground that the large questions were those raised and decided when it was originally determined that it was right to try to make a hydrogen bomb. This decision was reached by due process. Should we not regard this test, however striking its results may be, as the natural and routine consequence of the earlier decision? The question is important, because Government cannot permit itself the luxury of perpetual self-doubt.

We think that it may be more accurate to conceive of the decision to conduct a thermonuclear test in November as essentially a new decision, deserving the close attention and mature consideration of the highest officers of the Government. We think that much has changed since 1950, and we think also that the very magnitude of the technical accomplishment urges a review of its meaning.

Many relevant changes have occurred since 1950. First, the course of thermonuclear research has modified one set of fears which lent urgency to the quest for a hydrogen bomb. It no longer seems likely that Fuchs could have been of much help to the Russians in this field, since the information he could have supplied them has turned out in our experience to be misleading.

Second, we now think we know how to make a thermonuclear device that works, and we also think we can make it into a weapon fairly soon. In 1950 the decision to proceed could not but be stimulated in part by the very uncertainty and ignorance that surrounded the problem; now we know what we are trying to do. The decision to learn about a matter is quite different from a decision to act on what has been learned.

Third, our own stockpile of atomic weapons is very much larger than it was in 1950, and it will be larger still by the time the present thermonuclear device can be turned into a weapon. Moreover, extensions of atomic weapons techniques are making available fission weapons of a yield thirty-fold greater than that of the original bombs; weapons of this size are large enough to deal with nearly all important Russian targets. While these changes could in large measure be foreseen in 1950, a stockpile on hand is quite different in its impact on thought from one which is merely on order.

Fourth, present thinking about development of actual weapons with a thermonuclear component is aimed at a set of bombs very much smaller in yield than the projected test will be if it measures up to its reasonable possibilities. There is something odd in the prospect of a test which may be some ten times as powerful as any weapon we plan to produce for at least the next few years.

Fifth, our experience in Korea and in building NATO has deepened our national understanding of the complex task of resisting Soviet aggression and working for freedom. It is now much more clear than it was two years ago that it is vitally important to distinguish among different kinds of strength and force, using only those which effectively advance our chosen purposes.

Sixth, since the decision of 1950 the United States has made a major effort in the United Nations to assert and demonstrate the American interest in the balanced reduction of armaments. On the whole this effort, so far, has had good results on world opinion; but its future may be sharply, perhaps decisively, related to the proposed thermonuclear test. This connection is emphasized by the fact that the General Assembly will be meeting in November, at the very time when the test is now scheduled to take place.

Seventh, it has turned out, quite by accident, that if it goes off on schedule, the test will take place either just before or just after Election Day. In either case, it will come in the last months of what the world now knows to be an outgoing Administration. This accident of timing may affect the impact of the test in a number of ways.

Taken together, these changes from the situation of 1950 persuade us that it is proper to raise the question whether or not the projected test should proceed on the present schedule. We turn, then, to the principal considerations which seem to us to argue for a postponement into 1953.

. . .

V. CONCLUSION: LET US POSTPONE THE TEST IF SUCH A DECISION CAN BE UNDERSTOOD, EXPLAINED, AND PROPERLY SUPPORTED

Taken together, the arguments for a postponement of the projected thermonuclear test seem to us persuasive. We think that November is not a good time, and we think that the decision should be made by the next Administration. We think that this is a fateful step, and that before it is taken the next Administration should be quite sure that there is no better use to be made of all that we have learned since 1950. We are not persuaded by the claim that postponement would bring unacceptable dangers, and while we admit that it is not clear where a postponement would lead, we have to note that this ignorance applies to any effort to limit the current power struggle. We think the test should be postponed, and though our first concern is with the limitation of armaments, we think that postponement remains desirable when judged from the broad standpoint of the national security.

The reservation which we set to our conclusion is that we cannot urge a decision to postpone the test unless it proves possible to obtain for such a decision some measure of support and understanding from the senior government officials primarily concerned, to make the decision reasonably intelligible among those who have worked to make the test possible, and to explain it publicly without seriously limiting the freedom of the next Administration. We fully understand that it may not be possible to meet these conditions, but it is not for us to judge such a question. We cannot by a prejudgment of the temper of the Government excuse ourselves from the obligation to record our considered opinion that under the conditions we have stated, the postponement of the scheduled test not only is desirable, but could become a decisive act of statesmanship.

SOURCE: U. S. Department of State, *Foreign Relations of the United States, 1952–1954,* Vol. 2, Part 2 (Washington, D.C.: U.S. Government Printing Office, 1984) pp. 994–1008.

APPENDIX E

The Teapot Report on ICBMs
Recommendations of the Committee on Strategic Missiles
February 10, 1954

I. INTRODUCTION: SOME GENERAL REMARKS ON THE LONG-RANGE
MISSILE PROGRAMS

1. The Committee's assignment has been limited to that of studying long-range intercontinental strategic missiles under development by the Air Force and making suitable recommendations for improving this program. Specific recommendations are made of changes for the improvement of the present Snark, Navaho, and Atlas programs.

2. Unusual urgency for a strategic missile capability can arise from one of two principal causes: a rapid strengthening of the Soviet defenses against our SAC manned bombers, or rapid progress by the Soviet in his own development of strategic missiles which would provide a compelling political and psychological reason for our own effort to proceed apace. The available intelligence data are insufficient to make possible a positive estimate of the progress being made by the Soviet in the development of intercontinental missiles. Evidence exists of an appreciation of this field on the part of the Soviet and of activity in some important phases of guided missiles which could have as an end objective the development by the Soviet of intercontinental missiles. While the evidence does not justify a conclusion that the Russians are ahead of us, it is also felt by the Committee that this possibility certainly cannot be ruled out.

3. Generally speaking, important aspects of the present long-range missile program consisting of the three projects, Snark, Navaho, and Atlas, are believed to be unsatisfactory. While specific recommendations for improving each of these programs are made in the following sections of this memorandum, certain weaknesses generally common to all programs are noted here.

   a. It is believed that all three missile systems have thoroughly out-of-date military specifications on target C.E.P.'s. This results from the very recent progress toward larger yield warheads which could hardly have been predicted when these specifications were originally established.

   b. The problem of reduction of base vulnerability needs much more careful study, particularly with respect to the influence on missile design that might be exerted by a better handling of this base vulnerability matter.

    c. Closely related to base vulnerability is the problem of readiness and firepower; in general, the present plans for each of the three missiles result in discouragingly low-rate single and multiple missile launchings in view of the importance of destroying enemy SAC bases quickly at the start of the war.

    4. The specific recommendations made by this Committee on the long-range intercontinental missiles have been based on the conviction that only nuclear warheads are appropriate, and that the designs of the missiles should not be made more difficult by the added requirement to accommodate other types of warheads.

    5. Two peripheral items seem to require mention as exceptions to the policy of this Committee not to make recommendations on programs other than the intercontinental missile programs:

    a. Certain recommendations are made, in connection with the Snark program, for the use of Simplified Snarks as an aid to the SAC manned-bomber program. Generally speaking, any program proposals that offer possibilities of prolonging the use of manned bombers are worthy of serious consideration. This has not been an assignment of this Committee; these recommendations merely developed naturally out of the Committee's search for means of modifying the Snark program to permit it to lead to useful results in a reasonable time.

    b. There is to the Committee's knowledge no current Air Force program for ballistic missiles of medium range (say, 200–1,500 miles). Whether or not this is a serious omission in the overall Defense Department plans has not been studied by this Committee, but should be considered by some qualified agency. It is pertinent for this Committee to note that such missile capability is not necessarily automatically attained, nor most rapidly and economically attained, by the development of the longer-range missiles.

    6. In the investigations leading to the recommendations in this memorandum, the Committee acknowledges the aid received from the latest Rand proposals on an intercontinental ballistic missile system (IBMS).

SOURCE: Alfred Rockefeller Documents, 1951–1959, History Office, Air Force Systems Command Headquarters, Andrews Air Force Base, Maryland.

APPENDIX F

Killian's Charter for PSAC

December 1957

I. TERMS OF REFERENCE FOR PROPOSED APPOINTMENT OF SPECIAL AS-
SISTANT TO THE PRESIDENT FOR SCIENCE AND TECHNOLOGY

1. The title of the new post shall be Special Assistant to the President
   for Science and Technology. The appointee shall have White House
   status.
2. The duties of this Special Assistant would be:

   (a) To keep himself informed on the progress of scientific endeavor
       in the various agencies of Government, giving primary atten-
       tion to the use of science and technology in relation to national
       security.
   (b) To find and present facts to the President and to present evalu-
       ations and recommendations with respect to scientific and tech-
       nological matters.
   (c) To advise on scientific and technological matters at the policy-
       making level; to be available as an advisor on scientific and
       technological matters to Cabinet members and other policy-
       making officers of Government when appropriate and practi-
       cal, and when approved by the President; to work in close as-
       sociation with the Director of the Office of Defense Mobiliza-
       tion and the Special Assistant to the President for National
       Security.
   (d) To try to anticipate future trends or developments in the area
       of science and technology and to suggest future actions in re-
       gard thereto.
   (e) To aid in the collection of information about the relative
       progress of Soviet and U.S. science and technology.
   (f) To work closely with the National Science Foundation and its
       Director.
   (g) To be concerned with maintaining good and close relations
       with the U.S. scientific and engineering community and to fur-
       ther in every appropriate way the strength and morale of the
       scientific community.
   (h) To be concerned with the interchange, when feasible and
       proper, of scientific and technological information with scien-
       tists and officials, military and non-military, of our allies, and
       to encourage science in the free world.

The Special Assistant would be authorized to be in attendance at meetings of the National Security Council, the Cabinet, and the OCB and to attend or to be represented at meetings of the NSC Planning Board, the State Policy Planning Group, the Defense Science Board, the Interdepartmental Committee on Scientific Research and Development, and the Science Advisory Committee (described below). It is the intent of the President that the Special Assistant for Science and Technology will have full access to all plans, programs, and activities involving science and technology in the Government, including the Department of Defense, AEC, and CIA.

The Special Assistant to the President shall be authorized to nominate a full-time Deputy and to appoint a small supporting staff.

II. TERMS OF REFERENCE FOR PROPOSED PRESIDENT'S SCIENCE ADVISORY COMMITTEE

The President's Advisory Committee shall have the following characteristics:

(a) The members of the Committee to be recommended to the President by the Special Assistant to the President for Science and Technology with the approval of the Chairman and appointed by the President.
(b) The members of the Committee to have fixed terms of membership on the Committee, the intent being to provide for a rotation of membership.
(c) The Committee to be broadly representative of those fields of science and technology most important to Government and at this juncture, most relevant to national security. The number of members on this Committee should not be arbitrarily set at this time, but a committee of seventeen to twenty members is contemplated. In addition to regular members the Committee will have a group of consultants. The Committee should have its own executive officer. For a period it would be highly desirable if a few members of this Committee could serve full-time or nearly full-time.
(d) The Committee to be advisory to the President and to his Special Assistant for Science and Technology. It will have White House status.
(e) The Committee to nominate its chairman annually.

SOURCE: James Killian, *Sputnik, Scientists, and Eisenhower* (Cambridge, Mass: MIT Press, 1977), pp. 275–76.

APPENDIX G

Ruina-Gell-Mann Paper
December 1965

J. P. Ruina and M. Gell-Mann

BALLISTIC MISSILE DEFENCE AND THE ARMS RACE

This paper discusses briefly the possible harmful consequences that deployment of a ballistic missile defence system by either the U.S. or the U.S.S.R. may have on the arms race.

Both the U.S.S.R. and the U.S. have had extensive research and development programmes in ballistic missile defence, but neither country has to this date deployed in any meaningful quantity such defence systems to protect its population centres. Therefore, the cities of both powers are conspicuously vulnerable to ballistic missile attack.

On the other hand, by hiding, hardening, or making mobile the sites of their ballistic missiles both countries have become relatively invulnerable to offensive forces.

Under these conditions a state of mutual deterrence is reached where neither side dare attack the other. The consequences to an attacker are clear and unmistakable and so the danger of miscalculation is very small.

In this situation where offensive weapons are invulnerable to attack while cities are extremely vulnerable, a curious and unprecedented stability is maintained in two different senses.

1. The military balance is insensitive to the number and kind (as long as they are invulnerable) of offensive weapons in the arsenal of each country.
2. The danger of miscalculation on either side of the consequences of a nuclear attack are minimized.

Since, under these conditions, there is no great pressure for either country to have large quantities of nuclear armaments, the setting is excellent for taking positive steps towards a reduction in nuclear arms.

In regard to ballistic missile defence, it is well known that the technical problems faced in developing such a system are staggering. The offense, by saturating the defence and using a wide variety of penetration devices, has both the technical and economic factors in its favour. It would be far less costly and take far less time for the offense to overcome effectively a defensive measure than for the defending side to implement the measure initially.

Surely, a ballistic missile defence can be developed and deployed which will have some degree of effectiveness, but it would offer little protection against an all-out attack designed to penetrate such a system. Why then would the U.S. or U.S.S.R. consider deploying such a costly system? There are several possible reasons:

(a) Governments are very uncomfortable about a strategic balance which involves keeping their populations as hostages. It is natural, therefore, for a government to consider employing whatever protection can be bought, however meagre, on the assumption that if there is a nuclear exchange, damage would be reduced.
(b) Since neither power would know with certainty the capability of the other's defensive system, it may be thought that this would discourage an attacker in that he would be uncertain of the outcome of this attack.
(c) The government may expect that cities would not be the primary targets in a nuclear exchange and a defensive system would only have to operate against a small residual force, the main attacks being against strategic bases.
(d) A ballistic defence system may provide effective protection against the missile force of a smaller power.

The first two of these arguments require the deluding assumption that full deployment of a ballistic missile defense system for population protection on the part of one power would involve no consequent increase in the offensive force level of the other side.

Now let us consider what may be the consequence if one power deploys a ballistic missile defence system for population protection. There are several reactions one can expect on the part of the other power:

(i) The size of its deterrent force would be increased to take into account the existence of the defence system. The size of the increase would not only be compensatory but would also have to take into account all the uncertainties about the capability of the defence system and, therefore, over-compensation is very likely.
(ii) To maintain the balance and to respond to pressure at home the second power would also deploy a defence system which would cause the first power to increase his nuclear forces.
(iii) There would now be a premium on missiles that can penetrate defence systems. These are clearly more difficult to harden or to make mobile than missiles that do not have this requirement. Therefore, the arsenals of each power would tend to be more vulnerable than they need be otherwise.

The net result would be that the strategic balance would still be maintained but in a much less obvious manner than originally. The numbers and kinds of offensive weapons would now figure heavily in determining the balance. Population centres would still be vulnerable and populations would still in essence be kept as hostages. Therefore, no substantial gain will have been achieved by either side and yet the cost to each side would be great and the added dangers significant. Uncertainty and suspicion will be increased. Since the deterrent forces may be more vulnerable, each side would be more nervous and a pr emptive first strike would become more attractive than before. The leadership of one nation may attribute a greater capability to its own defence system than it really has and may consider risking an attack in a crisis. In general, adding this complicating factor to the current strategic balance would accelerate the pace of the arms race, add to the economic burden of both sides, decrease the possibility of substantial strategic arms reductions, and increase the dangers of escalation from crisis to nuclear war—all this with very modest compensating gains.

This leads us to the conclusion, perhaps surprising to many, that deployment of a ballistic missile defence system may not be desirable. Traditionally, one thinks of defensive steps as being reasonable, unaggressive, and stabilizing measures. Defence measures have generally been considered to discourage aggression, or at least to minimize damage from war if it comes. These sentiments about defensive measures are so prevalent that governments would be considered irresponsible and negligent if they did not take whatever defensive measures they can to protect their populations. Indeed these arguments would have merit if (1) full deployment of a ballistic missile defence system involved no consequent change in the number and kinds of offensive weapons the other side felt it necessary to have to maintain his deterrent; or if (2) the defensive system really provided adequate protection so as to make ballistic missiles ineffective for city destruction.

But this is clearly not the case. In times past, prior to the nuclear age, defensive systems were more effective and less costly relative to the offence and, therefore, did play stabilizing roles. With the new technological situation, where ballistic missiles are cheap and can do devastating damage, while defence is costly with very limited effectiveness, our sentiments about the role of defence must be re-examined.

The two superpowers should seriously consider refraining from the deployment (though not necessarily the research and development) of active city defences against missiles. A ban on ballistic missile defence, whether formally agreed to or tacitly followed, would have in its favour the fact that the inspection requirements would not be severe. The systems are large, employing heavy radars and large quantities of anti-missile missiles, and would be located near major cities. This makes clandestine deployment difficult.

In conclusion, it is important to stress the point that after many years of research and development on missile defence both powers must now be at the point of deciding on deployment. Once deployment takes place, it will be very difficult to negotiate back to the situation that we have today. Therefore, it is urgent that this important matter gets immediate consideration by both governments.

SOURCE: J. P. Ruina, manuscript.

APPENDIX H

Rathjens-Ruina Memorandum to Henry Kissinger

June 2, 1969

A Moratorium on the Testing of Multiple Warheads

The present strategic balance is in jeopardy primarily because of three developments: (1) the possibility of an ABM deployment (for defense of cities); (2) the possibility that the Soviet ICBM force, and particularly the SS-9 force, will continue to grow; and (3) MIRV development by the United States and possible MIRV development by the USSR. What happens in these areas will also have a bearing on the levels of armaments that might be negotiated in the Strategic Arms Limitation Talks and indeed on the prospects for success of those talks.

Neither of the first two possibilities above are time-urgent problems. If the Soviet Union goes ahead with either a further ABM deployment or a large SS-9 build-up, we will see adequate evidence long before the deployment becomes serious. Hopefully, these problems will be dealt with in the Strategic Arms Limitation Talks. If they are and there is a prohibition on either further ABM or ICBM deployment or both, we can have high confidence in our ability to monitor compliance.

The MIRV development is far more troublesome in that we really are just about at a point of no return. We see no way of precluding deployment of MIRV's by agreement, and of having sufficient confidence in our ability to verify compliance, once test programs have proceeded to the point where such systems are ready for deployment, or even possibly if there are just a modest number of additional tests. This does not mean that either side will have developed MIRV's in the near future to the point where they would be effective counterforce weapons. But if we have not already reached the point where we could go ahead with MIRV deployment that would be adequate for penetration of possible ABM defenses, we soon will. Much more extensive test programs, and indeed new development programs, will be required before either the U.S. or the Soviet Union would have a counterforce capability. The yield/accuracy combinations available with first generation MIRV's will be inadequate. We are concerned, however, that if tests are permitted to continue on these first generation systems possibly even for only a few more weeks, the point will have been passed where we could have the required high confidence that the Soviet Union might not develop a counterforce capability some years hence without it being obvious to unilateral intelligence collection efforts. The inverse problem is also worrisome in a way. The Soviet Union ought not to be as concerned about a few more American tests because if we can reach agreement to prohibit further development and deployment later on, they could probably have adequate confidence in our compliance, given our more open society. (JPR [Ruina] is more persuaded of this than GWR [Rathjens].) But continued U.S. testing would be worrisome because (1) it is simply not in the cards for the Soviet Union to stop if we continue, and (2) with each succeeding U.S. test the pressure from the military for deployment will increase; and once we deploy MIRV's there would be no doubt that the Soviet Union would be concerned, and legitimately so— evolutionary improvements in accuracy, reliability, and yield could result in a genuine U.S. counterforce capability. Because of the foregoing, it may not do to wait until Strategic Arms Limitation Talks take action on the MIRV question. Even if a moratorium should perhaps be the first order of Strategic Arms Limitations Talks business, it may be too late. Failure to achieve a MIRV moratorium may well foreordain those talks to failure.

For the United States, and probably for the Soviet Union as well, what is really at issue, besides the possibility of successful arms limitation talks, is the question of whether we will be able to rely on fixed-base ICBM's as a significant part of our deterrent in the mid-70's. If MIRV programs continue, we will almost certainly not wish to do so. Neither super-hardening nor active defense will offer the kind of security for our retaliatory force that we will want when the number of warheads that can be delivered against us is indeterminate. This means, at least as far as we can now see, that a decision to go ahead with MIRV tests probably also implies eventual abandonment of Minuteman missiles by the United States, and probably almost exclusive reliance on submarines for our deterrent including possibly implementation of the Navy's ULMS proposal. For the Soviet Union it will more likely mean reliance on a combination of submarines and land-mobile ICBM's. We believe that submarine-based forces are now so invulnerable, and so likely to remain so, that we would not be particularly concerned at having all or nearly all of our retaliatory strength at sea. Nevertheless, it is not quite as comforting a prospect as being able to rely on a multiplicity of systems each with radically different vulnerabilities.

Thus, we see the short-term objectives of a MIRV moratorium to be two: (1) prevention of development of Soviet capabilities that will in the long term force us to rely almost exclusively on SLBM [Submarine-Launched Ballistic Missile] forces as a deterrent; and (2) halting developments on both sides that could seriously prejudice the possibility that the Strategic Arms Limitation Talks will be successful.

We do not see any great disadvantage for the United States in stopping MIRV tests at this time. The test programs are already far enough along so that we have an adequate hedge against the possibility of a massive ABM deployment. If we were to see indications of the latter at any time during the next few years, our MIRV programs could be reactivated, and our MIRV deployment could keep well ahead of any Soviet ABM deployment, This would be particularly true if the conversion of the 31 Polaris to Poseidon submarines were to continue as scheduled.

That conversion would also provide us with an additional hedge. The Poseidon missile will be able to carry quite a heavy warhead to a considerably greater distance than can the Polaris A-3 missile. Thus, with the Poseidon conversion, the possibility of an effective Soviet ASW capability being developed will be much reduced (below what we anticipate will be a very low level anyway), a desirable development if attempts to stop MIRV programs fail and we are forced to rely primarily on our sea-based forces for deterrence.

Presumably we would want to reactivate programs to develop single warheads for both the Poseidon and Minuteman missiles.

With these factors in mind, we believe that the simplest MIRV moratorium that should be acceptable to the United States would be one prohibiting only the further testing by the United States and the Soviet Union of MIRV's and any kind of multiple warheads, respectively. There is an obvious problem of asymmetry here. We would presumably not want to stop confidence firings of the Polaris A-3 missile; on the other hand, we cannot accept continued firing of multiple warheads with the SS-9 despite the fact that there is still ambiguity as to whether or not they are individually targeted. Because of this problem, any formal agreement would not be easily negotiable. Therefore, we will probably simply want to state that we will stop our MIRV tests provided the Soviet Union does not continue its multiple warhead tests.

It would be advantageous if the moratorium could also apply to SS-9 and other Soviet missile and submarine production as well, but we see no need for that and consider that any attempt to include such developments would lead to a possibly unacceptable delay on the critical issue: the prohibition on MIRV tests. Thus, in our judgment, continued production of Soviet missiles and submarines should be permitted, as would be conversion of Polaris to Poseidon submarines and production of Poseidon and Minuteman III missiles, those problems to be dealt with in the Strategic Arms Limitation Talks.

Obviously a MIRV moratorium could not remain in effect with the deployment by either side of an extensive ABM system. This problem could be dealt with either by specifying that the moratorium would be of limited duration or by specifying that it would remain in effect only provided that there were no further ABM deployment. Either option would seem acceptable. Neither side could do much in the way of an ABM deployment on a short time scale, and the Strategic Arms Limitation Talks will presumably deal with longer-term problems.

SOURCE: George Rathjens, manuscript.

APPENDIX I

Garwin Letter to President Carter

August 15, 1978

President Jimmy Carter   August 15, 1978
The White House
Washington, D.C.

Dear Mr. President:

As individuals long involved in the conception, design, manufacture, test, and maintenance of many of the United States' nuclear and thermonuclear weapons, we want you to know of our judgment on a question which has assumed considerable prominence in connection with the Comprehensive Test Ban Treaty ("CTBT"). That is the question of the degree of assurance in the continued operability of our stockpiled nuclear weapons in the absence of any possibility of testing with significant nuclear yield (for instance, with testing limited to laboratory-type experiment).

As you know, the assurance of continued operability of stockpiled nuclear weapons has in the past been achieved almost exclusively by non-nuclear testing—by meticulous inspection and disassembly of the components of the nuclear weapons, including their firing and fuzing equipment. Problems encountered in this inspection are normally validated by additional sampling and solved by the remanufacture of the affected components. This program is, of course, supplemented by the instrumented firing of the entire nuclear weapon with inert material replacing the fissile materials, and the entire program thus far described would be unaffected by the requirements of a CTBT. It has been exceedingly rare for a weapon to be taken from stockpile and fired "for assurance."

It has also been rare to the point of nonexistence for a problem revealed by the sampling and inspection program to require a nuclear test for its resolution. There are three acceptable approaches to the correction of deficiencies without requiring nuclear testing:

(1) Remanufacture to precisely the original specifications.

(2) Remanufacture with minor modifications in surface treatment, protective coatings, and the like, after thorough review by experienced and knowledgeable individuals.

(3) Replace the nuclear explosive by one which has previously been tested and accepted for stockpile.

A fourth option, to replace the troubled nuclear system by one not already proof-tested, may result in improved performance, lesser use of special nuclear materials, or the like, virtues which have more to do with improvement of the stockpile than with confirming its operability.

We believe that the key question to be answered by those responsible for making and maintaining nuclear weapons is:

"Can the continued operability of our stockpile of nuclear weapons be assured without future nuclear testing? That is, without attempting or allowing improvement in performance, reductions in maintenance cost, and the like, are there non-nuclear inspection and correction programs which will prevent the degradation of the reliability of stockpiled weapons?

Our answer is "yes," and we now discuss the reasons why knowledgeable people may have answered "no" to seemingly similar questions.

First, we confined ourselves essentially to the question, "If the stockpile is not required to improve, can it be kept from degrading?" Others may have had in mind the normal work of the weapons laboratories, by which nuclear weapons are continuously made somewhat more efficient, less costly in terms of nuclear materials, adapted to new packaging requirements, and safer to handle—for instance by the substitution of insensitive explosion. We have participated in such programs and find them both interesting and useful. Were these "improvement programs" carried out long enough without nuclear testing, the weapons thus affected would indeed have uncertain performance; the solution under a CTBT would be to forego such programs in order not to sacrifice stockpile reliability to a desire for minor improvement in performance.

Second, it is true that certain deficiencies have in the past been corrected by the replacement of the affected nuclear system by another one, following a test certifying the replacement model as ready for stockpile. This corrective measure would not be available under a CTBT. But the examples normally cited need not have been corrected in this way; for instance, one Polaris warhead problem could readily have been solved by remanufacture with an acceptable change of surface treatment on the component which had caused the problem. The change of nuclear system was not absolutely necessary for the correction of the problem observed.

Finally, it is sometimes claimed that remanufacture may become impossible because of increasingly severe restrictions by EPA or OSHA to protect the environment of the worker. We note that additional protective measures which might be an intolerable cost burden in the manufacture of cardboard or of lightbulbs or of aircraft brakes are easily affordable in connection with the nuclear stockpile. Thus, if the worker's environment acceptable until now for the use of asbestos, spray adhesives, or beryllium should be forbidden by OSHA regulations, those few workers needed to continue operations with such material could wear plasticfilm suits (supplied with external air) commonly used for isolation against germs and against certain pharmaceuticals. It would be wise also to stockpile in appropriate storage facilities certain commercial materials used in weapons manufacture which might in the future disappear from the commercial scene.

It has been suggested that under a CTBT a President or Congress or the Department of Energy might not provide funds for stockpile maintenance inspection and correction, or that a President might not provide a requested exemption from OSHA or EPA requirements. We see no reason to assume that the national security bureaucracy will not continue to serve the national interest, and we would welcome a statement in conjunction with a CTBT that non-nuclear testing, inspection, and remanufacture where necessary will be fully supported in order to ensure the continued operability of stockpiled nuclear weapons.

We believe that the Department of Energy, through its contractors and laboratories, can through the measures described provide continuing assurance for as long as may be desired of the operability of the nuclear weapons stockpile. We are making this statement available to others in the Executive and the Congress.

Sincerely yours,

J. Carson Mark
Norris E. Bradbury
Richard L. Garwin

SOURCE: U. S. Congress, *Congressional Record,* Senate, August 17, 1978, pp. 26, 706–7.

APPENDIX J

The "Insert"
President Reagan's Announcement of SDI

March 23, 1983

Address to the Nation on Defense and National Security

My fellow Americans, thank you for sharing your time with me tonight.

The subject I want to discuss with you, peace and national security, is both timely and important. Timely, because I've reached a decision which offers a new hope for our children in the 21st century, a decision I'll tell you about in a few minutes. And important because there's a very big decision that you must make for yourselves. This subject involves the most basic duty that any President and any people share, the duty to protect and strengthen the peace.

. . .

Now, thus far tonight I've shared with you my thoughts on the problems of national security we must face together. My predecessors in the Oval Office have appeared before you on other occasions to describe the threat posed by Soviet power and have proposed steps to address that threat. But since the advent of nuclear weapons, those steps have been increasingly directed toward deterrence of aggression through the promise of retaliation.

This approach to stability through offensive threat has worked. We and our allies have succeeded in preventing nuclear war for more than three decades. In recent months, however, my advisers, including in particular the Joint Chiefs of Staff, have underscored the necessity to break out of a future that relies solely on offensive retaliation for our security.

Over the course of these discussions, I've become more and more deeply convinced that the human spirit must be capable of rising above dealing with other nations and human beings by threatening their existence. Feeling this way, I believe we must thoroughly examine every opportunity for reducing tensions and for introducing greater stability into the strategic calculus on both sides.

One of the most important contributions we can make is, of course, to lower the level of all arms, and particularly nuclear arms. We're engaged right now in several negotiations with the Soviet Union to bring about a mutual reduction of weapons. I will report to you a week from tomorrow my thoughts on that score. But let me just say, I'm totally committed to this course.

If the Soviet Union will join with us in our effort to achieve major arms reduction, we will have succeeded in stabilizing the nuclear balance. Nevertheless, it will still be necessary to rely on the specter of retaliation, on mutual threat. And that's a sad commentary on the human condition. Wouldn't it be better to save lives than to avenge them? Are we not capable of demonstrating our peaceful intentions by applying all our abilities and our ingenuity to achieving a truly lasting stability? I think we are. Indeed, we must.

After careful consultation with my advisers, including the Joint Chiefs of Staff, I believe there is a way. Let me share with you a vision of the future which offers hope. It is that we embark on a program to counter the awesome Soviet missile threat with measures that are defensive. Let us turn to the very strengths in technology that spawned our great industrial base and that have given us the quality of life we enjoy today.

What if free people could live secure in the knowledge that their security did not rest upon the threat of instant U.S. retaliation to deter a Soviet attack, that we could intercept and destroy strategic ballistic missiles before they reached our own soil or that of our allies?

I know this is a formidable technical task, one that may not be accomplished before the end of this century. Yet current technology has attained a level of sophistication where it's reasonable for us to begin this effort. It will take years, probably decades of effort on many fronts. There will be failures and setbacks, just as there will be successes and breakthroughs. And as we proceed, we must remain constant in preserving the nuclear deterrent and maintaining a solid capability for flexible response. But isn't it worth every investment necessary to free the world from the threat of nuclear war? We know it is.

In the meantime, we will continue to pursue real reductions in nuclear arms, negotiating from a position of strength that can be ensured only by modernizing our strategic forces. At the same time, we must take steps to reduce the risk of a conventional military conflict escalating to nuclear war by improving our nonnuclear capabilities.

America does possess—now—the technologies to attain very significant improvements in the effectiveness of our conventional, nonnuclear forces. Proceeding boldly with these new technologies, we can significantly reduce any incentive that the Soviet Union may have to threaten attack against the United States or its allies.

As we pursue our goal of defensive technologies, we recognize that our allies rely upon our strategic offensive power to deter attacks against them. Their vital interests and ours are inextricably linked. Their safety and ours are one. And no change in technology can or will alter that reality. We must and shall continue to honor our commitments.

I clearly recognize that defensive systems have limitations and raise certain problems and ambiguities. If paired with offensive systems, they can be viewed as fostering an aggressive policy, and no one wants that. But with these considerations firmly in mind, I call upon the scientific community in our country, those who gave us nuclear weapons, to turn their great talents now to the cause of mankind and world peace, to give us the means of rendering these nuclear weapons impotent and obsolete.

Tonight, consistent with our obligations of the ABM treaty and recognizing the need for closer consultation with our allies, I'm taking an important first step. I am directing a comprehensive and intensive effort to define a long-term research and development program to begin to achieve our ultimate goal of eliminating the threat posed by strategic nuclear missiles. This could pave the way for arms control measures to eliminate the weapons themselves. We seek neither military superiority nor political advantage. Our only purpose—one all people share—is to search for ways to reduce the danger of nuclear war.

My fellow Americans, tonight we're launching an effort which holds the promise of changing the course of human history. There will be risks, and results take time. But I believe we can do it. As we cross this threshold, I ask for your prayers and your support.

Thank you, good night, and God bless you.

Note: The President spoke at 8:02 p.m. from the Oval Office at the White House. The address was broadcast live on nationwide radio and television.

Following his remarks, the President met in the White House with a number of administration officials, including members of the Cabinet, the White House staff, and the Joint Chiefs of Staff, and former officials of past administrations, to discuss the address.

SOURCE: *Public Papers of the Presidents: Ronald Reagan,* 1983, Book 1 (Washington, D.C.: U.S. Government Printing Office, 1984), pp. 437–43.

APPENDIX K

Members of SAC/ODM and PSAC, 1951–73

Members of President's Science Advisory Committee and of
Science Advisory Committee of the Office of Defense
Mobilization from 1951 to 1973

NAME	AFFILIATION[a]	YEARS	FIELD
Alvarez, Luis W.	Lawrence-Berkeley Laboratory University of California at Berkeley	1973	Physics
Bacher, Robert F.	California Institute of Technology	1953–56, 1957–59	Physics
Baker, William O.	Bell Telephone Laboratories	1957–59	Physical chemistry
Baldeschwieler, John D.	Stanford University	1969–73	Chemistry
Bardeen, John	University of Illinois	1959–62	Physics
Beadle, George W.	California Institute of Technology	1960	Biology
Bennett, Ivan L., Jr.	Johns Hopkins University	1966–70	Pathology
Berkner, Lloyd W.	Associated Universities, Inc.	1957–58	Physics
Bethe, Hans A.	Cornell University	1956–59	Theoretical physics
Bradbury, Norris E.	Los Alamos Scientific Laboratory	1955–57	Physics
Branscomb, Lewis M.	Joint Institute for Laboratory Astrophysics	1965–67	Physics
Bronk, Detlev W.	The Rockefeller Institute	1951–62	Physiology, biophysics
Brooks, Harvey	Harvard University	1960–64	Physics
Buckley, Oliver E.[b]	Bell Telephone Laboratories	1951–55	Electrical engineering
Buchsbaum, Solomon J.	Sandia Laboratories (1971) Bell Telephone Lab. (1972–73)	1971–73	Physics
Cairns, Theodore L.	E. I. DuPont de Nemours & Co.	1971–73	Chemistry
Calvin, Melvin	University of California	1963–66	Organic chemistry
Chance, Britton	University of Pennsylvania	1959	Biophysics, biochemistry
Coleman, James S.	Johns Hopkins University (1971–72) University of Chicago (1973)	1971–73	Sociology
Conant, James B.	Harvard University	1951–53	Chemistry

NAME	AFFILIATION	YEARS	FIELD
David, Edward E., Jr.	Science Adviser to the President	1971–73	Physics, electrical engineering
Doolittle, James H.	Shell Oil Company	1957–58	Aeronautical engineering
Doty, Paul M.	Harvard University	1961–64	Biochemistry
Drell, Sidney D.	Stanford Linear Accelerator Center	1966–70	Theoretical physics
Dryden, Hugh L.	NASA	1951–56	Physics
DuBridge, Lee A.[b]	California Institute of Technology Science Adviser to the President (1969–70)	1951–56, 1969–73	Physics
Ference, Michael, Jr.	Ford Motor Company	1967–70	Physics
Fisk, James B.	Bell Telephone Laboratories	1951–60	Physics
Fitch, Val L.	Princeton University	1970–73	Physics
Fletcher, James C.	University of Utah	1967–70	Physics
Friedman, Herbert	E. O. Hulburt Center for Space Research, U.S. Naval Research Laboratory	1970–73	Physics
Garwin, Richard L.	IBM Corporation	1962–65, 1969–72	Physics
Gell-Mann, Murray	California Institute of Technology	1969–73	Theoretical physics
Gilliland, Edwin R.	Massachusetts Institute of Technology	1961–64	Chemical engineering
Goldberger, Marvin L.	Princeton University	1965–69	Physics
Haggerty, Patrick E.	Texas Instruments, Inc.	1969–71	Electrical engineering
Handler, Philip	Duke University Medical Center	1964–67	Biochemistry
Haskins, Caryl P.	Carnegie Institute of Washington	1955–58	Genetics, physiology
Hewlett, William R.	Hewlett-Packard Company	1966–69	Electrical engineering
Hornig, Donald F.	Princeton University (1960–64) Science Adviser to the President (1964–69)	1960–69	Chemistry
Killian, James R., Jr.	Massachusetts Institute of Technology (1951–57, 1960–) Science Adviser to the President (1957–59)	1951–61	Administration
Kistiakowsky, George B.	Harvard University (1957–59, 1961–63) Science Adviser to the President (1959–61)	1957–63	Physical Chemistry
Land, Edwin M.	Polaroid Corporation	1956–59	Physics
Lauritsen, Charles C.	California Institute of Technology	1952–57	Physics

NAME	AFFILIATION	YEARS	FIELD
Loeb, Robert F.	Columbia University	1951–55, 1960–62	Internal medicine
Long, Franklin A.	Cornell University	1961–62, 1963–66	Physical chemistry
MacDonald, Gordon J. F.	Institute for Defense Analyses (1966–68) University of California (1968–69)	1965–69	Geophysics
MacLeod, Colin M.	New York University	1961–64	Microbiology
McElroy, William D.	Johns Hopkins University	1963–66	Biology, biochemistry
Moynihan, Daniel P.	Harvard University	1971–73	Economics
Old, Bruce S.	Arthur D. Little, Inc.	1951–56	Metallurgy
Olsen, Kenneth M.	Digital Equipment Corporation	1971–73	Electrical engineering
Oppenheimer, J. Robert	Institute for Advanced Study	1951–54	Physics
Pake, George E.	Washington University	1965–69	Physics
Panofsky, Wolfgang K. H.	Stanford University	1963–64	Physics
Pierce, John R.	Bell Telephone Laboratories	1963–66	Electrical engineering
Piore, Emanuel R.	IBM Corporation	1959–62	Physics
Pitzer, Kenneth S.	Rice University	1965–68	Physical chemistry
Press, Frank	California Institute of Technology	1961–64	Geophysics
Purcell, Edward M.	Harvard University	1957–60, 1962–65	Physics
Rabi, Isidor I.[b]	Columbia University	1952–60	Physics
Robertson, H. P.	California Institute of Technology	1957–59	Mathematical physics
Seaborg, Glenn T.	University of California	1959–61	Chemistry
Seitz, Frederick	National Academy of Sciences	1962–70	Physics
Simon, Herbert A.	Carnegie-Mellon University	1968–71	Psychology, computer science
Slichter, Charles P.	University of Illinois	1964–69	Physics
Smith, Cyril	University of Chicago	1959	Physical metallurgy
Smith, Lloyd H., Jr.	University of California at San Francisco	1970–73	Physician
Tape, Gerald F.	Associated Universities, Inc.	1969–73	Physics
Thomas, Charles A.	Monsanto Chemical Corporation	1951–55	Chemistry
Thomas, Lewis	NYU Medical School (1967–68) Yale University Medical School (1969–70)	1967–70	Physician

NAME	AFFILIATION	YEARS	FIELD
Townes, Charles H.	Massachusetts Institute of Technology (1966–67) University of California at Berkeley (1967–70)	1966–70	Physics
Truxal, John G.	State University of New York, Stony Brook	1970–73	Electrical engineering
Tukey, John W.	Princeton University	1960–63	Mathematics
Turner, Howard S.	Turner Construction Company	1972	Chemistry
Waterman, Alan T.	National Science Foundation	1951–56	Physics
Webster, William	New England Electric System	1951	Physics
Weinberg, Alvin M.	Oak Ridge National Laboratory	1960–62	Nuclear physics
Weiss, Paul A.	The Rockefeller Institute	1958–59	Biology
Westheimer, F. H.	Harvard University	1967–70	Chemistry
Whitman, Walter G.	Massachusetts Institute of Technology	1951–55	Chemical engineering
Wiesner, Jerome B.	Massachusetts Institute of Technology Science Adviser to the President (1961–64)	1956-64	Electrical engineering
Wood, Harland G.	Case Western Reserve University	1968–72	Biochemistry
Wyngaarden, James B.	Duke University Medical School	1972–73	Medicine, biochemistry
York, Herbert F., Jr.	Livermore Laboratory	1957–58, 1964–67	Physics
Zacharias, Jerrold R.	Massachusetts Institute of Technology	1952–58, 1961–64	Physics
Zinn, Walter H.	Combustion Engineering, Inc.	1960–62	Physics

[a] Affiliation is at time of service.

[b] Chairmen of the Science Advisory Committee, ODM, were also Presidential Science Advisers, including Oliver E. Buckley (1951–52), Lee A. DuBridge (1952–56), and Isidor I. Rabi (1956–57).

SOURCE: William Golden, ed., *Science Advice to the President* (New York: Pergamon Press, 1980), pp. viii–ix.

Reference Matter

Notes

Since the dispersal of presidential libraries around the country makes it difficult for the general reader to conduct his or her own research on this topic, most document citations are to the Declassified Documents Reference System (DDRS)—a microfilmed collection of declassified U.S. government documents available at many major libraries. The National Security Archive, in Washington, D.C., promises to eventually fill the gaps in this collection and to remedy the problem of the unwieldy DDRS index, with its own comprehensive sets of declassified documents on topics pertaining to national defense. The *Foreign Relations of the United States* volumes, available at most university libraries, remain the best and most comprehensive source for government documents up to the mid-1950s. A collection of the President's Science Advisory Committee (PSAC) documents from the Eisenhower era has recently become available on microfilm.

Another relatively new and underutilized research source in this field is audio and videotaped interviews. The Alfred Sloan Foundation of New York has conducted a series of such interviews as part of its Videohistory Project, dealing with subjects like science advice to president and the H-bomb decision. The American Institute of Physics in New York has compiled a library of taped interviews with eminent physicists. The tapes and transcripts of the interviews conducted for this book are available to researchers at the Department of Space History, National Air and Space Museum, Smithsonian Institution, Washington, D.C.

Following is a list of abbreviations used in the Notes:

AEC	U.S. Atomic Energy Commission
ARPA	Advanced Research Projects Agency
DDR&E	Director Defense Research and Engineering
DDRS	Declassified Documents Reference System
Archives	U.S. Department of Energy Archives, Germantown, Maryland

FRUS	U.S. Department of State, *Foreign Relations of the United States*
GAC	General Advisory Committee, U.S. Atomic Energy Commission
IGCC	Institute on Global Conflict and Cooperation, University of California, San Diego
IDA	Institute for Defense Analyses
JCAE	Joint Committee on Atomic Energy, U.S. Congress
JFK Library	John F. Kennedy Presidential Library, Boston, Massachusetts
LANL RC/A	Los Alamos National Laboratory, Records and Archives
OST	Office of Science and Technology
OSTP	Office of Science and Technology Policy
OTA	Office of Technology Assessment, U.S. Congress
PSAC Records	Records of the President's Science Advisory Committee, National Archives, Record Group 359
SAC/ODM	Science Advisory Committee of the Office of Defense Mobilization

Preface

1. C. P. Snow, *Science and Government* (Cambridge, Mass.: Harvard University Press, 1961), p. 1.

2. Ibid. Snow later extended his thesis to include the notion of "two cultures," the Scientific and the Literary, arguing that scientists and engineers were well suited as advisers, being more likely to possess the gift of "foresight." Snow, *Science and Government,* pp. 80–82. On Snow's thesis and its critics, see Albert Wohlstetter, "Scientists, Seers and Strategy," *Foreign Affairs,* April 1963, pp. 466–78.

Chapter 1

1. H. G. Wells, *The World Set Free* (New York: Dutton, 1914). On this and other predictions of atomic power and nuclear war appearing in science fiction, see H. Bruce Franklin, *War Stars: The Superweapon and the American Imagination* (New York: Oxford, 1988); and Spencer Weart, *Nuclear Fear: A History of Images* (Cambridge, Mass.: Harvard University Press, 1988).

2. Spencer Weart and Gertrud Weiss Szilard (eds.), *Leo Szilard: His Version of the Facts* (Cambridge, Mass.: MIT Press, 1978), pp. 38–40. See also Bernard Feld and Gertrud Weiss Szilard (eds.), *The Collected Works of Leo Szilard—Scientific Papers* (Cambridge, Mass.: MIT Press, 1972), pp. 183–89. Concerning Szilard's later life and work, see Helen Hawkins and Allen Greb (eds.), *Toward a Livable World: Leo Szilard and the Crusade for Nuclear Arms Control* (Cambridge, Mass.: MIT Press, 1987).

3. Concerning Wells's influence upon Szilard, see Richard Rhodes, *The Making of the Atomic Bomb* (Simon & Schuster, 1986), pp. 14, 21–22.

4. In his letter, Szilard articulated an ethical dilemma that would later become commonplace for atomic scientists: the realization that their discovery could be both a boon and a curse to humanity. Szilard tacitly acknowledged this paradox by subsequently filing two patent applications—a public patent for an atomic reactor to gen-

erate electricity and a secret patent for an atomic bomb. Herbert York, *Making Weapons, Talking Peace* (New York: Basic Books, 1987), pp. 3–4.

5. L. Badash, E. Hodes, and A. Tiddens, "Nuclear Fission: Reaction to the Discovery in 1939," IGCC Research Paper no. 1, 1985.

6. Weart and Szilard, *Leo Szilard,* p. 54.

7. On Rabi, see Jeremy Bernstein, *Experiencing Science* (New York: Basic Books, 1978), pp. 38–129, especially pp. 42–43.

8. Weart and Szilard, *Leo Szilard,* p. 54.

9. On Strauss's career and his involvement with Szilard, see Richard Pfau, *No Sacrifice Too Great: The Life of Lewis Strauss* (Charlottesville: University Press of Virginia, 1985), pp. 55–80; and Lewis Strauss, *Men and Decisions* (New York: Doubleday, 1962), pp. 164–66.

10. Weart and Szilard, *Leo Szilard,* pp. 62–65; Rhodes, *The Making of the Atomic Bomb,* p. 292.

11. Weart and Szilard, *Leo Szilard,* p. 55.

12. Ibid., pp. 56–57.

13. Rhodes, *The Making of the Atomic Bomb,* pp. 303–4; Richard Hewlett and Oscar Anderson, Jr., *The New World: A History of the United States Atomic Energy Commission, 1939/1946* (Washington, D.C.: U.S. Atomic Energy Commission, 1972), pp. 15–17.

14. Weart and Szilard, *Leo Szilard,* pp. 83–84; Rhodes, *The Making of the Atomic Bomb,* pp. 303–4.

15. On the prewar status of science advising, see A. Hunter Dupree, *Science in the Federal Government: A History of Politics and Activities to 1940* (Cambridge, Mass.: Harvard University Press, 1957); Rexmond Cochrane, *The National Academy of Sciences: The First Hundred Years, 1863–1963* (Washington, D.C.: National Academy Press, 1978); and William Wells, "Science Advice and the Presidency, 1933–1976" (University Microfilms, 1977), pt. 1, pp. 191–213.

16. Dupree, *Science in the Federal Government,* pp. 326–43.

17. Hewlett and Anderson, *The New World,* pp. 19–20; James Katz, *Presidential Politics and Science Policy* (New York: Praeger, 1978), pp. 7–10.

18. Rhodes, *The Making of the Atomic Bomb,* p. 312.

19. Edward Teller and Allen Brown, *The Legacy of Hiroshima* (New York: Doubleday, 1962), pp. 10–11; Ralph Lapp, "The Einstein Letter That Started It All," *The New York Times Magazine,* August 2, 1964; Weart and Szilard, *Leo Szilard,* pp. 94–96.

20. Lapp, "The Einstein Letter"; Rhodes, *The Making of the Atomic Bomb,* pp. 306–8, 313.

21. Hewlett and Anderson, *The New World,* pp. 17–21; Rhodes *The Making of the Atomic Bomb,* pp. 313–14.

22. Weart and Szilard, *Leo Szilard,* pp. 14, 84–86.

23. Ibid., pp. 120–21; Daniel Kevles, *The Physicists: The History of a Scientific Community in Modern America* (New York: Knopf, 1978), p. 324; Rhodes, *The Making of the Atomic Bomb,* p. 331.

24. Hewlett and Anderson, *The New World,* pp. 23–24; Rhodes, *The Making of the Atomic Bomb,* p. 280.

25. On the formation of the NDRC, see Hewlett and Anderson, *The New World,* pp. 24–26; and Vannevar Bush, *Pieces of the Action* (New York: Morrow, 1970), pp. 40–49.

26. Ibid. On the wartime mobilization of science and the NDRC, see Wells, "Science Advice and the Presidency, 1933–1976," pt. 1, pp. 213–21; James P. Baxter, *Scientists Against Time* (Boston: Little, Brown, 1946); and A. Hunter Dupree, "National Security and the Post-War Science Establishment in the United States," *Nature,* September 18, 1986, pp. 213–16.

27. Rhodes, *The Making of the Atomic Bomb,* pp. 365–66; Bush, *Pieces of the Action,* pp. 59–60.

28. Hewlett and Anderson, *The New World,* p. 49.

29. Weart and Szilard, *Leo Szilard,* p. 152.

30. On the British effort, see Rhodes, *The Making of the Atomic Bomb,* pp. 329–31.

31. Weart and Szilard, *Leo Szilard,* p. 147.

32. Szilard, "What Is Wrong with Us?" September 21, 1942, LANL RC/A; also in Weart and Szilard, *Leo Szilard,* pp. 153–60.

33. Albert Wattenberg, "December 2, 1942: The Event and the People," *Bulletin of the Atomic Scientists,* December 1982, p. 32; Rhodes, *The Making of the Atomic Bomb,* p. 442.

34. Peter Wyden, *Day One: Before Hiroshima and After* (New York: Simon & Schuster, 1984), p. 54.

35. Arthur Compton, *Atomic Quest* (New York: Oxford, 1956), pp. 29–30.

36. Interview with Isidor Rabi.

37. Weart and Szilard, *Leo Szilard,* p. 84; Ralph Lapp, *The New Priesthood: The Scientific Elite and the Uses of Power* (New York: Harper & Row, 1965), p. 61.

38. Interview with Robert Serber. Szilard, in fact, played only a minor part in the bomb's actual development. Profoundly disliked by Groves, he was never invited to join the laboratory in the New Mexican desert. Remaining behind at Chicago, Szilard would routinely buttonhole colleagues in the university's cafeteria with original ideas on the bomb, but characteristically declined to do any experimental work himself. Szilard's notorious absentmindedness also presented difficulties for the security-minded director of the Manhattan Project. The Army counterintelligence agents whom Groves assigned to discreetly shadow the scientists complained of the difficulty of tailing Szilard—who would routinely leave a building, remember something he had left behind, and reenter the building by the same door, in the process bumping into his "tail." After the war, Groves blocked the awarding of a special government citation to Szilard. Wyden, *Day One,* p. 79.

39. Concerning the status of atomic research in Nazi Germany, see Mark Walker, *German National Socialism and the Quest for Nuclear Power* (New York: Cambridge University Press, 1989); David Irving, *The German Atomic Bomb: The History of Nuclear Research in Nazi Germany* (New York: Simon & Schuster, 1968); Malcolm MacPherson, *Time Bomb* (New York: Dutton, 1986); and Arnold Kramish, *The Griffin* (Boston: Houghton Mifflin, 1986).

40. Weart and Szilard, *Leo Szilard,* p. 180.

Chapter 2

1. Spencer Weart and Gertrud Weiss Szilard (eds.), *Leo Szilard: His Version of the Facts* (Cambridge, Mass.: MIT Press, 1978), p. 181.

2. Ibid., pp. 196–204; also in M. Grodzins and E. Rabinowitch (eds.), *The*

Atomic Age: Scientists in National and World Affairs (New York: Simon & Schuster, 1965), pp. 13–18.

3. Weart and Szilard, *Leo Szilard,* p. 182.

4. Richard Hewlett and Oscar Anderson, Jr., *The New World: A History of the United States Atomic Energy Commission, 1939/1946* (Washington, D.C.: U.S. Atomic Energy Commission, 1972), p. 355; James Byrnes, *All in One Lifetime* (New York: Harper, 1958), p. 284; Richard Rhodes, *The Making of the Atomic Bomb* (New York: Simon & Schuster, 1986), pp. 637–38.

5. Weart and Szilard, *Leo Szilard,* pp. 183–85. The June 1945 Franck Report concluded: "Russia is known to be mining radium on its own territory; and even if we do not know the size of the deposits discovered so far in the USSR, the probability that no large reserves of uranium will be found in a country which covers 1/5 of the land area of the earth (and whose sphere of influence takes in additional territory), is too small to serve as a basis for security." As some scientists predicted, and Groves subsequently discovered, the Russians obtained the uranium for their first bomb, which they tested in 1949, from Saxony in eastern Germany. On the Jeffries and Franck Reports, see ibid., pp. 196–204; and Alice Kimball Smith, *A Peril and a Hope: The Scientists' Movement in America, 1945–1947* (Chicago: University of Chicago Press, 1965). On Groves's mistaken estimate of the monopoly's duration, see Gregg Herken, *The Winning Weapon: The Atomic Bomb in the Cold War, 1945–1950* (Princeton, N.J.: Princeton University Press, 1988), p. 341; J. E. Helmreich, *Gathering Rare Earths: The Diplomacy of Uranium Acquisition* (Princeton, N.J.: Princeton University Press, 1986); and Tad Szulc, "The Untold Story of How Russia 'Got the Bomb,'" *Los Angeles Times,* August 26, 1984.

6. Weart and Szilard, *Leo Szilard,* p. 184; Byrnes, *All in One Lifetime,* p. 284; Rhodes, *The Making of the Atomic Bomb,* p. 638.

7. Weart and Szilard, *Leo Szilard,* pp. 186–87.

8. Historian Richard Dallek speculates that Roosevelt may have deliberately deceived Bohr into thinking he planned to cooperate with the Russians—in the expectation that Bohr, through his worldwide scientific contacts, would in turn delude the Soviets. On Bohr's meetings, see Martin J. Sherwin, *A World Destroyed: The Atomic Bomb and the Grand Alliance* (New York: Knopf, 1975), pp. 107–8; and Richard Dallek, *Franklin D. Roosevelt and American Foreign Policy* (New York: Oxford, 1979), pp. 479–82.

9. Rhodes, *The Making of the Atomic Bomb,* p. 537. On the Anglo-American agreement, see R. C. Williams and P. L. Cantelon (eds.), *The American Atom: A Documentary History, 1939–1984* (Philadelphia: University of Pennsylvania Press, 1984), pp. 43–45.

10. The Bush–Conant memorandum is in Sherwin, *A World Destroyed,* pp. 286–88. On Bush's declining role after Roosevelt's death, see Vannevar Bush, *Pieces of the Action* (New York: Morrow, 1970), pp. 303–4.

11. The Franck Report is in Smith, *A Peril and a Hope,* pp. 371–83.

12. Sherwin, *A World Destroyed,* pp. 144–45, 287–88.

13. Ronald Clark, *The Greatest Power on Earth: The International Race for Nuclear Supremacy* (New York: Harper & Row, 1980), pp. 187–88.

14. Interview with Robert Wilson. On this point, see also Weart and Szilard, *Leo Szilard,* p. 185.

15. Wilson later claimed that he warned Oppenheimer "there'll be hell to pay" if the bomb were built without telling the Russians. In 1983, Wilson admitted that

Oppenheimer might have thought his idea of inviting the Russians "a little bit nutty." He believed Oppenheimer's strongly negative response was prompted by concern that anyone suggesting an approach to Russian scientists might be fired from the project—"or he may have suspected that I was testing him, not knowing me very well," Wilson said. Wilson interview.

16. Ibid.

17. On the consideration given the demonstration option, see Sherwin, *A World Destroyed,* pp. 304–5; Arthur Compton, *Atomic Quest* (New York: Oxford, 1956), pp. 238–40; and McGeorge Bundy, *Danger and Survival: Choices About the Bomb in the First Fifty Years* (New York: Random House, 1988), pp. 68–77. On a possible use of radiological warfare, see Rhodes, *The Making of the Atomic Bomb,* pp. 510–11. Concerning expectations of the Trinity test, see F. M. Szasz, *The Day the Sun Rose Twice: The Story of the Trinity Site Nuclear Explosion* (Albuquerque: University of New Mexico Press, 1984), pp. 115–44; and S. Glasstone and P. J. Dolan (eds.), *The Effects of Nuclear Weapons* (Washington, D.C.: U.S. Government Printing Office, 1977), pp. 27–28.

18. Lewis Strauss, *Men and Decisions* (New York: Doubleday, 1962), pp. 192–93.

19. "Memorandum for Brigadier General T. F. Farrell," May 11, 1945, Series 1, Box 17–1, LANL RC/A.

20. Groves to Oppenheimer, untitled, April 27, 1945; and Oppenheimer to Groves, untitled, June 27, 1945, Series 2, Box 22–5, LANL RC/A.

21. Hewlett and Anderson, *The New World,* pp. 378–80; David Hawkins, Edith Truslow, and Ralph C. Smith, *Project Y: The Los Alamos Story* (San Francisco: Tomash Press, 1983), pp. 237–41.

22. The idea, however, would come up again ten days later in a meeting of Compton, Lawrence, Fermi and Oppenheimer. Compton, *Atomic Quest,* pp. 238–39.

23. Interview with Robert Serber.

24. Sherwin, *A World Destroyed,* pp. 213–15; Rhodes, *The Making of the Atomic Bomb,* pp. 696–97.

25. Sherwin, *A World Destroyed,* pp. 304–5.

26. Hawkins et al., *Project Y,* pp. 241–43.

27. For scientists' eyewitness accounts of Trinity, see ibid. and Series 2, Box 22–6, LANL RC/A.

28. Sherwin, *A World Destroyed,* pp. 311–12. Coincidentally, a witness to the test of the Soviet Union's first atomic bomb, in August 1949, similarly remarked upon its "blinding light, brighter than the brightest sunlit day." I. N. Golovin, *I. V. Kurchatov: A Socialist-Realist Biography of the Soviet Nuclear Scientist* (Bloomington, Ind.: Selbstverlag Press, 1968), p. 64.

29. Maurice Shapiro, "Observations of the Trinity Test," July 23, 1945, Series 2, Box 22–6, LANL RC/A.

30. The authors of the memorandum were Norris Bradbury, George Kistiakowsky, and Max Roy. See "Proposal for a Modified Tactical Use of the Gadget," July 17, 1945, LANL RC/A.

31. Weart and Szilard, *Leo Szilard,* p. 186.

32. The scientific panel's report is in Sherwin, *A World Destroyed,* pp. 304–5.

33. On Oppenheimer's views after Hiroshima, see Ralph Lapp, *The New Priesthood: A Scientific Elite and the Uses of Power* (New York: Harper & Row,

1965), p. 76; and the transcript of Warner Schilling's interview with Oppenheimer, June 11–12, 1957, Box 65, Robert Oppenheimer Papers, Library of Congress, Washington, D.C.

34. Sherwin, *A World Destroyed,* pp. 212–13.

35. July 2, 1945 entry, Stimson diary, vol. 51, Henry Stimson Papers, Sterling Library, Yale University, New Haven, Conn.; Robert Ferrell (ed.), *Off the Record: The Private Papers of Harry S. Truman* (New York: Harper & Row, 1980), p. 56.

36. Rhodes, *The Making of the Atomic Bomb,* p. 692.

37. Weart and Szilard, *Leo Szilard,* pp. 185–87; Sherwin, *A World Destroyed,* p. 201.

38. Weart and Szilard, *Leo Szilard* p. 187.

39. Ibid., pp. 211–13.

40. Ibid.; Wyden, *Day One,* p. 179 fn.; Hewlett and Anderson, *The New World,* pp. 399–400.

41. Teller's views on the demonstration may not have differed from Oppenheimer's. See Sherwin, *A World Destroyed,* p. 218; Teller, "Seven Hours of Reminiscences," *Los Alamos Science,* Winter/Spring 1983, pp. 190–95.

42. Strauss, *Men and Decisions,* p. 194.

43. Weart and Szilard, *Leo Szilard,* p. 188.

44. Ibid., p. 218.

45. Ibid., pp. 219–20.

46. On Bush's September 1945 memorandum, see Harry Truman, *Year of Decisions: Memoirs* (New York: Doubleday, 1955) p. 579; and Herken, *The Winning Weapon,* pp. 36–37.

47. Bush to Conant, November 8, 1945, "Conant" Correspondence File, Box 27, Vannevar Bush Papers, Library of Congress, Washington, D.C.

48. Ibid. By the summer of 1946, virtually all communications between Truman and Bush and Conant had ceased—due to what seemed, at least in part, a clash of personalities. Truman twice refused Stimson's request that Bush be given the Distinguished Service Medal for his work on behalf of the Manhattan Project—citing, on one occasion, the fact that Bush had not attended a previous ceremony awarding him the Legion of Honor Medal. On his troubles with Truman, see Bush, *Pieces of the Action,* pp. 302–3, and Herken, *The Winning Weapon,* pp. 347–48 fn.

49. Bush, *Science: The Endless Frontier* (Washington, D.C.: U.S. Government Printing Office, 1945). On Bush's ideas for the postwar reorganization of science, see also William Wells, "Science Advice and the Presidency, 1933–1976" (University Microfilms, 1977), pt. 1, pp. 265–68.

50. Hewlett and Anderson, *The New World,* pp. 409–10; Hunter Dupree, "National Security and the Post-War Science Establishment in the United States," *Nature,* September 18, 1986, pp. 213–16.

51. On other plans for the postwar organization of defense research, see Daniel Kevles, "Scientists, the Military, and the Control of Postwar Defense Research: The Case of the Research Board for National Security, 1944–1946," *Technology and Culture,* January 1975; and Herbert York and Allen Greb, "Military Research and Development: A Postwar History," *Bulletin of the Atomic Scientists,* January 1977.

52. Dupree, "National Security . . . ," p. 214; Thomas Sturm, *The USAF Scientific Advisory Board: Its First Twenty Years, 1944–64* (Washington, D.C.: U.S. Government Printing Office, 1977). On the origins of the GAC, see Richard Sylves, *The Nuclear Oracles: A Political History of the General Advisory Committee of the*

Atomic Energy Commission, 1947–1977 (Ames: Iowa State University, 1987), pp. 16–44.

53. On the Steelman Report, see Wells, "Science Advice and the Presidency," pt. 1, pp. 310–18.

54. Truman to Bush, August 2, 1946, "Atomic Energy Control Commission, UN" folder, Box 112, PSF, Harry S. Truman Library, Independence, Missouri; Truman to Acheson, May 3, 1946, Box 201, ibid.

55. Interview with Gordon Arneson. Arneson's report is in *FRUS, 1947* (Washington, D.C.: U.S. Government Printing Office, 1972), vol. 1, pp. 487–88.

56. On Einstein's postwar views, see Wyden, *Day One,* p. 342 fn.; and Ronald Clark, *Einstein: The Life and Times* (New York: Crowell, 1971).

57. On the Einstein interview, see *FRUS, 1948* (Washington, D.C.: U.S. Government Printing Office, 1973), vol. I, pp. 388–99.

58. On the activities of Szilard after 1945, see Hawkins and Greb (eds.), *Toward a Livable World: Leo Szilard and the Crusade for Nuclear Arms Control* (Cambridge, Mass.: MIT Press, 1987); Bernard Feld and Gertrud Weiss Szilard (eds.), *The Collected Works of Leo Szilard—Scientific Papers* (Cambridge, Mass.: MIT Press, 1972), pp. 189–90; and Weart and Szilard, *Leo Szilard,* pp. 223–29.

59. Herken, *The Winning Weapon,* p. 400 fn.

60. Weart and Szilard, *Leo Szilard,* p. 225.

61. On the role of the "reluctant lobby," see Smith, *A Peril and a Hope,* pp. 203–26.

62. Ibid., pp. 347–60.

63. On Rabi's postwar views, see Jeremy Bernstein, *Experiencing Science* (New York: Basic Books, 1978), p. 102; and John Rigden, *Rabi: Scientist and Citizen* (New York: Basic Books, 1987), pp. 193–210.

Chapter 3

1. On the origins of the superbomb concept, see Richard Rhodes, *The Making of the Atomic Bomb* (New York: Simon & Schuster, 1986), pp. 150, 415; David Hawkins, Edith Truslow, and Ralph C. Smith, *Project Y: The Los Alamos Story* (San Francisco: Tomash Press, 1983), pp. 14–16, 184–88; Jeremy Bernstein, *Prophet of Energy: Hans Bethe* (New York: Dutton, 1981), pp. 92–114; and Edward Teller, *Better a Shield Than a Sword: Perspectives on Defense and Technology* (New York: Free Press, 1987), pp. 66–84.

2. On the story of the H-bomb, see Hawkins et al., *Project Y,* pp. 86–88; Rhodes, *The Making of the Atomic Bomb,* p. 374; and Peter Galison and Barton Bernstein, "In any light: Scientists and the decision to build the Superbomb, 1952–1954," *Historical Studies in the Physical and Biological Sciences,* vol. 19, pt. 2, pp. 267–347.

3. Bethe's subsequent calculations put that particular fear to rest. However, the question came up again in 1946 in relation to the hydrogen bomb. Rhodes, *The Making of the Atomic Bomb,* pp. 418–19; Edward Teller et al., "Ignition of the Atmosphere with Nuclear Bombs," August 14, 1946, DDRS-1975 Retrospective-8C.

4. Ben Diven et al., "Nuclear Data," *Los Alamos Science,* Winter/Spring 1983, p. 121.

5. That June, when Teller still had not completed the calculations assigned to

him concerning the plutonium-implosion bomb, the work was given to other scientists at the lab—among whom was Klaus Fuchs, the quiet British physicist later found to be spying for the Russians. No one at Los Alamos suspected Fuchs's double role. Following a visit to Columbia in the winter of 1944, Teller had written to a colleague about meeting "a very nice man by the name of Fuchs. . . . In talking, his spontaneous emission is very low but his induced emission is quite satisfactory." Teller to M. Mayer, February 8, 1944, LANL RC/A. On Fuchs at Los Alamos, see Robert Chadwell Williams, *Klaus Fuchs: Atom Spy* (Cambridge, Mass.: Harvard University Press, 1987), pp. 75–91.

6. The Bush-Conant memorandum is in Martin Sherwin, *A World Destroyed: The Atomic Bomb and the Grand Alliance* (New York: Knopf, 1975), pp. 286–88.

7. Ibid., pp. 297–98.

8. Ibid., p. 315; Roger Anders (ed.), *Forging the Atomic Shield: Excerpts from the Office Diary of Gordon E. Dean* (Chapel Hill: University of North Carolina Press, 1987), p. 57.

9. Sherwin, *A World Destroyed*, p. 315. Compton's letter continued: "Ten years from now the question of developing the super bomb can be assessed again. . . . Probably the effort required for its development will then be considerably less. Perhaps there may be then an international government adequate to make its development under world auspices safe or perhaps unnecessary for further consideration." Compton to Wallace, September 27, 1945, Washington University Archives, St. Louis, Missouri. The author would like to thank Barton Bernstein for a copy of the Compton letter. For its impact, see Galison and Bernstein, "In any light," pp. 276–77.

10. For example, it seemed more difficult than previously suspected to ignite deuterium. Not only were the necessary temperatures higher, but the method of ignition proposed proved inadequate for the purpose. In the fusion bomb originally envisioned in 1942, energy from an exploding atomic bomb would be used to ignite the Super's deuterium fuel. But subsequent calculations at Los Alamos showed that the same phenomenon that protected the atmosphere and the earth from being ignited by atomic bombs—the loss of heat through radiation—might also prevent a fission reaction from igniting a mass of deuterium; an intermediary element, tritium, would be necessary to start the thermonuclear "burn." Even so, the concern at Los Alamos was that the thermonuclear "flame" would flicker only briefly and then go out. On the state of superbomb research just after the war, see "Report of Conference on the Super," February 16, 1950, LA-575, LANL RC/A; Hawkins et al., *Project Y*, pp. 184–87; Rhodes, *The Making of the Atomic Bomb*, pp. 770–73; J. Carson Mark, "A Short Account of Los Alamos Theoretical Work on Thermonuclear Weapons, 1946–1950." July 1974, LA-5647-MS, LANL RC/A, pp. 1–2; Chuck Hansen, *U.S. Nuclear Weapons: The Secret History* (New York: Orion Books, 1988), pp. 42–49; Galison and Bernstein, "In any light," pp. 275–80; and Herbert York, *The Advisors: Oppenheimer, Teller, and the Superbomb* (New York: Freeman, 1976), pp. 13–28.

11. Teller was apparently the principal author of the 1946 report. In 1984, Robert Serber, who attended the 1946 conference, characterized the thinking on the H-bomb at that time as "incredibly optimistic at every point." Serber interview. On the 1946 conference and report, see Galison and Bernstein, "In any light," pp. 279–80.

12. Teller's new concept for the Super still relied upon the energy of a fission bomb to start the thermonuclear reaction. But in this second design, alternating rings or layers of fissionable uranium and a tritium-deuterium mixture surrounded an

atomic trigger. In theory, the fission trigger would provide enough energy to ignite the deuterium-tritium in the adjacent ring, which would in turn initiate fission in the next uranium ring, and so on. On the Alarm Clock, see "Report of Conference on the Super," p. 46; Mark, "A Short Account," p. 5; and Hansen, *U.S. Nuclear Weapons,* pp. 43–49. The term "Alarm Clock" also later referred to another thermonuclear weapon. See ibid., pp. 61–62.

13. Interview with Hans Bethe. Concerning doubts about the feasibility of Teller's design, see Hans Bethe, "Memorandum on the History of the Thermonuclear Program," May 28, 1952, Record Group 326, File 4930, DOE Archives, Germantown, MD; and "Comments on the History of the H-bomb," *Los Alamos Science,* Fall 1982, pp. 43–53.

14. Mark, "A Short Account," pp. 9–10; Hansen, *U.S. Nuclear Weapons,* pp. 45–50.

15. Mark, "A Short Account," p. 9.

16. Richard Hewlett and Francis Duncan, *Atomic Shield: A History of the United States Atomic Energy Commission, 1947/1952* (University Park, Pennsylvania: State University Press, 1969), p. 374.

17. Concerning the evolution of the GAC, see Hewlett and Duncan, *Atomic Shield,* pp. 5–7, 15–16; and Richard Sylves, *The Nuclear Oracles: A Political History of the General Advisory Committee of the Atomic Energy Commission, 1947–1977* (Ames: Iowa State University, 1987), pp. 16–44.

18. On the resignations of Stimson and Byrnes, see Gregg Herken, *The Winning Weapon: The Atomic Bomb in the Cold War, 1945–1950* (Princeton, N.J.: Princeton University Press, 1988), pp. 89–93, 236, 355–56.

19. "The Atom General Answers His Critics," *Saturday Evening Post,* June 19, 1948; *The New York Times,* February 2, 1948; CIA, "Status of the USSR Atomic Energy Project," July 1, 1949, DDRS-1979–18B. On Bush's relationship with Truman, see Vannevar Bush, *Pieces of the Action* (New York: Morrow, 1970), pp. 302–3.

20. On early efforts to detect nuclear explosions, see Bruce Bolt, *Nuclear Explosions and Earthquakes: The Parted Veil* (New York: Freeman, 1976), pp. 1–18. On the origins of the Long-Range Detection Program, see Hewlett and Duncan, *Atomic Shield,* pp. 362–64; Lewis Strauss, *Men and Decisions* (New York: Doubleday, 1962), pp. 201–7; Jeffrey Richelson, *American Espionage and the Soviet Target* (New York: Quill Press, 1987), pp. 115–17; and Charles Ziegler, "Waiting for Joe-1," *Social Studies of Science,* vol. 18, no. 2, May 1988, pp. 197–229.

21. CIA, untitled report, September 9, 1949, DDRS-1978-340B.

22. Naval Research Laboratory, "Collection and Identification of Fission Products of Foreign Origins," September 26, 1949, Box 199, President's Secretary's Files, Harry Truman Library, Independence, Missouri; CIA, "Status of the Soviet Atomic Energy Program," March 6, 1952, DDRS-1980-135C; "The Bradbury Years," *Los Alamos Science,* Winter/Spring 1983, p. 36.

23. Naval Research Laboratory, "Collection and Identification," pp. 5–6. Recently published Soviet and American sources pinpoint the Russian test, codenamed *Pervaya Moiniya* (First Lightning), as taking place at 4 A.M. on August 29, near Semipalatinsk, in Kazakhstan, Soviet Central Asia. Concerning development of the Soviet atomic bomb, see Tad Szulc, "The Untold Story of How Russia 'Got the Bomb,'" *Los Angeles Times,* August 26, 1984; David Holloway, *The Soviet Union and the Arms Race* (New Haven, Conn.: Yale University Press, 1984), pp. 15–20;

and Vasily Yemelyanov, "The Making of the Soviet Bomb," *Bulletin of the Atomic Scientists,* December 1987, pp. 39–41.

24. Truman's demand was noted in an interview with Robert Bacher. On Truman's announcement of the Soviet test, see *The New York Times,* September 25, 1949. Truman's doubts are noted in *FRUS, 1952–54* (Washington, D.C.: U.S. Government Printing Office, 1984), vol. II, pt. 2, p. 1113 fn.

25. Strauss, *Men and Decisions,* p. 217.

26. Ibid. On early fears concerning the Soviet Super, see also Hewlett and Duncan, *Atomic Shield,* pp. 375–76; "The Bradbury Years," *Los Alamos Science,* Winter/Spring 1983, p. 36; and Galison and Bernstein, "In any light," pp. 286–88.

27. Strauss, *Men and Decisions,* pp. 216–17.

28. McMahon to AEC, October 17, 1949, DOE Archives.

29. Glenn Seaborg was in Sweden at the time of this meeting but sent Oppenheimer a letter giving conditional support to development of the H-bomb. In interviews, surviving members of the GAC could not recollect whether Oppenheimer read Seaborg's letter at the October meeting. Interviews: Cyril Smith, Glenn Seaborg, and Lee DuBridge. Seaborg's letter to the GAC is reprinted in U.S. Atomic Energy Commission, *In the Matter of J. Robert Oppenheimer* (Cambridge, Mass.: MIT Press, 1971), pp. 238–39. On GAC meetings, see Hewlett and Duncan, *Atomic Shield,* pp. 381–85; R. C. Williams and P. L. Cantelon (eds.), *The American Atom: A Documentary History, 1939–1984* (Philadelphia: University of Pennsylvania Press, 1984), pp. 117–20; and Galison and Bernstein, "In any light," pp. 290–95.

30. Mark, "A Short Account," p. 7; Bethe, "Comments on the History of the H-bomb," pp. 43–53.

31. Williams and Cantelon (eds.), *The American Atom,* p. 124; York, *The Advisors; pp. 46–56;* and Steven Rearden, *History of the Office of the Secretary of Defense: The Formative Years, 1947–1950,* vol. I (Washington, D.C.: U.S. Government Printing Office, 1984), pp. 439–40.

32. Thomas Cochran, William Arkin, and Milton Hoenig, *Nuclear Weapons Databook,* vol. I (New York: Ballinger Press, 1984), pp. 6–11; Bethe, "Comments on the History of the H-bomb," pp. 43–53; Hansen, *U.S. Nuclear Weapons,* pp. 31–41.

33. Hewlett and Duncan, *Atomic Shield,* p. 397.

34. Ibid., p. 383; "Report of Conference on the Super," pp. 4–5; Galison and Bernstein, "In any light," pp. 292–93.

35. Williams and Cantelon (eds.), *The American Atom,* p. 126. The committee later changed its mind about the carbon-14 danger. A letter the GAC sent to Truman on December 7, 1949, noted that further studies had shown the danger of radioactive pollution of the atmosphere to be exaggerated, since it would take at least five hundred and perhaps fifty thousand H-bombs to reach a danger point. But a concurrent study of the long-range radiological effects that atomic explosions might have upon life on earth—undertaken at the request of AEC General Manager Carroll Wilson, and aptly titled Project Gabriel—concluded that the fallout from fission bombs would contaminate crops over a wide area and might make much of the United States temporarily uninhabitable after a war. Hawkins et al., *Project Y,* p. 187. On Project Gabriel, see Hewlett and Duncan, *Atomic Shield,* pp. 499, 518; AEC, "Report of the Gabriel Project Study," May 21, 1949, and "Report on Project Gabriel," July 1954, Box 3363, Record Group 326, DOE Archives.

36. The GAC reports are reprinted in York, *The Advisors,* pp. 156–57; and Williams and Cantelon (eds.), *The American Atom,* pp. 120–27.

37. York, *The Advisors,* p. 157.

38. In a 1984 interview, Rabi conceded that he and Fermi erred in not spelling out in more detail how such a ban would work. Hence, because fission and fusion reactions have distinctively different "signatures" in terms of the fallout they leave behind, the same technology that allowed American scientists to detect the 1949 Soviet atomic test—and to know both the approximate date of the explosion and the relative sophistication of the bomb's design—could be trusted, they felt, to reveal any clandestine Russian H-bomb test. Moreover, many tests would be necessary before either side had an operational weapon.

Hans Bethe, in a secret 1954 "history" of the H-bomb that was not declassified until almost thirty years later, also emphasized this point: "Thermonuclear weapons are so complicated that nobody will be confident that he has the correct solution before he has tested such a device. But it is well known that any test of a bomb of such high yield is immediately detected. Therefore, without any inspection, each side would know immediately if the other side had broken the agreement." Bethe, "Comments on the History of the H-bomb," p. 53. On the proposal by Rabi and Fermi, see also McGeorge Bundy, "The H-Bomb: The Missed Chance," *The New York Review of Books,* May 13, 1982, pp. 13–21.

39. Interviews: Isidor Rabi, Cyril Smith, John Manley, and Carson Mark. Gordon Dean's comment is in Anders (ed.), *Forging the Atomic Shield,* p. 59.

40. The Oppenheimer-Conant letter is quoted in Williams and Cantelon (eds.), *The American Atom,* p. 1; and Hewlett and Duncan, *Atomic Shield,* pp. 378–79.

41. Rabi interview.

42. Barton Bernstein, "Truman and the H-bomb," *Bulletin of the Atomic Scientists,* March 1984, p. 15. Concerning Conant's opposition to the H-bomb, see James Hershberg, "Over my dead body: James B. Conant and the hydrogen bomb," in E. Mendelsohn et al. (eds.), *Science, Technology, and the Military* (New York: Barton, 1989).

43. Hewlett and Duncan, *Atomic Shield,* pp. 378–79.

44. Ibid., pp. 388–89.

45. Ibid., p. 374.

46. *FRUS, 1949* (Washington, D.C.: U.S. Government Printing Office, 1976), vol. I, pp. 576–85. Concerning Dean and the H-bomb decision, see Anders (ed.), *Forging the Atomic Shield,* pp. 49–64.

47. *FRUS, 1949,* vol. I, pp. 597–99.

48. Ibid., pp. 595–96.

49. Dean Acheson, *Present at the Creation: My Years in the State Department* (New York: Norton, 1969), p. 348.

50. Gordon Arneson, "The H-Bomb Decision," *Foreign Service Journal,* May 1969, pp. 27–43; Arneson interview.

51. Manley to AEC, December 3, 1949, "Thermonuclear Weapons Program Chronology," DOE Archives.

52. In 1985, Manley claimed that the impetus for this letter had been concern that the president was about to be confronted with a "false choice" over the H-bomb—in that Truman had yet to be told that a decision to proceed with research would probably also commit the nation, perhaps irretrievably, to building the bomb, so great were the pressures gathering on its behalf. Manley interview.

53. Pike to Truman, December 7, 1949, DOE Archives. Acheson's early think-

ing on the H-bomb is noted in *FRUS, 1949,* I, p. 576. On the deliberations of the superbomb committee, see Galison and Bernstein, "In any light," pp. 302–5.

54. Bernstein, "Truman and the H-bomb," p. 16.

55. Lilienthal to AEC files, January 31, 1950, DOE Archives.

56. *FRUS, 1950,* vol. I, pp. 513–17. The end of the cold war, and the subsequent availability of previously closed Soviet sources, has cast new light upon the question of which side was first in developing the hydrogen bomb. According to these sources, work on a Soviet H-bomb was proposed in 1946 and begun in 1948 under the direction of physicists Igor Tamm and Andrei Sakharov. On August 12, 1953, the Soviets tested a single-stage fission weapon whose 200–300-kiloton yield was "boosted," or enhanced, by a thermonuclear reaction. The first true Soviet multimegaton Super was tested on November 22, 1955. By comparison, work in the United States on an H-bomb was proposed in 1942 and began in earnest in 1946. In a May 1951 test, code-named Item, the United States exploded the first "boosted" fission-fusion weapon. On November 1, 1952, Mike, with a yield of 10.5 megatons, was the first U.S. test of the staged principle behind the true Super. While the Soviet Super tested in 1955 was small enough to be dropped by an airplane, the two-stage Mike device weighed 65 tons and was meant only as a proof of the superbomb concept. The United States had a "weaponized" or air-droppable version of the Super by 1954. Thus, the United States was the first to develop and test a boosted fission weapon, as well as the first to develop, test, and deploy a multimegaton Super. On Soviet H-bomb developments, see Andrei Sakharov, *Memoirs* (New York: Knopf, 1990), pp. 180–81, 190–91; Thomas Cochran and Robert Norris, "Soviet Nuclear Warhead Production," Nuclear Databook Working Papers, Natural Resources Defense Council, Washington, D.C.; and Cochran et al., *Nuclear Weapons Databook,* vol. IV, pp. 336–37. On development of the U.S. H-bomb, see Rhodes, *The Making of the Atomic Bomb,* p. 422; and Hansen, *U.S. Nuclear Weapons,* pp. 44–61.

57. David Lilienthal, *The Journals of David E. Lilienthal: The Atomic Energy Years, 1945–50* (New York: Harper & Row, 1964), pp. 623–32.

58. *FRUS, 1950,* vol. I, p. 518.

59. On the view of the JCS, see Rearden, *The Formative Years, 1947–1959,* pp. 451–52; and *FRUS, 1950,* vol.I, pp. 503–11.

60. Concerning the announcement of Truman's January 31 decision, see *FRUS, 1950,* vol. I, p. 513; and Herken, *The Winning Weapon,* pp. 319–20.

61. Rabi, for example, believed that Truman either never read the letter or failed to understand its proposal for a test ban. Rabi interview.

62. Strauss to Truman, January 31, 1950, DOE Archives.

63. Lilienthal, *The Atomic Energy Years,* p. 633.

64. Ibid., p. 635.

65. Ibid., p. 636.

Chapter 4

1. DuBridge to AEC, December 5, 1949; Dean to AEC, January 16, 1950; "Memorandum for the Secretary of Defense," January 13, 1950, DOE Archives.

2. Richard Hewlett and Francis Duncan, *Atomic Shield: A History of the United*

States Atomic Energy Commission, 1947/1952 (University Park: Pennsylvania State University Press, 1969), pp. 411–13.

3. On Fuchs, see Robert Chadwell Williams, *Klaus Fuchs: Atom Spy* (Cambridge, Mass.: Harvard University Press, 1987), pp. 115–16, 151–55. Fuchs also attended the November 1947 Anglo-American conference on declassification—where, ironically, the German-born Soviet agent had opposed the release of any more information on the bomb to the American public. Gregg Herken, *The Winning Weapon* (Princeton, N.J.: Princeton University Press, 1988), p. 323.

4. Williams, *Klaus Fuchs,* p. 116. Recently available Soviet sources are either silent or inconsistent on the extent and value of the contribution that espionage made to their H-bomb project. Sakharov, for example, claims that Fuchs's information on the atomic bomb was "exceptionally important," but he makes no such claim concerning the latter's contribution to the Soviet H-bomb project. Andrei Sakharov, *Memoirs* (New York: Knopf, 1990), pp. 94 fn., 176. On Soviet nuclear and thermonuclear weapons development, see Chapter 3 note 56.

5. "Basis for Estimating Maximum Soviet Capabilities for Atomic Warfare," February 20, 1950, Box 201, President's Secretary's File, Harry S. Truman Library, Independence, Missouri.

6. Hewlett and Duncan, *Atomic Shield,* pp. 415–16.

7. *FRUS, 1950* (Washington, D.C.: U.S. Government Printing Office, 1977), vol. I, pp. 538–39.

8. Ibid., pp. 541–42.

9. NSC memorandum, untitled, February 24, 1950, DDRS-1977-108A.

10. Harry Truman, *Years of Trial and Hope: Memoirs* (New York: Doubleday, 1956), p. 354. Since the tritium required for the H-bomb would be produced at the expense of plutonium required for the atomic stockpile, Truman was apparently misinformed in thinking that thermonuclear research would necessarily benefit fission bomb production.

11. Public opinion polls showed that a bare majority of those Americans queried—48 percent vs. 45 percent—gave support to efforts to seek cooperative control of nuclear weapons with the Soviet Union before the H-bomb was added to the U.S. arsenal. Barton Bernstein, "Truman and the H-bomb," *Bulletin of the Atomic Scientists,* March 1984, p. 18.

12. In his confession to the British, Fuchs admitted that he had given the Russians "information about the principles of the design of the plutonium bomb," but claimed that it was his Russian contact who, in 1947, first brought up the subject of a "tritium bomb"—about which Fuchs said he knew nothing. Williams, *Klaus Fuchs,* pp. 188–94.

13. In the aftermath of Truman's approval of the all-out effort, confidential assessments of what Fuchs could have told the Russians about the H-bomb became markedly less alarmist. In a June 16, 1950, letter to Truman, Hoover admitted that Fuchs had not been able to furnish much useful information on the H-bomb because he "did not have a clear understanding of the research being done in this regard" and was even "generally confused" about the concepts behind the weapon. A "damage assessment" by the AEC the following month similarly concluded that Fuchs's value to the Soviets had probably been exaggerated even in the case of atomic secrets, since the spy's information was "of an early vintage." A top-secret CIA report on July 4 on the "Status of the Soviet Atomic Energy Program" noted that although Fuchs began supplying information to the Russians as early as 1942, the

Soviets did not launch a crash program to develop the atomic bomb until 1945: "Likewise, the information obtained by them on thermonuclear weapons must of necessity have been scanty as far as the solution of the many complex problems are concerned." Concerning Fuchs's contribution to the Soviet effort, see ibid.; Joint Atomic Energy Intelligence Committee, "Status of the Soviet Atomic Energy Program," July 4, 1950, DDRS-1979-20A. On the Soviet atomic bomb, see also Tad Szulc, "The Untold Story of How Russia 'Got the Bomb,'" August 26, 1984, *Los Angeles Times;* and Thomas Cochran, William Arkin, and Milton Hoenig, *Nuclear Weapons Databook,* vol. IV (New York: Ballinger Press, 1984), pp. 4–6.

14. Bethe, "Memorandum on the History of the Thermonuclear Program," p. 5; J. Carson Mark, "A Short Account of Los Alamos Theoretical Work on Thermonuclear Weapons, 1946–1950," July 1974, LA-5647-MS, LANL RC/A, pp. 8–12. Edward Teller contests Bethe's assertion that Fuchs would have learned nothing of value from U.S. thermonuclear research prior to 1950. According to Teller, therefore, the concept of radiation implosion—which proved key to the theoretical breakthrough that made the Super possible—was discussed at the 1946 Los Alamos conference, which Fuchs attended. As of this writing, the relevant minutes of that meeting remain classified. On the Bethe-Teller dispute regarding the Super, see Hans Bethe, "Memorandum on the History of the Thermonuclear Program," May 28, 1952, Record Group 326, File 4930, DOE Archives, Germantown, MD; and Edward Teller, "Comments on Bethe's History of the Thermonuclear Program," August 14, 1952, JCAE Document DLIX, Legislative Branch, National Archives; and Sakharov, *Memoirs,* p. 100.

15. *FRUS, 1950,* vol. I, p. 173.

16. Ibid., p. 178; Edward Teller, *Better a Shield Than a Sword,* p. 76.

17. Hewlett and Duncan, *Atomic Shield,* p. 440.

18. Ibid.

19. An unclassified account of the Teller-Ulam design, which appeared in a 1983 issue of *Los Alamos Science,* notes that it is "based on the application of x-rays produced by a primary nuclear device to compress and ignite a physically distinct secondary nuclear assembly." "The Weapons Program," *Los Alamos Science,* Winter/Spring 1983, p. 112. On the Teller-Ulam breakthrough, see also Chuck Hansen, *U.S. Nuclear Weapons: The Secret History* (New York: Orion Books, 1988), pp. 49–50.

20. By the meeting's end, most participants agreed that Teller and Ulam had found a way to make the H-bomb work. Bethe subsequently characterized the so-called Teller-Ulam discovery as "a stroke of genius." In a comment that would later come to haunt him, Oppenheimer described it as "technically so sweet that you could not argue about it." To Rabi, it was simply a *"Witz"*—a German word meaning a clever trick. For differing versions of the Princeton meeting, see Hewlett and Duncan, *Atomic Shield,* pp. 542–45; and Teller, *Better a Shield Than a Sword,* pp. 81–82. Oppenheimer's comment is in U.S. AEC, *In the Matter of J. Robert Oppenheimer* (Cambridge, Mass.: MIT Press, 1971), p. 81. Interviews: Hans Bethe and Isidor Rabi.

21. On the significance of the George test to the H-bomb's development, see Hansen, *U.S. Nuclear Weapons,* pp. 51–52; NSC, untitled memorandum, January 31, 1951, DDRS-1978-191A; Roger Anders (ed.), *Forging the Atomic Shield: Excerpts from the Office Diary of Gordon E. Dean* (Chapel Hill: University of North Carolina Press, 1987), pp. 143–44; and Bethe, "Comments on the History of the H-bomb," *Los Alamos Science,* Fall 1982, p. 48.

22. Hewlett and Duncan, *Atomic Shield,* pp. 562–64; Hansen, *U.S. Nuclear*

Weapons, pp. 50–51; Cochran et al., *Nuclear Weapons Databook,* vol. 1, pp. 31–34; and U.S. Department of Energy, "Announced United States Nuclear Tests," NVO-209, January 1980, p. 5.

23. In December 1951, Teller presented his case for the Livermore lab to the GAC, where it was opposed by both the scientists and Dean, who expressed concern that a second lab would mean a wasteful and unnecessary diversion of effort and resources from the work on the H-bomb being done at Los Alamos. On Teller's case for the Livermore lab, see Edward Teller, "Statement to the General Advisory Committee on Need of Second Weapons Laboratory," December 7, 1951, AEC Secretariat Files, L951–58, Box 4930, DOE Archives. On Pike's troubles, see Hewlett and Duncan, *Atomic Shield,* pp. 446–47.

For a time, Strauss had even thought of going to Truman directly with his charges against Oppenheimer. Persuaded by LeBaron against taking so drastic a step, Strauss had gone instead to Dean that February, even before the breakthrough by Teller and Ulam, with a draft of a lengthy memorandum to the president urging another redoubling of effort for the Super. The fact that Strauss ended up burning his memorandum in Dean's fireplace showed the passions aroused by the superbomb controversy. On the H-bomb lobby's charges against Oppenheimer, see *Atomic Shield,* p. 536; Anders (ed.), *Forging the Atomic Shield,* pp. 117–18; and "Policy and Progress in the H-Bomb Program: A Chronology of Leading Events," January 1, 1953, JCAE Doc. DLXXXIV, Legislative Branch, National Archives.

24. On Mike, see Hansen, *U.S. Nuclear Weapons,* pp. 56–58.

25. Stephen Rearden, *History of the Office of the Secretary of Defense: The Formative Years, 1947–1950,* vol. 1 (Washington, D.C.: U.S. Government Printing Office, 1984), p. 533. On Vista, see David Elliot, "Project Vista and Nuclear Weapons in Europe," *International Security,* Summer 1986, pp. 163–83. On Conant's concerns, see James Hershberg, "Over my dead body: James B. Conant and the hydrogen bomb," in E. Mendelsohn et al. (eds.), *Science, Technology, and the Military* (New York: Barton, 1989), pp. 38–48.

26. Rabi interview.

27. Concerning Bethe's shifting position on the Super, see Peter Galison and Barton Bernstein, "In any light: Scientists and the decision to build the Superbomb, 1952–1954," *Historical Studies in the Physical and Biological Sciencss,* vol. 19, pt. 2, p. 336.

28. Hewlett and Duncan, *Atomic Shield,* pp. 486, 518.

29. Concerning the status of science advising at this time, see "Resume of Activities of the Science Advisory Committee," June 8, 1954, Box 18, PSAC Records; and Hunter Dupree, "National Security and the Post-war Science Establishment in the United States," *Nature,* September 18, 1986, pp. 213–16.

30. "Résumé of Activities. . . ."

31. William Golden, "Mobilizing Science for War: A Scientific Adviser to the President" [The Golden Report], William Golden papers, Library of Congress, pp. 2, 392–404. The author is indebted to William Golden for a copy of his report and related documents.

32. On Bush's study and its fate, see James R. Killian, Jr., *Sputnik, Scientists, and Eisenhower* (Cambridge, Mass.: MIT Press, 1977), p. 60–62.

33. On opposition to the founding of a science advisory committee in the White House, see D. W. Bronk, "Science Advice in the White House," in William Golden (ed.), *Science Advice to the President* (Elmsford, N.Y.: Pergamon Press, 1980), pp. 245–56; and Dupree, "National Security . . . ," pp. 213–16.

34. Killian, *Sputnik, Scientists, and Eisenhower,* p. 65; Bronk, "Science Advice in the White House," pp. 245–56. Interview with William Golden. "Memo of Conversation with Oppenheimer," December 21, 1950, William Golden papers.

35. Killian, *Sputnik, Scientists, and Eisenhower,* p. 65; Golden interview.

36. Buckley objected to SAC's original title—Advisory Committee on Defense Scientific Research—as too militaristic. Golden Report, p. 377. Besides Buckley, Oppenheimer, Conant, and DuBridge, the charter members of SAC/ODM were Detlev Bronk, president of the National Academy of Sciences; William Webster, chairman of the Pentagon's Research and Development Board; Alan Waterman, director of the National Science Foundation; Hugh Dryden of the Interdepartmental Committee on Scientific Research and Development; James Killian, president of MIT; Robert Loeb of Columbia University's medical school; and Charles Thomas, vice president of Monsanto Chemical. Killian, *Sputnik, Scientists, and Eisenhower,* pp. 60–65.

37. Killian, *Sputnik, Scientists, and Eisenhower,* p. 66.

38. Golden interview.

39. In June 1951, presumably as a result of this rapid expansion of the atomic stockpile, the AEC ordered a reevaluation of the 1949 Project Gabriel. On the growth of the atomic stockpile, see Cochran et al., *Nuclear Weapons Databook,* vol. I, p. 15. On the updating of Project Gabriel, see "Note by the Secretary: Project Gabriel," February 14, 1952, DOE Archives; and Richard Sylves, *The Nuclear Oracles: A Political History of the General Advisory Committee of the Atomic Energy Commission, 1947–1977* (Ames: Iowa State University Press, 1987), pp. 171–88.

40. On the GAC's "swan song," see GAC to Truman, June 14, 1952, DOE Archives; and Hewlett and Duncan, *Atomic Shield,* pp. 518–20.

41. On the Panel of Consultants on Disarmament and its work, see McGeorge Bundy, "Early Thoughts on Controlling the Nuclear Arms Race: A Report to the Secretary of State, January 1953," *International Security,* Fall 1982, pp. 3–27; and *FRUS, 1952–1954* (Washington, D.C.: U.S. Government Printing Office, 1984), vol. II, pt. 2, pp. 992–93.

42. The sensitivity attached to the question of a delay in testing the H-bomb is demonstrated by the fact that Bush destroyed the only copy of the memorandum he prepared on the "standstill" for Acheson and neglected to even mention the proposal in his memoirs. A recently declassified memorandum—undated and unsigned, but titled "The Timing of the Thermonuclear Test"—summarizes the arguments for and against the standstill, and is very likely a draft of the document written by Bush. *FRUS, 1952–1954,* vol. II, pt. 2, pp. 994–1008. On the standstill proposal, see also Barton Bernstein's "Crossing the Rubicon: A Missed Opportunity to Stop the H-Bomb?" *International Security,* Fall 1989, pp. 132–60.

43. *FRUS, 1952–1954,* vol. II, pt. 2, pp. 994–1008.

44. A March 6, 1952, CIA analysis of the three atomic tests that the Soviets had conducted since August 1949 noted that more than two years passed between the explosion of their first and second atomic bombs. The second Soviet bomb, tested on September 24, 1951, and detected by the Army's acoustic sensors as well as by the Air Force's Long-Range Detection Program, was a plutonium-implosion weapon of improved efficiency. The third test, conducted just three weeks later, was the first Russian "composite" bomb, using both plutonium and enriched uranium, and hence similar in design to the advanced fission weapons tested by the United States in the spring of 1948 as part of Operation Sandstone. On the Soviet nuclear weapons program, see Allen Dulles to Sidney Souers, October 1, 1951, DDRS-1979-234B; CIA,

"Status of the Soviet Atomic Energy Program," July 28, 1951, DDRS-1980-135B; CIA, "Status of the Soviet Atomic Energy Program," March 6, 1952, DDRS-1980-135C; and Cochran et al., *Nuclear Weapons Databook,* vol. IV, pp. 336–37.

45. Asked in 1954 why he and Bush's panel had urged the postponement of Mike, Oppenheimer said: "We thought [the Russians] would get a lot of information out of it." AEC, *In the Matter of J. Robert Oppenheimer,* p. 248. Indeed, it did occur to Sakharov and his colleagues working on the Soviet H-bomb that they might learn some of the secrets of the American Super by analyzing a fallout sample from Mike. However, according to Sakharov, their efforts came to nought when a Soviet chemist—distracted by some personal crisis—absentmindedly poured the sample down the drain. Sakharov, *Memoirs,* p. 158. According to Hans Bethe, Sakharov "probably developed the idea [for the Super] independently" and not from espionage or from analysis of the fallout from U.S. thermonuclear tests. Bethe, "Sakharov's H-bomb," *Bulletin of the Atomic Scientists,* October 1990, pp. 8–9.

46. In early April 1951, after receiving intelligence reports that the Russians might be preparing to enter the Korean War, Truman approved the transfer of nine nuclear weapons from the custody of the AEC to the Air Force. Possible targets for the bombs included Chinese troops in Manchuria and Soviet submarine pens at Vladivostok. Anders (ed.), *Forging the Atomic Shield,* pp. 136–37.

47. Dean Acheson, *Present at the Creation: My Years in the State Department* (New York: Norton, 1969), pp. 359–61.

48. On Teller and the second laboratory, see Anders (ed.), *Forging the Atomic Shield,* pp. 201–13; and *FRUS, 1952–1954,* vol. II, pt. 2, pp. 880–81.

49. *FRUS, 1952–1954,* vol. II, pt. 2, pp. 880–81.

50. Ibid., pp. 958–63.

51. Bernstein, "Crossing the Rubicon," p. 147.

52. *FRUS, 1952–1954,* vol. II, pt. 2, p. 957. Interview with Gordon Arneson.

53. *FRUS, 1952–1954,* vol. II, pt. 2, p. 990.

54. Hewlett and Duncan, *Atomic Shield,* p. 591.

55. Bethe's second letter to Dean is noted in Hewlett and Duncan, *Atomic Shield,* p. 662 fn.

56. *FRUS, 1952–1954,* vol. II, pt. 2, pp. 1017–25.

57. AEC, *In the Matter of J. Robert Oppenheimer,* p. 247. In fact, Oppenheimer had asked Los Alamos director Norris Bradbury whether postponing Mike for a week or two would seriously affect the H-bomb program. Bradbury—who on June 30 would brief Truman in the Oval Office on the forthcoming test—told Oppenheimer that, because of changing weather patterns in the Pacific testing area, a postponement beyond October might delay the test until the following March and would also upset the schedule for subsequent nuclear tests. Interview with Norris Bradbury. On the failure to postpone Mike, see Hewlett and Duncan, *Atomic Shield,* pp. 591–93.

58. *FRUS, 1952–1954,* vol. II, pt. 2, pp. 1032–33.

59. Hewlett and Duncan, *Atomic Shield,* pp. 590–93.

60. Hansen, *U.S. Nuclear Weapons,* pp. 58–60.

61. A declassified memorandum from Dean, dated October 30, 1952, acknowledges: "Continuing study of [Mike] has revealed the need for last minute changes . . . in order to secure a substantially less [sic] probability of failure from one specific cause." Bethe notes: "This redesign came at the latest moment compatible with meeting the test date of November 1952; had Teller's test date (of spring or summer 1952) been accepted, redesign would have been impossible and the test would very probably

have failed." AEC, "Approval for Operation Ivy," October 30, 1952, President's Secretary's Files, Truman Library, Independence, Missouri. Bethe, "Comments on the History of the H-bomb," pp. 47–48. On the continuing controversy over the H-bomb, see William Broad, "Rewriting the History of the H-bomb," November 19, 1982, *Science*, pp. 769–72.

62. Teller, *Better a Shield Than a Sword*, pp. 83–84. Interviews: Hans Bethe and Lee DuBridge.

63. Killian, *Sputnik, Scientists, and Eisenhower*, pp. 66–67.

64. AEC, *In the Matter of J. Robert Oppenheimer*, p. 562.

65. *FRUS, 1952–1954*, vol. II, pt. 2, pp. 1038, 1056–91.

66. Ibid., pp. 1049–56.

67. While the Finletter statement appears to have been destroyed, the recently declassified minutes of this meeting note that its main points were to have been: "1. That the American people should be informed of the order of magnitude of the thermonuclear explosion; 2. That the American people should be brought to realize the seriousness of the problem raised by this new development; and 3. That no clear solution to these difficulties seemed at hand." Ibid., p. 1051.

68. Ibid., pp. 1051–55.

69. What the panel originally intended to be an unprecedented warning from two presidents was reduced to the familiar homilies of a farewell address. Truman's speech referred only to "a new era of destructive power, capable of creating explosions of a new order of magnitude, dwarfing the mushroom clouds of Hiroshima and Nagasaki." *Public Papers of the Presidents, Harry S. Truman, 1952–53* (Washington, D.C.: U.S. Government Printing Office, 1966), pp. 1124–26.

Chapter 5

1, "Memorandum of Conversation," November 18, 1952, DDRS-1976-303D; and "Memorandum of Meeting at the White House," November 18, 1952, DDRS-106C; Roger Anders (ed.), *Forging the Atomic Shield: Excerpts from the Office Diary of Gordon E. Dean* (Chapel Hill: University of North Carolina Press, 1987), p. 31. On the Mike briefings, see also R. G. Hewlett and J. M. Holl, *Atoms for Peace and War, 1953–1961* (Berkeley: University of California Press, 1989), pp. 1–3.

2. Vannevar Bush, *Pieces of the Action* (New York: Morrow, 1970), p. 306.

3. Stephen Ambrose, *Eisenhower: The President* (New York: Simon & Schuster, 1984), p. 617.

4. Ibid., p. 38

5. Ibid, pp. 123, 135.

6. *FRUS, 1952–1954*, vol. II, pt. 2 (Washington, D.C.: U.S. Government Printing Office, 1984), pp. 1106–9.

7. Ibid, pp. 1110–14.

8. Ibid.

9. Ibid., pp. 1135–37.

10. Ibid., pp. 1169–74.

11. During the Truman administration the number of bombs in the stockpile was deleted even from "eyes only" briefing papers for the president—who was simply told the latest figure by an AEC officer. Initially, despite repeated requests, Truman

also denied the stockpile numbers to senior members of the JCAE. On the secrecy surrounding the early stockpile, and evidence of its subsequent growth, see Anders (ed.), *Forging the Atomic Shield,* p. 233; David Rosenberg, "U.S. Nuclear Stockpile, 1945 to 1950," *Bulletin of the Atomic Scientists,* May 1982, pp. 25–30; and Thomas Cochran, Willian Arkin, and Milton Hoenig, *Nuclear Weapons Databook,* vol. I (New York: Ballinger Press, 1984), p. 15.

12. On NSC-30, see *FRUS, 1948,* vol. I, pt. 2 (Washington, D.C.: U.S. Government Printing Office, 1976), pp. 625–28.

13. Ambrose, *Eisenhower: The President,* pp. 123–24.

14. Cutler to Adams, April 10, 1953, DDRS-1979-327B.

15. *FRUS, 1952–1954,* vol. II, pt. 2, pp. 1184–85.

16. Robert Oppenheimer, "Atomic Weapons and American Policy," *Foreign Affairs,* July 1953, pp. 525–35.

17. Lewis Strauss, *Men and Decisions* (New York: Doubleday, 1962), pp. 345–47.

18. Herbert York, *The Advisors: Oppenheimer, Teller, and the Superbomb* (San Francisco: Freeman, 1976), pp. 89–93.

19. Ibid. On misunderstandings concerning the 1953 Soviet test, which was of a fusion-boosted fission bomb and not a true Super, see Hewlett and Holl, *Atoms for Peace and War,* p. 59.

20. The fact that the Russian bomb had used dry lithium-deuteride instead of liquid deuterium for its thermonuclear fuel was also less significant than Soviet claims indicated, since the advantage of dry lithium-deuterium—shrinking the size and weight of the bomb—had been recognized as early as 1943 at Los Alamos and by 1952 was incorporated into the design of almost all U.S. bombs scheduled for testing. In interviews, three of the scientists who analyzed the radioactive debris from the August 1953 Soviet test confirmed that, unlike Mike, most of the Russian bomb's energy had come from fission. While initial estimates were that the yield of the August 12 explosion was about 1.5 megatons, a recalculation of the data two years later, using refined analytical techniques, concluded that the actual yield had been more like 300–600 kilotons, or only slightly more powerful than the advanced pure-fission bomb the United States had exploded in the November 1952 King test. The Soviet bomb had also used a prodigious amount of tritium, making it much more expensive and far less efficient than the American H-bomb. Said one scientist of the first Soviet H-bomb: "It was a dead end technologically." Interviews: Hans Bethe, Herbert Scoville, and Herbert York. Hewlett and Holl, *Atoms for Peace and War;* York, *The Advisors,* pp. 90–92. On the Soviet H-bomb program, see Chapter 3, note 56.

21. *FRUS, 1952–1954,* vol. II, pt. 2, pp. 1185–86.

22. Strauss, *Men and Decisions,* p. 356.

23. *FRUS, 1952–1954,* vol. II, pt. 2, p. 1213.

24. In the personal diary he kept while in office, Eisenhower confided that there was always a pragmatic as well as an idealistic motive behind Atoms for Peace: "The United States could unquestionably afford to reduce its atomic stockpile by two or three times the amounts that the Russians might contribute to the United Nations agency, and still improve our relative position in the cold war and even in the event of the outbreak of war." But the president also made plain in the same entry that his own hopes took a larger view: "Underlying all this, of course, is the clear conviction that as of now the world is racing toward catastrophe—that some-

thing must be done to get a brake on this movement." Robert Ferrell (ed.), *The Eisenhower Diaries* (New York: Norton, 1981), pp. 261–62. One of the closely guarded secrets of the cold war at this time was the fact that the United States was able to gauge the rate of Soviet plutonium production by the amount of a radioactive byproduct—krypton-85—released into the air over Russia and monitored by the Long-Range Detection Program. The importance of the krypton discovery is noted, for example, in Jeffrey Richelson, *American Espionage and the Soviet Target* (New York: Morrow, 1987), p. 120.

25. Strauss also directed Eisenhower's attention to the AEC's latest intelligence, which estimated that the Russians might have ten thermonuclear weapons of the power of Joe-4 by 1954, thirty such weapons in 1955, and more than a hundred a year later. *FRUS, 1952–1954,* vol. II, pt. 2, pp. 1218–20.

26. Ibid., pp. 1224–26.

27. When an early draft of the speech by Jackson proposed the joint withdrawal of all NATO and Warsaw Pact forces from Germany, for example, Eisenhower criticized it for not going far enough. Ibid. On the transformation of Atoms for Peace, see Peter Pringle and James Spiegelman, *The Nuclear Barons* (New York: Holt, Rinehart and Winston, 1981), pp. 118–21; and J. F. Pilat (ed.), *Atoms for Peace: An Analysis after Thirty Years* (Boulder, Colo.: Westview Press, 1985).

28. *FRUS, 1952–1954,* vol. II, pt. 2, p. 1232.

29. Ibid., p. 1243

30. Ambrose, *Eisenhower: The President,* p. 133.

31. Ibid.

32. Ibid., pp. 148–51; *Public Papers of the Presidents: Dwight D. Eisenhower, 1953–54* (Washington, D.C.: U.S. Government Printing Office, 1955), pp. 813–22.

33. Untitled memorandum, January 14, 1954, DDRS-1979-331B. By fall 1954, the Soviet Union was complaining that Atoms for Peace had been reduced to isotopes and fertilizer. Hewlett and Holl, *Atoms for Peace and War,* p. 231.

34. Ferrell (ed.), *The Eisenhower Diaries,* pp. 260–61. Wilson's warning was, in part, a response to the allegation that Oppenheimer was "more probably than not . . . functioning as an espionage agent" contained in a recent letter to FBI Director J. Edgar Hoover by William Borden, Brian McMahon's aide on the JCAE. Portions of Borden's letter are in Stanley Blumberg and Gwinn Owens, *Energy and Conflict: The Life and Times of Edward Teller* (New York: Putnam, 1976), pp. 317–18. Borden, Strauss, and apparently others believed that Oppenheimer was the unidentified "second scientist" whom Klaus Fuchs suspected of working at Los Alamos during the war. On this charge in Fuchs's confession, see Robert C. Williams, *Klaus Fuchs: Atom Spy* (Cambridge, Mass.: Harvard University Press, 1987), p. 192. Concerning the possibility that Strauss may have used the Oppenheimer case to discredit Operation Candor, see Hewlett and Holl, *Atoms for Peace and War,* p. 50.

35. Concerning Eisenhower's "blank wall" order, see Ambrose, *Eisenhower: The President,* pp. 141–42; Ferrell (ed.), *The Eisenhower Diaries,* pp. 260–61; and Peter Goodchild, *J. Robert Oppenheimer: "Shatterer of Worlds"* (Boston: Houghton Mifflin, 1981), p. 224.

36. In a 1985 interview, former Los Alamos director Norris Bradbury recalled that Strauss kept his own private file of derogatory information on Oppenheimer in a safe at his AEC office. Bradbury said he was "unimpressed" when Strauss once showed him what the AEC chairman considered to be an especially incriminating document. Bradbury interview. On Strauss and his relationship with Oppenheimer,

see Richard Pfau, *No Sacrifice Too Great: The Life of Lewis Strauss* (Charlottesville: University Press of Virginia, 1985); and Pringle and Spiegelman, *The Nuclear Barons,* pp. 147–64.

37. Rabi interview. On the relationship between Rabi and Eisenhower, see John Rigden, *Rabi: Scientist and Citizen* (New York: Basic Books, 1987), pp. 238–39.

38. Rabi interview. Rabi made this point in a subsequent article, "The Cost of Secrecy," *Atlantic,* August 1960, pp. 39–42.

39. In an interview, Rabi confessed to feeling guilty about taking up the president's time on those occasions when Eisenhower called on him for advice. Once, for example, when what was supposed to be a fifteen-minute appointment in the Oval Office stretched into almost an hour because of Eisehower's volubility, Rabi felt compelled to break off the meeting—since Secretary of State John Foster Dulles was being kept waiting outside. Rabi interview.

40. James Killian, *Sputnik, Scientists, and Eisenhower* (Cambridge, Mass.: MIT Press, 1977), pp. 65–67.

41. "Strauss became his link for a time, as far as there was one, between the President and American science," Bush later wrote of the relationship between Eisenhower and Strauss. Vannevar Bush, *Pieces of the Action* (New York: Morrow, 1970), p. 307. On Strauss's influence with Eisenhower, see also McGeorge Bundy, *Danger and Survival: Choices About the Bomb in the First Fifty Years* (New York: Harper & Row, 1988), pp. 316–18. Observes Bundy of Eisenhower's first term: "Eisenhower never reviewed the record for himself or looked behind what he heard from Strauss. He never sought out others who could have told him what Strauss left out."

42. All three scientists also served on the Air Force's Scientific Advisory Board—where first von Neumann and later Teller headed the important Nuclear Panel. On von Neumann's role as a science adviser, see Steven Heims, *John von Neumann and Norbert Wiener: From Mathematics to the Technologies of Life and Death* (Cambridge, Mass.: MIT Press, 1984), pp. 230–77. On the activities of the Air Force's Scientific Advisory Board, see Thomas Sturm, *The USAF Scientific Advisory Board: Its First Twenty Years, 1944–1964,* USAF Historical Division Liaison Office (Washington, D.C.: Government Printing Office, 1967).

43. On the Teapot panel and its report, see Jacob Neufeld, *Ballistic Missiles in the United States Air Force, 1945–1960* (Washington, D.C.: Office of Air Force History, 1990), pp. 98–102. The importance of the Teapot panel report is noted in Dwight Eisenhower, *Waging Peace, 1956–1961* (New York: Doubleday, 1965), pp. 208–9. On the origins of von Neumann's report, see also Simon Ramo to Trevor Gardner, "Recommendations of the Committee on Strategic Missiles," February 10, 1954, Albert Simpson Historical Research Center, Maxwell Air Force Base, Alabama; and Simon Ramo, *The Business of Science: Winning and Losing in the High-Tech Age* (New York: Hill & Wang, 1988), pp. 85–88.

44. Cochran et al., *Nuclear Weapons Databook,* vol. I, p. 27.

45. On the history of the U.S. international ballistic missile program, see Neufeld, *Ballistic Missiles in the United States Air Force;* and Edmund Beard, *Developing the ICBM* (New York: Columbia University Press, 1976).

46. Bush is quoted in Walter McDougall, *The Heavens and the Earth: A Political History of the Space Age* (New York: Basic Books, 1985), p. 98.

47. Eisenhower, *Waging Peace,* pp. 207–8.

48. Beard, *Developing the ICBM,* pp. 37–39.

49. On the controversies surrounding ICBM development, see also McDougall, *The Heavens and the Earth,* pp. 97–101; Ramo, *The Business of Science,* pp. 78–114; Eugene Emme (ed.), *The History of Rocket Technology* (Detroit: Wayne State University Press, 1964), pp. 142–61; Major General John Medaris, *Countdown for Decision* (New York: Putnam, 1960); and Herbert York, *Race to Oblivion* (New York: Simon & Schuster, 1970), pp. 75–105.

50. Beard, *Developing the ICBM,* pp. 157–63; and John Greenwood, "The Air Force Ballistic Missile and Space Program, 1954–74," *Aerospace Historian,* Winter 1974, pp. 190–200.

51. Greenwood, "The Air Force Ballistic Missile and Space Program, 1954–74," pp. 190–200.

52. Ramo to Gardner, "Recommendations," p. 2. On RAND's study see Fred Kaplan, *The Wizards of Armageddon* (New York: Simon & Schuster, 1983), pp. 111–17. The Teapot panel report is in Neufeld, *Ballistic Missiles in the United States Air Force,* pp. 249–65.

53. At least three different prototype ICBM warheads were tested in Operation Castle. Bravo tested a bomb nicknamed "Shrimp" by its designers. Koon—the test of the first thermonuclear weapon to be developed at the new Livermore laboratory, nicknamed "Morgenstern"—fizzled. Beard, *Developing the ICBM,* p. 165; Robert Divine, *Blowing on the Wind: The Nuclear Test Ban Debate, 1954–1960* (New York: Oxford, 1978), pp. 3–18; U.S. Department of Energy, "Announced United States Nuclear Tests" (Washington, D.C.: U.S. Government Printing Office, 1980), p. 7; and Chuck Hansen, *U.S. Nuclear Weapons: The Secret History* (New York: Orion Books, 1988), pp. 61–68.

54. In a 1985 interview, Herbert Scoville, who was assigned responsibility for measuring the fallout from Bravo, recalled that members of an Air Force meteorological unit near the test reported their dosimeters off the scale in the red shortly after the explosion. On the unexpected fallout from Bravo, see Bernard O'Keefe, *Nuclear Hostages* (Boston: Houghton Mifflin, 1983), pp. 158–208, and Hewlett and Holl, *Atoms for Peace and War,* pp. 173–76.

55. Divine, *Blowing on the Wind,* pp. 27–35.

56. Ambrose, *Eisenhower: The President,* p. 168

57. *FRUS, 1952–1954,* vol. II, pt. 2, p. 1379.

58. Frank Wisner to Lewis Strauss, April 29, 1954, DDRS-1984-2256.

59. Ambrose, *Eisenhower: The President,* pp. 168–69.

60. Ibid.

61. Ibid., p. 132. Concerning the role of nuclear weapons in the Eisenhower administration, see John Lewis Gaddis, *Strategies of Containment* (New York: Oxford, 1982), pp. 148–52; Hewlett and Holl, *Atoms for Peace and War,* pp. 179–82; and H. W. Brands, "The Age of Vulnerability: Eisenhower and the National Insecurity State," *American Historical Review,* October 1989, pp. 963–89.

62. The Air Force, the AEC, and Livermore continued to propose testing even more powerful bombs. York interview. In Cherokee, a test on May 20, 1956, the United States air dropped an H-bomb with a yield of more than ten megatons. On nuclear testing after Bravo, see U.S. Department of Energy, "Announced United States Nuclear Tests," p. 8; Cochran et al., *Nuclear Weapons Databook,* vol. I, p. 34 fn; and Hansen, *U.S. Nuclear Weapons,* pp. 69–89.

63. Ambrose, *Eisenhower: The President,* p. 170.

Chapter 6

1. Thomas Murray, *Nuclear Policy for War and Peace* (Chicago: World Publishers, 1960), pp. 15–17.

2. Ibid.

3. Murray to Eisenhower, March 14, 1955, DDRS-1983-000009.

4. Eisenhower's letter is cited in Murray, *Nuclear Policy for War and Peace,* pp. 55–57.

5. Ibid., pp. 75–77; Robert Divine, *Blowing on the Wind: The Nuclear Test Ban Debate, 1954–1960* (New York: Oxford, 1978), p. 24.

6. Murray, *Nuclear Policy for War and Peace,* pp. 75–77.

7. *FRUS, 1952–1954* (Washington, D.C.: U.S. Government Printing Office, 1984), vol. II, pt. 2, pp. 1383, 1387–92, 1418–19.

8. Ibid., pp. 1423–29.

9. Ibid., pp. 1452–56.

10. Ibid., pp. 1457–58.

11. Ibid., pp. 1467–72.

12. Ibid.

13. On Eisenhower, Strauss, and the Oppenheimer case, see Stephen Ambrose, *Eisenhower: The President* (New York: Simon & Schuster, 1984), p. 166; *FRUS, 1952–1954,* vol. II, pt. 2, pp. 1472–73; and R. G. Hewlett and J. M. Holl, *Atoms for Peace and War, 1953–1961* (Berkeley: University of California Press, 1989), pp. 73–112.

14. Ambrose, *Eisenhower: The President,* pp. 166–67.

15. On the verdict of the Gray board, and Murray's opinion, see U.S. Atomic Energy Commission, *In the Matter of J. Robert Oppenheimer* (Cambridge, Mass.: MIT Press, 1971), pp. 1049-65. Concerning Teller's testimony, see Ibid., p. 710.

16. Ambrose, *Eisenhower: The President,* p. 170.

17. Oppenheimer had also suggested that SAC/ODM brief Eisenhower on the ICBM. James R. Killian, *Sputnik, Scientists, and Eisenhower* (Cambridge, Mass.: MIT Press, 1977), pp. 68–69; and Dwight Eisenhower, *The White House Years: Waging Peace, 1956–1961* (New York: Doubleday, 1965), p. 208.

18. Edmund Beard, *Developing the ICBM* (New York: Columbia University Press, 1976), pp. 163–64.

19. William Burrows, *Deep Black: Space Espionage and National Security* (New York: Random House, 1986), pp. 66–67.

20. CIA, "Soviet Capabilities for Attack on the United States through Mid-1955," August 3, 1953, DDRS-1980-136A.

21. Stephen Ambrose and Richard Immerman, *Ike's Spies: Eisenhower and the Espionage Establishment* (New York: Doubleday, 1981), pp. 205–7.

22. Ibid.; Ambrose, *Eisenhower: The President,* p. 560.

23. Ambrose, *Eisenhower: The President,* p. 89

24. Killian, *Sputnik, Scientists, and Eisenhower,* pp. 67–68.

25. Ibid.

26. James Killian and A. G. Hill, "For a Continental Air Defense," *Atlantic,* April 1948. On Killian's role in the study that led to the DEW (Distant-Early-Warning) line, see the transcript of "Project *Charles,*" Videotape History Project, Alfred Sloan Foundation, New York, New York.

27. On the origins of the TCP, see Killian, *Sputnik, Scientists, and Eisenhower,* pp. 67–71; and Burrows, *Deep Black,* pp. 69–71. Concerning reaction to the panel's report in the White House, see Robert Cutler, *No Time for Rest* (Boston: Little, Brown, 1965), pp. 350–51.

28. Dominating the White House Broadcast Room where the NSC and Killian's panel assembled was a blackboard featuring a scale drawing of a 110-foot-high ICBM, the subject that had also been at the forefront of the panel's concerns for the past nine months. Killian interview.

29. Killian's panel warned that the United States might be the victim of a devastating, if unorthodox, kind of surprise attack within the next few years—since it was "technically feasible," the panel wrote, "for the USSR to deliver, by ship or submarine, very large and heavy, though expensive, bombs having yields of up to about 1000 megatons." Smaller bombs—"of several megatons" apiece—might also be secretly smuggled into American cities by enemy agents. Department of Defense, Office of Defense Mobilization, "Report to the President by the Technological Capabilities Panel of the Science Advisory Committee" [The Killian Report], February 14, 1955, DDRS-1975 Retrospective-965A. See also Killian, *Sputnik, Scientists, and Eisenhower,* pp. 72–76.

30. Ibid.

31. On the ICBM and IRBM decisions, see Dwight Eisenhower, *The White House Years* (New York: Doubleday, 1965), p. 208; Beard, *Developing the ICBM,* pp. 184–89; Michael Armacost, *The Politics of Weapons Innovation: The Thor-Jupiter Controversy* (New York: Columbia University Press, 1969), pp. 51–56; and Simon Ramo, *The Business of Science: Winning and Losing in the High-Tech Age* (New York: Hill & Wang, 1988), pp. 78–114. On the origins of Polaris, see Killian, *Sputnik, Scientists, and Eisenhower,* pp. 77, 89, 92.

32. Killian Report, DDRS-1975 Retrospective-965A. Besides Land and Killian, other members of Project Three, the panel dealing specifically with intelligence, were Harvard's Edward Purcell and James Baker, Joseph Kennedy of Washington University, Allen Latham of Arthur Little Associates, and Princeton's John Tukey. Burrows, *Deep Black,* p. 70.

33. On the origins of the U-2 program, see Burrows, *Deep Black,* pp. 71–77; and Michael Beschloss, *Mayday: Eisenhower, Khrushchev, and the U-2 Affair* (New York: Harper & Row, 1986), pp. 85–93.

34. Ambrose and Immerman, *Ike's Spies,* pp. 267–72; Beschloss, *Mayday,* pp. 92–93.

35. Purcell interview. Beschloss, *Mayday,* pp. 81–83.

36. Part of Eisenhower's enthusiasm for the U-2 may have been because a last-minute overflight of the Normandy beaches in 1944 had shown the German defenders unalerted to the impending invasion and thus had allowed Operation Overlord to proceed on schedule. Ambrose and Immerman, *Ike's Spies,* pp. 265–66; Burrows, *Deep Black,* p. 71.

37. Ibid. In a 1985 interview, Purcell reflected that he, Killian, and Land should have seen the mishaps that befell them on the way to the Oval Office as a portent of the trouble to come over the U-2. The Air Force plane carrying them from Boston had almost skidded off the icy runway in Washington; two members of their motorcycle escort had collided, without injury, on the way from the airport to the White House. Purcell interview.

38. Burrows, *Deep Black,* pp. 62–63; Beschloss, *Mayday,* pp. 111–12.

39. On the balloon overflights, see Burrows, *Deep Black*, pp. 78–79; W. W. Rostow, *Open Skies: Eisenhower's Proposal of July 21, 1955* (Austin: University of Texas Press, 1982), pp. 189–93 fn.

40. Memorandum of meeting, February 10, 1956, DDRS-1982-798.

41. Concerning early overflights of the Soviet Union, see Burrows, *Deep Black*, pp. 57–59; Beschloss, *Mayday*, pp. 77–79; and Jeffrey Richelson, *American Espionage and the Soviet Target* (New York: Quill Press, 1987), pp. 127–52.

42. Burrows, *Deep* Black, p. 67; Beschloss, *Mayday*, p. 81.

43. On the origin and activities of the Vulnerability Panel, see Rostow, *Open Skies*, pp. 26–33.

44. Concerning Open Skies, see Beschloss, *Mayday*, pp. 98–107.

45. Killian interview.

46. Memorandum of conversation, June 25, 1956, DDRS-1976-241A.

47. Killian interview.

48. Beschloss, *Mayday*, pp. 123–24; Thomas Powers, *The Man Who Kept the Secrets: Richard Helms and the CIA* (New York: Knopf, 1979), pp. 96–98; Ambrose and Immerman, *Ike's Spies*, pp. 265–66.

49. Memorandum of conversation, July 10, 1956, DDRS-1979-333D. The comment, by Land, is in the transcript of "The Science Advisers," Videotape History Project, Alfred Sloan Foundation, New York, New York.

50. Ambrose and Immerman, *Ike's Spies*, p. 273; Farrell (ed.), *The Eisenhower Diaries*, pp. 330–31.

51. Burrows, *Deep Black*, p. 102; Ambrose, *Eisenhower: The President*, p. 374.

52. Ambrose, *Eisenhower: The President*, p. 374; Ambrose and Immerman, *Ike's Spies*, p. 273.

53. Divine, *Blowing on the Wind*, pp. 60, 66–68.

54. On Stassen's Nuclear Task Force, see Hewlett and Holl, *Atoms for Peace and War*, pp. 296–97; and Allen Greb, "Science Advice to Presidents: From Test Bans to the Strategic Defense Initiative," IGCC Research Paper No. 3, p. 6.

55. Interviews: Hans Bethe and Ernie Plesset.

56. Herbert York, *The Advisors: Oppenheimer, Teller, and the Superbomb* (New York: Freeman, 1976), p. 92.

57. CIA, "Report of the Joint Atomic Energy Intelligence Committee," November 7, 1955, DDRS-1979-472B.

58. Murray to Eisenhower, March 14, 1955, DDRS-1983-9. On the revival of the test-ban issue that spring, see Divine, *Blowing on the Wind*, pp. 70–72; Earl Voss, *Nuclear Ambush: The Test-Ban Trap* (New York: Henry Regnery, 1963), pp. 76–78; and Murray, *Nuclear Policy for War and Peace*, p. 86.

59. Divine, *Blowing on the Wind*, pp. 72–73; Ambrose, *Eisenhower: The President*, pp. 343–44.

60. Ambrose, *Eisenhower: The President*, pp. 343–44.

61. Ibid., p. 344.

62. Ibid.

63. Divine, *Blowing on the Wind*, p. 105.

64. Ibid.

65. Memorandum of meeting, October 9, 1956, DDRS-1980-383A.

66. Eisenhower, *The White House Years*, p. 208.

67. Killian, *Sputnik, Scientists, and Eisenhower*, pp. 83–84; Beschloss, *Mayday*, pp. 132–33.

68. Divine, *Blowing on the Wind*, p. 157; Ambrose, *Eisenhower: The President*, pp. 403–4.

69. Ambrose, *Eisenhower: The President*, p. 398.

70. Ibid.

71. Divine, *Blowing on the Wind*, p. 148.

72. Ibid.

73. Memorandum of conversation, June 24, 1957, DDRS-1977-253C. On this meeting and the clean bomb, see also Katherine Magraw, "Teller and the 'Clean Bomb' Episode," *Bulletin of the Atomic Scientists*, May 1988, pp. 32–37; and Hewlett and Holl, *Atoms for Peace and War*, pp. 398–402.

74. Magraw, "Teller and the 'Clean Bomb' Episode," pp. 32–37.

75. Ambrose, *Eisenhower: The President*, pp. 399–400.

76. What Strauss did not explain to Eisenhower was that the dramatic reduction in fallout from Plumbbob, compared to earlier atomic tests, was achieved by the simple expedient of carrying the bombs aloft by balloon rather than exploding them on a tower close to the earth and by removing their uranium casing—which accounts for much of the yield and most of the fallout of modern thermonuclear weapons. Divine, *Blowing on the Wind*, p. 150; Carson Mark interview.

77. Khrushchev is quoted in Divine, *Blowing on the Wind*, p. 151.

78. Ibid., p. 152.

79. Ambrose, *Eisenhower: The President*, p. 401.

80. Memorandum of meeting, August 9, 1957, DDRS-1978-311B.

81. Ibid. In rejecting Strauss's appeal for a test during Hardtack of a bomb yielding twenty megatons or more, Eisenhower revealed that he was now relying upon someone else—probably Rabi—for advice on nuclear weapons. Thus, when Strauss tried to justify the big bomb on the grounds that the destructiveness of such a weapon would compensate for inaccuracies in delivery, the president pointed out that "the scaling laws apply on a cube root basis," and hence that the damage caused by a forty-megaton bomb would be only half again that of a ten-megaton bomb.

82. Strobe Talbott (trans. and ed.), *Khrushchev Remembers: The Last Testament* (Boston: Little, Brown, 1974), pp. 47–48.

83. "Chronology of Significant Events in the U.S. Intermediate and Intercontinental Ballistic Missile Program," November 8, 1957, DDRS-1983-11. On problems in the American missile program at this time, see also Walter McDougall, *The Heavens and the Earth: A Political History of the Space Age* (New York: Basic Books, 1985), pp. 129–31.

84. McDougall, *The Heavens and the Earth*, pp. 129–31.

85. Burrows, *Deep Black*, pp. 92–96.

86. Ibid.; McDougall, *The Heavens and the Earth*, pp. 121–23.

87. On the RAND report, see McDougall, *The Heavens and the Earth*, p. 102.

88. The CIA's Richard Bissell had cautioned the Eisenhower administration about the potentially serious psychological and military consequences of finishing second in a satellite race. Bissell interview; Ambrose, *Eisenhower: The President*, pp. 427–28.

89. Ibid.

90. Ibid. Eisenhower also received a progress report at this meeting on Project Corona, the CIA's reconnaissance satellite program.

91. Ibid., p. 430.

Chapter 7

1. Memorandum of conference, October 15, 1957, PSAC Records, National Archives; Stephen Ambrose, *Eisenhower: The President* (New York: Simon & Schuster, 1984), pp. 430–31.

2. Rabi to Gray, Octber 28, 1957, DDRS-1983-621. Concerning Rabi's proposal and his meeting with Eisenhower, see also Robert H. Ferrell (ed.), *The Eisenhower Diaries* (New York: Norton, 1981), pp. 348–49; and Memorandum of conversation, October 30, 1957, DDRS-1981-631A.

3. A. Dulles to Goodpaster, October 28, 1957, DDRS-1980-8B.

4. Rabi claimed that a test ban could be monitored by the same means that brought the flaw in Russian warheads to light—namely, atmospheric sampling—as well as by the half dozen on-site inspection stations to which the Russians had agreed in principle at Geneva. As an additional safeguard, Rabi suggested that work continue in the United States on more conventional ways of defending against missiles. Memorandum of meeting, October 29, 1957, DDRS-1984-1297.

5. On December 26, 1957, Eisenhower was sent a four-page memorandum containing the results of the study by the "ad hoc Scientific Panel" established to investigate Rabi's thesis concerning the vulnerability of Soviet warheads. Despite repeated appeals by the author, this document remains classified as of this writing. The question of whether Russian ICBM warheads were vulnerable to preinitiation was rendered moot shortly after this report, according to Bethe, who served on the ad hoc panel. Thus, nuclear tests conducted by the Soviets in the spring of 1958 showed that the suspected flaw had been identified and corrected. The flaw in Soviet warheads was apparently the lack of a boosted fission trigger. "Report of the *ad hoc* Scientific Panel . . . ," December 26, 1957, DDRS-1982-1. Interviews: Hans Bethe and Spurgeon Keeny.

6. Ferrell (ed.), *The Eisenhower Diaries,* pp. 348–49.

7. On the creation of PSAC, see James R. Killian, *Sputnik, Scientists, and Eisenhower* (Cambridge, Mass.: MIT Press, 1977), pp. 21–23, 107–9.

8. Eisenhower's speech is in *Public Papers of the President: Dwight D. Eisenhower* (Washington, D.C.: U.S. Government Printing Office, 1958), pp. 789–99.

9. Memorandum of meeting, November 7, 1957, DDRS-1979-331A. On the origins of the Gaither Report, its recommendations, and their fate, see Fred Kaplan, *The Wizards of Armageddon* (New York: Simon & Schuster, 1983), pp. 125–43; and U.S. Congress, Joint Committee on Defense Production, "Deterrence and Survival in the Nuclear Age: The Gaither Report" (Washington, D.C.: U.S. Government Printing Office, 1976). Gaither, stricken with cancer, gradually dropped out of the panel's deliberations. His place was taken by Paul Nitze, a prominent administration critic—and a chief author of the subsequent Gaither Report.

10. A CIA estimate of Soviet missile strength sent to Eisenhower later in the month also seemed to confirm the Gaither Report's grim prognosis. Thus, the CIA thought the Russians might have an "initial operating capability" of 10 ICBMs as early as 1958, a force of 100 missiles between mid-1959 and early 1960, and as many as 500 ICBMs between 1960 and 1962. See CIA, "Briefing to Senate Armed Services Committee," November 26–27, 1957, DDRS-1984-1544.

11. Kaplan, *Wizards of Armaggedon,* pp. 125–43.

12. On reaction to the Gaither Report, see Memorandum of conversation,

Eisenhower and Dulles, November 7, 1957, DDRS-1984-1630. A leaked account of the Gaither Report, appearing some six weeks later in the *Washington Post,* spoke of a "missile-bristling Soviet Union," "rocketing Soviet military might," and "a powerful, growing Soviet economy." See Chalmers Roberts, "Enormous Arms Outlay Is Held Vital to Survival," December 20, 1957, *Washington Post.* Sprague was so worried by the Gaither Report that he suggested to Dulles the United States might wish to consider a preventive war against the Soviet Union—a suggestion that the secretary of state promptly rejected, noting that he "had long felt that no man should arrogate the power to decide that the future of mankind would benefit by an action entailing the killing of tens of millions of people, and he believed the President agreed with this." Memorandum of conversation, Dulles and Sprague, January 3, 1958, DDRS-1984-1631.

13. Wiesner interview.

14. Cutler to Killian, November 14, 1957, DDRS-1982-2917; Killian, *Sputnik, Scientists, and Eisenhower,* pp. 30–32.

15. On PSAC's terms of reference, see Killian, *Sputnik, Scientists, and Eisenhower,* pp. 275–76; and Killian to Eisenhower, December 20, 1957, DDRS-1982-2918-9. Killian interview.

16. Other SAC/ODM veterans to join PSAC were Detlev Bronk, president of the National Academy of Sciences; Lloyd Berkner, president of Associated Universities, Inc.; Caryl Haskins, president of the Carnegie Institution of Washington, D.C.; MIT physicist Jerrold Zacharias; Bell Labs' William O. Baker and James Fisk; and Caltech's H. P. Robertson. The new members of PSAC were George Kistiakowsky, Edward Purcell, Robert Bacher, General James Doolittle, and Herbert York. In his memoirs, York speculates on the reason he was selected for PSAC: "Evidently they wanted someone from inside the current nuclear weapons establishment. Edward Teller, who might otherwise have been considered, was *persona non grata* with many of the other members because of his role in the Oppenheimer hearings. . . ." Herbert York, *Making Weapons, Talking Peace* (New York: Basic Books, 1987), p. 105. On the origins of PSAC, see also Killian, *Sputnik, Scientists, and Eisenhower,* pp. 277–79.

17. Minutes, December 9–11, 1957, PSAC Records, National Archives.

18. Minutes of meeting, February 10, 1958, DDRS-1984-718.

19. The PSAC report, "Introduction to Outer Space," is reprinted in Killian, *Sputnik, Scientists, and Eisenhower,* pp. 288–99.

20. Killian, *Sputnik, Scientists, and Eisenhower,* pp. 120–21; Walter McDougall, *The Heavens and the Earth: A Political History of the Space Age* (New York: Basic Books, 1985), pp. 168–69.

21. Killian, *Sputnik, Scientists, and Eisenhower,* p. 112.

22. Herbert York, *Race to Oblivion* (New York: Simon & Schuster, 1970), pp. 53–58.

23. PSAC's "Missile Panel" had recently reported that both the ICBM and IRBM programs were now proceeding in a satisfactory manner. Killian, *Sputnik, Scientists, and Eisenhower,* pp. 145–48, 221; York, *Making Weapons, Talking Peace,* pp. 110–11.

24. Killian, *Sputnik, Scientists, and Eisenhower,* pp. 152–54; "*Aide-Memoire* on Major Activities of the PSAC, November 1957–May 1959," May 9, 1959, DDRS-1977-205A. In March, Eisenhower received two reports that confirmed the U.S. advantage in nuclear weapons. A study by the CIA's Office of Scientific Intelli-

gence noted that the Soviets had exploded eleven H-bombs between their first test in 1955 and the most recent one at the end of February 1958. Not only was this but a fraction of the number of American tests thus far, but the efficiency of at least four of the Russian bombs had been poor. A Pentagon report at the end of the month concurred that the United States had "an advantage in yield vs. weight ratios, in flexibility of application," and "in knowledge of weapons effects of a specialized nature," but noted that the United States lacked knowledge of weapons effects "at ultra-high altitudes." See CIA, "Impact of 1 September 1958 Nuclear Test Moratorium on Soviet Nuclear Weapons Capabilities," March 18, 1958, DDRS-1980-20B; and DOD, "Ad Hoc Panel on Nuclear Test Cessation," March 21, 1958, DDRS-1982-1545.

25. Report, Dearborn to Eisenhower, February 14, 1958, DDRS-1977-254C. Another AEC recommendation, forwarded to Eisenhower by Cutler, proposed adding a six-megaton clean bomb test to Hardtack and inviting an international group of distinguished scientists to witness the explosion and confirm its low radioactivity. Teller also lobbied for the clean bomb in the February 10 issue of *Life* magazine. Memorandum, Cutler to Eisenhower, March 24, 1958, DDRS-1977-255A.

26. Memorandum of meeting, March 24, 1958, DDRS-1978-124A.

27. "Report of NSC Ad Hoc Working Group on the Technical Feasibility of a Cessation of Nuclear Testing" [The Bethe Report], March 27, 1958, DDRS-1984-2702. General Herbert Loper, one of two Pentagon representatives on Bethe's panel, disavowed the report's conclusion on the grounds that the United States should continue testing. Livermore physicist Harold Brown—who was coauthor, with Bethe, of an appendix to the report dealing with verification of underground testing—initially balked at signing the report, but later overcame his doubts about the possibility of detecting clandestine tests underground. Bethe interview. On the Bethe report, see also Harold Jacobson and Eric Stein, *Diplomats, Scientists, and Politicians: The United States and the Test Ban Negotiations* (Ann Arbor: University of Michigan Press, 1966), pp. 44–47; and Charles Appleby, "Eisenhower and Arms Control, 1953–1961: A Balance of Risks," unpublished Ph.D. dissertation, 1987, pp. 261–65. My thanks to Mr. Appleby for providing me with a copy of his dissertation.

28. On April 7, 1958, Mark Mills, associate director at Livermore and a chief advocate of the clean bomb, was killed in a helicopter crash on his way to investigate a problem with one of the devices at the Pacific testing range. The unusual circumstances of the crash—the helicopter was flying at night in a storm—suggest the urgency of Mills's mission. Both Teller and Mills were concerned that Eisenhower might announce a moratorium before Hardtack could be completed; if the clean bomb test failed, they feared he might cancel the program altogether. The clean bomb test that was to be witnessed by foreign scientists was subsequently canceled, due to delays and a lack of interest on the part of the scientists. On problems with the clean bomb tests, see Chuck Hansen, *U.S. Nuclear Weapons: The Secret History* (New York: Orion Books, 1988), pp. 73–78.

29. Ambrose, *Eisenhower: The President*, pp. 451–52; Robert A. Divine, *Blowing on the Wind: The Nuclear Test Ban Debate, 1954–1960* (New York: Oxford, 1978), p. 202.

30. Minutes, April 8–10, 1958, PSAC Records.

31. York is quoted in Killian, *Sputnik, Scientists, and Eisenhower*, p. 157; see also York, *Making Weapons, Talking Peace*, pp. 117–19.

32. York, *Making Weapons, Talking Peace,* pp. 117–19. York interview.

33. Minutes, April 8–10, 1958, PSAC Records; Memorandum of meeting, March 6, 1958, DDRS-1975 Retrospective-904B.

34. York, *Making Weapons, Talking Peace,* p. 76. Operation Argus was the inspiration of Nicholas Christofilos, a brilliant and eccentric Livermore physicist, who theorized that the high-energy electrons produced by a nuclear explosion in the upper atmosphere would be spread out in a broad belt by the earth's magnetic field. The "Christofilos effect," its inventor believed, would severely damage or destroy the delicate electronics in an ICBM warhead—creating, in essence, a kind of temporary antimissile *cordon sanitaire* around the earth. Concerning the origins and outcome of Argus, see York, *Making Weapons, Talking Peace,* pp. 128–32.

35. Memorandum of meeting, April 17, 1958, DDRS-1975 Retrospective-906C.

36. Ibid.

37. Killian interview. There were other indications of PSAC's growing importance. Within days of becoming science adviser, Killian received a luncheon invitation from Strauss—who used the occasion to ask for assurances that PSAC would not reopen the Oppenheimer investigation. Although Killian characterized his relations with the AEC chairman as "cordial," he acknowledged that it seemed Strauss's "policy to oppose any PSAC recommendation." Killian remembered, for example, that Strauss was the only one at an NSC meeting to object to an early PSAC report on the state of American science. Killian interview. Strauss also complained to John Foster Dulles at this time about PSAC's growing influence. See Hewlett and Holl, *Atoms for Peace and War,* p. 479.

38. Dwight Eisenhower, *The White House Years: Waging Peace,* 1956–1961 (New York: Doubleday, 1965), p. 476; memorandum, Twining to McElroy, April 30, 1958, DDRS-1979-37C.

39. In January 1958, Strauss had written Eisenhower offering to step down when his renomination as AEC chairman came up that summer. Strauss acknowledged that "he had accumulated a number of liabilities, including most of the columnists in the Washington press." The president—noting he "shared these liabilities"— was sympathetic and the following November picked Strauss to be secretary of commerce. Strauss was subsequently denied confirmation, however, by senators outraged over his role in the Oppenheimer controversy. Memorandum of conversation, January 22, 1958, DDRS-1977-254B; Lewis Strauss, *Men and Decisions* (New York: Doubleday, 1962), pp. 375–403.

40. Lawrence, seriously ill with colitis at the time he joined the Committee of Experts, died in August 1958, the day after the Conference of Experts finished its report. On Lawrence's role in Geneva, see York, *Making Weapons, Talking Peace,* pp. 163–64. Concerning the Conference of Experts, see Appleby, "Eisenhower and Arms Control," pp. 273–81; and Jacobson and Stein, *Diplomats, Scientists, and Politicians,* pp. 54–55.

41. Memorandum of meeting, June 18, 1958, DDRS-1975 Retrospective-914A. The clean bomb project was deemphasized at Livermore after Hardtack. See Hansen, *U.S. Nuclear Weapons,* pp. 73–78; and memorandum of meeting, July 24, 1958, DDRS-1978-311C. Shortly before his meeting with Bethe, Eisenhower had denied Strauss's request for a new series of above-ground tests—Operation Millrace—to follow Hardtack. See memorandum, Strauss to Eisenhower, June 12, 1958, DDRS-1983-10; and memorandum of meeting, June 13, 1958, DDRS-1984-2747.

42. DDRS-1975 Retrospective-914A; Ambrose, *Eisenhower: The President,* p. 457.

43. Minutes, June 17–18, 1958, PSAC Records.

44. Ambrose, *Eisenhower: The President,* p. 477.

45. On August 1, 1958, the United States exploded a four-megaton bomb almost fifty miles above Johnston Island in the Pacific in a test code-named Teak, which was designed to study certain weapons effects—including the radiation hazard to Strategic Air Command bomber crews from high-altitude nuclear explosions. Unexpectedly, Teak blacked out radar and radio communications over a wide area. A second high-altitude test two weeks later, code-named Orange, confirmed the nuclear "blackout" effect. Albert Latter interview. On the discovery of the "blackout" effect and its impact upon the test ban, see Kaplan, *Wizards of Armageddon,* pp. 344–45; and Appleby, "Eisenhower and Arms Control," p. 240 fn.

46. Memorandum of meeting, August 14, 1958, DDRS-1982-1289.

47. Memorandum of meeting, August 19, 1958, DDRS-1984-528.

48. Ambrose, *Eisenhower: The President,* pp. 477–78. On the origins of the moratorium, see Appleby, "Eisenhower and Arms Control," pp. 263, 283–84; and Robert Divine, "Early Record on Test Moratoriums," *Bulletin of the Atomic Scientists,* May 1986, pp. 24–26.

49. On the Committee of Principals, see Killian, *Sputnik, Scientists, and Eisenhower,* pp. 160–63; and Jacobson and Stein, *Diplomats, Scientists, and Politicians,* pp. 85–87. Britain apparently made its support of the moratorium conditional upon receiving technical assistance from the United States in making its nuclear weapons invulnerable to neutron preinitiation, the flaw that had earlier afflicted Soviet ICBM warheads. Against AEC objections, Eisenhower promised such cooperation. See Appleby, "Eisenhower and Arms Control," pp. 283–84. On PSAC's involvement in a "Surprise Attack" Conference being held in Geneva at the same time, see Appleby, "Eisenhower and Arms Control," pp. 288–95.

50. Interview with Jerry Johnson.

51. "Report of Ad Hoc Panel . . . ," November 18, 1958, DDRS-1982-1290; memorandum of meeting, undated, DDRS-1984-2376.

52. Memorandum, Killian to Eisenhower, November 3, 1958, DDRS-1977-355D. In March 1959, *The New York Times* published an exclusive series of articles on Operation Argus, which it described as "the greatest scientific experiment of all time." The *Times* article only vaguely alluded to Argus's potential military application. Twelve days earlier, an article in the Soviet newspaper *Izvestia* reported that a Russian satellite had detected a previously undiscovered band of radiation circling the earth. The *Izvestia* story attributed the effect to an unannounced nuclear test. On the reporting of Argus, see "U.S. Atom Blasts 300 Miles Up Mar Radar, Snag Missile Plan," *The New York Times,* March 19, 1959; "Quarles Says Atom Shots Aided Weapons Research in Attack and Defense," *The New York Times,* March 20, 1959; and York, *Making Weapons, Talking Peace,* pp. 149–50. Concerning PSAC's role in Operation Argus, see memorandum of meeting, March 6, 1958, DDRS-1975 Retrospective-904B.

53. "Report, PSAC Panel on AICBM," December 17, 1958, DDRS-1981-88A.

54. Memorandum, Skolnikoff to Killian, November 24, 1958, DDRS-1984-2377.

55. Edward Teller and Albert Latter, *Our Nuclear Future: Facts, Dangers, and Opportunities* (New York: Criterion Books, 1958). Latter interview.

56. Latter interview. In February 1959, physicist Wolfgang Panofsky, whom

Killian had asked to head a study of clandestine testing in outer space, reported to PSAC that the practical difficulties of conducting such tests far outweighed the value of the information that could be gained from them. Panofsky interview.

57. Latter calculated that decoupling might reduce the seismic signal from a nuclear explosion by a factor of 300. Latter interview.

58. In their appendix to the 1958 Bethe Report, Bethe and Harold Brown wrote: "The digging of underground caves large enough to give a substantial reduction of the seismic signal from a 50-kiloton explosion will be very costly and may in fact be impossible." See "Appendix C: Concealment and Detection of Nuclear Tests Underground," DDRS-1984-1975; and Edward Teller and Allen Brown, *The Legacy of Hiroshima* (New York: Doubleday, 1962), p. 196. Latter claims that after he pointed out at the Livermore briefing how Bethe's earlier calculations had overlooked one physical effect of decoupling, Bethe "bent over backward" in accepting his theory. Interviews: Hans Bethe and Albert Latter.

59. Bruce Bolt, *Nuclear Explosions and Earthquakes: The Parted Veil* (San Francisco: Freeman, 1976), pp. 103–5.

60. Memorandum of meeting, January 5, 1959, DDRS-1984-530; Jacobson and Stein, *Diplomats, Scientists, and Politicians,* pp. 76–77. Edward Teller evidently considered resigning as director of Livermore in order to publicize the "flawed" advice that Eisenhower was receiving from PSAC on the test ban. See Appleby, "Eisenhower and Arms Control," p. 298.

61. Memorandum of meeting, January 19, 1959, DDRS-1980-216B; Jacobson and Stein, *Diplomats, Scientists, and Politicians,* pp. 135–37. Part of the confusion over the rival interpretations of seismic data by Soviet and American experts stemmed from the geologic differences between test sites in the United States and Russia. Underground tests carried out in the hard granite at the Soviet proving grounds near Semipalatinsk typically gave off a much stronger seismic signal than tests conducted in the porous alluvia tuff characteristic of Nevada. The part that geology played in the different estimates of test yields was not fully appreciated until the late 1970s and early 1980s. The Berkner Report was the first study to draw attention to this phenomenon. My thanks to Hans Bethe for pointing out the importance of the Berkner Report in a letter of December 11, 1987. See Chapter 11 on the improvement of seismic detection techniques and its consequences.

62. Memorandum of meeting, February 28, 1959, DDRS-1975 Retrospective-911D.

63. "Report of the Panel on Seismic Improvement," January 7, 1959, DDRS-1984-2025. Berkner's panel concluded, for example, that decoupling was likely to reduce the seismic signal of an underground explosion by a factor of 10, not 300, and that the act of digging such an enormous cavern would probably be detected. "It would be like putting the Yale Bowl underground," said one scientist who looked at the practical difficulties of decoupling. Scoville interview. On the Berkner Report, see Killian, *Sputnik, Scientists, and Eisenhower,* pp. 165–66; and Howard Rodean, *Nuclear-Explosion Seismology* (Washington, D.C.: U.S. Atomic Energy Commission, 1971), pp. 1–5. The Russians subsequently accepted some decoupling as theoretically feasible. See Bethe to Fisk, December 12, 1959, "Status of Discussions on the Latter Hole," PSAC Records, Box 42.

64. Memorandum of meeting, March 16–17, 1959, DDRS-1981-349B.

65. At this meeting, Killian also poured cold water on Macmillan's idea for a

yearly quota of on-site inspections to distinguish between bomb tests and earth-quakes: "Unless there were authority to visit the site of the shocks, there could be no confidence that they were not underground tests." Ibid.; Killian, *Sputnik, Scientists, and Eisenhower,* p. 168–70.

66. Goodpaster wrote of Eisenhower at this time: "He is coming to the conclusion that our position should be that we will not test in the atmosphere." Memorandum of conversation, March 20, 1959, DDRS-1980-448C.

67. Memorandum of meeting, May 6, 1959, DDRS-1980-113C.

68. Memorandum of meeting, June 8, 1959, DDRS-1980-114A.

69. Memorandum of meeting, May 19, 1959, DDRS-1981-349D.

70. Memorandum of meeting, February 12, 1959, DDRS-1982-1400.

71. On the establishment of the Advanced Research Projects Agency and the Office of the Director of Defense Research and Engineering, see York, *Making Weapons, Talking Peace.* pp. 132–42, 168–92. Responding in March 1959 to the recommendations contained in a PSAC report, Eisenhower also created a Federal Council for Science and Technology to promote federally funded scientific research. Killian, *Sputnik, Scientists, and Eisenhower,* pp. 185–86.

72. Concerning the origins and activities of the Defense Science Board, see U.S. Department of Defense, Office of Secretary of Defense, "Defense Science Board: Background, Biographical Sketches, and Activities" (Washington, D.C.: U.S. Government Printing Office, 1985); and Kevin Cunningham, "Scientific Advisors and Defense Decision-Making: The Case of the Defense Science Board," unpublished manuscript. The author would like to thank Mr. Cunningham for a copy of his manuscript on the DSB.

73. York, *Making Weapons, Talking Peace,* pp. 166–68, 179–81.

74. Killian, *Sputnik, Scientists, and Eisenhower,* p. 168.

75. Killian gave his wife's illness and the need to get back to MIT as reasons for leaving the post. Killian, *Sputnik, Scientists, and Eisenhower,* pp. 205–7.

76. In a 1985 interview, Killian voiced regret that he had not been more aggressive in countering the technical arguments used to block progress toward the test ban. Killian interview.

77. Concerning continuing problems with the U.S. missile program, see memorandum of meeting, July 1, 1959, DDRS-1975 Retrospective-905A; and memorandum, Kistiakowsky to Killian, June 19, 1958, DDRS-1980-172A.

78. George B. Kistiakowsky, *A Scientist at the White House* (Cambridge, Mass.: Harvard University Press, 1976), pp. 9–11.

79. Ibid.

80. Ibid., pp. 17–18, 23.

81. Ibid., pp. 21–22. Earlier, Kistiakowsky had aroused McCone's ire by discounting the AEC's argument that a particular weapon in the U.S. nuclear stockpile was not "one-point-safe," or immune from accidental detonation. McCone cited the safety issue as a reason to resume nuclear testing. In a 1985 interview, PSAC physicist Edward Purcell, whom Kistiakowsky had appointed to a panel to resolve the one-point-safe question, claimed that the controversy was an "absolutely transparent . . . gimmick" that McCone and McElroy hoped to use to end the moratorium. Purcell credited Kistiakowsky with "beating back the attack." Purcell interview. On the one-point-safe controversy, see "Nuclear Weapons Accidents," *Defense Monitor* (Center for Defense Information, Washington, D.C.), vol. X, no. 5, 1981, pp. 1–3; Kisti-

akowsky, *A Scientist at the White House,* pp. 55, 79–80, 213; and memorandum, McElroy to Eisenhower, September 14, 1959, DDRS-1979-154A.

82. Kistiakowsky, *A Scientist at the White House,* pp. 71–72; Twining to McElroy, August 14, 1959, DDRS-1979-38A; Divine, *Blowing on the Wind,* pp. 284–85.

83. Kistiakowsky, *A Scientist at the White House,* p. 150.

84. Ibid., p. 214.

85. Ibid., p. 198. A threshold test ban, PSAC pointed out, might also prevent Soviet development of a lightweight, high-yield missile warhead. See Appleby, "Eisenhower and Arms Control," p. 299.

86. Kistiakowsky, *A Scientist at the White House,* p. 213.

87. Ibid., p. 14. Early in 1959, Kistiakowsky admitted that his "impressions ran counter to our best intelligence estimates," which had yet to identify a tangible Soviet ICBM threat. Kistiakowsky believed the Russians "now have an operational long-range missile force." Memorandum of meeting, January 14, 1959, DDRS-1975 Retrospective-904E.

88. Letter, Eisenhower to Swede Haslett, November 18, 1957, DDRS-1982-2931.

89. For example, the CIA's National Intelligence Estimate for June 1958 reported that the Soviets' testing program for the SS-6 appeared to have stalled, but nonetheless went on to predict that the Russians would have 100 SS-6s by 1959, 500 by 1960, and 1,000 by 1961—or twice what the agency had predicted only six months earlier. William Burrows, *Deep Black: Space Espionage and National Security* (New York: Random House, 1986), pp. 96–97.

90. John Prados, *The Soviet Estimate: U.S. Intelligence Analysis and Russian Military Strength* (New York: Dial Press, 1982), pp. 83–85. In an October 1958 memorandum to the Senate's Guided Missile Intelligence Committee, CIA Director Allen Dulles noted "the likelihood that the apparent slow rate of [Soviet] ICBM test firings represents serious difficulty and delay in the development program." The previous May, Democratic Senator Stuart Symington, a prominent believer in the missile gap, had predicted the Soviets might have as many as 500 operational ICBMs by 1961. In a December 1958 briefing of Symington by the CIA director, Allen Dulles acknowledged feeling "puzzlement and concern" over the slow rate of Russian missile development. An Air Force officer at the briefing speculated that "maybe they had gone back to the drawing board to fix something." Observed Symington: "It sounded as if Nikita Khrushchev was violating Theodore Roosevelt's principle of speaking softly but carrying a big stick, since he has virtually given the United States an ultimatum but at the same time is reducing his armament." See memorandum, Dulles to Symington, October 9, 1958, DDRS-1984-1545; and memorandum of briefing, December 16, 1958, DDRS-1982-2350. Goodpaster, too, acknowledged the "growing necessity for a project aimed at finding out more of the story regarding___, whether they exist in anything like the numbers previously estimated, where they are, what their readiness is, etc." Memorandum of conversation, October 26, 1958, DDRS-1979-334A.

91. Kistiakowsky, *A Scientist at the White House,* p. 115.

92. Ibid., p. 149. Killian, for example, remembered a telephone call from the president "out of the blue," reassuring him "that the Soviets were not as strong as many claimed." Killian, *Sputnik, Scientists, and Eisenhower,* p. 222.

93. Kistiakowsky, *A Scientist at the White House,* p. 219.

94. Memorandum of meeting, March 14, 1960, DDRS-1978-124C.

95. Ambrose, *Eisenhower: The President,* pp. 567–68.

96. Ibid.

97. Interviews: Herbert York and George Rathjens. It was not until the spring of 1960 that CIA analysts felt they had finally solved the mystery of the missing Soviet missiles. That March, the agency sent Eisenhower the first comprehensive report on the problems the Russians had encountered in their missile program. The CIA noted that early theoretical work on ICBMs was done at a Moscow facility called the Scientific Research Institute, whereas the actual building of the rockets had taken place at Kaliningrad's "Experimental Factory 88 for Guided Missile Development." The CIA's experts concluded that the Russians, like their American counterparts, had relied on captured German rocket scientists and that the Soviets, too, had decided to defer mass production of early model ICBMs, preferring to await development of a smaller and more reliable version. See CIA, "Scientific Research Institute and Experimental Factory 88 for Guided Missile Development, Moskva/Kaliningrad," March 4, 1960, DDRS-1979-234C; and Andrew Cockburn, *The Threat: Inside the Soviet Military Machine* (New York: Random House, 1983), pp. 187–221.

98. On the setbacks in the Discoverer program, see U.S. Department of Defense, "Military Space Projects Report," April 11, 1960, DDRS-1977-288A; and Burrows, *Deep Black,* pp. 109–10.

99. The CIA's estimate that the Russians might have a jet interceptor capable of shooting down the U-2 before the end of the year accounted in part for the urgent request for more overflights. The previous February, citing "the opinion of the Joint Chiefs of Staff that our planes will not be shot down," McElroy had asked that the overflights be resumed on a regular basis. Joint Chiefs of Staff Chairman Nathan Twining observed at this meeting that the military "would certainly like more information" and "pointed out that the Soviets have never fired a missile at one of our reconnaissance aircraft." On Eisenhower's concern with the U-2, see "Notes on special meeting," January 1958, DDRS-1979-334B; memorandum of meeting, January 14, 1959, DDRS-1975 Retrospective-904E; memorandum of meeting, February 12, 1959, DDRS-1981-622A; and memorandum for record, March 4, 1959, DDRS-1982-2934.

100. Concerning the U-2 shootdown and its effect upon U.S.-Soviet relations, see memorandum of meeting, May 12, 1960, DDRS-1979-104B; memorandum of meeting, May 15, 1960, DDRS-1982-1222; and Michael Beschloss, *Mayday: Eisenhower, Khrushchev, and the U-2 Affair* (New York: Harper & Row, 1986), pp. 273–304. The downing of the U-2 occurred only weeks before the first success of Project Corona, the CIA's satellite reconnaissance program. On August 10, Discoverer 13 was successfully launched and its payload recovered the following day. To the CIA's surprise—and Eisenhower's relief—the Russians did not protest the orbiting spacecraft above their skies: a forebearance that hinted at Soviet plans to follow suit, and that also established a legal precedent critical in subsequent verification of arms control agreements by "national technical means." See Burrows, *Deep Black,* pp. 109–11.

101. Kistiakowsky, *A Scientist at the White House,* p. 375.

102. Memorandum of meeting, January 12, 1961, DDRS-1981-398C.

103. Ibid.

104. Herbert York believed that Eisenhower's second warning referred to the "hard-sell technologists" who perennially proposed new weapons to the Pentagon. Spurgeon Keeny, then a PSAC consultant, speculates that Eisenhower had scientists like Edward Teller in mind. Interviews: York and Keeny.

Chapter 8

1. The Oval Office briefing was also a sign of things to come. Kennedy's first inquiry concerned the Communist insurgency in Laos—which Eisenhower said might be just "the cork in the bottle," and the "beginning of the loss of most of the Far East." Kennedy's other questions focused on the Congo, Cuba, the Caribbean, the war against the French in Algeria, the possibility of another confrontation with the Russians over Berlin, and the nation's ability to conduct limited wars in the Far East—where Kennedy asked Eisenhower if "we could put troops in there fast." Memorandum of conversation, January 19, 1961, DDRS-1984-728.

2. In his letter to Nitze, Kistiakowsky also alluded to the "good progress" that had been made in the talks at Geneva due to the contribution of scientists, but conceded that they had not been able to overcome every obstacle: "The AEC . . . under Strauss and McCone had gone its own independent way, playing off the Joint Committee against the President and vice versa." Memorandum of conversation, November 12, 1960, Box 86, President's Office Files, JFK Library, Boston, Massachusetts.

3. Interview with Jerome Wiesner. Eisenhower's willingness to agree to this arrangement, Wiesner believed, reflected his lack of enthusiasm for a Nixon presidency. Even before becoming science adviser, Wiesner was engaged in international diplomacy on Kennedy's behalf. During a meeting of scientists in Moscow, Wiesner and another Kennedy aide met with Soviet Deputy Foreign Minister Vladimir Kuznetsov, who agreed—as a sign of his government's desire for better relations with the new president—to release two Air Force crewmen whose plane had been shot down over Russia near the end of Eisenhower's term.

4. Wiesner proposed a flight-testing ban on ballistic missiles, on the grounds that both sides now had an operational liquid-fueled ICBM reliable enough for deterrence but too slow reacting and too inaccurate for a surprise attack. A missile test ban, he argued, would prevent the development of a second-generation, solid-fueled ICBM—which would be inexpensive, easily concealed, and suitable for a first strike. A Pentagon memorandum criticized Wiesner's report as "a waste of time since we obviously wouldn't touch such an agreement." See "The Urgency of a Complete Missile Test Ban," undated, DDRS-1980-172A-C; and "Comments on Weisner's [sic] Paper," DDRS-1980-171A-C.

5. On the connection between the Joint Committee on Atomic Energy and the neutron bomb, see Sam Cohen, *The Truth about the Neutron Bomb* (New York: Morrow, 1983), pp. 65, 81.

6. Wiesner interview.

7. PSAC's new members were to be physicists Harold Brown and Jerrold Zacharias, biochemist Paul Doty, and geophysicist Frank Press. When Brown became DDR&E director that May, his place on the committee was taken by Edwin Gilliland, a chemical engineer at MIT. Wiesner to Kennedy, January 23, 1961, Box 204, White House Central Files, JFK Library.

8. Later, in 1962, the pesticide problem was brought to the president's attention by Rachel Carson's best-selling book *Silent Spring*. In early 1963, Wiesner invited Carson to a PSAC meeting on the pesticide threat, where one committee member congratulated her for "pulling the bung out of the barrel." In response to *Silent Spring*, PSAC created a Pesticide Committee and in May 1963 published a report, "The Use of Pesticides," which essentially echoed the warning contained in Carson's book. Interview with Paul Doty. On the pesticides controversy and the influence of

Carson's book, see Paul Brooks, *The House of Life: Rachel Carson at Work* (Boston: Houghton Mifflin, 1972). The report on pesticides and supporting documents are in Box 86A, President's Office Files, JFK Library.

9. "PSAC, 5/6–12/61," Box 86A, President's Office Files, JFK Library.

10. Purcell interview. On the Space Council and the Wiesner Report, see Walter McDougall, *The Heavens and the Earth: A Political History of the Space Age* (New York: Basic Books, 1985), pp. 309, 315–18.

11. McDougall, *The Heavens and the Earth,* pp. 309, 315–18; "The Urgency of a Complete Missile Test Ban," undated, DDRS-1980-172C.

12. McDougall, *The Heavens and the Earth,* pp. 309, 315–18. In a 1985 interview, Wiesner claimed that Kennedy eventually came to agree with PSAC's assessment of the space race: "Several times Kennedy asked me if there wasn't something on earth he could find to do with that money that would be more productive. I said no—because people were always equating military missiles and space."

13. On the Apollo decision and its critics, see McDougall, *The Heavens and the Earth,* pp. 389–94.

14. Wiesner interview and his taped comments on draft manuscript.

15. On changes at DDR&E and ARPA during the Kennedy administration, see "The Advanced Research Projects Agency, 1958–1974," J. Barber Associates, December 1975, National Technical Information Service, vol. V, pp. 1–16; and Herbert York, *Making Weapons, Talking Peace* (New York: Basic Books, 1987), pp. 166–71.

16. On cancellation of the B-70, see Nick Kotz, *Wild Blue Yonder: Money, Politics, and the B-1 Bomber* (New York: Pantheon, 1988), pp. 48–49. The secretary of defense proved, in fact, to be a more stalwart promoter of the test ban than either Secretary of State Dean Rusk or Arms Control and Disarmament Agency Director William Foster. At one Committee of Principals meeting, for example, McNamara—exasperated by Foster's suspicion that the Soviets were cheating on the moratorium—snapped, "Bill, you're supposed to worry about disarmament. Let me worry about defending the security of the United States." Transcript of "The Nuclear Test Ban," Tape 2, p. 25, Sloan Videotape History Project, Alfred Sloan Foundation, New York, N.Y.

17. Other PSAC members on the panel were Hans Bethe, Harold Brown, and Herbert York. On the panel, see Glenn Seaborg, *Kennedy, Khrushchev, and the Test Ban* (Berkeley: University of California Press, 1981), pp. 35–37.

18. Besides Joint Chiefs of Staff Chairman General Lyman Lemnitzer, the new members of the Committee of Principals were McGeorge Bundy, Kennedy's national security adviser, and Edward R. Murrow, the new head of the U.S. Information Agency. That March, the committee agreed, at McCloy's urging, to a compromise on the number of on-site inspections. Instead of the twenty inspections a year demanded under Eisenhower, the committee called for twelve annual inspections, leaving open the possibility of an additional eight inspections if warranted by unexplained seismic events. On Wiesner's and PSAC's role as advisers to the Committee of Principals, see Seaborg, *Kennedy, Khrushchev, and the Test Ban,* pp. 41–43; and Cecil Uyehara, "Scientific Advice and the Nuclear Test Ban Treaty," in Sanford Lakoff (ed.), *Knowledge and Power: Essays on Science and Government* (New York: Free Press, 1966), pp. 134–35.

19. Seaborg interview. On Seaborg's admitted ambivalence toward the test ban as AEC chairman, see Seaborg, *Kennedy, Khrushchev, and the Test Ban,* p. 35.

20. Ibid., pp. 46–48.

21. The RAND report and Air Force reaction is in Box 99a–100, "Disarmament—Nuclear Test Ban Negotiations" folder, President's Office Files, JFK Library.

22. In February, Wiesner had cautioned Kennedy concerning Plowshare "that the proponents of this project may be overly optimistic over its immediate prospects, and that this project could be oversold by them in much the same manner as were controlled thermonuclear reactors and aircraft nuclear propulsion." Wiesner to Kennedy, February 23, 1961, DDRS-1975 Retrospective-911F.

23. Concerning Plowshare in the Kennedy years, see Seaborg, *Kennedy, Khrushchev, and the Test Ban,* pp. 39–40.

24. Ibid., p. 63.

25. In a May letter, Kennedy responded to JCAE Chairman Chet Holifield's claim that correction of a recently discovered safety defect in the Mark 7, a tactical nuclear weapon already in the U.S. arsenal, required the immediate resumption of nuclear testing. Kennedy rejected Holifield's effort to resurrect the so-called one-point-safe controversy by noting that additional safety devices had since been added to the Mark 7, making the resumption of testing unnecessary. Kennedy to Holifield, May 3, 1961, DDRS-1975 Retrospective-913C.

26. Early in his administration, Kennedy said he was puzzled by the shift in public concern with fallout. A 1957 Gallup poll, for example, had shown 63 percent support for a nuclear test ban. Seaborg, *Kennedy, Khrushchev, and the Test Ban,* pp. 31, 73–74.

27. Ibid., pp. 66–68.

28. Interviews: York and Scoville. Concerning charges of Soviet cheating, see Seaborg. *Kennedy, Khrushchev, and the Test Ban,* p. 34.

29. Observed Panofsky of his 1958 inquiry into the likelihood of Soviet testing in outer space: "The doves were saying 'No, they can't,' and the hawks were saying 'Yes, they can,' and I was saying 'That's the wrong question.'" Panofsky interview. Concerning the conclusions of Panofsky's first panel, see "Report of the Technical Working Group on the Detection and Identification of High-Altitude Nuclear Explosions," undated, Box 43, PSAC Records.

30. "Report of the Ad Hoc Panel on Nuclear Testing" [The Panofsky Report], July 21, 1961, DDRS-1981-636A. The panel's findings on Soviet compliance was, in Panofsky's words, "basically a 'Scotch verdict'"—that is, no evidence could be found of Russian cheating. Panofsky interview.

31. Panofsky's panel concluded that the United States would maintain its lead in the arms race if the moratorium continued; that the Soviets "could become superior in 3–4 years" if they cheated and tested secretly underground; and that both countries would eventually wind up even in the race if unrestricted testing resumed. Panofsky Report.

32. Seaborg, *Kennedy, Khrushchev, and the Test Ban,* pp. 75–76.

33. In announcing his decision to resume nuclear testing, Khrushchev noted that the Soviet Union in Geneva had promised to abide by the moratorium so long as the "Western powers" did so. France tested its first atomic bomb in the Pacific during February 1960. As Wiesner and Seaborg have both pointed out, the French test meant that, technically, the Soviets were no longer bound by the terms of the moratorium. Interviews: Seaborg and Wiesner. On the controversy over the end of the moratorium, see Wiesner, "Setting the Moratorium Record Straight," and the reply by Robert Squire in *The New York Times,* January 9 and 19, 1986; and Robert Divine, "Early Record on Test Moratoriums," *Bulletin of the Atomic Scientists,* May 1986, pp. 24–26.

34. Divine, "Early Record on Test Moratoriums."

35. The CIA, in fact, notified Wiesner and Kaysen of the moratorium's impending end just before Khrushchev's announcement—having learned of the Soviets' intentions from a civilian Russian radio broadcast announcing that certain stations in Siberia would go off the air for a specified period. In the past this had been a telltale sign of preparations for a nuclear test. Rushing to the White House to deliver the news in person, the two found the president in his bedroom taking a nap. While Kaysen argued that the Soviet decision presented "the opportunity for us to make a grand gesture"—a unilateral declaration that the United States, despite the Russian action, would continue to refrain from testing—Kennedy's reaction was altogether different. "We had hardly got half the words out of our mouths," Kaysen said, "when Kennedy's response was, 'Kicked in the nuts again.'" Kaysen thought the president's remark "underlined the difference between the political perceptions of a couple of professors and the political perceptions of the president." Transcript of "The Nuclear Test Ban," Tape 2, p. 24, Sloan Videotape History Project. A slightly different version of this incident appears in Arthur Schlesinger, *A Thousand Days: John F. Kennedy in the White House* (Boston: Houghton Mifflin, 1965), p. 451.

36. Wiesner remembered, for example, a meeting with the president on the fallout hazard where Kennedy—gazing out the Oval Office window during a heavy downpour—asked, "You mean that stuff is in the rain out there?" Wiesner interview.

37. Kennedy's notes are in the "Disarmament—Nuclear Test Ban Negotiations, 7/30/62 Meeting" folder, Box 100a, President's Office Files, JFK Library.

38. "Transcript of William Foster Interview for the Kennedy Library," DDRS-1979-109C.

39. Seaborg, *Kennedy, Khrushchev, and the Test Ban,* pp. 81–85. Wiesner claims that Kennedy emerged from the forty-five-minute meeting "obviously shaken" by Teller's plan for a system of deep underground shelters. Teller, in his own account, confirms merely that the meeting was strained for both men. Wiesner interview. On Teller's first meeting with Kennedy, see Fred Kaplan, *The Wizards of Armageddon* (New York: Simon & Schuster, 1983), pp. 313–14; and Teller's letter in *Science,* November 19, 1982, p. 1270.

40. On the resumption of testing by the United States, see Seaborg, *Kennedy, Khrushchev, and the Test Ban,* pp. 86–88, 132–39.

41. On the test of the Soviet "Big Bomb," see Andrei Sakharov, *Memoirs* (New York: Knopf, 1990), pp. 218–23. The giant Russian bomb fueled speculation in the United States that the Soviets were experimenting with an antimissile shield, similar in concept to Project Argus. Other scientists hypothesized that such a bomb, if exploded high above the United States, might set fire to an area as large as four states. Concern that the Russians could put an even larger bomb into orbit reportedly prompted McNamara's decision to approve deployment of a primitive antisatellite capability early in 1962. The United States stationed one or more nuclear-tipped Thor missiles on Kwajalein atoll to intercept bombs-in-orbit until 1975, when the system was declared obsolete and dismantled. On the Soviet test and the U.S. reaction, see Seaborg, *Kennedy, Khrushchev, and the Test Ban,* p. 83; and Jack Manno, *Arming the Heavens: The Hidden Military Agenda for Space, 1945–1995* (New York: Dodd, Mead, 1984), pp. 142–43.

42. Seaborg, *Kennedy, Khrushchev, and the Test Ban,* p. 115.

43. Ibid., p. 117.

44. Ibid., p. 120.

45. Ibid., p. 121.

46. Concerning the early technical debate over the ABM, see "Warning and Defense in the Missile Age," June 3, 1959, DDRS-1978-195A; Avco Corporation, "Effect of Nuclear Blast on the Penetration Problem," December 1959, Box 67, PSAC Records; and York, *Making Weapons, Talking Peace,* pp. 142–43.

47. On Project Defender, see "The Advanced Research Projects Agency," vol. IV, pp. 21–23, and vol. V, pp. 16–30; and John Bosma, "Space and Strategic-Defense Reorientation: Project Defender," *Defense Science and Electronics,* September 1983, pp. 58–65. Concerning other advanced concepts for the antiballistic missile, and PSAC's involvement, see Kaplan, *The Wizards of Armaggedon,* pp. 344–45.

48. Ruina interview.

49. Rathjens interview. On the creation of the Arms Control and Disarmament Agency, see York, *Making Weapons, Talking Peace,* pp. 218–20; and James R. Killian, *Sputnik, Scientists, and Eisenhower* (Cambridge, Mass.: MIT Press, 1977), pp. 176–77. Wiesner claims that contrary to expectations the agency and its director proved "very cautious, very conservative" in their support of the test ban: "When we pushed for a disarmament agency it was to try to get the technical and policy responsibility [for the test ban] out of the White House. And here I suddenly found that we had built another barrier into the system." Wiesner interview.

50. Beckler written comments on draft manuscript. On the origins of the Office of Science and Technology, see James Katz, *Presidential Politics and Science Policy* (New York: Praeger, 1978), pp. 39–41; and U.S. Congress, "The Office of Science and Technology: A Report Prepared by the Science Policy Research Division" (Washington, D.C.: U.S. Government Printing Office, March 1967).

51. Observed Wiesner in a 1985 interview: "The most important reason for the Office of Science and Technology was to permit the science adviser to have two lives—that of the science adviser to the president, which would be protected by presidential privilege, and a life in which he could deal with the Congress on the many issues where [executive privilege] was not at stake."

52. Seaborg, *Kennedy, Khrushchev, and the Test Ban,* pp. 150–52; U.S. Department of Energy, "Announced United States Nuclear Tests, July 1945–December 1979," p. 14.

53. Kaysen to Kennedy, January 5, 1962, DDRS-1975 Retrospective-912A.

54. Ibid.; Seaborg, *Kennedy, Khrushchev, and the Test Ban,* pp. 126–31.

55. "The U.S.-U.S.S.R. Military Balance With and Without a Test Ban," undated, DDRS-1976-238B.

56. On the U.S. decision to resume atmospheric testing, see Kaysen to Kennedy, January 5, 1962, DDRS-1975 Retrospective-912A; transcript of "The Nuclear Test Ban," Tape 2, p. 24, Sloan Videotape History Project; and Seaborg, *Kennedy, Khrushchev, and the Test Ban,* p. 135–39.

57. Wiesner taped comments on draft manuscript. On Project Vela, see "The Advanced Research Projects Agency, 1958–1974," vol. IV, pp. 37–40, vol. V, pp. 31–34, and vol. VI, pp. 26–33.

58. Seaborg, *Kennedy, Khrushchev, and the Test Ban,* pp. 145–46.

59. Concerning the purpose of U.S. nuclear tests conducted in 1962 and their effects, see Chuck Hansen, *U.S. Nuclear Weapons: The Secret History* (New York: Orion Books, 1988), pp. 81–89; "Minutes of Meeting on the Status of U.S. and Soviet Nuclear Tests," February 2, 1962, DDRS-1981-637A; U.S. Department of Energy,

"Announced United States Nuclear Tests, July 1945–December 1979," pp.14–18; "Proposed Atmospheric Test Program," February 12, 1962, DDRS-1978-1B; and transcript of "The Nuclear Test Ban," Tape 2, p. 31, Sloan Videotape History Project.

60. In May, Wiesner had informed Kennedy that PSAC, while unenthusiastic about Urraca, and unconvinced of the need for the test, believed that it would have no lasting harmful effects. Sloan Videotape History Project. On these tests, see Hansen, *U.S. Nuclear Weapons,* pp. 84–89.

61. Foster to Kennedy, July 30, 1962, Box 100a, President's Office Files, JFK Library; Seaborg, *Kennedy, Khrushchev, and the Test Ban,* p. 162.

62. Seaborg, *Kennedy, Khrushchev, and the Test Ban,* pp. 162–63; and transcript of "The Nuclear Test Ban," Tape 3, p. 31, Sloan Videotape History Project.

63. Seaborg, *Kennedy, Khrushchev, and the Test Ban,* p. 188. When Harold Brown was quoted by a newspaper as believing that only five on-site inspections were needed to verify a test ban, Kennedy quickly disassociated himself from Brown's remark in a press conference—noting that the head of DDR&E had spoken "as a scientist." Interviews: Jack M. Ruina and Spurgeon Keeny.

64. "Memorandum on Relative Technical and Military Advantages of Testing or Non-Testing Under Various Testing Constraints," July 29, 1962, DDRS-1978-49A.

65. Wiesner is quoted in Seaborg, *Kennedy, Khrushchev, and the Test Ban,* p. 42.

66. Uyehara, "Scientific Advice and the Nuclear Test Ban Treaty," in Sanford Lakoff, ed. *Knowledge and Power: Essays on Science and Government* (New York: Free Press, 1966), p. 113.

67. Concerning the effect of the Cuban missile crisis on the Kennedy administration, see, for example, McGeorge Bundy, *Danger and Survival* (New York: Random House, 1989), pp. 391–462; and John Newhouse, *War and Peace in the Nuclear Age* (New York: Knopf, 1989), pp. 183–84.

68. China's first atomic bomb was actually tested in October 1964. On U.S. fears of the Chinese bomb, see Gordon Chang, "JFK, China, and the Bomb," *Journal of American History,* vol. 74, 1988, pp. 1287–1310.

69. "Minutes of NSC Meeting," January 21–22, 1963, Box 313, National Security Files, JFK Library; Seaborg, *Kennedy, Khrushchev, and the Test Ban,* p. 188.

70. At this meeting, ACDA proposed consideration of an agreement "to take radical steps, in cooperation with the USSR, to prevent the further proliferation of nuclear capabilities." The Pentagon raised the possibility of a Soviet-American "Non-Diffusion Agreement with Sanctions." Concerning discussion in the Kennedy administration of possible preemptive action against China, see Chang, "JFK, China, and the Bomb"; "Briefing Book on U.S.-Soviet Non-Diffusion Agreement for Discussion at the Moscow Treaty," undated, "ACDA—Disarmament—Briefing Book" folder, Box 265–270A, National Security Files, JFK Library; and "Transcript of William Foster Interview for the Kennedy Library," DDRS-1979-109C. In September 1964, when a Chinese nuclear test appeared imminent, McGeorge Bundy approached President Lyndon Johnson regarding "a possible agreement to cooperate in preventive military action" against China's nuclear facilities. Bundy's memorandum is quoted in Glenn Seaborg and Benjamin Loeb, *Stemming the Tide: Arms Control in the Johnson Years* (Lexington, Mass.: Lexington Books, 1987), pp. 112–17. For an account of China's atomic bomb project, see John Lewis and Xue Litai, *China Builds the Bomb* (Stanford, Calif.: Stanford University Press, 1988). On subsequent U.S. concern over China's nuclear potential, see Seaborg and Loeb, *Stemming the Tide,* pp. 111–12; and Newhouse, *War and Peace in the Nuclear Age,* pp. 193–95.

71. "The Diffusion of Nuclear Weapons With and Without a Test Ban," February 12, 1963, DDRS-1978-49B.

72. Seaborg, *Kennedy, Khrushchev, and the Test Ban,* pp. 199–200; Wiesner interview. Since the United States was demanding seven on-site inspections and the Russians would allow only three, "the logical compromise was five," observed Wiesner in taped comments on this manuscript. Alva Myrdal, Sweden's delegate to the eighteen-nation Geneva disarmament negotiations in the 1960s, subsequently claimed that Prime Minister Macmillan personally intervened with the Swedish government in the spring of 1963 to prevent Myrdal from proposing a compromise based upon five on-site inspections. Myrdal—who died in 1986—made her accusation in a Swedish television documentary. In his memoir of the test-ban talks, Seaborg writes that, in March 1963, Macmillan raised "the possibility of an offer at Geneva of five inspections but felt a rejection by the Soviets would also hurt the president politically." Seaborg, *Kennedy, Khrushchev, and the Test Ban,* p. 208. The author is grateful to Professor Milton Leitenberg of Stockholm's Utrikespolitiska Institut for pointing out Myrdal's allegation.

73. Minutes of conversation, May 16, 1963, DDRS-1981-637B. According to Wiesner, the Russians, too, seemed to believe that the impasse over the number of on-site inspections was more political than technical in nature. Told that it would be far easier to detect cheating with six inspections than three, Dobrynin, Wiesner said, "got impatient and said that they don't examine the matter in such detail in the Soviet Union and that he thought we paid too much attention to calculations on what he regarded to be a political matter." Wiesner interview.

74. As late as February 1963, the State Department and the Arms Control and Disarmament Agency had still not agreed on guidelines for on-site inspection. One ACDA plan called for a team of fourteen experts plus an undetermined number of "support personnel" at each inspection. The inspection might last as long as six weeks, with the ACDA team roaming over an elliptical plot some 500 square miles in area. Inspectors would search for evidence of clandestine underground testing with giant drilling rigs and by helicopter overflights. Project Cloud Gap, a secret U.S. program to identify problems likely to be encountered in on-site inspections, was abandoned in 1967 after several members of a mock inspection team were killed in a helicopter crash. Concerning disagreements within the United States over on-site inspections, see Dean Rusk to U.S. Mission at Geneva, February 18, 1963, "Meetings with the President—Test Ban Treaty" folder, Box 317–318, National Security Files, JFK Library. On Cloud Gap, see "Project Cloud Gap: Final Report," June 1967, Box 687, PSAC Records.

75. Cohen, *The Truth about the Neutron Bomb,* p. 87; transcript of "The Nuclear Test Ban," Tape 3, p. 19, Sloan Videotape History Project.

76. Wiesner comments on draft manuscript. It was also by reason of his long-standing association and friendship with his British counterpart—Macmillan's science adviser, Lord Solly Zuckerman—that Wiesner remained apprised of the significant contributions of British scientists to the seismic detection program, and likewise of Macmillan's efforts to rally support for the test ban in Britain. Wiesner interview.

77. Concerning Harriman's visit, see Seaborg, *Kennedy, Khrushchev, and the Test Ban,* pp. 235–53.

78. On the impact of the American University speech, see Seaborg, *Kennedy, Khrushchev, and the Test Ban,* pp. 216–18. The new attitude was also evident in ACDA Director Foster's report to Kennedy that July: "In the perspective of the next

ten years, the significance of a nuclear test-ban lies more in the political doors which it might assist in opening than in the military doors which it might close." Foster to Kennedy, "Political Implications of a Nuclear Test Ban," July 12, 1963, Box 265–270A, National Security Files, JFK Library.

79. Ronald Terchek, *The Making of the Test Ban Treaty* (The Hague: M. Nijhjoff, 1970), p. 101.

80. As late as July, Kennedy found the Joint Chiefs of Staff still divided on a partial test ban—with Air Force General Curtis LeMay "solidly opposed." On military opposition to the ban, see Uyehara, "Scientific Advice and the Nuclear Test Ban Treaty," p. 123; and "Memorandum of Conversation," July 22, 1963, "Meetings with the President—Harriman Mission to Moscow" folder, Box 317–318, National Security Files, JFK Library.

81. After the meeting with Teller, Kennedy asked Wiesner why reputable scientists differed so widely on the feasibility of a verifiable test ban. "The fact is that we're both talking about something that hasn't been done," Wiesner said he told Kennedy, "and so we both make assumptions. You have to look at the assumptions. Are they reasonable, or aren't they?" Wiesner interview.

82. Harold K. Jacobson and Eric Stein, *Diplomats, Scientists, and Politicians* (Ann Arbor: University of Michigan Press, 1966), p. 448.

83. One of the biggest unknowns about a partial test ban remained the effectiveness of decoupling. After numerous delays, Salmon—a test designed to prove the feasibility of decoupling—was carried out near Hattiesburg, Mississippi, in October 1964. Salmon showed that decoupling was only about a third as effective in masking seismic signals as previously assumed and much more expensive than earlier estimated. Wiesner interview; Department of Energy, "Announced U.S. Nuclear Tests," p. 21.

84. Khrushchev failed to respond to another overture that Harriman made, at Kennedy's request, on possible action by the United States and the Soviet Union to prevent China from getting the bomb. In a reply to a cable from Harriman on July 15, Kennedy said he remained "convinced that Chinese problem is more serious than Khrushchev suggests and believe you should press question with him in private meeting. . . . You should try to elicit K[hrushchev]'s views of means of limiting or preventing Chinese nuclear development and his willingness either to take Soviet action or to accept U.S. action aimed in this direction." Seaborg, *Kennedy, Khrushchev, and the Test Ban,* p. 239. One plan reportedly discussed in the Kennedy administration was to have a Soviet and an American plane fly together over the Chinese test site, with only one dropping a bomb. Wiesner interview.

85. Ibid., pp. 254–55.

86. The scientists' press release is in "Disarmament—Nuclear Test Ban, Part II, 7/63" folder, Box 99a–100, President's Office Files, JFK Library.

87. Teller opposed the treaty on the grounds that it would "prohibit . . . the acquisition of knowledge about effects of weapons. This is particularly true of those effects that are of vital importance to ballistic missile defense." Teller's testimony is in U.S. Congress, Senate, Committee on Foreign Relations, *Nuclear Test Ban Treaty: Hearings,* 88th Cong., 1st sess., 1963 (Washington, D.C.: U.S. Government Printing Office, 1963), pp. 417–27. In 1985, Teller acknowledged that his 1963 argument— namely, "that 'the United States research on defense hardly could be accomplished without opportunities to test in the atmosphere'—proved to be overstated. Ingenious underground experimentation allowed for finding out far more about defensive weapons than I originally expected." The author is grateful to Dr. Teller's office for

making available "Notes Added in 1985" concerning his 1963 test-ban testimony. On Kennedy's concern about Teller's opposition to the test ban, see "Winning Support for the Nuclear Test Ban Treaty, 1963," Presidential Recording Transcripts, JFK Library. In a telephone conversation with Kennedy on August 23, 1963, Fulbright compared Teller to "John L. Lewis and Billy Sunday all wrapped in one."

88. The August 24 press statement by PSAC is in the "Disarmament—Nuclear Test Ban, Part II, 7/63" folder, Box 99A–100, President's Office Files, JFK Library.

89. Bundy's memorandum is in "PSAC 1963" folder, Box 204, White House Central Files, JFK Library.

90. Terchek, *The Making of the Test Ban Treaty,* pp. 101–3.

91. Interviews: Wiesner and Keeny.

92. Wiesner, for example, claims that Kennedy was surprised when the latter's impromptu mention of the test ban was widely cheered during a subsequent cross-country speaking tour, while the actual theme of the president's speeches—the growing hazard of environmental pollution—received only polite applause. Had he realized the depth of popular support for arms control, Kennedy reportedly told Wiesner, he might not have retreated from a comprehensive test ban. Wiesner interview.

93. Kennedy's speech is quoted in Jerome Wiesner, *Where Science and Politics Meet* (New York: McGraw-Hill, 1965), p. 11. Frederick Seitz, a member of PSAC in the Kennedy and Johnson administrations, argues that "President Kennedy supported those things which emerged from the scientific community that he felt made political sense from his own viewpoint but that he was by no means enchanted with scientists as such since he recognized their failings as well as their strengths." Letter, Seitz to author, July 28, 1988.

Chapter 9

1. Wiesner interview.

2. Hornig interview.

3. Johnson's attitude toward intellectuals is noted, for example, in Doris Kearns, *Lyndon Johnson and the American Dream* (New York: Signet, 1976), pp. 44–45. Wiesner described his relations with Johnson as "ambivalent—alternately friendly and quite hostile." Seaborg agreed that the president's attitude toward scientists was mercurial, but noted that he enjoyed unusually good relations with Johnson. "I think if Glenn had wanted to put a reactor on top of the White House LBJ would have said OK," observed a former member of Johnson's staff. Interviews: Wiesner and Seaborg. The White House aide is quoted in James Katz, *Presidential Politics and Science Policy* (New York: Praeger, 1978), p. 69.

4. Wiesner interview.

5. Hornig interview.

6. Interviews: Seaborg, Wiesner, Harvey Brooks.

7. Johnson personally, if tersely, acknowledged this debt in a brief telegram—"Thank you very much"—to Herbert York on the day after the election. During the campaign, a portion of York's Senate testimony had been used in a Democratic television commercial implying that Johnson's Republican opponent, Barry Goldwater, could not be trusted with nuclear weapons. York interview.

8. In January 1966, PSAC's Spurgeon Keeny recommended in a memorandum to McGeorge Bundy that Oppenheimer's security clearance be restored. Bundy

opposed this symbolic gesture as likely to rekindle emotions over the Oppenheimer case. Oppenheimer's death the following year rendered the question moot. Memorandum, Keeny to Bundy, January 13, 1966, DDRS-1975 Retrospective-913D.

9. Herbert York recalls the contrast between PSAC's first meeting with President Johnson, shortly after the inauguration, and its last one, some four years later. On the first occasion, Johnson talked with enthusiasm about what he and his scientists needed to get done. At the last meeting, Johnson had complained bitterly: "You people tell me how to get things done and what to do, but you don't have any appreciation of how difficult it is to do it." York's comments at American Association for the Advancement of Science meeting, January 18, 1989, San Francisco. Concerning the alienation of Johnson from his scientists, see also "After the Pentagon Papers: Talk with Kistiakowsky, Wiesner," *Science,* November 26, 1971, p. 927. The number of reports is noted in William Golden (ed.), *Science Advice to the President* (Elmsford, N.Y.: Pergamon Press, 1980), p. 49.

10. Interviews: Hornig; Brooks; Paul Doty. The official history of the Office of Science and Technology confirms the diminished role that OST and PSAC had during the Johnson administration—where there was, it notes, "a visible effort to avoid the danger of 'self-perpetuation' by looking to [PSAC] as the primary but not the exclusive source of recommendation." See "OST During the Administration of Lyndon Baines Johnson," vol. I, Box 1, PSAC Records.

11. On the blackout episode, see W. Henry Lambright, *Presidential Management of Science and Technology: The Johnson Presidency* (Austin: University of Texas Press, 1985), pp. 26–27.

12. Ibid.; letter, Donald Hornig to author, November 21, 1985; Franklin Long interview.

13. Katz, *Presidential Politics and Science Policy,* pp. 46–47.

14. During the Johnson administration, PSAC and OST published the following reports: "Restoring the Quality of the Environment" (1965); "The Space Program in the Post-Apollo Period" (1965); "Effective Use of the Sea" (1966); "The World Food Study" (1967); and "Computers in Education" (1967). In July 1964, Johnson advised Hornig and PSAC that he was also interested in distributing federal research and development funds more broadly throughout the states. This inspiration, which many saw as politically motivated and patronage related, led the following year to the "New Centers of Excellence" program. Lambright, *Presidential Management of Science and Technology,* p. 80.

15. Katz, *Presidential Politics and Science Policy,* pp. 46–47. Said Hornig of the problem of coming up with a weekly press release: "The president can say that a man has landed on the moon. But the president is not going to announce that one of our people has just discovered the 'Z' particle." Hornig interview.

16. Jerome Wiesner and Herbert York, "National Security and the Nuclear Test Ban," in Herbert York (ed.), *Arms Control: Readings from Scientific American* (San Francisco: Freeman, 1973), pp. 129–39; interviews: Wiesner and York.

17. Wiesner contends that he and York did not see the article as a break with the tradition of silence maintained by former PSAC and DDR&E chairmen: "We felt that we were in fact supporting the government by making this public statement." Wiesner interview.

18. Concerning the letter, see "After the Pentagon Papers," p. 923.

19. Ibid.

20. The President's Task Force on Preventing the Spread of Nuclear Weapons,

also known as the Gilpatrick Committee, met in late 1964 and early 1965. Its report urged Johnson to seek a comprehensive test-ban treaty; to try to establish nuclear-free zones in Latin America, Africa, and the Middle East; and to negotiate a "freeze," with eventual reductions, on the number of strategic missiles and bombers. On the Gilpatrick Report and its significance, see Glenn Seaborg and Benjamin Loeb, *Stemming the Tide: Arms Control in the Johnson Years* (Lexington, Mass.: Lexington Books, 1987), pp. 136–45; and Herbert York, *Making Weapons, Talking Peace* (New York: Basic Books, 1987), pp. 228–32. Significantly, the Gilpatrick Committee's attempt to present its report to the president, on January 21, 1965, was sidetracked by Johnson's diatribe against professors who had recently signed a published letter condemning the administration's policy in Vietnam.

21. Wiesner interview.

22. Notes of the January 1966 PSAC meeting are in "1966 OST Status Reports," Box 1, PSAC Records.

23. Foster's idea is noted in ibid. Another controversial—and ultimately unsuccessful—attempt to harness technology to win in Vietnam was ARPA's Project Agile. See "The Advanced Research Projects Agency, 1958–1974," vol. V (Washington, D.C.: Richard Barber Associates), pp. 35–43.

24. Concerning ideas advanced at this time for applying technology to win the war in Vietnam, see Sam Cohen, *The Truth about the Neutron Bomb* (New York: Morrow, 1983), pp. 97–98; and Paul Dickson, *The Electronic Battlefield* (Bloomington: Indiana University Press, 1976).

25. Operation Ranch Hand, a controversial program for the defoliation of Vietnam's rain forests using Agent Orange, began in 1962 and was the focus of protests by the Federation of American Scientists two years later. Popeye remained secret until 1973, when its existence was revealed in the course of Senate testimony. On the origins and fate of Ranch Hand and Popeye, see Lambright, *Presidential Management of Science and Technology*, pp. 69–72.

26. Dickson, *The Electronic Battlefield*, pp. 36–37.

27. Norris Bradbury interview.

28. Wiesner interview.

29. This section on the origins of the Cambridge-Jason study of the barrier is taken from William Nierenberg, "DCPG—The Genesis of the Concept;" Gordon MacDonald, "Jason and DCPG—Ten Lessons"; and author's interviews. The author is grateful to William Nierenberg and Gordon MacDonald for copies of their unpublished papers.

30. Dickson, *The Electronic Battlefield*, p. 21.

31. Indirectly, the Jasons were a spinoff of Sputnik—in that they were created in lieu of a new national laboratory and as a response to the Russian achievement. Partly as a result of controversy over Vietnam, the Jasons split from IDA. The group's activities were later administered by MITRE, an independent think tank previously affiliated with MIT. On the Jasons, see Chapter 8; York, *Making Weapons, Talking Peace*, pp. 153, 233–35; "Jason Division: Division Consultants Who Are Also Professors Attacked," *Science*, February 2, 1973, pp. 459–505; and Barber Associates, "The Advanced Research Projects Agency, 1958–1974," vol. V, pp. 33–35. The author thanks Finn Aaserud of the American Institute of Physics for information on the Jasons.

32. In 1961, Jason physicist Murray Gell-Mann organized the so-called White Tiger seminar at Maine's Bowdoin College to discuss the contribution that the

Jasons might make to counterinsurgency warfare. Since no conclusions were reached, no report was written. A second study of Vietnam by the Jasons in 1964, chaired by William Nierenberg, called upon outside experts on Southeast Asia—including journalist Bernard Fall—but was, in essence, "a repeat of the first," claims Nierenberg. Its report on the role the Jasons might play in the war was "broad, all-inclusive, and from the technical point of view, largely negative," according to another participant. Indeed, so great was the "educational shock" of the second study, he notes, "that, by common agreement, no systematic work was done on the subject in 1965." In 1966, Nierenberg was the leader once again of the Jason part of the IDA Vietnam study. Letter, Nierenberg to author, May 9, 1989; Gell-Mann interview.

33. Nierenberg, "DCPG . . ."; and MacDonald, "Jason and DCPG . . ."

34. Ibid.

35. Letter, Nierenberg to author; interviews: Gordon MacDonald and Marvin Goldberger.

36. One participant in the final meetings at Dana Hall remembered "shouting matches" between the Cambridge group and the Jasons. Another seminar goer, a Second World War veteran, thought some of his younger colleagues' ideas for reinventing infantry tactics—such as putting iron covers on foxholes—"incredibly naive." Interviews.

37. MacDonald, "Jason and DCPG," and Nierenberg, "DCPG"; MacDonald interview.

38. MacDonald interview.

39. The classified IDA study was included in the Defense Department's "History of Decision-Making in Vietnam," which became better known as the *Pentagon Papers* when it was leaked to the press in 1971. See Neil Sheehan et al., *The Pentagon Papers: The New York Times Edition* (New York: Bantam, 1971), pp. 502–9.

40. Dickson, *The Electronic Battlefield,* pp. 27–29, 38.

41. The technology for the barrier's acoustic sensors was derived from the sonubuoys used by the Navy to detect Russian submarines. A plan to disguise the button bomblets to look like dog droppings was withdrawn after a Pentagon analyst pointed out that North Vietnamese troops traveling the Ho Chi Minh Trail were seldom accompanied by dogs. Eventually, seismic, magnetic, infrared, and chemical sensors—the notorious "people-sniffers"—augmented the acoustic detectors. Enemy countermeasures, though far less sophisticated, proved more effective than the designers of the barrier had foreseen. Among the measures reportedly used to fool the sensors, for example, was a tape recording of truck engines. Ibid., pp. 43–45, 95–96. Nierenberg claims that the "electronic barrier worked perfectly—exactly as predicted. It did not accomplish its objectives because McNamara consistently refused to buy and stock the special munitions needed to complement the barrier." Letter, Nierenberg to author.

42. "After the Pentagon Papers," p. 926; Nierenberg, "DCPG," pp. 5–6.

43. MacDonald later described the scene at Zacharias' house: "Maps were spread on the floor, drinks were served, a dog kept crossing the demilitarized zone as top-secret matters were discussed." MacDonald interview.

44. Sheehan et al., *The Pentagon Papers,* pp. 483–85. According to the Pentagon history, McNamara's attitude toward the war shifted from "hesitancy" in the winter of 1965 to "perplexity" in the spring of 1966 to "disenchantment" in the wake of the Jason report. *The Pentagon Papers,* p. 484.

45. Dickson, *The Electronic Battlefield,* p. 36.

46. Ibid., pp. 50–51.

47. "After the Pentagon Papers," pp. 923–25.

48. Richard Blankenbechler interview.

49. The Jasons, for example, became a target of criticism in 1967 when a student newspaper published the purloined notes of a conference called by Murray Gell-Mann to discuss the creation of a social science division of the group to work in Thailand. Several Jasons who were also PSAC members—including Sidney Drell, chairman of PSAC's Ground Warfare Panel—were prevented by protesters from speaking at scientific conferences in Europe at this time. "Jason Division," pp. 923–25; interviews: Drell and Gell-Mann.

50. Dickson, *The Electronic Battlefield,* pp. 73–76. A Marine Corps captain who was targeting and gunnery officer at Khe Sahn had coincidentally taken part in the Dana Hall study. Nierenberg, "DCPG—The Genesis of the Concept," p. 5.

51. Even after Kistiakowsky's resignation, work continued on the barrier concept under the direction of Caltech physicist Charles Lauritsen. On the fate of the barrier, see U.S. Congress, Senate, Committee on the Armed Services, *Hearing before the Electronic Battlefield Subcommittee,* 91st Cong., 2d sess., 1970 (Washington, D.C.: U.S. Government Printing Office, 1970).

52. Wiesner interview.

53. Hornig interview.

54. "Scientists Protest Viet Crop Destruction," *Science,* January 21, 1966, p. 309

55. "1967 OST Status Reports," Box 1, PSAC Records.

56. Ibid.

57. The Military Aircraft Panel acknowledged the fact that a certain technology worked in the laboratory was no proof that it would work—or should be deployed—on the battlefield. According to their March 1967 Status Report to PSAC, members of the panel "were impressed with the quality of a videotape of a test of helicopter night-vision equipment in Vietnam, although some of the targets observed by the Panel in the conference room were not observed by pilots and observers in the helicopters in Vietnam. It is not clear at the present time whether this was due to vibration or to other causes. However, the resolution obtained was excellent." In a subsequent report, the panel concluded that while it would be both feasible and cheaper to use helicopters exclusively for transportation inside Vietnam, such a plan "was said to be incompatible with the long range objective of 'nation building.'" Ibid.

58. "1966 OST Status Reports" and "1967 OST Status Reports." On the work of other PSAC panels on Vietnam, see, for example, "Ground Warfare—Working Paper," January 6, 1969, Box 1147; and "Report of the Panel on Southeast Asia," July 6–14, 1967, Box 691, PSAC Records.

59. Hornig interview.

60. "CBW, Vietnam Evoke Scientist's Concern," *Science,* January 20, 1967, p. 302.

61. Hornig interview. Secrecy added further barriers to protest. PSAC scientists who knew of the Pentagon's secret "weather war" in Vietnam could not share their concerns with colleagues who lacked security clearances.

62. Ibid. Writes Johnson PSAC member Frederick Seitz: "This disenchantment on the part of President Johnson made the situation quite difficult for Don Hornig who did his very best to keep matters in line. I believe on good grounds that Presi-

dent Johnson would have terminated PSAC had he had another term in office." Letter, Seitz to author, July 28, 1988.

63. Memorandum, Hornig to Rostow, February 17, 1967, DDRS-1984-1645. On the controversy over chemical warfare in Vietnam, see also Lambright, *Presidential Management of Science and Technology*, p. 115. While members of PSAC and the Jasons were unable to prevent the employment of chemical agents in Vietnam, the fact that a far more destructive weapon was not used may have been due in part to their influence. The only IDA-Jason study reportedly exploring the use of nuclear weapons in Vietnam remains classified, but it is said to have concluded that such use would be to the distinct disadvantage of the United States—since U.S. bases would be even more vulnerable to reprisal nuclear attacks. "That paper gives all the reasons why you wouldn't use nuclear weapons in Vietnam," observed one of its authors. "Jason Division," p. 461. In February 1968, a planned visit to Vietnam by PSAC's Richard Garwin and three other scientists—members of a secret IDA-Jason project codenamed Mussel Shoals—sparked rumors that Johnson was considering the use of nuclear weapons in defense of Khe Sahn, prompting Kistiakowsky and Rabi to write to the president urging him not to use nuclear weapons in Vietnam. In actuality, Garwin and his colleagues were on the way to Vietnam to review the performance of the electronic barrier when their visit was canceled because of the Tet offensive. Dickson, *The Electronic Battlefield*, p. 75 fn.; Richard Garwin interview.

64. Hornig interview.

65. "1967 OST Status Reports." According to Jason Marvin Goldberger, McNamara in 1967 invited a select number of the group to undertake another secret study of the war in Vietnam, posing the question: "It's ten years after the war in Vietnam. The United States has won—and withdrawn. What is the successful means to conclude the war, and how do you get there from here?" He and his colleagues responded, Goldberger said, that McNamara's question had overlooked the obvious issue—namely, that victory in Vietnam was not going to be possible to achieve by any means likely to be acceptable to the American public. Goldberger interview.

66. Hornig interview.

67. MacDonald interview.

68. Ibid.; "Jason Division," p. 462.

69. MacDonald claims that both the Air Force and the White House were "furious" at his report, which remains classified. When he attempted to brief National Security Adviser Walt Rostow on the study, "Rostow just pulled out of his desk the latest body count. There was no way to reach him." MacDonald interview.

70. "Jason Division," p. 462; letter, Hornig to author, November 21, 1985.

71. "[Johnson's] response [to Hornig's briefing] was to listen very intently," Hornig remembers. "Then he asked, 'Are you saying the Air Force is pulling the wool over my eyes?'" The president proposed calling General John McConnell, the Air Force chief of staff, into the Oval Office to resolve the dispute, but McConnell—reached by telephone—suggested that both he and Hornig submit a joint written report instead. While his meeting with McConnell was genial, Hornig says, neither man yielded on his respective point: McConnell insisted that the Air Force was doing a lot of damage to enemy supply columns, while Hornig pointed out that it still wasn't enough to stop vital supplies from getting through. Hornig interview.

72. Concerning the role of the Senior Advisory Group, see Walter Isaacson and Evan Thomas, *The Wise Men* (New York: Simon & Schuster, 1986), pp. 681–91.

73. Telephone interview with Harry McPherson.

74. By 1967, PSAC's efforts were increasingly divided between the Vietnam War and the neglected home front. In its June "Status Report," for example, PSAC noted that while its Military Aircraft Panel was investigating a new type of antiradar missile, other panels were preparing reports on "Water for Peace" and "Ice and Snow Control in Urban Areas." A year later, the Military Aircraft Panel was still studying ways to improve the electronic barrier, while other panels were looking at pollution problems and how to deal with "oil spill emergencies." "OST Status Reports," Box 1, PSAC Records.

75. Ruina interview.

76. Ibid.; J. P. Ruina and M. Gell-Mann, "Ballistic Missile Defence and the Arms Race," unpublished paper. The author is grateful to Dr. Ruina for a copy of his and Dr. Gell-Mann's paper.

77. Ibid.

78. Ibid.

79. "Damage Limiting—A Rationale for the Allocation of Resources by the U.S. and U.S.S.R.," January 21, 1964, DDRS-1979-137A. So impressed was McNamara with the DDR&E study that two months later he asked each of the military services to participate in a comprehensive review of U.S. nuclear strategy. The six-month study concluded that damage to the United States in a nuclear war, even with an ABM, would be "unacceptable." See "A Summary Study of Strategic Offensive and Defense Forces of the U.S. and U.S.S.R.," September 8, 1964, DDRS-1979-137B.

80. On the ABM debate in the Johnson administration, see Fred Kaplan, *The Wizards of Armageddon* (New York: Simon & Schuster, 1973), pp. 321–24.

81. Bethe interview.

82. Another reason for pessimism regarding the ABM was the "Pen-X" study conducted by DDR&E in July 1965. While the purpose of this study was to develop "penetration aids" for U.S. offensive missiles, its conclusion was that the Russians as well would, in time, be able to use the same techniques to defeat an ABM. On Project Defender and the "Pen-X" study, see Chapter 8 and "The Advanced Research Projects Agency, 1958–1974," vol. VII, pp. 9–10.

83. By 1966, Project Defender envisioned two possibilities for an ABM defense—a thin "area" or nationwide defense coupled with a thick "terminal" defense of twenty-five American cities, or a more ambitious plan that would attempt to protect some fifty-two American cities from missile attack. Ashton Carter and David Schwartz (eds.), *Ballistic Missile Defense* (Washington, D.C.: Brookings Institution, 1984), pp. 336–37.

84. On McNamara on the SST, see Lambright, *Presidential Management of Science and Technology,* pp. 131–32.

85. So hastily called was the meeting that McNamara's summons reached Hornig on vacation in the Caribbean; the science adviser had to be flown back to Washington by an Air Force jet. Hornig interview.

86. As Wiesner pointed out at this meeting, the difficulty of distinguishing between the "thin" anti-Chinese defense that McNamara had in mind and the "thick" anti-Soviet ABM that the Joint Chiefs wanted to build was likely to prove as thorny a problem for Congress as for the Russians. Wiesner interview. Ironically, the inspiration for McNamara's "austere" ABM may have come, indirectly, from PSAC. In its most recent review of the ABM, the Strategic Military Panel had reportedly looked at those instances in which a limited deployment might make sense. Included in this category was the possibility of an accidental missile launch or a "rudimenta-

ry" attack by twenty to thirty ICBMs. China was thought the only country likely to have such a force by the mid-1970s. Interviews: Hornig, Bethe, York.

87. On the January 4 meeting with the president, see Herbert York, *Race to Oblivion: A Participant's View of the Arms Race* (New York: Clarion Press, 1970), pp. 194–95. Concerning Johnson's ABM decision, see also Anne Cahn, "American Scientists and the ABM: A Case Study in Controversy," in Albert Teich (ed.), *Scientists and Public Affairs* (Cambridge, Mass.: MIT Press, 1974), pp. 41–51.

88. Cahn, "American Scientists and the ABM," pp. 41–51.

89. Hornig interview.

90. Lyndon Johnson, *The Vantage Point: Perspectives of the Presidency, 1963–1969* (New York: Holt, Rinehart and Winston, 1971), pp. 479–80.

91. On the Glassboro summit, see Seaborg and Loeb, *Stemming the Tide*, pp. 423–30.

92. Significantly, McNamara later chose to distance himself from Johnson's ABM decision by separating the Sentinel announcement from the text of his 1967 speech in his book, *The Essence of Security: Reflections in Office* (New York: Harper & Row, 1968).

93. Wiesner interview.

94. In his ABM announcement, McNamara noted that those scientists who had been present at the Oval Office meeting supported the administration's decision not to deploy "an ABM system designed to protect our population against a Soviet attack." As Kistiakowsky pointed out in his telegram, McNamara's comment seemed to suggest that the scientists had endorsed a limited version of Sentinel—when in fact they had opposed all versions of the ABM. Kistiakowsky's telegram and Bethe's comments are cited in Cahn, "American Scientists and the ABM," pp. 50–51.

95. Interviews: Bethe and Richard Garwin.

96. Wiesner interview; "After the Pentagon Papers," p. 928.

97. Cahn, "American Scientists and the ABM," p. 71.

98. Richard Garwin and Hans Bethe, "Anti-Ballistic-Missile Systems," March 1968, in York (ed.), *Arms Control: Readings from Scientific American*, pp. 164–76; Cahn, "American Scientists and the ABM," pp. 76–77.

99. Hornig interview.

100. Cahn, "American Scientists and the ABM," p. 71.

101. Kistiakowsky's letter is cited in "After the Pentagon Papers," p. 927.

102. Hornig interview.

103. On the political affiliation of PSAC's members, see Cahn, "American Scientists and the ABM," p. 73.

104. "1968 OST Status Reports," Box 1, PSAC Records.

Chapter 10

1. George Kistiakowsky, *A Scientist at the White House* (Cambridge, Mass.: Harvard University Press, 1976), p. 191. In the same entry, Kistiakowsky wrote of Nixon: "Generally, I had a feeling that although I was invited to come in order to provide information and express my views, actually he was trying to impress me and, should I add, successfully. I still wonder, however, whether he would have the strength of his convictions if an occasion arises."

2. Many PSAC scientists were, like Kistiakowsky, surprised by Nixon's affability and openness at private meetings, which was in considerable contrast to his public persona. In a 1985 interview, Marvin Goldberger recalled that, during PSAC's first meeting with the president, in June 1969, he had planned to read a statement announcing the Strategic Military Panel's unanimous opposition to the ABM. But Nixon disarmed the protest when, at the start of the meeting, he told the group that since he already knew how they felt about the ABM, they should talk about more agreeable subjects. Goldberger admitted "to being very impressed with Nixon, and very ashamed of myself." Goldberger interview.

3. Baker interview.

4. DuBridge interview.

5. Gordon MacDonald, who sat next to DuBridge on the flight to Washington, D.C., and the PSAC swearing-in ceremony, recalled that the science adviser-designate pointed with pride to a White House organization chart showing him coequal in authority with presidential aides John Ehrlichman and Robert Haldeman. MacDonald interview.

6. William Wells, "Science Advice and the Presidency, 1933–1976," unpublished dissertation (Ann Arbor, Mich.: University Microfilms, 1977), pt. II, pp. 642–43.

7. According to former PSAC member Frederick Seitz, Melvin Laird told Nixon at the Pierre Hotel meeting "that he would accept the position of Secretary of Defense if and only if PSAC were kept away from dealing with military problems." Letter, Seitz to author, July 28, 1989. On the "Long incident," see "Nixon Admits Error on Science Nominee," *The New York Times*, April 19, 1969. Long interview.

8. *Science*, April 18, 1969, p. 283.

9. On the neglect of PSAC during the Nixon administration, see William Golden (ed.), *Science Advice to the President* (Elmsford, N.Y.: Permagon Press, 1980), pp. 115–18, 208–12; and Wells, "Science Advice and the Presidency, 1933–1976," pt. II, pp. 678–79.

10. John Newhouse, *Cold Dawn: The Story of SALT* (New York: Holt, Rinehart and Winston, 1973), pp. 146–48; "Preliminary Strategic Arms Limitation Talks," November 12, 1967, DDRS-1982-567.

11. Concerning public opposition to the ABM and its effect, see Newhouse, *Cold Dawn*, pp. 150–51; Henry Kissinger, *The White House Years* (Boston: Little, Brown, 1979), pp. 205–6; and Ernest Yanarella, *The Missile Defense Controversy* (Lexington: University of Kentucky Press, 1977), pp. 148–53.

12. Kissinger reportedly told Packard that the Defense Department study should find the administration's version of Sentinel cheaper and more effective in shooting down ICBMs than any of the alternate ABMs being considered. On the administration's lobbying for Safeguard, see Fred Kaplan, *Wizards of Armageddon* (New York: Simon & Schuster, 1983), p. 350; and Anne Cahn, "American Scientists and the ABM: A Case Study in Controversy," Albert Teich (ed.), *Scientists and Public Affairs* (Cambridge, Mass.: MIT Press, 1974), pp. 109–11.

13. On the origins of Safeguard, see "Nixon for Limited Missile Plan to Protect U.S. Nuclear Bases," *The New York Times*, March 15, 1969; and Kissinger, *The White House Years*, pp. 209–10.

14. Foster's subsequent admission that his estimate of Soviet MIRV capabilities proved to be exaggerated further weakened the Pentagon's credibility, which was already under attack because of the ABM and Vietnam. See Thomas Powers, *The*

Man Who Kept the Secrets (New York: Knopf, 1979), pp. 211–12. On the Foster study, see Yanarella, *The Missile Defense Controversy*, pp. 170–73; Joel Primack and Frank von Hippel, *Advice and Dissent: Scientists in the Political Arena* (New York: Basic Books, 1974), pp. 68–71; and "Nixon Staff Had Central Role in Missile Decision," *The New York Times*, March 19, 1969.

15. U.S. Congress, Senate, Committee on Foreign Relations, *Hearings: Strategic and Foreign Policy Implications of ABM Systems*, 91st Cong., 1st sess., March 1969 (Washington, D.C.: U.S. Government Printing Office, 1969), pp. 612–13; Cahn, "American Scientists and the ABM," p. 110.

16. Cahn, "American Scientists and the ABM," p. 110.

17. "Nixon Science Unit Cites ABM Flaws," *The Washington Post*, March 14, 1969.

18. Yanarella, *The Missile Defense Controversy*, p. 145. During the hearings, Senator Edward Kennedy announced that he was assembling his own distinguished group of experts to advise on the question of missile defense, to be headed by Jerome Wiesner and Abram Chayes, a Cambridge, Massachusetts, lawyer. Later in the year, the two edited an anti-ABM book that contained essays by Wiesner, Hans Bethe, and George Rathjens, among others. See Abram Chayes and Jerome Wiesner (eds.), *Why ABM? An Evaluation of the Decision to Deploy an Anti-ballistic Missile System* (New York: Harper & Row, 1969).

19. *Hearings: Strategic and Foreign Policy Implications of ABM Systems*, pp. 87–90.

20. Ibid., p. 85.

21. Ibid., p. 121.

22. Challenged in the hearings to name one non-Pentagon scientist who supported Safeguard, Packard mentioned Wolfgang Panofsky. However, Panofsky in his testimony pointed out that he had discussed the ABM with Packard only briefly—during a chance encounter at an airport—and, furthermore, his highly qualified endorsement pertained to Sentinel, not Safeguard. See ibid., pp. 307, 326–28 and Primack and von Hippel, *Advice and Dissent*, pp. 66–68. Panofsky interview.

23. Concerning the effect of the ABM debate on PSAC, see Wells, "Science Advice and the Presidency, 1933–1976," pt. II, pp. 675–76; and Primack and von Hippel, *Advice and Dissent*, p. 72. DuBridge also promised in the letter that he would "endeavor to make clear to my scientific colleagues that the Safeguard plan represents a sound and a reasonable approach to our strategic defense problem." DuBridge's letter is reprinted in *The Weekly Compilation of Presidential Documents*, vol. 5 (Washington, D.C.: U.S. Government Printing Office, 1969), p. 430.

24. Sidney Drell, for example, reportedly told DuBridge, "No, that's not our function" when he was asked to sign the letter. Marvin Goldberger similarly balked, stating that the letter was an effort by the administration "to deliver PSAC." Interviews: Drell and Goldberger.

25. Earlier, a delegation of his former Cambridge, Massachusetts, colleagues had visited Kissinger at his invitation to advise against the ABM. According to one of the scientists, Kissinger reportedly misinterpreted their support for the principle of a "hard-point" defense as an endorsement of Safeguard. Subsequently, Kissinger was said to have felt "betrayed" when the scientists came out against Safeguard. Cahn, "American Scientists and the ABM," p. 110; interviews: Drell and Panofsky.

26. Two of the seven members of the O'Neill panel—Goldberger and Drell—were also members of PSAC's Strategic Military Panel; a third, physicist Lewis

Branscomb, was a member of PSAC from 1965 to 1967. In the summer of 1970, during the second round of Senate ABM hearings, a controversy erupted when Goldberger and Drell flatly contradicted Foster's claim that the O'Neill report had endorsed Safeguard, prompting ABM opponents to charge the Pentagon and Foster with creating "a missile credibility gap. " See U.S. Congress, Senate, Committee on Foreign Relations, *Hearings: ABM, MIRV, SALT, and the Nuclear Arms Race,* 91st Cong., 2d sess., March–June 1970 (Washington, D.C.: U.S. Government Printing Office, 1970), pp. 507, 521–24; and Primack and von Hippel, *Advice and Dissent,* pp. 70–71. On the O'Neill Report, see Cahn, "American Scientists and the ABM," p. 63; and *Congressional Record,* Senate, 1970, pp. 27723–28.

27. Cahn, "American Scientists and the ABM," pp. 63–65.

28. The senators' comments are in *Hearings: Strategic and Foreign Policy Implications of ABM Systems,* pp. 434, 442.

29. On the origins of MIRV, see Ted Greenwood, *Making the MIRV: A Study of Defense Decision Making* (New York: Ballinger Press, 1975), pp. 27–36; Fred Kaplan, *Wizards of Armageddon,* pp. 325–26; and Gregg Herken, *Counsels of War* (New York: Knopf, 1985), pp. 200–203.

30. According to Kissinger's account, Nixon was frequently "bored to distraction" by technical briefings. "His glazed expression showed that he considered most of the arguments esoteric rubbish." Kissinger, *The White House Years,* p. 542.

31. Interviews: Panofsky, Drell, Doty. Carl Kaysen and George Rathjens also were asked to join the Doty group. Kaysen declined; Rathjens attended only a few initial meetings. On the Doty group, see Seymour Hersh, *The Price of Power: Kissinger in the Nixon White House* (New York: Summit Books, 1983), pp. 151–52.

32. Interviews: Panofsky and Drell.

33. Greenwood, *Making the MIRV,* pp. 110–11. The irony of the MIRV debate, as Edward David has pointed out, is that it was not MIRV but the advent of cruise missiles—whose development was welcome by dovish scientists—that complicated the verification of arms control measures. Letter, David to author, May 22, 1989.

34. Greenwood, *Making the MIRV,* p. 113.

35. Interviews: Ruina and Rathjens. On other early warnings about MIRV, see Michael Krepon, *Strategic Stalemate: Nuclear Weapons and Arms Control in American Politics* (New York: St. Martin's Press, 1984), pp. 98–101.

36. Krepon, *Strategic Stalemate,* pp. 98–101.

37. Hersh, *The Price of Power,* p. 151.

38. Shortly after his meeting with Brooke, Nixon ordered an acceleration of the testing schedule for MIRV; on June 17, 1969—the day Brooke introduced his resolution to the Senate—the Pentagon issued the first contract for the production of MIRV once testing was completed. Ibid., pp. 160–61.

39. Panofsky, for example, at one of these meetings proposed an annual quota of missile flight tests for the United States and the Soviet Union. Since it generally took about twenty tests to develop a new weapon, Panofsky suggested a quota of six tests a year, which would substantially delay the development of a weapon like MIRV on both sides. Panofsky interview.

40. Letter, Ruina and Rathjens to Kissinger, June 2, 1969. The author is grateful to George Rathjens for a copy of this letter.

41. Ibid.

42. Kissinger is quoted in an August 17, 1969, *New York Times* article. Declassified National Security Council memoranda suggest that as late as November 1969—

only five days before the Strategic Arms Limitation Talks began in Helsinki—U.S. negotiators were still considering the idea of a MIRV flight-testing moratorium. See untitled memoranda, DDRS-1982-566-7.

43. Since April 1969, DDR&E's John Foster and Defense Secretary Melvin Laird had been claiming that recent tests of the Russians' latest SS-9 ICBM showed it to be the "functional equivalent" of the MIRV. PSAC scientists and the CIA's analysts concluded, on the other hand, that the Soviet warheads were not independently targetable and hence not sufficiently accurate to pose a threat to America's land-based Minuteman force. On the "functional equivalent" controversy, see Newhouse, *Cold Dawn*, pp. 160–61; and John Prados, *The Soviet Estimate: U.S. Intelligence Analysis and Russian Military Strength* (New York: Dial Press, 1982), pp. 208–18.

44. Fink interview. Aerospace executive Daniel Fink, who was Foster's choice to investigate the verification question, concluded that the Soviets could cheat on a MIRV flight-testing ban. Kissinger's MIRV panel failed to resolve the controversy over the SS-9 threat. Most of its members—including its head, Laurence Lynn, a National Security Council attorney who had earlier served on a Kissinger ABM panel—had insufficient knowledge of modern weaponry and consequently were compelled to turn for advice to the CIA's analysts and members of the Doty group. Some of the latter reacted "as if close questioning by nonexperts was improper," Lynn complained. On the Fink report, see "Nixon Confronts a Momentous Decision on the Hydra-Headed MIRV," *The New York Times*, August 17, 1969. Lynn is quoted in U.S. Congress, *Commission on the Organization of the Government for the Conduct of Foreign Relations [The Murphy Commission]*, June 1975, vol. 7 (Washington, D.C.: U.S. Government Printing Office, 1975), p. 47.

45. Raymond Garthoff, *Detente and Confrontation: American-Soviet Relations from Nixon to Reagan* (Washington, D.C.: Brookings Institution, 1985), p. 135 fn.

46. Under pressure from Kissinger and Laird, CIA Director Richard Helms agreed to delete a controversial paragraph appearing in a CIA assessment of the SS-9, which challenged the contention that the Soviet missile was the "functional equivalent" of a MIRVed ICBM. See Prados, *The Soviet Estimate*, pp. 217–18.

47. Newhouse, *Cold Dawn*, pp. 173–74; Herken, *Counsels of War*, pp. 255–56.

48. Letter, Garwin to author, July 31, 1986.

49. Letter, Rathjens to Kissinger, April 13, 1970. The author thanks George Rathjens for a copy of this letter.

50. Greenwood, *Making the MIRV*, p. 134.

51. Letter, Garwin to author, July 31, 1986.

52. Interviews: Panofsky and Doty. Panofsky notes that as late as 1974 the group was still sending Kissinger reports on different subjects, including one in 1973 proposing limits on MIRV in a future SALT agreement. Among other topics were "An Analysis of Alternative ABM Limitations in SALT" (1970); "Suggestions for an Early SALT II Agreement" (1973); "SALT I Comments" (1973); and "A Proposal Involving Flight Test Quotas and Reductions in Aggregates of Strategic Offensive Forces" (1974). Letter, Panofsky to author, August 27, 1986.

53. Interview: Doty.

54. Panofsky interview. The Doty group survived long enough to see many of its predictions concerning MIRV vindicated. In 1972, Kissinger admitted that the failure to ban MIRV flight testing was a significant missed opportunity. Two years later, he expressed regret for not having previously "thought through the implica-

tions of a MIRVed world more thoughtfully in 1969 and 1970." Concludes one biographer, Seymour Hersh: "Kissinger knew all he needed to know about MIRV and its implications in mid-1969, but he chose not to act on his knowledge." Greenwood, *Making the MIRV,* p. 133; and Hersh, *The Price of Power,* pp. 155 fn., 167.

55. Nonetheless, the Doty group continued, according to Panofsky, on the premise that "it was better to be used than not to be used." Drell also considered the scientists' role "a no-lose game." He and his colleagues persisted, Garwin said, "because this is what we wanted to do for our country." Only Rathjens, who was an early dropout from the Doty group, regarded the endeavor as futile: "We weren't doing anything useful; it was like talking into a void." Letter, Garwin to author, July 31, 1986. Interviews: Panofsky, Drell, and Rathjens.

56. Concerning the phenomenon of "invoking the experts on the ABM," see Primack and von Hippel, *Advice and Dissent,* pp. 59–73.

57. Kissinger, *The White House Years,* p. 540.

58. Dubridge now seemed to be going out of his way to avoid antagonizing either Nixon or PSAC. For example, in January 1970, DeBridge wrote to Kissinger to deny a *New York Times* claim that he had "entered the technical controversy" over MIRV and now supported a unilateral ban on testing the weapon. "I certainly did nothing to enter any controversy," DuBridge protested. DuBridge also sent a copy of his letter to Nixon's Domestic Council. See "Memorandum for Henry Kissinger," January 16, 1970, Box 944, PSAC Records. Kissinger's memoirs has only a brief reference to DuBridge; Nixon failed to mention any of his three science advisers in his memoirs.

59. "OST Status Reports, 1967–71," Box 1, PSAC Records. On Operation Phoenix, see Powers, *The Man Who Kept the Secrets,* p. 181.

60. "OST Status Reports, 1969–71," Box 1, PSAC Records.

61. Wells, "Science Advice and the Presidency, 1933–1976," pt. II, p. 656.

62. Interviews: DuBridge and MacDonald. Stopping by DuBridge's office on an unscheduled visit at this time, Gordon MacDonald was surprised to find the science adviser alone in his office, his appointment calendar virtually blank.

63. The showdown came at the end of a contentious meeting on the creation of the Environmental Protection Agency when Haldeman, Ehrlichman, and Kissinger took DuBridge aside. "'You don't understand the politics of this thing' was their message," recalled DuBridge—who responded that the environment was "a scientific problem, not a political one." DuBridge interview.

64. Ibid.

65. Interviews: David and Baker. On the selection of David, see Wells, "Science Advice and the Presidency, 1933–1976," pt. II, pp. 660–62.

66. Ibid., p. 660.

67. James Katz, *Presidential Politics and Science Policy* (New York: Praeger, 1978), p. 54.

68. Within weeks of becoming science adviser, David invited his predecessors to a meeting in Cambridge where the future of PSAC was discussed. David interview.

69. "The cancer thing is something the president decided on without any strong advice from me," David recalled. "But there was a general belief that something good would come out of it." David interview.

70. Ibid.

71. Newhouse, *Cold Dawn,* p. 230.

72. On Clements's appointment and its effects, see Katz, *Presidential Politics and Science Policy,* p. 184.

73. The "new technologies" program investigated ideas for improving mail delivery, video communications, and air traffic control. Controversy erupted when it was discovered that the program was also sponsoring research into weather modification and the use of mind-altering drugs for the purpose of crowd control. Disappointed by the program's failure to come up with new and marketable ideas, and also disturbed by its cost, Nixon canceled it at the end of 1971—reportedly when Magruder and his staff were away on their Christmas vacations. See Katz, *Presidential Politics and Science Policy,* p. 207; and "Magruder in White House: SST Man Plans New Technology Take-Off," *Science,* October 22, 1971, pp. 386–87.

74. Letter, Panofsky to author, October 21, 1986.

75. David, on the other hand, claims that having a staff member present at such meetings was "standard procedure." Letter to author, August 22, 1989.

76. Wells, "Science Advice and the Presidency, 1933–1976," pt. II, p. 663.

77. David interview.

78. Daniel Greenberg, "David and Indifference," *Saturday Review/Science,* September 30, 1972, pp. 41–43.

79. Ibid., p. 43.

80. Ibid.

81. On the origins of the SST debate, see Mel Horwitch, *Clipped Wings: The American SST Conflict* (Cambridge, Mass.: MIT Press, 1982); and Mary Ames, *Outcome Uncertain: Science and the Political Process* (New York: Communications Press, 1978), pp. 50–53.

82. Untitled memorandum, Federal Aviation Administration to McNamara, August 1, 1966, "SST 1966" folder, Box 617, PSAC Records. The results of earlier NASA-Air Force tests to gauge popular reaction to sonic booms did not engender confidence that the public would find the SST's noise acceptable. In Operation Heat Rise, for example, on March 5, 1962, a Strategic Air Command bomber left behind a wake of broken windows, irate citizens, and more than 5,000 damage claims in its supersonic dash from coast to coast. Operation Bongo some two years later—which rattled Oklahoma City with eight sonic booms a day for six days—transformed many previously pro-SST residents into opponents of the plane. On the importance of public opposition to the SST, see Ames, *Outcome Uncertain,* p. 102; and Primack and von Hippel, *Advice and Dissent,* p. 14.

83. Horwitch, *Clipped Wings,* pp. 158–70.

84. The month before the Boeing contract was awarded, the first of what would become a myriad of citizen groups against the SST—the Citizens' League Against the Sonic Boom—was created by a Harvard physicist and a biologist. The physicist, William Shurcliff, subsequently published an *SST/Sonic Boom Handbook.* See Primack and von Hippel, *Advice and Dissent,* pp. 14–16.

85. See Horwitch, *Clipped Wings,* pp. 261–69. As well as belonging to the Jasons and the Doty group, Garwin had been a member of Kennedy's PSAC and was appointed to a second four-year term on the committee in 1969. Even when not a member of PSAC, Garwin served as consultant for a variety of PSAC panels dealing with intelligence and military matters.

86. On the dispute over Beggs's report, see *Congressional Record,* House, 1970, pp. 32599–613. On the Garwin report, see *Congressional Record,* House, 1971, pp. 32125–29.

87. Horwitch, *Clipped Wings,* p. 271.

88. When the Beggs report was finally released, it showed that DuBridge had opposed the SST in a March 1969 letter to the committee on the grounds that "the government should not be subsidizing a device which has neither commercial attractiveness nor public acceptance." DuBridge nonetheless continued to defend both the plane—and Nixon's decision—in public. *Congressional Record,* House, 1970, pp. 32599–613.

89. The question of whether a dissenting alumnus of PSAC could properly take a public stand against the declared policy of an administration he served had been raised earlier when Wiesner—then a consultant-at-large—had asked Nixon, through DuBridge, whether he should resign before speaking out against the ABM. Nixon had answered that Wiesner's resignation was not necessary. The important difference in Garwin's case, of course, was that the protester was still a member of PSAC. On Garwin's role in the SST controversy, see Horwitch, *Clipped Wings,* p. 238; and Primack and von Hippel, *Advice and Dissent,* p. 22.

90. In a 1980 retrospective on the incident, Garwin wrote: "At most times, and in most cases, the purpose of the President and the purpose of the nation are coincident. When they are not, advisers and advisory committees are faced with a serious problem. When an adviser or such a committee can no longer carry out its function, it is conventional and appropriate for the individual to resign. When there is a serious threat to the nation (as in a President gone wrong and committing illegal acts day after day) the problem is not simply one of resignation but to ask in what way the individual, by fulfilling his oath of office, can serve the Constitution, giving one's best efforts in the performance of one's job, trying his best within the administration to return things to the right track while being vigilant in determining when the threat to the nation becomes critical. At that time the adviser must act, no longer as adviser but as citizen." Concerning Garwin's side of the incident, see Golden (ed.), *Science Advice to the President,* pp. 115–28.

91. Garwin's letter continued: "That one portion of the government seeks advice on a particular question from . . . an individual is not adequate reason for denying the provision of advice to others in the administration or to the Congress and the public." Garwin informed his colleagues that, within limitations, he considered them "free to advise or speak publicly either in support of or in opposition to the supersonic transport program. Indeed, you are among those in the country best able to lend wisdom to the deliberations of the Congress and of the public." Ibid., p. 124.

92. Primack and von Hippel, *Advice and Dissent,* pp. 53–54; Ames, *Outcome Uncertain,* pp. 74–76; *Congressional Record,* House, 1971, pp. 32125–29.

93. On the administration's response to Garwin, see Horwitch, *Clipped Wings,* p. 291; and Horace Sutton, "Is the SST Really Necessary?" *Saturday Review,* August 15, 1970, p. 14.

94. The 1970 hearings also focused on a new discovery about the SST that proved to be the most worrisome yet: evidence that the SST's jet exhaust would deplete the ozone layer in the atmosphere, resulting in a higher incidence of skin cancer on earth. See Primack and von Hippel, *Advice and Dissent,* pp. 21–22; and Horwitch, *Clipped Wings,* pp. 287–89.

95. Interviews: DuBridge and Hornig.

96. Interviews: Panofsky and Drell. The ambiguity that PSAC felt toward Garwin's action was mirrored in the scientific community at large. In a poll conducted

under the auspices of Congress, members of the National Academies of Science and Engineering were asked their opinions of when PSAC scientists "'went public' with personal views on an issue examined by PSAC." Respondents were almost evenly split in characterizing the action as "appropriate" or "inappropriate." Wells, "Science Advice and the Presidency, 1933–1976," pt. II, pp. 687–88.

97. Ibid., p. 650; Greenberg, "David and Indifference," p. 42; and Katz, *Presidential Politics and Science Policy*, p. 185.

98. Golden (ed.), *Science Advice to the President*, p. 119.

99. For Stever's own account of the transition, see Golden (ed.), *Science Advice to the President*, pp. 61–75.

100. In November 1972, David had been informed at Camp David by Nixon's aides that the post of science adviser would be moved out of the White House and perhaps abolished outright. William O. Baker was told of PSAC's impending demise around Christmas by Treasury Secretary George Shultz, who reportedly argued that PSAC's contribution did not justify its cost. Rabi, too, held Shultz at least partly responsible for the abolition of PSAC. Interviews: David and Baker. On the abolition of PSAC, see Wells, "Science Advice and the Presidency, 1933–1976," pt. II, pp. 722–24; and transcript of "I. I. Rabi," p. 9, Videotape History Project, Alfred Sloan Foundation, New York, New York.

101. Rabi interview.

102. Interviews: David and DuBridge.

103. As evidence for his thesis, Stever pointed to a 1972 PSAC study of industry's damage to the environment and to another controversial report that same year on chemicals and health by PSAC consultant John Tukey, which identified alcohol and nicotine as two of the greatest threats to public health. Stever interview.

104. On the role of Vietnam in Nixon's decision, see James Killian, *Sputnik, Scientists, and Eisenhower* (Cambridge, Mass.: MIT Press, 1977), pp. 255–56. Former PSAC member Harvey Brooks argues that another element in the abolition of PSAC was passage of the Freedom of Information Act and the Federal Advisory Committee Act during the Nixon administration. As Brooks writes, "In my view it was the passage of those laws, fortuitously coincident with the expiration of the President's reorganization authority in February 1983, that undoubtedly led Nixon to hurriedly abolish OST about a week before the expiration of his legislative authority to do so, and return the authority to where it has always belonged by statute, the NSF." Letter, Brooks to author, August 10, 1989. Jerome Wiesner and Edwin Land were put on Nixon's "enemies list" for their opposition to the ABM. One administration staffer also suggested cutting off federal research funds to MIT as a way of getting back at Wiesner. Interviews: Stever, Wiesner, David. Concerning the scientists on the "enemies list," see Katz, *Presidential Politics and Science Policy*, p. 186.

105. *Science*, February 2, 1973, p. 455; and Golden (ed.), *Science Advice to the President*, pp. 66–67, 70–71.

106. Golden (ed.), *Science Advice to the President*, pp. 64, 68–69; Stever interview.

107. Ibid., pp. 69–70; Stever interview.

108. So sudden was the switch from David to Stever that it took the Russians, too, by surprise. At the first of these exchanges, Soviet scientists presented Stever with a rare-mineral collection that had plainly been intended as a gift for David, who was known to be an avid rock collector. Stever interview.

109. Stever interview.

110. Ibid.

111. Golden (ed.), *Science Advice to the President,* p. 61. On the National Academy of Sciences report, see Killian, *Sputnik, Scientists, and Eisenhower,* pp. 256–58.

112. Stever interview.

113. On the origins of the Office of Technology Assessment, see Primack and von Hippel, *Advice and Dissent,* pp. 273–75.

114. Interview with OTA Director Jack Gibbons.

115. Golden (ed.), *Science Advice to the President,* p. 63.

116. On the passage of the National Science and Technology Policy, Organization, and Priorities Act of 1976, see ibid., pp. 65–66, and Killian, *Sputnik, Scientists, and Eisenhower,* pp. 258–59.

117. Hoping that PSAC might be recreated in Ford's second term, Baker and Ramo proposed an ambitious agenda of some twenty-five studies and projects for the commission, almost all of which dealt with domestic issues, such as the revitalization of agricultural research and the rebuilding of the nation's railroads. When their study was not completed until after the 1976 election, Baker and Ramo presented it instead to President Jimmy Carter—who ignored the recommendations of what he regarded as a Republican-dominated committee. Interviews: Baker and Stever.

118. The task of reworking the nation's military strategy was assigned to John Foster, then-DDR&E director, and an interagency panel of civilian strategists. The directive creating what became known as the Foster panel was sent to the NSC in February 1973, and specified that the review of strategy was to be conducted by "a special ad hoc group" with representatives from the Defense Department, State Department, CIA, and NSC. See NSSM-169, February 13, 1973, DDRS-1982-565.

119. Wells, "Science Advice and the Presidency, 1933–1976," pt. II, p. 737.

120. Ibid., pp. 712–13; Katz, *Presidential Politics and Science Policy,* p. 181.

121. Katz, *Presidential Politics and Science Policy,* p. 181.

Chapter 11

1. "Search for a Science Adviser: The Names on the List," *Science,* January 7, 1977, pp. 31–33.

2. Interview with Jerome Wiesner. Brown may have shared Wiesner's concern. According to a subsequent *Science* article, Brown submitted his own list of five candidates for the post of science adviser. "Harold Brown and Defense: From Scientist to Secretary," *Science,* February 4, 1977, pp. 463–66.

3. "Frank Press, Long-Shot Candidate, May Become Science Adviser," *Science,* February 25, 1977, pp. 763–66.

4. For a comparison of the careers of Brown and Press, see John Edwards, *Super Weapon: The Making of MX* (New York: Norton, 1982), pp. 141–42.

5. "Frank Press," *Science,* pp. 763–66. Within a week of President Kennedy's assassination, Press resigned from PSAC, several months before his term on the committee was to expire.

6. Ibid.

7. U.S. Congress, Senate, Committee on Commerce, Science, and Transportation, *Hearings on the Confirmation of Frank Press as Science Adviser,* 95th Cong.,

1st sess., April 7, 1977 (Washington, D.C.: U.S. Government Printing Office, 1977), pp. 40–42.

8. Interview with Frank Press.

9. Letter, Press to author, May 19, 1988.

10. On Brown's role in the B-1 decision, see "Death of the B-1: The Events Behind Carter's Decision," *Science,* August 5, 1977, pp. 536–38; Harold Brown, *Thinking About National Security* (Boulder, Colo.: Westview Press, 1983), pp. 72–74; and Nick Kotz, *Wild Blue Yonder: Money, Politics, and the B-1 Bomber* (New York: Pantheon, 1988), pp. 169–70.

11. Carter wrote of the B-1 decision: "If I had had absolute power, the answer would have been simple: do not build it, because it would be a gross waste of money. My problem was that I would have to win the argument not merely in the Oval Office, but also in the public arena—indirectly with the American people, and then directly with a majority of Congress." Jimmy Carter, *Keeping Faith: Memoirs of a President* (New York: Bantam Books, 1982), p. 81.

12. Press interview; Carter, *Keeping Faith,* p. 146. On Carter and the ASAT issue, see Raymond Garthoff, *Détente and Confrontation* (Washington, D.C.: Brookings Institution, 1985), pp. 759–60.

13. Frank Press, "Science and Technology in the White House, 1977 to 1980: Part 2," *Science,* January 16, 1981, pp. 249–56. The author thanks Dr. Press for a list of the OSTP committees relating to national security and international and space affairs. Letter, Press to author, December 26, 1986. For a list of OSTP consultants, see William Lanouette, "Carter's Science Adviser—Doing Part of His Job Well," *National Journal,* January 6, 1979, pp. 14–19.

14. This scheme called for the missiles to be continuously moved along the 4,000-mile length of the trenches to make it more difficult for the enemy to pinpoint their location. Members of the panel included Jack Ruina, Daniel Fink, Richard Garwin, Wolfgang Panofsky, and Solomon Buchsbaum, a Bell Labs physicist and member of PSAC during the Nixon administration. On early ideas for basing the MX, see Edwards, *Super Weapon,* pp. 111–17; and Office of Technology Assessment, "MX Missile Basing" (Washington, D.C.: U.S. Government Printing Office, 1981), pp. 3–32. The author thanks Dr. Buchsbaum for a list of the members of the OSTP Missile Vulnerability Panel.

15. The panel also discovered that the Air Force plan had a serious flaw: shock waves from a nuclear blast could travel the length of the trench, destroying the missiles in it. Edwards, *Super Weapon,* p. 143.

16. "Science and Technology in the White House," *Science,* January 16, 1981, p. 252.

17. U.S. Congress, Senate, Committee on Commerce, Science, and Transportation, *Hearings: Regulations of Recombinant DNA Research,* 95th Cong., 1st sess., November 2, 8, 10, 1977 (Washington, D.C.: U.S. Government Printing Office, 1977), p. 120.

18. On the concern with "competitiveness" and OSTP's other activities in the domestic realm, see Claude Barfield, *Science Policy from Ford to Reagan* (Washington, D.C.: American Enterprise Institute, 1982); Frank Press, "Science and Technology in the White House, 1977 to 1980: Part I," *Science,* January 9, 1981, pp. 139–45; and "President and Science Adviser Push for a Foundation for Development," *Science,* June 16, 1978, pp. 1252–53.

19. On the history of the CTB since 1963 and the origins of the Treaty on the

Nonproliferation of Nuclear Weapons, see National Academy of Sciences, *Nuclear Arms Control: Background and Issues* (Washington, D.C.: National Academy Press, 1983), pp. 222–73. In July 1973, a Threshold Test-ban Treaty allowing the underground testing of weapons with yields up to 150 kilotons had been signed at Moscow, in one of the last successes of the Nixon administration's policy of détente. Due in part to the subsequent deterioration of relations with Russia, however, the treaty had yet to be ratified by the Senate. Ibid.

20. "We could explode a kiloton in Nevada and not see it 800 miles away. The Soviets said they could explode 300 pounds of TNT and see it at that distance. We could never conceive of such a thing, so we suspected the veracity of their statements. They, I'm sure, thought that we were lying." Press interview. On the arguments over seismic verification of a CTB, see "Seismic Methods for Verifying Nuclear Test Bans," in D. W. Hafemeister and D. Schroeer, *Physics, Technology and the Nuclear Arms Race* (New York: American Institute of Physics, 1983), pp. 86–133; and W. J. Hannon, "Seismic Verification of a Comprehensive Test Ban," *Science,* January 18, 1985, pp. 251–57.

21. Interview with Warren Heckrotte.

22. On the CTB negotiations, see Allen Greb and Warren Heckrotte, "The Long History: The Test Ban Debate," *Bulletin of the Atomic Scientists,* August/September 1983, pp. 36–43; and Neil Joeck and Herbert York, "Countdown on the Comprehensive Test Ban," IGCC, University of California, San Diego, 1986.

23. Interview with Jack Ruina. In another move seemingly intended to defuse opposition to the CTB from the national laboratories, Carter appointed former Livermore director Herbert York the U.S. representative to the negotiations at Geneva.

24. Greb and Heckrotte, "The Long History," p. 42 fn.

25. The argument for proof testing to guarantee stockpile reliability rested in part on the fact that the volatile chemicals and radioactive materials used in nuclear weapons deteriorate over time. Advocates also claimed that as materials became unavailable and laws controlling the handling of hazardous materials changed, it might become impossible to correct flaws or to remanufacture the weapons. At the extremes of the CTB debate were opponents who charged that only a ban of "zero-length" could assure reliability, and proponents who argued that reduced reliability might be a positive good—since it would undermine the confidence of both sides in their ability to carry out a successful first strike. On the stockpile reliability argument, see U.S. Congress, House, Committee on Armed Services, *Hearings: Effects of a Comprehensive Test Ban Treaty on U.S. National Security Interests,* 95th Cong., 2d sess., August 14–15, 1978 (Washington, D.C.: U.S. Government Printing Office, 1978). On the technical arguments behind the anti-CTB position, see J. W. Rosengren, "Some Little-Publicized Difficulties with a Nuclear Freeze," U.S. Department of Energy, October 1983; Ray Kidder, "Evaluation of the 1983 Rosengren Report . . .," June 17, 1986, Lawrence Livermore National Laboratory; and the reply by Rosengren, "Stockpile Reliability and Nuclear Test Bans: A Reply to a Critic's Comments," LLNL. The author thanks Warren Heckrotte for copies of the Rosengren and Kidder reports.

26. "Defense Scientists Differ on Nuclear Stockpile Testing," *Science,* September 22, 1978, pp. 1105–6.

27. Experts still disagree over the smallest detectable yield; the claim by pro-CTB geophysicists that detection was feasible down to the subkiloton level was challenged by anti-CTB scientists, who have also disputed the smallest yield that is

"militarily significant," or useful in designing new nuclear weapons. In 1973, for example, former DDR&E director John Foster testified in Congress that the ability to detect yields down to 0.25 kiloton was necessary for national security, whereas former Los Alamos director Harold Agnew argued that 0.1 kiloton was the threshold of military significance. On the other hand, in testimony at congressional hearings in 1978, there was almost universal agreement among scientists that only nuclear testing in the range of 5–10 kilotons was militarily significant. See *Hearings: Effects of a Comprehensive Test Ban Treaty on U.S. National Security Interests,* August 14–15, 1978, and "Defense Scientists Differ on Nuclear Stockpile Testing," pp. 1105–6.

28. "Defense Scientists Differ on Nuclear Stockpile Testing," *Science,* p. 1106.

29. Interviews: Agnew, Brown, Press, Aaron. Letter, Press to author, May 19, 1988; letter, Brown to author, July 6, 1989.

30. Interviews: Agnew, Brown, Press. In a 1981 interview, Agnew boasted that he and Batzel had a direct effect on Carter in the 1978 Cabinet Room meeting: "We influenced Carter with facts so that he did not introduce the CTB, which we subsequently learned he had planned to do. There's no question in my mind that Roger and I turned Carter around because we incurred so many enemies from the other side! It was obvious we had an impact." *Los Alamos Science,* Summer/Fall 1981, p. 154. On the debate over the laboratories' influence on national policy, see California Legislature, Senate Committee on Health and Human Services, "Forum on the Involvement of the University of California in Nuclear Testing at Lawrence Livermore and Los Alamos National Laboratories," February 11, 1987.

31. Ruina interview.

32. Interviews: Ruina, Panofsky, York, Drell, and Mark.

33. On the hearings, see U.S. Congress, House, Armed Services Committee, *Effects of a Comprehensive Test Ban Treaty on U.S. National Security Interests,* August 14–15, 1978. Kerr's testimony is reprinted in the *Congressional Record,* Senate, August 17, 1978, p. 26706.

34. Letter, Garwin to author, October 29, 1986.

35. Garwin's letter is reprinted in the *Congressional Record,* Senate, August 17, 1978, pp. 26706–7.

36. Letter, Garwin to author, October 29, 1986.

37. *Congressional Record,* Senate, October 12, 1978, pp. 36003–4.

38. *Hearings: Effects of a Comprehensive Test Ban Treaty on U.S. National Security Interests,* October 15, 1978, p. 38. Neither Garwin's letter nor the brief volley of accusations that followed the printed debate over stockpile reliability caused Carter to change his mind on the CTB—but the incident nonetheless had the beneficial effect of "smoking out" the arguments against the treaty, Carson Mark argues. Mark interview. *Hearings,* ibid.

39. Ibid.

40. Carter, *Keeping Faith,* p. 231.

41. Interviews: Ruina and Heckrotte.

42. Press interview.

43. Letter, Garwin to author, October 29, 1986. Brown later argued that questions about stockpile reliability "are not easily answerable without (or even with) access to information on U.S. and Soviet nuclear weapons designs." Brown, *Thinking About National Security,* p. 191.

44. Earlier in the year, Carter had inadvertently added to his political troubles

with a controversial decision on the so-called neutron bomb—which, in a turnabout that satisfied none of his critics, Carter decided to develop but not to deploy. See Cyrus Vance, *Hard Choices* (New York: Simon & Schuster, 1983), pp. 67–69. On Brzezinski and the MX, see Zbigniew Brzezinski, *Power and Principle: Memoirs of the National Security Adviser, 1977–1981* (New York: Farrar, Straus & Giroux, 1983), pp. 333–34.

45. Edwards, *Super Weapon,* p. 148. Since in peacetime aircraft can easily be counted by satellites, air basing answered Press's concern about verifiability under the terms of SALT. However, as Brown pointed out, air-based missiles would be just as vulnerable to attack as land-based bombers. On the air-basing concept, see Office of Technology Assessment, "MX Missile Basing," pp. 217–34.

46. Known as "multiple aim points," or MAPs, this basing plan called for the continuous moving of MXs among as many as ten thousand widely dispersed shelters in the southwestern desert. In the Air Force version of the plan the shelters would be vertical silos; May's panel believed that horizontal shelters would be cheaper and easier to build. Edwards, *Super Weapon,* pp. 144–50.

47. Ibid., p. 167.

48. Ibid., p. 165–68.

49. Ibid., pp. 184–85. In another change of nomenclature, the Advanced Research Projects Agency (ARPA) had meanwhile been renamed Defense Advanced Research Projects Agency (DARPA).

50. On the Perry study, see "Cost of Airborne Mobile Missile May Be Prohibitive," *The New York Times,* April 3, 1979.

51. On the thinking behind the "racetrack," see Office of Technology Assessment, "MX Missile Basing," pp. 261–65; and Edwards, *Super Weapon,* pp. 204–13.

52. Brzezinski, *Power and Principle,* pp. 334–36. Brzezinski approved the larger missile, apparently not realizing that it would be too big for the missile launcher he proposed to carry it.

53. "I could have been more forceful on [the MX]. I should have gone to see the president personally on it, instead of having only a comment—which he read—through the normal White House staff commentary," Press remarked in a 1986 interview. By the time he thought of confronting Carter face to face with his objections to the MX, Press said, "it was already too late."

54. Edwards, *Super Weapon,* pp. 189, 199. On Brown's concern with the MX decision as a reflection of U.S. resolve, see Brown, *Thinking About National Security,* p. 67. Brzezinski wrote in his memoirs that Carter by late 1978 was "increasingly unhappy over Harold's pressure to increase defense spending and on several occasions complained to me that Brown did not make his own position clear and instead propounded uncritically the Defense Department perspective." Brzezinski, *Power and Principle,* pp. 44–46.

55. Carter, *Keeping Faith,* p. 241. Carter's MX announcement is in *Public Papers of the President, Jimmy Carter,* 1979, v. II (Washington, D.C.: U.S. Government Printing Office, 1980), pp. 1599–1601.

56. Edwards, *Super Weapon,* p. 247.

57. Perry is quoted in Edwards, *Super Weapon,* p. 199.

58. Brown interview.

59. Letter, Press to author, May 19, 1988.

60. Herbert Scoville, *MX: Prescription for Disaster* (Cambridge, Mass.: MIT Press, 1982); Scoville interview.

61. See "MX Missile to Roam 200 Racetracks," *Science,* October 12, 1979, pp. 198–200.

62. Ibid.

63. On shallow underwater mobile (SUM) basing and Garwin's testimony to Congress, see *Congressional Record,* Senate, November 9, 1979, pp. 31852–55; and Office of Technology Assessment, "MX Missile Basing," pp. 167–216.

64. *Congressional Record,* ibid.; "MX on Land or Sea?" *Science,* April 11, 1980, p. 155; Drell interview; and letter, Garwin to author, July 17, 1989.

65. *Congressional Record,* ibid.; "Congress Challenges MX Basing Plans," *Science,* May 30, 1980, pp. 1007–9.

66. Letter, Garwin to author, October 29, 1986; and "MX on Land or Sea?" *Science,* p. 155. Wrote Garwin to Brzezinski: "I do believe the President should have available the results of [the SUM] analysis in case the MX racetrack basing cannot go forward for some reason." Letter, Garwin to Brzezinski, February 12, 1980. The author thanks Richard Garwin for a copy of this letter.

67. On the debate in the Carter administration over the United States as a "reliable supplier," see Edward Markey, *Nuclear Peril* (New York: Ballinger, 1982).

68. Press interview.

69. Brzezinski, *Power and Principle,* p. 226.

70. Garthoff, *Détente and Confrontation,* p. 706 fn. OSTP also played a role in the Carter administration's subsequent "normalization" of relations with China. Letter, Press to author, May 19, 1988.

71. The energy summit is noted in Carter, *Keeping Faith,* pp. 116–17. Wiesner said that while he was impressed by Carter's knowledge of the energy crisis at the summit, "the experts were not prepared for it." Wiesner interview.

72. Letter, Press to author, May 19, 1988.

73. Ibid.; "Flash Not Missed by Vela Still Veiled in Mist," *Science,* November 30, 1979, pp. 1051–52; "Scientists Fail to Solve Vela Mystery," *Science,* February 1, 1980, pp. 504–6; Panofsky interview. On the sonic booms, see "East Coast Mystery Booms: A Scientific Suspense Tale," *Science,* March 31, 1978, pp. 1416–17; and Richard Garwin, "Speculation on Long-Range Effects of Supersonic Flight," March 14, 1978, unpublished paper.

74. Aaron interview. On *Cosmos 954,* see William Burrows, *Deep Black: Space Espionage and National Security* (New York: Random House, 1986), pp. 271–72.

75. Letter, Press to author; Lanouette, "Carter's Science Adviser . . . ," pp. 14–19.

76. Office of Technology Assessment, "The Effects of Nuclear Weapons" (Washington, D.C.: U.S. Government Printing Office, 1979). MX opponent Senator Mark Hatfield was one of those who requested a congressional study of the MX. See *Congressional Record,* Senate, November 9, 1979, p. 31856. On other studies of Three Mile Island for Congress, see, for example, General Accounting Office, "Three Mile Island: The Financial Fallout" (Washington, D.C.: U.S. Government Printing Office, July 1980).

77. At Press's request, the National Academy of Sciences conducted two separate studies of the "greenhouse" effect and the phenomenon of planet warming. Press later wrote of the controversy: "Informed policy decisions about this potentially significant environmental problem will require greater knowledge and sophistication than now exist." "Science and Technology in the White House," *Science,* January 16, 1981, p. 254.

78. Press interview. On the acid rain debate in the Reagan administration, see Chapter 12.

79. William Golden, "PSAC: Reestablish It Now," *Science*, October 10, 1980, p. 1.

Chapter 12

1. Other members of the Task Force were Edward Teller; Harold Agnew; former PSAC physicist Frederick Seitz; Wilson Talley, president of the Hertz Foundation; General Electric vice president Arthur Bueche; William Nierenberg, director of the Scripps Institute of Oceanography; and retired Air Force General Bernard Schriever. Ramo interview.

2. Interview with William O. Baker; telephone interview with William Nierenberg.

3. Baker interview.

4. Interviews: Baker, Nierenberg, Edward David, Simon Ramo.

5. Interview with Paul Doty.

6. Baker interview.

7. Reagan's Livermore tour is noted, for example, in Edward Teller, "SDI: The Last, Best Hope," *Insight*, October 28, 1985, pp. 75–79.

8. See Edward Teller, "Technology: The Imbalance of Power," in Peter Duignan and Alvin Rabushka (eds.), *The United States in the 1980s* (Stanford, Calif.: Hoover Institution, 1980), pp. 497–534.

9. Keyworth had already befriended others who would have an important impact on the new administration—including former Los Alamos director Harold Agnew and William Wilson, a long-time Reagan friend and member of the president's informal but influential "Kitchen Cabinet." In 1979, all three men had served on a University of California committee seeking a replacement for Agnew, who was about to step down as head of the New Mexico laboratory. Interviews: Harold Agnew and George Keyworth.

10. "Science Adviser Post Has Nominee in View," *Science*, May 22, 1981, pp. 903–4.

11. Ibid.

12. Keyworth interview. On his view of the science adviser's role, see "Keyworth Gives First Policy Speech," *Science*, July 10, 1981, pp. 183–84.

13. On the Reagan administration's early budget cuts affecting research, see "House Science Panel Throws Down Gauntlet," *Science*, April 10, 1981, p. 144. On Stockman's proposed 10 percent cut, see George Keyworth, "Giving Good Counsel at the White House," *Issues in Science and Technology*, Spring 1988, pp. 37–43.

14. U.S. Congress, House, Committee on Commerce, Science, and Transportation, *Hearings: Nominations . . .*, 97th Cong., 1st sess., July 20–21, 1981, pp. 6–12.

15. In an interview, Keyworth said that he had intended WHSC to be "totally and fundamentally different from PSAC." On the origins of WHSC, see "Pared Down PSAC Proposal," *Science*, December 18, 1981, p. 1324.

16. "The Making of a Science Adviser," *Science*, November 12, 1982, p. 659.

17. On the yellow rain controversy, see Peter Pringle, "Political Science," *Atlantic*, October 1985, pp. 67–81; and Elisa Harris, "Sverdlovsk and Yellow Rain: Two Cases of Soviet Noncompliance?" *International Security*, Spring 1987, pp.

41–95. The author thanks Elisa Harris for commenting on an early draft of this chapter. Letter, Harris to the author, January 6, 1988.

18. "U.S. Says Data Show Toxin Use in Asia Conflict," *The New York Times,* September 14, 1981.

19. U.S. Congress, Senate, Committee on Foreign Relations, *Hearings: 'Yellow Rain,'* 97th Cong., 1st sess., November 10, 1981, p. 29.

20. Pringle, "Political Science"; "Yellow Rain: Filling in the Gaps," *Science,* July 2, 1982, pp. 31–34.

21. Pringle, "Political Science." See also "Bugs in the Yellow Rain Theory," *Science,* June 24, 1983, pp. 1356–58.

22. Pringle, "Political Science."

23. Ibid.

24. Ibid.; "The Apology of Yellow Rain," *Science,* July 15, 1983, p. 242.

25. Nor did the government concede that its analysis might be in error. As late as 1987, a Reagan administration report to Congress still blamed the Russians for yellow rain. "Yellow Rain Evidence Slowly Whittled Away," *Science,* July 4, 1986, p. 18; letter, Elisa Harris to author, January 6, 1988.

26. On the conflict over acid rain, see Ernest Yanarella and Randal Ihara (eds.), *The Acid Rain Debate: Scientific, Economic, and Political Dimensions* (Boulder, Colo.: Westview Press, 1985). See also U.S. Congress, House, Committee on Interstate and Foreign Commerce, *Hearings: Acid Rain,* 96th Cong., 2d sess., February 26, 1980.

27. "Science Advisers to the Government," *Science,* February 19, 1982, p. 921.

28. See U.S. Congress, House, *First Annual Report of Inter-Agency Task Force on Acid Precipitation* (Washington, D.C.: U.S. Government Printing Office, January 1982).

29. On the congressional response to the acid rain controversy, see U.S. Congress, Senate, Committee on Environmental and Public Works, *Hearings: Acid Rain, A Technical Inquiry,* 97th Cong., 2d sess., May 25, 27, 1982; and Committee on Foreign Relations, *Hearings: Acid Rain,* 97th Cong., 2d sess., February 10, 1982. On the growing concern of outside scientists, see "Acid Rain, A Year Later," *Science,* July 15, 1983, pp. 241–42.

30. Interview with John Gibbons. A 1984 OTA study on acid rain conceded that its "analysis cannot provide an unambiguous answer" to the problem, and that "even substantial additional scientific research is unlikely to provide significant, near-term policy guidance, or resolve value conflicts." U.S. Congress, Office of Technology Assessment, "Acid Rain and Transported Air Pollutants: Implications for Public Policy" (Washington, D.C.: U.S. Government Printing Office, June 1984), p. 3. By 1990, the deleterious effects of acid rain were still being debated. See "Primary Ingredient of Acid Rain May Counteract Greenhouse Effect," *The Washington Post,* September 17, 1990.

31. National Academy of Sciences, *Acid Deposition: Atmospheric Processes in Eastern North America* (Washington, D.C.: National Academy Press, 1983).

32. The author thanks Dr. Nierenberg for a copy of the draft OSTP report, "General Comments on Acid Rain," June 27, 1983, and for comments on an earlier version of this chapter. Letter, Nierenberg to author, June 8, 1988. On the OSTP report, see "Acid Rain, A Year Later," *Science,* pp. 241–42. Coincidentally, a few weeks after Nierenberg's study began, a group of outside scientists warned of an altogether different—but potentially even more serious—threat to the global envi-

ronment: the phenomenon of "nuclear winter," whereby the aftermath of a nuclear war would enshroud the earth in a thick pall of dust and smoke, cutting off the warmth and light of the sun. While the conclusion of the so-called TTAPS study was subsequently challenged by other experts, the fact that Pentagon scientists had missed the nuclear winter phenomenon was "embarrassing," conceded a Defense Department spokesman, and yet another reminder of how important issues may be overlooked when the government becomes scientifically uncurious. On the TTAPS study and nuclear winter, see Paul Ehrlich et al., *The Cold and the Dark: The World After Nuclear War* (New York: Norton, 1984); P. J. Crutzen and J. W. Birks, "The Atmosphere After a Nuclear War: Twilight at Noon," *Ambio,* No. 11, pp. 114–25; and Carl Sagan and Richard Turco, *A Path Where No Man Thought* (New York: Random House, 1990). The author thanks Dr. Richard Turco of R & D Associates for a copy of the draft TTAPS report.

33. "Acid Rain Report Allegedly Suppressed," *Science,* September 21, 1984, p. 1374; "Acid Rain Report," *Science,* November 16, 1984, p. 780; and "The Knives Are Out for OSTP," *Science,* December 21, 1984, p. 1400. Nierenberg claims that while it was "completely clear . . . that the president was strongly in favor of doing something about the problem, [i]t was equally clear . . . that Stockman, on the contrary, was strongly opposed." According to Nierenberg, Stockman argued, in effect, "It makes no sense to spend one hundred dollars to save a five dollar fish." Letter, Nierenberg to author, June 8, 1988.

34. "Silos and Vulnerability," *The New York Times,* October 3, 1981.

35. U.S. Congress, Office of Technology Assessment, "MX Missile Basing" (Washington, D.C.: U.S. Government Printing Office, 1981).

36. Keyworth interview.

37. On the work of the first Townes panel, see John Edwards, *Super Weapon: The Making of MX* (New York: Norton, 1982), pp. 228–40; and "Reagan's Plan for MX Attracts Fire," *Science,* April 9, 1982, pp. 150–52.

38. On reaction to the proposals for the MX, see "Air Force Takes Aim at Big Bird," *Science,* April 16, 1982, pp. 270–73; and "A Doomsday Plan for the 1990's," *Science,* April 25, 1982, pp. 388–90.

39. "Silos and Vulnerability," *The New York Times,* October 3, 1981.

40. Edwards, *Super Weapon,* pp. 242–44.

41. "MX Missile Deployment," *The New York Times,* November 23, 1982. The opponents of the MX on the second Townes panel were Nierenberg and Admiral Worth Bagley. Letter, Nierenberg to author, June 8, 1988. On the second Townes report and Densepack, see U.S. Congress, Senate, Armed Services Committee, *Hearings: The MX Missile and Associated Basing Decision,* 97th Cong., 2d sess., December 8, 1982.

42. "President Urges Support for Dense Pack Deployment of MX Missile," *The New York Times,* November 23, 1982.

43. There was, for example, widespread confusion over the efficacy of super-hardening. Air Force representatives at the hearings admitted that even superhardened silos could resist overpressures no greater than 15,000 to 30,000 pounds per square inch. Keyworth, however, argued that superhardening was effective to 45,000 psi, while Weinberger claimed 60,000 to 80,000 psi. See *Hearings: The MX Missile . . . ,* p. 58. "Congress Ducks the MX," *Science,* January 14, 1983, pp. 151–52.

44. Keyworth interview.

45. The text of the unclassified portion of the Scowcroft Report appears in *The New York Times,* April 12, 1983. A second Scowcroft Report, implicitly critical of the president's SDI concept, was sent to Reagan a year after his "Star Wars" speech. See "President's Commission on Strategic Forces," March 21, 1984 (Washington, D.C.: U.S. Government Printing Office, 1984). On the renewed controversy over the MX, see "The Newly Improved MX Missile," *Science,* April 29, 1983, p. 486. The question of what to do about the missile was reopened in the fall of 1986 when the commander of the Strategic Air Command proposed that the entire MX force be put on rail cars and moved around military reservations in a time of crisis. See "SAC Head Seeks to Put MX Missiles on Trains," *The New York Times,* October 23, 1986.

46. Keyworth interview. On the opposition of Stockman and Keyworth to the space station, see "Squabbling Over the Space Policy," *Science,* July 23, 1982, pp. 331–33.

47. Keyworth interview; ibid.

48. The text of Reagan's address appears in *The New York Times,* March 24, 1983.

49. For Teller's account of his role in SDI, see Edward Teller, *Better a Shield Than a Sword: Perspectives on Defense and Technology* (New York: Free Press, 1987), pp. 37–41.

50. Robert Scheer, *With Enough Shovels: Reagan, Bush and Nuclear War* (New York: Random House, 1982), pp. 232–33. On the origins of SDI, see Philip Boffey et al., *Claiming the Heavens: The New York Times Complete Guide to the Star Wars Debate* (New York: Times Books, 1988), pp. 3–25; and Don Baucom, "Origins of the Strategic Defense Initiative," unpublished manuscript. The author thanks Dr. Baucom for a copy of his forthcoming book and comments on this chapter.

51. Boffey et al., *Claiming the Heavens,* pp. 3–25.

52. Ibid.

53. On the technical roots of SDI before Reagan, see Jack Manno, *Arming the Heavens: The Hidden Military Agenda for Space, 1945–95* (New York: Dodd, Mead, 1984), pp. 145–49; and John Bosma, "Space and Strategic Defense Reorientation: Project Defender," *Defense Science and Electronics,* September 1983, pp. 58–65.

54. "Debate on Missile-Destroyer Aims Picks Up Heat Over Soviet Moves," *The New York Times,* December 5, 1978. Agnew subsequently became a critic of Reagan's SDI. See "What Is the Right SDI Approach?" *San Diego Union,* December 18, 1988.

55. York interview. For an example of this enthusiasm, see Daniel Graham et al., "High Frontier: A New National Strategy" (Washington, D.C.: The Heritage Foundation, 1982); and Graham, *A Defense That Defends: Blocking Nuclear Attack* (Greenwich, Conn.: Devin-Adair Publishers, 1983).

56. These included concepts like BAMBI (Ballistic Missile Boost Interceptor) and SAINT (Satellite Inspector-Interceptor). See Manno, *Arming the Heavens,* pp. 47–49; and Paul Stares, *The Militarization of Space* (Ithaca, N.Y.: Cornell University Press, 1985), pp. 239–42.

57. On Teller's contribution to SDI and Excalibur, see William Broad, *Star Warriors* (New York: Simon & Schuster, 1985); Boffey et al., *Claiming the Heavens,* pp. 3–25; and Gregg Herken, "How Reagan Was Sold Star Wars," *Bulletin of the Atomic Scientists,* October 1987, pp. 20–28.

58. On the ideas of the laser lobby, see Angelo Codevilla, *While Others Build: A Commonsense Approach to the Strategic Defense Initiative* (New York: Free Press, 1988).

59. In theory, Teller's Excalibur would physically disintegrate space targets at light speed with a focused beam of high-energy x-rays. The space-based system favored by Graham's organization, High Frontier, would rely on kinetic-kill weapons, which would destroy missiles by colliding with them in space. The laser lobby intended to use the heat of a chemical laser to burn a hole in the missile's outer skin. On the various proposals for "Star Wars," see Office of Technology Assessment, *Strategic Defenses* (Princeton, N.J.: Princeton University Press, 1985).

60. Interview with Daniel Graham.

61. Interviews: Keyworth, Bendetsen, and Wood. At a White House meeting on January 8, 1982, Bendetsen and three other members of Reagan's inner circle presented the president with a copy of their report. Baucom, "Origins of the Strategic Defense Initiative," pp. 291–92. Keyworth described Teller's meeting with Reagan on September 14, 1982 as a "disaster." Scheduled for thirty minutes, the meeting was reportedly cut short by the president's aides, William Clark and Edwin Meese, when Teller asked Reagan to dramatically increase funding for the x-ray laser project at Livermore. In December 1984, Teller wrote to Paul Nitze, the Reagan administration's chief arms control adviser, claiming that "a single x-ray laser module the size of an executive desk which applied this technology could potentially shoot down the entire Soviet land-based missile force, if it were to be launched into the module's field-of-view." Letter, Teller to Nitze, December 28, 1984. Similar claims for Excalibur were made by Teller in letters to Keyworth and Robert McFarlane. Teller's claims were subsequently challenged by Roy Woodruff, associate director for SDI research at Livermore, as "overly optimistic." The author thanks the office of Congressman Edward Markey for copies of the letters from Teller and Woodruff. On the controversy surrounding the claims for the x-ray laser, see "X-ray Laser Budget Grows as Public Information Declines," *Science,* April 11, 1986, pp. 152–53; and "Teller Gave Flawed Data on X-Ray Laser, Scientist Says," *Los Angeles Times,* October 21, 1987.

62. Malcolm Wallop, "Opportunities and Imperatives of Ballistic Missile Defense," *Strategic Review,* Fall 1979, pp. 13–21.

63. "Laser Wars on Capitol Hill," *Science,* June 4, 1982, pp. 1082–83.

64. Interviews: Drell and Panofsky.

65. Keyworth interview.

66. Ibid.

67. "Edward Teller told me about the x-ray laser the first day I took office," DeLauer claimed in a 1986 interview.

68. Letter, Malcolm Wallop to James Baker, November 13, 1981. The author thanks Dr. Keyworth for a copy of this letter and of his appointment calendar for March 17–23, 1983.

69. "Throngs Fill Manhattan to Protest Nuclear Weapons," *The New York Times,* June 13, 1982; "House Supports Reagan on Arms," *The New York Times,* August 6, 1982; and "Bishops Endorse Stand Opposed to Nuclear War," *The New York Times,* May 4, 1983.

70. On Watkins' role in the origins of SDI, see Admiral James Watkins, "The Strategic Defense Initiative," *Defense/85,* March 1985, pp. 14–18; and "Enhanced Role of Religious Faith at Pentagon Raises Questions, Doubts," *Los Angeles Times,*

December 30, 1984. Weinberger's doubts are noted in John Newhouse, *War and Peace in the Nuclear Age* (New York: Knopf, 1989), pp. 360–61.

71. Watkins, "The Strategic Defense Initiative"; Keyworth interview. Reagan was reminded of the public's growing concern about the arms race during a 1982 White House dinner. George Gallup reportedly told the president that opinion polls showed the American people were losing patience with the strategic stalemate. At a subsequent New Year's Eve party that Reagan attended, discussion was said to have focused on ways of counteracting the administration's hawkish image. Interviews: George Chapline and Simon Ramo.

72. In 1988 testimony before Congress, McFarlane, though noting that "the President has had an interest in strategic defense for a long time," claimed to be the first to propose SDI to Reagan. But McFarlane also acknowledged that while he and others at the Pentagon were talking "frankly about just stressing the Soviet system," their concept was subsequently transformed by the president into a much more ambitious nationwide missile defense. See U.S. Congress, Armed Services Committee, May 17, 1988, *Hearings on U.S. Strategic Forces and START* (Washington, D.C.: U.S. Government Printing Office, 1988), pp. 167–68. On McFarlane's role in SDI, see also Frank Greve, "'Star Wars': How Reagan's Plan Caught Many Insiders by Surprise," San Jose *Mercury News,* November 17, 1985.

73. Keyworth interview; telephone interview with Gil Rye.

74. Ibid. NSC aide Gil Rye, one of the original drafters of the Insert, claims that the decision to inform Keyworth of Reagan's pending SDI announcement was almost an afterthought: "How can the president go on the tube directing a major high-technology initiative and tell his science adviser nothing?" Rye said he and his colleagues asked themselves.

75. Keyworth had commissioned the so-called Defense Technologies Study at the suggestion of Edwin Meese, Reagan's close friend and domestic adviser, who urged the science adviser to follow up on the report that Teller and the "Kitchen Cabinet" had earlier given the president on strategic defense. Keyworth interview; telephone interview with Edward Frieman.

76. Interview with Victor Reis. Reis carried out his study of lasers for the Pentagon at the end of the Carter administration. For the laser lobby's critical view of Reis's study, see Codevilla, *While Others Build,* pp. 71, 75.

77. Frieman interview.

78. A Defense Department-funded experiment in Hawaii to devise improved methods of photographing Russian satellites from the ground was reportedly indirectly responsible for the interest in applying adaptive optics to lasers. Interviews: Keyworth and Frieman. On the technology of atmospheric compensation and "rubber mirrors," see Jeff Hecht, *Beam Weapons: The Next Arms Race* (New York: Plenum, 1985), pp. 99–105.

79. Keyworth interview.

80. "This is too big, too much of a change, too dramatic," Keyworth said he told McFarlane and Poindexter regarding SDI when he returned to McFarlane's office that afternoon. At the end of an intense hour-long discussion, however, Keyworth became a convert to the cause of strategic defense: "What I needed was that talk with them to start putting science and strategy together. When I went out of that room I had absolutely no more doubts." Keyworth interview.

81. Reis refused to work on SDI, but under an arrangement worked out with

Keyworth, agreed to stay on at OSTP until the term of his appointment lapsed at the end of August 1983. In a June 13, 1988 letter to the author, Reis wrote of Keyworth's reasons for supporting "Star Wars": "I believe fundamentally that Keyworth decided to endorse the program because he felt that the President's political instincts were superior to his own scientific uncertainties, and his job was to ensure that the science was up to the task."

82. Frieman interview.

83. Telephone interview with Solomon Buchsbaum.

84. Frieman interview.

85. The most controversial assertion in Reagan's speech—the claim that SDI might make not only ICBMs but also nuclear weapons impotent and obsolete— "received more attention than anything else," Keyworth said. "Those words 'nuclear weapons' stayed because that's what the president wanted." Keyworth interview.

86. For the text of Reagan's SDI announcement, see *The New York Times,* March 24, 1983. Interviews: Frieman, Ramo, and Keyworth. According to Ramo, Shultz claimed at the White House dinner that he learned of SDI only that afternoon. The scientists invited to the White House were Harold Agnew, William O. Baker, Hans Bethe, Solomon Buchsbaum, John Foster, Edward Frieman, William Nierenberg, Frank Press, Charles Townes, Victor Weisskopf, Simon Ramo, and Edward Teller. On the dinner and the president's speech, see "Reagan Plans New ABM Effort," *Science,* April 8, 1983, pp. 170–71; and Simon Ramo, *The Business of Science: Winning and Losing in the High-Tech Age* (New York: Hill & Wang, 1988), pp. 171–75.

87. Interviews: Ramo, Buchsbaum, Frieman, and Bethe.

88. "Reagan Plans New ABM Effort," *Science,* pp. 170–71.

89. Ibid.

90. Bethe interview.

91. Garwin, "Reagan's Riskiness," *The New York Times,* March 30, 1983. For the views of other scientists critical of SDI, see, for example, Franklin Long, Donald Hafner, and Jeffrey Boutwell (eds.), *Weapons in Space* (New York: Norton, 1986); and the Federation of American Scientists, *Empty Promise: The Growing Case Against Star Wars* (Boston: Beacon Press, 1986).

92. "100% Defense? Hardly," *The New York Times,* March 27, 1983.

93. The Defensive Technologies Study Team, headed by former NASA administrator James Fletcher, assessed the technical feasibility of "Star Wars." Two other commissions of experts—the first led by a private defense consultant, Fred Hoffman, the second by Franklin Miller, director of the Pentagon's Office of Strategic Forces Policy—looked at SDI's military and strategic implications. See Future Security Strategy Study, "Ballistic Missile Defenses and U.S. National Security" [The Fletcher Report] (Washington, D.C.: U.S. Government Printing Office, 1983). On the technical reviews of SDI, see Donald Hafner, "Assessing the President's Vision: The Fletcher, Miller, and Hoffman Panels," *Daedalus,* Spring 1985, pp. 91–108; and Tina Rosenberg, "The Authorized Version," *Atlantic,* February 1986, pp. 26–30; see also the response to Rosenberg by Miller in *Atlantic,* March 1986.

94. On the reports by the Federation of American Scientists and the American Physical Society, see "Reduced Short-Term Goal Set on Reagan's Plan for Space Defense System," *The New York Times,* December 23, 1984; and "Physicists Express 'Star Wars' Doubt; Long Delays Seen," *The New York Times,* April 22, 1987.

95. Keyworth interview. Keyworth ultimately proved to be more of a "Star

Wars" enthusiast than those in the Pentagon charged with responsibility for strategic defense. See Allen Greb, "Science Advice to Presidents: From Test Bans to the Strategic Defense Initiative," IGCC Research Paper No. 3, 1987, University of California, San Diego, pp. 19–20.

96. "The Knives Are Out for OSTP," *Science,* December 21, 1984, p. 1400.

97. "Keyworth Attacks the Press," *Science,* March 15, 1985, p. 1319.

98. "Reagan Versus the Social Sciences," *Science,* November 30, 1984, pp. 1052–54; "Keyworth Quits White House Post," December 13, 1985, *Science.*

99. "The Knives Are Out for OSTP," *Science,* p. 1400. The effort to fire Keyworth was apparently connected with the pending departure of Edwin Meese—Keyworth's superior and his chief ally in the White House—whose appointment as attorney general had just been announced. But other observers note that OSTP had never received much support within the White House and was virtually ignored by the president's first chief of staff, James Baker. Simon Ramo claims, for example, that although Keyworth technically reported to Meese, the science adviser rarely saw Reagan's friend and domestic adviser; Keyworth was reportedly not even invited to sit down when he gave his final report, in December 1985, to Reagan chief of staff Don Regan. Ramo interview and Ramo, *The Business of Science,* pp. 171–75.

100. "McTague Quits White House Post," *Science,* June 6, 1986, p. 1185.

101. On the controversy over Graham's appointment, see U.S. Congress, Senate, Committee on Commerce, Science, and Transportation, *Hearings: Nominations . . . ,*" 99th Cong., 2d sess., pp. 9–34; "Ex-NASA Head Picked as Science Adviser," *The New York Times,* June 3, 1986; and Jerome Wiesner and Kosta Tsipis, "Put 'Star Wars' Before a Panel," *The New York Times,* November 11, 1986.

102. This was the case, for example, with a planned OTA study of nuclear targeting policy. "It's terribly important for us to have access when we really need it, so we haven't followed up on that," the OTA director admitted. Gibbons interview.

103. For example, in 1986, the Natural Resources Defense Council (NRDC)—a citizens' lobby concerned with national security and environmental issues—sponsored an exchange of Soviet and American scientists to study the problem of seismic verification of a comprehensive test ban. NRDC organized the exchange after the Reagan administration announced that it was no longer interested in pursuing a comprehensive test ban. In 1989, NRDC-sponsored scientists took part in a similar experiment aimed at proving the feasibility of a ban on sea-launched cruise missiles. See "Soviet, U.S. Scientists Reach Seismic Agreement," *Science,* June 13, 1986, p. 1338; and "Americans Examine a Soviet Warhead," *The Washington Post,* July 6, 1989.

104. On the renewed call for a science adviser in the White House, see William Golden (ed.), *Science and Technology Advice to the President, Congress, and Judiciary* (Elmsford, N.Y.: Pergamon Press, 1988); and Hans Bethe and John Bardeen, "Back to Science Advisers," *The New York Times,* May 17, 1986.

105. "Put 'Star Wars' Before a Panel," *The New York Times.*

106. "A Department of Science?" *Science,* September 21, 1984, p. 1372.

Conclusion

1. "Yale Nuclear Physicist Picked as Bush Adviser," *The Washington Post,* April 20, 1989; "Bromley in Line for Science Adviser," *Science,* April 21, 1989, p. 283; "Science Adviser Gets First Formal Look," *Science,* July 21, 1989, pp. 247–48.

2. As assistant to the president, Bromley also served on the Economic Policy Council, the Domestic Policy Council, and the National Space Council.

3. The fact that the Bush administration filled four previously vacant associate directorships in OSTP with recognized professionals was likewise seen as a promising indication of its seriousness in seeking scientific advice. See "Bush's Science Adviser Gains Visibility; Bromley Sounds Call for Action, Caution," *The Washington Post,* December 26, 1989. On the creation and membership of Bush's PCAST, see "Bush Names Science Committee," *Science,* February 9, 1990, p. 629.

4. "Bromley Promises Small Science Focus," *Science,* April 20, 1990, p. 297.

5. "A Conversation with D. Allan Bromley," *Science,* October 13, 1989, pp. 203–4. Ironically, even this rather circumscribed role was frequently denied him, Bromley confided in a candid memoir, published in 1994. Bureaucratic infighting and resistance from the president's own chief of staff were among the obstacles that Bromley listed as impediments to his initiatives as science adviser. See D. Allan Bromley, *The President's Scientists: Reminiscences of a White House Science Advisor* (New Haven: Yale University Press, 1994).

6. Bromley, *The President's Scientists,* p. 2.

7. Ibid., pp. 30, 238.

8. Ibid., p. 186.

9. Ibid., p. 98.

10. Ibid., pp. 237–38. On the debate over space-station "Freedom," see Bromley's op-ed article, "Embrace a New Age of Exploration," and the reaction by U.S. Representative Bob Traxler, *The Washington Post,* July 10 and July 25, 1991.

11. On the reaction to Gibbons, see John Horgan, "The Nicest Guy in Washington," *Scientific American,* April 1993, pp. 42–43.

12. Concerning the difficulty of making prompt presidential appointments, see G. Calvin Mackenzie, "Starting Over: The Presidential Appointment Process in 1997," letter published by The Twentieth Century Fund, 1997.

13. "Without President to Voice R & D Agenda, PCAST Seeks Relevance and Receptivity," *Physics Today,* February 1995, pp. 45–46.

14. Under Clinton, PCAST stood for the President's *Committee* of Advisers on Science and Technology, to distinguish it from NSTC, the National Science and Technology *Council.* On the origins and work of PCAST, see "Clinton's PCAST Promises to Offer New Perspectives on Science and Technology," *The Scientist,* September 5, 1994; and "PCAST Plunges into Its Work," *Science,* November 4, 1994, p. 723.

15. On Gore's particular interest in global warming, see "Gore Walks a Political Tightrope at Kyoto Talks," *The New York Times,* December 9, 1997.

16. As of this writing, updated information on OSTP, PCAST, and NSTC is available on line at www.ostp.eop.gov.

17. In keeping with the administration's emphasis on sophisticated technology, Gibbons would describe NSTC as a "virtual" agency. Its creation was inspired by the Bush administration's success in using the Federal Coordinating Council for Science, Engineering, and Technology (FCCSET) for research on global climate change. On the origins of NSTC, see "White House Plans New Science Council," *Science,* September 17, 1993, p. 1513; and "Conversation with Jack Gibbons on Coordinating Science Policy," *Physics Today,* August 1994, pp. 47–53.

18. "Clinton Fuels 'Clean Car' Initiative," *Chicago Tribune,* September 19, 1993; "U.S. Opens Satellites to Civilians," *The Washington Post,* March 31, 1996.

19. NSTC was used, successfully, as an argument against replacing these offices. On the renewed proposal for a Department of Science, see "Agency Merger Plan Faces High Hurdles," *Science,* March 31, 1995, p. 1990; and "Robert Walker: The Speaker's Right Hand on Science," *Science,* August 11, 1995, pp. 749–50.

20. "Crippling American Science," *The New York Times,* May 23, 1995; "Congress's Science Agency Prepares to Close Its Doors," *The New York Times,* September 24, 1995.

21. "Some politicians saw just stating facts as taking sides," observed Gibbons, OTA's director for fourteen years (author's interview with John Gibbons, February 20, 1996). In 1996, an on-line archive of all OTA publications was established at www.ota.nap.edu.

22. On the difficulty of finding a replacement for Gibbons, see "Wanted: The Ideal Science Adviser," *Science,* December 12, 1997, pp. 1872–73.

23. See, for example, Gregg Herken, " 'Secret No More': A Report on the Security Implications of Global Transparency," manuscript, May 28, 1998, National Air and Space Museum, Smithsonian Institution, Washington, D.C.

24. Regarding this trend, and the reaction to it, see Alan Sokal and Jean Bricmont, *Fashionable Nonsense: Postmodern Intellectuals' Abuse of Science* (New York: St. Martins, 1998); and Paul Gross (ed.), *The Flight from Science and Reason* (Baltimore: Johns Hopkins University Press, 1997).

25. The argument in Congress, according to Gibbons, was that global warming "was just so much liberal claptrap" (author's interview with Gibbons).

26. On proposed reforms, see U.S. Congress, House, *Hearings: A Proposed National Science Policy and Organization Act of 1975,* 94th Cong., 1st sess. (Government Printing Office, 1974); and National Academy of Sciences, "Science and Technology in Presidential Policymaking: A Proposal," June 1974. Concerning the history of the idea of a Department of Science, see "A Department of Science and Technology: In the National Interest?" *Technology in Society,* vol. 8, nos. 1 and 2 (1986). On the proposal for a science court, see "The Science Court Experiment: An Interim Report," *Science,* August 30, 1976, pp. 653–56.

27. In 1988, a Carnegie Commission study on presidential science advising noted that there were then some sixty presidential appointments requiring scientific or technical expertise. Carnegie Commission on Science, Technology, and Government, "Science and Technology and the President," October 24, 1988, pp. 22–24. The author would like to thank David Beckler for a copy of the Carnegie report.

28. Reestablishing a national security role for the president's science advisers was also the recommendation of a 1990 Carnegie report on presidential science advising. In January 1991, the Bush administration took a step in this direction by establishing a PCAST subcommittee on science and national security, which continued to exist into the Clinton administration. See Carnegie Commission on Science, Technology, and Government, "New Thinking and American Defense Technology," August 1990; and "Tech Security Panel Set," *Washington Technology,* January 24, 1991.

29. "Troubled Path Toward a National Shield," *The Washington Post,* April 27, 1998.

30. "Bromley Promises Small Science Focus," *Science,* April 20, 1990, p. 297. On the revival of the role of FCCSET, see "Science and Technology: From Eisen-

hower to Bush," a speech given by Bromley before the Center for the Study of the Presidency, in Austin, Texas, on October 27, 1990. My thanks to Sarah Keegan of OSTP for a copy of Dr. Bromley's speech.

31. William Golden, "Mobilizing Science for War: A Scientific Adviser to the President," December 18, 1950 (Papers of William Golden, Library of Congress, Washington, D.C.). For more on the Golden Report, see Chapter 4 and Appendix C.

32. Transcript of "The Science Advisers," Videotape History Project, Alfred Sloan Foundation, New York City.

33. Snow, *Science and Government,* pp. 68–69.

34. Author's interview with Jerome Wiesner, December 23–24, 1985.

35. Wilson is cited in Lapp, *The New Priesthood,* p. 1.

36. Snow, *Science and Government,* p. 2.

37. Donald Hornig, "The President's Need for Science Advice: Past and Future," in Golden (ed.), *Science Advice to the President,* p. 42.

Bibliography

Abrams, Nancy, and Stephen Berry. "Mediation: A Better Alternative to the Science Court." *Bulletin of the Atomic Scientists,* April 1977.

Acheson, Dean. *Present at the Creation: My Years in the State Department.* New York: Norton, 1969.

Ambrose, Stephen. *Eisenhower: The President.* New York: Simon & Schuster, 1984.

Ames, Mary. *Outcome Uncertain: Science and the Political Process.* New York: Communications Press, 1978.

Anders, Roger, ed. *Forging the Atomic Shield: Excerpts from the Office Diary of Gordon E. Dean.* Chapel Hill: University of North Carolina Press, 1987.

Appleby, Charles. "Eisenhower and Arms Control, 1953–1961: A Balance of Risks." Ann Arbor, Mich.: University Microfilms, 1987.

Armacost, Michael. *The Politics of Weapons Innovation: The Thor-Jupiter Controversy.* New York: Columbia University Press, 1969.

Arneson, Gordon. "The H-Bomb Decision." *Foreign Service Journal,* May 1969.

Badash, Lawrence, et al. "Nuclear Fission: Reaction to the Discovery in 1939." IGCC Research Paper No. 1. University of California, San Diego, 1985.

Barfield, Claude. *Science Policy from Ford to Reagan.* Washington, D.C: American Enterprise Institute, 1982.

Baucom, Don. "Origins of the Strategic Defense Initiative: Ballistic Missile Defense, 1944–1983." Draft manuscript, 1989.

Baxter, James. *Scientists Against Time.* Boston: Little, Brown, 1946.

Beard, Edward. *Developing the ICBM.* New York: Columbia University Press, 1976.

Bernstein, Barton. "Crossing the Rubicon: A Missed Opportunity to Stop the H-bomb?" *International Security,* Fall 1989.

———. "Truman and the H-bomb," *Bulletin of the Atomic Scientists,* March 1984.

Bernstein, Jeremy. *Experiencing Science.* New York: Basic Books, 1978.

———. *Prophet of Energy: Hans Bethe.* New York: Dutton, 1981.

Beschloss, Michael. *Mayday: Eisenhower, Khrushchev, and the U-2 Affair.* New York: Harper & Row, 1986.

Bethe, Hans. "Comments on the History of the H-Bomb." *Los Alamos Science,* Fall 1982.

———. "Sakharov's H-bomb." *Bulletin of the Atomic Scientists,* October 1990.

Blumberg, Stanley, and Gwinn Owens. *Energy and Conflict: The Life and Times of Edward Teller.* New York: Putnam, 1976.

341

Boffey, Philip, et al. *Claiming the Heavens: The New York Times Complete Guide to the Star Wars Debate*. New York: Times Books, 1988.

Bolt, Bruce. *Nuclear Explosions and Earthquakes: The Parted Veil*. San Francisco: Freeman, 1976.

Broad, William. "Rewriting the History of the H-bomb." *Science,* November 19, 1982.

———. *Star Warriors*. New York: Simon & Schuster, 1985.

Bronk, Detlev. "Science Advice in the White House." *Science,* October 11, 1974.

Brooks, Paul. *The House of Life: Rachel Carson at Work*. Boston: Houghton Mifflin, 1972.

Brown, Harold. *Thinking about National Security*. Boulder, Colo.: Westview Press, 1983.

Brzezinski, Zbigniew. *Power and Principle: Memoirs of the National Security Adviser, 1977–1981*. New York: Farrar, Straus & Giroux, 1983.

Bundy, McGeorge. *Danger and Survival: Choices about the Bomb in the First Fifty Years*. New York: Harper & Row , 1988.

———. "Early Thoughts on Controlling the Nuclear Arms Race: A Report to the Secretary of State, January 1953." *International Security,* Fall 1982.

———. "The H-Bomb: The Missed Chance." *The New York Review of Books,* May 13, 1982.

Burrows, William. *Deep Black: Space Espionage and National Security*. New York: Random House, 1986.

Bush, Vannevar. *Pieces of the Action*. New York: Morrow, 1970.

———. *Science: The Endless Frontier*. Washington, D.C.: U.S. Government Printing Office, 1945.

Byrnes, James. *All in One Lifetime*. New York: Harper, 1958.

Cahn, Anne. "American Scientists and the ABM: A Case Study in Controversy." In Albert Teich, ed. *Scientists and Public Affairs*. Cambridge, Mass.: MIT Press, 1974.

Carter, Ashton, and David Schwartz, eds. *Ballistic Missile Defense*. Washington, D.C.: Brookings Institution, 1984.

Carter, Jimmy. *Keeping Faith: Memoirs of a President*. New York: Bantam Books, 1982.

Chang, Gordon. "JFK, China, and the Bomb." *Journal of American History*. Vol. 74, 1988.

Chayes, Abram, and Jerome Wiesner, eds. *Why ABM? An Evaluation of the Decision to Deploy an Anti-ballistic Missile System*. New York: Harper & Row , 1969.

Clark, Ronald. *Einstein: The Life and Times*. New York: Crowell, 1971.

———. *The Greatest Power on Earth: The International Race for Nuclear Supremacy*. New York: Harper & Row , 1980.

Cochran, Thomas, et al. *Nuclear Weapons Databook*. Vol. 1. New York: Ballinger Press, 1984.

Cochrane, Rexmond. *The National Academy of Sciences: The First Hundred Years, 1863–1963*. Washington, D.C.: National Academy Press, 1978.

Cockburn, Andrew. *The Threat: Inside the Soviet Military Machine*. New York: Random House, 1983.

Codevilla, Angelo. *While Others Build: A Commonsense Approach to the Strategic Defense Initiative*. New York: Free Press, 1988.

Cohen, Sam. *The Truth about the Neutron Bomb*. New York: Morrow, 1983.

Compton, Arthur. *Atomic Quest*. New York: Oxford, 1956.

Conant, James. *My Several Lives: Memoirs of a Social Inventor.* New York: Harper and Row, 1970.

Condit, Kenneth. *The History of the Joint Chiefs of Staff.* Vol. II. Wilmington, Del.: Michael Glazier, 1979.

Cunningham, Kevin. "Scientific Advisors and Defense Decision-Making: The Case of the Defense Science Board." Unpublished dissertation, 1990.

Cutler, Robert. *No Time for Rest.* Boston: Little, Brown, 1965.

Dallek, Richard. *Franklin D. Roosevelt and American Foreign Policy.* New York: Oxford, 1979.

Dickson, Paul. *The Electronic Battlefield.* Bloomington: Indiana University Press, 1976.

Diven, Ben, et al. "Nuclear Data," *Los Alamos Science.* Winter/Spring 1983.

Divine, Robert. *Blowing on the Wind: The Nuclear Test Ban Debate, 1954–1960.* New York: Oxford, 1978.

————. "Early Record on Test Moratoriums." *Bulletin of Atomic Scientists,* May 1986.

Dupree, A. Hunter. "National Security and the Post-War Science Establishment in the United States." *Nature,* September 18, 1986.

————. *Science in the Federal Government: A History of Politics and Activities to 1940.* Cambridge, Mass.: Harvard University Press, 1957.

Edwards, John. *Super Weapon: The Making of MX.* New York: Norton, 1982.

Eisenhower, Dwight. *The White House Years: Waging Peace, 1956–1961.* New York: Doubleday, 1965.

Ehrlich, Paul, et al. *The Cold and the Dark: The World After Nuclear War.* New York: Norton, 1984.

Elliott, David. "Project Vista and Nuclear Weapons in Europe." *International Security,* Summer 1986.

Emme, Eugene, ed. *The History of Rocket Technology.* Detroit: Wayne State University Press, 1964.

Federation of American Scientists. *Empty Promise: The Growing Case Against Star Wars.* Boston: Beacon Press, 1986.

Feld, Bernard, and G. W. Szilard, eds. *The Collected Works of Leo Szilard— Scientific Papers.* Cambridge, Mass.: MIT Press, 1987.

Ferrell, Robert, ed. *The Eisenhower Diaries.* Norton, 1981.

————, ed. *Off the Record: The Private Papers of Harry S. Truman.* New York: Harper & Row , 1980.

Franklin, H. Bruce. *War Stars: The Superweapon and the American Imagination.* New York: Oxford, 1988.

Gaddis, John Lewis. *Strategies of Containment.* New York: Oxford, 1982.

Galison, Peter, and Barton Bernstein. "In any light: Scientists and the decision to build the Superbomb, 1952–1954." *Historical Studies in the Physical and Biological Sciences* 19, pt. 2, 1989.

Garthoff, Raymond. *Detente and Confrontation: American-Soviet Relations from Nixon to Reagan.* Washington, D.C.: The Brookings Institution, 1985.

Glasstone, S., and P. J. Dolan, eds. *The Effects of Nuclear Weapons.* Washington, D.C.: U.S. Government Printing Office, 1977.

Golden, William, ed. *Science Advice to the President.* Elmsford, N.Y.: Pergamon Press, 1980.

————, ed. *Science and Technology Advice to the President, Congress, and Judiciary.* Elmsford, N.Y.: Pergamon Press, 1988.

Golovin, I. N. *I. V. Kurchatov: A Socialist-Realist Biography of the Soviet Nuclear Scientist*. Bloomington, Ind.: Selbstverlag Press, 1968.

Goodchild, Peter. *J. Robert Oppenheimer: "Shatterer of Worlds."* Boston: Houghton Mifflin, 1981.

Graham, Daniel. *A Defense that Defends: Blocking Nuclear Attack*. Greenwich, Conn.: Devin-Adair Publishers, 1983.

Greb, Allen. "Science Advice to Presidents: From Test Bans to the Strategic Defense Initiative." IGCC Research Paper No. 3. University of California, San Diego, 1987.

———, and Warren Heckrotte. "The Long History: The Test Ban Debate." *Bulletin of the Atomic Scientists*, August/September 1983.

Greenberg, Daniel. "David and Indifference." *Saturday Review/Science*, September 30, 1972.

Greenwood, John. "The Air Force Ballistic Missile and Space Program, 1954–74." *Aerospace Historian*, Winter 1974.

———. *Making the MIRV: A Study of Defense Decision Making*. New York: Ballinger Press, 1975.

Grodzins, M., and E. Rabinowitch, eds. *The Atomic Age: Scientists in National and World Affairs*. New York: Simon & Schuster, 1965.

Hafemeister, D. W., and D. Schroeer. *Physics, Technology and the Nuclear Arms Race*. New York: American Institute of Physics, 1983.

Hafner, Donald. "Assessing the President's Vision: The Fletcher, Miller, and Hoffman Panels." *Daedalus*, Spring 1985.

Hannon, W. J. "Seismic Verification of a Comprehensive Test Ban." *Science*, January 18, 1985.

Hansen, Chuck. *U.S. Nuclear Weapons: The Secret History*. New York: Orion Books, 1988.

Harris, Elisa. "Sverdlovsk and Yellow Rain: Two Cases of Soviet Noncompliance." *International Security*, Spring 1987.

Hawkins, D., et al. *Project Y: The Los Alamos Story*. San Francisco: Tomash Press, 1983.

Hawkins, Helen, and Allen Greb, eds. *Toward a Livable World: Leo Szilard and the Crusade for Nuclear Arms Control*. Cambridge, Mass.: MIT Press, 1987.

Hecht, Jeff. *Beam Weapons: The Next Arms Race*. New York: Plenum Press, 1985.

Heims, Stephen. *John von Neumann and Norbert Wiener: From Mathematics to the Technologies of Life and Death*. Cambridge, Mass.: MIT Press, 1980.

Helmreich, J. E. *Gathering Rare Earths: The Diplomacy of Uranium Acquisition*. Princeton, N.J.: Princeton University Press, 1986.

Herken, Gregg. *Counsels of War*. New York: Knopf, 1985.

———. "How Reagan Was Sold 'Star Wars.'" *Bulletin of the Atomic Scientists*, October 1987.

———. *The Winning Weapon: The Atomic Bomb in the Cold War, 1945–50*. New York: Knopf, 1980.

Hersh, Seymour. *The Price of Power: Kissinger in the Nixon White House*. New York: Summit Books, 1983.

Hershberg, James. "Over my dead body: James B. Conant and the hydrogen bomb." In E. Mendelsohn, et al. *Science, Technology, and the Military*. New York: Barton, 1990.

Hewlett, Richard, and Oscar Anderson, Jr. *The New World: A History of the United*

States Atomic Energy Commission, 1939/46. University Park: Pennsylvania State University Press, 1962.

———, and Francis Duncan. *Atomic Shield: A History of the United States Atomic Energy Commission, 1947/52.* University Park: Pennsylvania State University Press, 1969.

———, and J. M. Holl. *Atoms for Peace and War, 1958–1961.* Berkeley: University of California Press, 1989.

Holloway, David. *The Soviet Union and the Arms Race.* New Haven, Conn.: Yale University Press, 1984.

Horwitch, Mel. *Clipped Wings: The American SST Conflict.* Cambridge, Mass.: MIT Press, 1982.

Immerman, Richard. *Ike's Spies: Eisenhower and the Espionage Establishment.* New York: Doubleday, 1981.

Irving, David. *The German Atomic Bomb: The History of Nuclear Research in Nazi Germany.* New York: Simon & Schuster, 1968.

Isaacson, Walter, and Evan Thomas. *The Wise Men.* New York: Simon & Schuster, 1986.

Jacobson, Harold, and Eric Stein. *Diplomats, Scientists, and Politicians: The United States and the Test Ban Negotiations.* Ann Arbor: University of Michigan Press, 1966.

Joeck, Neil, and Herbert York. "Countdown on the Comprehensive Test Ban." IGCC. University of California, San Diego, 1986.

Johnson, Lyndon. *The Vantage Point: Perspectives of the Presidency, 1963–1969.* New York: Holt, Rinehart and Winston, 1971.

Jungk, Robert. *Brighter Than a Thousand Suns: A Personal History of the Atomic Scientists.* New York: Harcourt, Brace, 1958.

Kaplan, Fred. *The Wizards of Armageddon.* New York: Simon & Schuster, 1983.

Katz, James. *Presidential Politics and Science Policy.* New York: Praeger, 1978.

Kearns, Doris. *Lyndon Johnson and the American Dream.* New York: Signet, 1976.

Kevles, Daniel. *The Physicists: The History of a Scientific Community in Modern America.* New York: Knopf, 1978.

———. "Scientists, the Military, and the Control of Postwar Defense Research: The Case of the Research Board for National Security, 1944–1946." *Technology and Culture,* January 1975.

Keyworth, George. "Giving Good Counsel at the White House." *Issues in Science and Technology,* Spring 1988.

Kidder, Ray. "Evaluation of the 1983 Rosengren Report." Washington, D.C.: U.S. Department of Energy, June 17, 1986.

Killian, James. *Sputnik, Scientists, and Eisenhower.* Cambridge, Mass.: MIT Press, 1977.

———, and A. G. Hill. "For a Continental Air Defense." *Atlantic,* April 1948.

Kissinger, Henry. *The White House Years.* Boston: Little, Brown, 1979.

Kistiakowsky, George. *A Scientist at the White House.* Cambridge, Mass.: Harvard University Press, 1976.

Kotz, Nick. *Wild Blue Yonder: Money, Politics, and the B-1 Bomber.* New York: Pantheon, 1988.

Kramish, Arnold. *The Griffin.* Boston: Houghton Mifflin, 1986.

Krepon, Michael. *Strategic Stalemate: Nuclear Weapons and Arms Control in American Politics.* New York: St. Martin's Press, 1986.

Lambright, W. Henry. *Presidential Management of Science and Technology: The Johnson Presidency.* Austin: University of Texas Press, 1985.

Laqueur, Walter. *A World of Secrets: The Uses and Limits of Intelligence.* New York: Basic Books, 1985.

Lanouette, William. "Carter's Science Adviser—Doing Part of His Job Well." *National Journal,* January 6, 1979.

Lapp, Ralph. "The Einstein Letter That Started It All." *The New York Times Magazine,* August 2, 1964.

———. *The New Priesthood: The Scientific Elite and the Uses of Power.* New York: Harper & Row , 1965.

Lewis, John, and Xue Litai. *China Builds the Bomb.* Stanford, Calif.: Stanford University Press, 1988.

Lilienthal, David. *The Journals of David E. Lilienthal: The Atomic Energy Years, 1945–59.* New York: Harper & Row , 1964.

Long, Franklin, et al. *Weapons in Space.* New York: Norton, 1986.

MacPherson, Malcolm. *Time Bomb.* New York: Dutton, 1986.

Magraw, Katherine. "Teller and the 'Clean Bomb' Episode." *Bulletin of the Atomic Scientists,* May 1988.

Manno, Jack. *Arming the Heavens: The Hidden Military Agenda for Space, 1945–1995.* New York: Dodd, Mead, 1984.

Mark, J. Carson. "A Short Account of Los Alamos Theoretical Work on Thermonuclear Weapons, 1946–1950." LA-5647-MS, Los Alamos National Laboratory, July 1974.

Markey, Edward. *Nuclear Peril.* New York: Ballinger, 1982.

McDougall, Walter. *The Heavens and the Earth: A Political History of the Space Age.* New York: Basic Books, 1985.

McNamara, Robert. *The Essence of Security: Reflections in Office.* New York: Harper and Row, 1968.

Medaris, John. *Countdown for Decision.* New York: Putnam, 1960.

Murray, Thomas. *Nuclear Policy for War and Peace.* New York: World Publishers, 1960.

National Academy of Sciences. *Acid Deposition: Atmospheric Processes in Eastern North America.* Washington, D.C.: National Academy Press, 1983.

———. *Nuclear Arms Control: Background and Issues.* Washington, D.C.: National Academy Press, 1985.

Neufeld, Jacob. *Ballistic Missiles in the United States Air Force, 1945–1960.* Washington, D.C.: Office of Air Force History,1990.

Newhouse, John. *Cold Dawn: The Story of SALT.* New York: Holt, Rinehart and Winston, 1973.

———. *War and Peace in the Nuclear Age.* New York: Knopf, 1989.

O'Keefe, Bernard. *Nuclear Hostages.* Boston: Houghton Mifflin, 1983.

Oppenheimer, Robert. "Atomic Weapons and American Policy." *Foreign Affairs,* July 1953.

Pfau, Richard. *No Sacrifice Too Great: The Life of Lewis Strauss.* Charlottesville: University Press of Virginia, 1985.

Pilat, J. F., et al. *Atoms for Peace: An Analysis after Thirty Years.* Boulder, Colo.: Westview Press, 1985.

Porter, Roger. *Presidential Decision Making: The Economic Policy Board.* Cambridge, Mass.: Harvard University Press, 1985.

Powers, Thomas. *The Man Who Kept the Secrets: Richard Helms and the CIA.* New York: Knopf, 1979.

Prados, John. *The Soviet Estimate: U.S. Intelligence Analysis and Russian Military Strength*. New York: Dial Press, 1982.

Press, Frank. "Science and Technology in the White House, 1977 to 1980." *Science*, January 9, 1981.

Price, Don. *The Scientific Estate*. Cambridge, Mass.: Harvard University Press, 1965.

Primack, Joel, and Frank von Hipple. *Advice and Dissent: Scientists in the Political Arena*. New York: Basic Books, 1974.

Pringle, Peter, and James Spiegelman. *The Nuclear Barons*. New York: Holt, Rinehart, and Winston, 1981.

———. "Political Science." *Atlantic*, October 1985.

Rabi, I. I. "The Cost of Secrecy." *Atlantic*, August 1960.

Ramo, Simon. *The Business of Science: Winning and Losing in the High-Tech Age*. New York: Hill & Wang, 1988.

Reardon, Steven. *History of the Office of the Secretary of Defense: The Formative Years, 1947–1950*. Vol. 1. Washington, D.C.: U.S. Government Printing Office, 1984.

Rhodes, Richard. *The Making of the Atomic Bomb*. New York: Simon & Schuster, 1986.

Richelson, Jeffrey. *American Espionage and the Soviet Target*. New York: Quill Press, 1987.

Rigden, John. *Rabi: Scientist and Citizen*. New York: Basic Books, 1987.

Rodean, Howard. *Nuclear-Explosion Seismology*. Washington, D.C.: U.S. Atomic Energy Commission, 1971.

Rosenberg, David A. "U.S. Nuclear Stockpile, 1945 to 1950." *Bulletin of the Atomic Scientists*, May 1982.

Rosenberg, Tina. "The Authorized Version." *Atlantic*, February 1986.

Rosengren, J. W. "Some Little-Publicized Difficulties with a Nuclear Freeze." Washington, D.C.: U.S. Department of Energy, October 1983.

Rostow, W. W. *Open Skies: Eisenhower's Proposal of July 21, 1955*. Austin: University of Texas Press, 1982.

Sakharov, Andrei. *Memoirs*. New York: Knopf, 1990.

———. *Sakharov Speaks*. New York: Knopf, 1974.

Scheer, Robert. *With Enough Shovels: Reagan, Bush and Nuclear War*. New York: Random House, 1982.

Schlesinger, Arthur. *A Thousand Days: John F. Kennedy in the White House*. Boston: Houghton Mifflin, 1965.

Schwiebert, Ernest. *History of the U.S. Air Force Ballistic Missiles*. New York: Praeger, 1965.

Scoville, Herbert, Jr. *MX: Design for Disaster*. Cambridge, Mass.: MIT Press, 1981.

Seaborg, Glenn, and Benjamin Loeb. *Kennedy, Khrushchev, and the Test Ban*. Berkeley: University of California Press, 1981.

———, and Benjamin Loeb. *Stemming the Tide: Arms Control in the Johnson Years*. Lexington, Mass.: Lexington Books, 1987.

Seitz, Frederick, ed. "A Department of Science and Technology in the National Interest?" *Technology in Society*, nos. 1 and 2, 1986.

Sheehan, Neil, et al. *The Pentagon Papers: The New York Times Edition*. New York: Bantam, 1971.

Sherwin, Martin. *A World Destroyed: The Atomic Bomb and the Grand Alliance*. New York: Knopf, 1975.

Smith, Alice Kimball. *A Peril and a Hope: The Scientists' Movement in America, 1945–1947*. Chicago: University of Chicago Press, 1965.

Snow, C. P. *Science and Government.* Cambridge, Mass.: Harvard University Press, 1961.

Stares, Paul. *The Militarization of Space.* Ithaca, N.Y.: Cornell University Press, 1985.

Strauss, Lewis. *Men and Decisions.* New York: Doubleday, 1962.

Strum, Thomas. *The USAF Scientific Advisory Board: Its First Twenty Years, 1944–1964.* Washington, D.C.: U.S. Government Printing Office, 1977.

Sutton, Horace. "Is the SST Really Necessary?" *Saturday Review,* August 15, 1970.

Sylves, Richard. *The Nuclear Oracles: A Political History of the General Advisory Committee of the Atomic Energy Commission, 1947–1977.* Ames: Iowa State University Press, 1987.

Szasz, F. M. *The Day the Sun Rose Twice: The Story of the Trinity Nuclear Explosion.* Albuquerque: University of New Mexico Press, 1984.

Szulc, Tad. "The Untold Story of How Russia 'Got the Bomb.'" *Los Angeles Times,* August 26, 1984.

Talbott, Strobe, ed. and trans. *Khrushchev Remembers.* Boston: Little, Brown, 1970.

———. *Khrushchev Remembers: The Last Testament.* Boston: Little, Brown, 1974.

Teller, Edward. *Better a Shield Than a Sword: Perspectives on Defense and Technology.* New York: Free Press, 1987.

———. "SDI: The Last, Best Hope." *Insight.* October 28, 1985.

———. "Seven Hours of Reminiscences." *Los Alamos Science,* Winter/Spring 1983.

———. "Technology: The Imbalance of Power." In Peter Duignan and Alvin Rabushka, eds., *The United States in the 1980s.* Stanford, Calif.: Hoover Institution Press, 1980.

———, and Allen Brown. *The Legacy of Hiroshima.* New York: Doubleday, 1962.

———, and Albert Latter. *Our Nuclear Future: Facts, Dangers, and Opportunities.* New York: Criterion Books, 1958.

Terchek, Ronald. *The Making of the Test Ban Treaty.* The Hague: M. Nijhjoff, 1970.

Truman, Harry. *Years of Trial and Hope.* New York: Doubleday, 1955.

U.S. Atomic Energy Commission. *In the Matter of J. Robert Oppenheimer.* Cambridge, Mass.: MIT Press, 1971.

U.S. Congress, Office of Technology Assessment. *Strategic Defenses.* Princeton, N.J.: Princeton University Press, 1985.

Uyehara, Cecil. "Scientific Advice and the Nuclear Test Ban Treaty." In Sanford Lakoff, ed. *Knowledge and Power: Essays on Science and Government.* New York: Free Press, 1966.

Vance, Cyrus. *Hard Choices.* New York: Simon & Schuster, 1983.

Voss, Earl. *Nuclear Ambush: The Test-Ban Trap.* New York: Regnery, 1963.

Wallop, Malcolm. "Opportunities and Imperatives of Ballistic Missile Defense." *Strategic Review,* Fall 1979.

Watkins, James. "The Strategic Defense Initiative." *Defense/85,* March 1985.

Wattenberg, Albert. "December 2, 1942: The Events and the People." *Bulletin of the Atomic Scientists,* December 1982.

Weart, Spencer. *Nuclear Fear: A History of Images.* Cambridge, Mass.: Harvard University Press, 1988.

———, and G. W. Szilard, eds. *Leo Szilard: His Version of the Facts.* Vol. 2. Cambridge, Mass.: MIT Press, 1978.

Wells, H. G. *The World Set Free.* New York: Dutton, 1914.

Wells, William. "Science Advice and the Presidency, 1933–1976." Ann Arbor, Mich.: University Microfilms, 1977.

Wiesner, Jerome. *Where Science and Politics Meet.* New York: McGraw-Hill, 1965.

Williams, Robert C. *Klaus Fuchs: Atom Spy.* Cambridge, Mass.: Harvard University Press, 1987.

Williams, R. C., and P. L. Cantelon, eds. *The American Atom: A Documentary History, 1939–1984.* Philadelphia: University of Pennsylvania Press, 1984.

Wohlstetter, Albert. "Scientists, Seers and Strategy," *Foreign Affairs,* April 1963.

Wyden, Peter. *Day One: Before Hiroshima and After.* New York: Simon & Schuster, 1984.

Yanarella, Ernest. *The Missile Defense Controversy.* Lexington: University of Kentucky Press, 1977.

———, and Randal Ihara, eds. *The Acid Rain Debate: Scientific, Economic, and Political Dimensions.* Boulder, Colo.: Westview Press, 1985.

Yemelyanov, Vasily. "The Making of the Soviet Atomic Bomb." *Bulletin of the Atomic Scientists,* December 1987.

York, Herbert. *The Advisors: Oppenheimer, Teller, and the Superbomb.* New York: Freeman, 1976.

———, ed. *Arms Control: Readings from Scientific American.* New York: Freeman, 1973.

———. *Making Weapons, Talking Peace.* New York: Basic Books, 1987.

———. *Race to Oblivion: A Participant's View of the Arms Race.* New York: Simon & Schuster, 1970.

———, and Allen Greb. "Military Research and Development: A Postwar History." *Bulletin of the Atomic Scientists,* January 1977.

Ziegler, Charles. "Waiting for Joe-1." *Social Studies of Science* 18, no. 2, May 1988.

Interviews

David Aaron, April 20, 1987, telephone

Gordon Arneson, July 11, 1984, and July 13, 1985, Washington, D.C.

Robert Bacher, March 12, 1985, Caltech

William O. Baker, April 24, 1986, Bell Labs

Karl Bendetsen, April 4, 1986, Washington, D.C.

Hans Bethe, March 14 and May 6, 1985, Caltech

Richard Bissell, May 15, 1980, Farmington, Connecticut

Richard Blankenbechler, February 2, 1986, Stanford

Harvey Brooks, November 19, 1985, Harvard

Harold Brown, April 22, 1986, Washington, D.C.

Norris Bradbury, March 28, 1985, Los Alamos

Solomon Buchsbaum, May 5, 1986, telephone

Edward David, April 24, 1986, Westminster, New Jersey

Richard DeLauer, April 22, 1986, Washington, D.C.

Paul Doty, November 19, 1985, Harvard

Sidney Drell, February 26 and August 22, 1986, Stanford

Lee Dubridge, March 12, 1985, Caltech

Daniel Fink, August 7, 1986, Rosslyn, Virginia

Edward Frieman, May 5, 1986, telephone

Murray Gell-Mann, May 20, 1987, Caltech

John Gibbons, April 16, 1986, and February 20, 1996, Washington, D.C.

Marvin Goldberger, March 12, 1985, Caltech

William Golden, October 26, 1984, New York, New York

Don Hornig, November 20, 1985, Harvard

Gerald Johnson, June 10, 1988, San Diego, California

Spurgeon Keeny, June 11, 1985, Washington, D.C.

George Keyworth, April 16 and April 22, 1986, Washington, D.C.

James Killian, January 16, 1985, MIT

Albert Latter, March 11, 1985, Marina Del Ray, California

Franklin Long, November 21, 1985, Boston

Gordon MacDonald, April 18, 1986, Washington, D.C.

Robert NcNamara, April 1, 1986, telephone

John Manley, March 29, 1985, Los Alamos

Carson Mark, March 30, 1985, Los Alamos

William Nierenberg, November 17, 1986, telephone

Wolfgang Panofsky, January 27 and August 22, 1986, Stanford

Ernie Plesset, May 14, 1988, Woodside, California

Frank Press, April 21, 1986, Woods Hole, Massachusetts

Edward Purcell, January 17, 1985, telephone

Isidor Rabi, October 26, 1984, Columbia

Simon Ramo, August 13, 1987, telephone

George Rathjens, December 23, 1985, MIT

Victor Reis, April 21, 1986, Washington, D.C.

Jack Ruina, December 23, 1985, MIT

Gil Rye, May 23, 1986, telephone

Herbert Scoville, June 12, 1985, Washington, D.C.

Glenn Seaborg, January 21, 1986, Berkeley, California

Robert Serber, October 26, 1984, New York, New York

Cyril Smith, January 17, 1985, Boston

Guyford Stever, April 21, 1986, Washington, D.C.

Jerome Wiesner, December 23–24, 1985, Boston

Robert Wilson, April 15, 1983, Los Alamos

Lowell Wood, June 11, 1986, Livermore, California

Herbert York, March 13, 1985, San Diego, California

Index

Aaron, David, 190
Acheson, Dean, 45–46, 51, 65
Acid rain, 198, 204–5
Adamson, Keith, 11
Adobe (code name), 136
Advanced Research Projects Agency, 117, 135
Advocacy: influence of on science advising, 218–20, 221, 222–24
Agent Orange, 174
Agnew, Harold, 189, 190, 191, 201, 208
Alarm Clock (code name), 36–37, 41
Alvarez, Luis, 40
Anderson, Martin, 208
Angels Project, 32
Antiballistic missile, 135–36, 159–64, 169–70
Antisatellite weapon, 186–87
Antiscience bias, 220
"Armaments and American Policy," 64
Arms control: Strategic Arms Limitation Talks, 167. *See also* Nuclear test ban; Treaties
Arms Control and Disarmament Agency, 136, 139, 167
Arms race, 74, 243–46; early view of, 18
Arneson, Gordon, 31, 45–46, 61
Ash, Roy, 181

Association of Scientific Collaboration, 6
Atomic bomb: Alarm Clock, 36–37, 41; Booster, 37; disclaimer from original scientists about, 32, 33, 34; early forecasts of, 4–5; effects of, 22–23, 24–25; first information to American government on, 7–13, 229–30; H–bomb, 35–65; Superbomb, 35, 36, 40, 231–32
"Atomic Bombs and the Postwar Position of the United States in the World" (Szilard), 18
Atomic energy: Oppenheimer and proposal for control, 33. *See also* Atomic bomb
Atomic Energy Commission, 31, 37
Atomic tests, 43, 74 , 94, 235–38; demonstration option, 21–25; H–bomb, 80–81; in space, 132–33; Trinity test, 24–25; underground testing, 114–15, 116, 121, 137, 141, 188. *See also* Nuclear test ban
"Atomic Weapons and American Policy" (Oppenheimer), 73
Atoms for Peace speech, 76–77

B–1 bomber, 186
Baker, William O., 183, 199–200
Bard, Ralph, 23, 27

Baruch, Bernard, 10
Batzel, Roger, 189, 190, 191
Bethe, Hans, 35, 48, 102–3, 108, 109, 161, 163–64, 191
Bohr, Niels, 20, 31
Booster, 37, 53
Bradbury, Norris, 191
Bravo (code name), 80–81
Brezhnev, Leonid, 187
Briggs, Lyman, 9, 10, 16
Bromley, Dr. Allen, 217–18
Brown, Harold, 185–86, 190, 192
Brzezinski, Zbigniew, 192, 196
Buchsbaum, Solomon, 213
Buckley, Oliver, 37, 56–57
Bulletin of the Atomic Scientists, 32
Bund, 4–5, 6, 8, 13, 14, 15, 16, 26, 29, 33
Burt, Richard, 202
Bush, George: and creation of PCAST, 217–18; science adviser to, 217
Bush, Vannevar, 12–13, 21, 29–30, 31, 32, 35, 39, 54
Byrnes, James, 18–19, 25, 27, 32, 35, 38

Cardinal choices: and the future, 219–20, 225–26; tensions surrounding, 223–24, 225
Carter, Jimmy: comprehensive test ban, 188–92; and MX missile, 193–95; relationship with scientists, 185–86; SALT II, 190, 192, 193, 194; science adviser to, 185–88
Challenger disaster, 216
Chemical warfare, 157–58, 202–3
China, 140–41
Churchill, Winston, 20
Clay, Lucius, 56
Clayton, William, 23
Clean bombs, 111
Clinton, William: and creation of NSTC, 219, 223; science advisers to, 218–19; and science advising, 218–19, 220, 221, 223

Codevilla, Angelo, 209
Committee of Principals, 112, 140
Committee on Atmospheric Testing, 135, 136–37
Comprehensive test ban, 188–92
Comprehensive Test Ban Treaty, 191, 250–52
Compton, Arthur, 15
Compton, Karl, 10
Conant, James, 12, 26, 29, 31, 35, 37, 44
Conference of Experts, 111, 112
Cosmos 954, 197
Council for a Liveable World, 32
Cousins, Norman, 144

David, Edward: President's Science Advisory Committee, 175–80
Dean, Gordon, 43, 45
Deaver, Michael, 214
Decoupling, 115–16
Defense Science Board, 206
Defense systems: antiballistic missile defense, 135–36, 159–64; anti–ICBM shield, 103–4, 113; anti–satellite weapon, 186–87; Ruina–Gell–Mann paper, 243–45; Safeguard, 168–70; Sentinel, 168: Strategic Defense Initiative, 199, 208–15, 253–55
DeLauer, Richard, 210
Densepack, 206–7
Disarmament Panel, 64–65, 71
Doolittle, James, 88
Doty, Jack, 170
Doty group, 170–71, 173, 179
Drell, Sidney, 170, 179, 196
DuBridge, Lee, 37, 56, 86, 87; President's Science Advisory Committee, 166–83
Dulles, John Foster, 69, 70, 84, 93, 105

Einstein, Albert, 3, 11, 18, 32, 48;

and early experiments, 7–8; letter to Roosevelt, 229–30

Eisenhower, Dwight: Atoms for Peace speech, 76–77; attitude towards science, 70; defense spending, 96; and nuclear test ban, 82–87, 94–98, 107–23; and Operation Candor, 71–77: and overflight program, 89–93, 120; President's Science Advisory Committee, 101, 104–7, 117–19

Energy czar, 181

Energy Research and Development Agency, 181

Energy summit, 196

Environmental issues, 218, 219, 220, 222, 225

Excalibur (code name), 209, 210, 212, 214

Fallout, 23

Federal Coordinating Council for Science, Engineering, and Technology (FCCSET), 221

Federation of American Scientists, 179, 191, 214, 215

Federation of Atomic Scientists, 33

Fermi, Enrico, 5–7, 11, 23, 35, 37, 42–43

Ford, Gerald, 181–84; and congressional science advisory, 182; Office of Science and Technology Policy, 182; presidential commission on science, 183

Forrestal, James, 22

Fortunate Dragon, 80

Foster, John, 150–51

Franck Report, 21, 24

Frieman, Edward, 211, 212, 213

Fuchs, Klaus, 50, 51, 52

Fusion, process of, 34–35

Gaither Report, 105

Garwin, Richard, 163–64, 170, 173, 178, 191, 196, 208

Gene splicing, 187

Geneva conference: nuclear test ban, 111–12, 118–21, 132, 133, 137–38, 142, 189

George (code name), 53

Gibbons, John, 204, 218–19

Golden, William, 55–57, 198, 223, 233–34

Goldhaber, Maurice, 7

Gore, Albert, 219

Graham, Daniel, 208–9, 210

Great Britain, 20

Great Depression, 5, 8

Greenhouse effect, 187, 197

Gromyko, Andrei, 192

Groves, Leslie, 13, 16, 17, 19, 20, 23, 29, 32, 38

Hahn, Otto, 5

Haig, Alexander, 202–3

Harrison, George, 23

H–bomb, 35–65; crash effort for, 51–59; development of, 36–37, 41–42, 52–53; first test of, 80–81; lobby for, 39–40, 45–47, 48, 61; power of, 35; scientists, opposition to, 42–47, 53–54, 57–58, 231–32; smaller model, 78–79; Truman decision to develop, 47–51

Herbicides, 203

Heritage Foundation, 209

High Frontier, 209

Hiroshima, 31, 34, 41

Hoover, J. Edgar, 50

Hornig, Donald, 225; President's Science Advisory Committee, 146–51, 154, 156–59

"Insert," 211, 212, 253–55

Intercontinental ballistic missile, 78–81, 86, 89; antimissile shield, 103–4; recommendations regarding (Teapot Report), 239–40; and Soviet Union, 99–100

Interim Committee, 23, 26, 27, 35, 37, 217
Intermediate–range ballistic missile, 89
Israel, 197

Japan, 22, 27; pre–bomb events, 27–30, 33
Jasons, 152–54, 195
Jeffries Report, 21
Johnson, Louis, 39, 45, 47, 50
Johnson, Lyndon: antiballistic missile issue, 159–64; President's Science Advisory Committee, 146–51, 154, 156–59, 163; relationship with scientists, 147, 148; Vietnam War, 149–60
Joint Committee on Atomic Energy, 40, 54, 74, 97, 143
Joint Research and Development Board, 31, 55
Joliot, Frederic, 7
"Junk science," 220

Kennedy, Edward, 191
Kennedy, John: nuclear test ban, 130–45; President's Science Advisory Committee, 128–31, 135–47
Kerr, Donald, 191
Keyworth, George, 201, 204, 205–8
Khrushchev, Nikita, 92, 93, 98, 110–11, 132, 134
Killian, James, 92, 93, 96, 104, 116, 181–82; President's Science Advisory Committee, 104–7, 110–12, 241–42; Technological Capabilities Panel, 87–90
Kissinger, Henry, 166, 170–74
Kistiakowsky, George, 118–22, 144, 145, 149–50, 152, 154, 164, 183
Kosygin, Aleksei, 162

Laird, Melvin, 168
Land, Edwin, 88, 90, 96, 147
Lanc, Neal, 219

Laser lobby, 209
Latter, Albert, 114
Latter hole theory, 115
Lawrence, Ernest, 15, 23, 40, 94, 97, 111
LeBaron, Robert, 50–51, 52
Libby, Willard, 55
Lilienthal, David, 44, 45, 47, 48, 49–50
Limited Test–ban Treaty, 144–45
Lindbergh, Charles, 9
Long, Franklin, 167
Long incident, 167
Long–Range Detection Program, 38, 50
Loper, Herbert, 50
Los Alamos laboratory, 15, 16, 20, 21–22, 28, 35, 36, 37, 53, 114

McCarthy, Joseph, 60
McCloy, John, 130
MacDonald Report, 158–59
McFarlane, Robert, 211, 212
McMahon, Brian, 40, 62
McNamara, Robert, 148, 153–55, 158–64
McNamara Line, 155–56, 174
McTague, John, 215
Magruder, William, 176
Manhattan Project, 15–16, 17, 20
Manley, John, 43, 46
Mark, Carson, 191
May, Michael, 191, 193
Meselson, Matthew, 202–3
Midgetman, 207
Mike (code name), 54, 58–59, 61, 62, 63, 65, 70, 81
Military Liaison Committee, 50
Minuteman, 195
Missiles: antiballistic missile, 135–36, 159–64, 169–70; intercontinental ballistic missile, 78–81, 99–100, 103–4; intermediate–range ballistic missile, 89; MX missile, 193–95, 205–7. See also Defense

systems
Missile Vulnerability Panel, 187, 193, 195
"Mobilizing Science for War: A Scientific Adviser to the President," 55, 233–34
Multiple Independently targetable reentry vehicles (MIRV), 170–73; moratorium on testing of, 247–49
Multiple protective shelters, 194
Murphree, Eger, 55
Murray, Thomas, 82–85, 94
MX missile, 193–195, 205–7, 222
Mycotoxins, 202

Nagasaki, 39, 41
National Academy of Science, 13
National Advisory Committee for Aeronautics, 107
National Aeronautics and Space Administration (NASA), 107
National Bureau of Standards, 9, 10, 16
National Defense Research Committee, 12, 29
National Research Board, 9
National Research Council, 8, 204
National Science and Technology Council (NSTC), 219, 223
National Science Foundation, 30–31, 55, 56, 167, 201
Neumann, John von, 40, 53
New Technologies Opportunity Program, 176
Nichols, Kenneth, 50
Nierenberg, William, 205
Nike–X, 136, 161–62
Nike–Zeus, 133, 135, 136
Nitze, Paul, 61–62
Nixon, Richard, 70; antiballistic missile issue, 169–70; President's Science Advisory committee, 166–83; relationship with scientists, 165–66, 167; Science and

Technology Policy Office, 181
North American Air Defense Command, 208
Nuclear arsenal, United States, 41, 59
Nuclear deterrence, 243–45; and development of MIRV, 248–49
Nuclear stockpile, 250–52
Nuclear Task Force, 94, 97
Nuclear test ban: Central Park demonstration, 210; cheating and evading detection, 114–15, 132; comprehensive test ban, 188–92; Eisenhower era, 82–87, 94–98, 107–23; Geneva conference 111–12, 118–21, 132, 133, 137–38, 142, 189; Kennedy era, 130–45; and nuclear detection, 108, 115–16, 138; and onsite inspection, 138, 141–42; opposition to, 110, 111, 114–15, 118, 119, 131, 132, 142–43; *Scientific American* article, 149

Objectivity: as goal of science advising, 220–22, 224–25
Office of Energy Policy, 181
Office of Energy Research, 196
Office of Science and Technology, 136, 182
Office of Scientific Research and Development, 12, 16, 29–31, 56
Office of Technology Assessment, 182, 197, 216, 218, 219, 223
Oil embargo, 183
O'Neill Report, 170
Open Conspiracy, The (Wells), 4
Open Skies initiative, 92
Operation Argus, 110, 113
Operation Buster, 53
Operation Candor, 71–77
Operation Castle, 81, 86
Operation Deadline, 113
Operation Dominic, 136–37, 138
Operation Hardtrack, 98, 108, 109–10

Operation Igloo White, 155
Operation Popeye, 151
"Opinion on the Development of the
    'Super,' An," 42–43, 231–32
Oppenheimer, Robert, 220; early
    work on the bomb, 15, 21–28,
    31, 33; and Eisenhower, 71–74;
    Enrico Fermi Medal, 148; and
    H–bomb, 33, 35–37, 41–48, 56,
    57, 58, 63–65; investigation into
    loyalty of, 85–86
Our Nuclear Future (Teller), 114
Overflights: U–2 overflights of Russia,
    89–93, 120

Panofsky, Wolfgang, 132–33, 140,
    170, 179, 189, 208
Panofsky Report, 132–33
Parsons, William, 25
Pearl Harbor, 13
Pegram, George, 7
Perle, Richard, 213
Perry, William, 193, 195
Pike, Sumner, 45, 50, 53
Population growth, 218, 220, 225
Potsdam ultimatum, 27
Powers, Francis Gary, 122
Presidential Review Memorandum,
    188
President's Council of Advisers on Sci-
    ence and Technology (PCAST),
    217–18, 219, 221
President's Science Advisory Commit-
    tee (PSAC), 101, 117–19, 217,
    218, 220–21 222, 225; abolition
    of, 180–83; charter for, 241–42;
    under David, 175–80; under
    DuBridge, 166–83; under
    Hornig, 146–51, 154, 156–59,
    163; under Killian, 104–7,
    110–12; members of, 256–59;
    under Weisner, 128–31, 135–47
Press, Frank, 185–90, 192, 204
Project Apollo, 129–30, 177
Project Aquatone, 89–93

Project Centering, 38–39, 50
Project Charles, 88
Project Corona, 122
Project Defender, 135
Project Gemini, 129
Project Genetrix, 91
Project Mercury, 129
Project MX–774, 79
Project Plowshare, 131–32
Project Rover, 147
Project Sunrise, 152
Project Vista, 54
"Proposal for a Modified Tactical Use
    of the Gadget" (Parsons), 25
"Proposal for Research and Devel-
    opment in the Field of Atomic
    Energy," 36

Rabi, Isidor, 6, 7, 15, 33, 37, 42–43,
    54, 77, 101–4, 109, 180
Ramo, Simon, 183, 199–200
Rathjens, George, 171–72, 214
Reagan, Ronald: and acid rain,
    204–5; and MX decision, 205–7;
    relationship with scientists,
    199–200; science adviser to, 201,
    204, 205–8, 210–15; Strategic
    Defense Initiative, 199, 208–15,
    252–54
Reis, Victor, 212
Rockerfeller, Nelson, 182
Roosevelt, Eleanor, 18
Roosevelt, Franklin, 3, 21, 30; re-
    sponse to information about
    bomb, 10–16
Rosenman, Samuel, 30
Rowe, Hartley, 37
Ruina, Jack, 170, 171–72, 189, 190,
    214

Sachs, Alexander 10, 11, 21
Safeguard, 168–70
SALT I, 167
SALT II, 190, 192, 193, 194
Schlesinger, James, 183, 189, 190

Science advisers: ideal role of, 220–26; recommendations regarding appointment of, 233–34, 241–42; traditional view of, 223–24. *See also* President's Science Advisory Committee, and individual presidents
Science advising: loss of faith in, 220–21, 224
Science Advisory Board, 8–9
Science Advisory Committee (SAC/ODM), 56–57, 63, 198; members of, 256–59
Science and Technology Policy Office, 181
Science: The Endless Frontier (Bush), 30, 55
Scowcroft Commission, 207
Seaborg, Glenn, 37, 55, 131, 147
Security Resources Panel, 105
Sentinel, 168
Serber, Robert, 16, 23
Shapiro, Maurice, 25
Shell game, 194
Shultz, George, 213
Smith, Cyril, 37, 43
Smyth, Henry, 45, 53
Snow, C.P., 220, 224, 225
Souers, Sidney, 37, 44, 47
South Africa, 197
Soviet Union: and intercontinental ballistic missile, 99–100; speculations about atomic energy, 18–19, 30, 39, 40, 46, 50–51, 52, 59–60, 73–74, 86, 89; Sputnik I, 99–101; U–2 overflights, 89–93; U.S. flights into airspace of, 91
Space: nuclear testing, 132–33
Space program: Eisenhower era, 107; Weisner Report, 129–30
Spies and spying, 60; Fuchs 50, 51, 52; and public discussion of nuclear weapons, 72; U–2 overflights of Russia, 89–93, 120
Sputnik I, 99–101, 218

SST program, 177–79
Stagg Field, 14–15
Starfish (code name), 138–39
Stassen, Harold, 94
Stealth bomber, 186
Steelmen, John, 31
Stever, H. Guyford, 180, 182
Stimson, Henry, 23, 26, 27, 38
Stockman, David, 200
Stolper, Gustav, 10
Strassman, Fritz, 5
Strategic Arms Limitation Talks, 167, 171, 173, 247, 248
Strategic Defense Initiative, 199, 208–15, 222, 225; announcement of (the "Insert"), 253–55
Strategic Missiles Evaluation Committee (Teapot panel), 78, 79–80
Strategic Review, 209
Strauss, Lewis, 6, 22, 38, 39–40, 44–45, 48, 72–74, 77, 96–97, 103–4, 111
Superbomb, 35, 36, 40, 43, 49, 51, 53, 62
Szilard, Leo, 3, 4–21, 28–29, 32, 224

Task Force on Acid Precipitation, 204
Task Force on Science and Technology, 199
Teapot panel, 78–79; report of, 239–40
Technological Capabilities Panel (TCP), 87–90
Teller, Edward, 6, 7, 28, 35, 36, 39, 59, 61, 94, 114, 143–45, 200–201, 208
Three Mile Island, 197
Townes, Charles, 206
Treaties: Comprehensive Test Ban Treaty, 191; Limited Test–ban Treaty, 144–45; Treaty on Non–proliferation of Nuclear Weapons, 188
Trinity test, 24–25
Tritium, 41

Truman, Harry, 18–20, 27, 29–30, 31–33, 37–39; decision on H–bomb, 47–51; scientific advisers, 54–60
Tsipis, Kosta, 216
Twining, Nathan, 92
TX–14 (Alarm Clock), 36–37
Ulam, Stanislaus, 53, 59
Underground testing, 114–15, 116, 121, 137, 141, 188; threshold agreement, 121
Uranium: discovery of fission, 5–8
Uranium Committee, 11–12, 15
Urraca (code name), 139

Verification Panel, 174
Vessey, John, 211
Vietnam Panel, 150–51
Vietnam War, 149–60; and Jasons, 152–54; MacDonald Report, 158–59; McNamara Line, 155–56; technological schemes for, 151–54, 156–59, 174; Vietnamization, 174
Vulnerability Panel, 92

Wallace, Henry, 8
Wallop, Malcolm, 209
Watkins, James, 211
Weapons proliferation, 219–20, 221–22, 225
Weinberger, Caspar, 201, 205
Wells, H.G., 4
White House Science Council, 201, 206, 211
Whitman, Walter, 55
Wiesner, Jerome, 149–50, 152, 196, 216, 223, 225; President's Science Advisory Committee, 128–31, 135–47; Wiesner Report, 129–30
Wigner, Eugene, 6, 7, 10, 11, 14
Wilson, Robert R., 21
Wood, Lowell, 209
World Set Free, The (Wells), 4

Yellow rain, 202–3
York, Herbert, 117, 130, 189
Yucca (code name), 108

Zacharias, Jerrold, 151–52, 154
Zhukov, Marshall G. K., 92
Zinn, Walter, 6

Library of Congress Cataloging-in-Publication Data

Herken, Gregg
    Cardinal choices : presidential science advising from the atomic bomb to SDI / Gregg Herken
        p. cm. — (Stanford nuclear age series)
    Originally published: New York : Oxford University Press, 1992.
    "A Century Foundation Book."
    Includes bibliographical references and index.
    ISBN 0-8047-3966-8 (alk. paper) — ISBN 0-8047-3770-3 (pbk. : alk paper)
      1. Science and state—United States—History—20th century. 2. Science
consultants—United States—History—20th century. 3. Presidents—United
States—Staff—History—20th century. I. Series.

Q127.U6 H394 2000
338.973'06—dc21

                                                                    00-026546

♾ This book is printed on acid-free paper.

Original printing 2000
Last figure below indicates year of this printing:
09 08 07 06 05 04 03 02 01 00